Willett Family

of

Pennsylvania

WILLETT HOUSE
COLLECTION

Albert J. Willett

HERITAGE BOOKS
2017

HERITAGE BOOKS
AN IMPRINT OF HERITAGE BOOKS, INC.

Books, CDs, and more—Worldwide

For our listing of thousands of titles see our website
at
www.HeritageBooks.com

Published 2017 by
HERITAGE BOOKS, INC.
Publishing Division
5810 Ruatan Street
Berwyn Heights, Md. 20740

Copyright © 1998 Albert James Willett, Jr.

International Standard Book Numbers
Paperbound: 978-0-7884-0903-5

DEDICATION

To the girlfriend of my childhood
and computer smitten wife of the present

ACKNOWLEDGEMENTS

This volume was not the work of one person. More hours of research and diligent study have been devoted to its creation than one person could provide. This volume would not have as much scope, be as complete, or as accurate, without the help of many friends. In particular:

Helen Barrett, Kent, Ohio, who did much of the research in Ohio census records, and additional research whenever asked not just for this volume but for the whole range of Willett House family records.

Patricia Louise Berzonsky, of Cambria County, Pennsylvania, has provided much information on descendants of Burgess Willett (1810-1870).

Nova Boyer, Bowie, Maryland, provided data which is incorporated in the chapter on Burgess Willett (1810-1870).

Margaret Ernest, Seattle, Washington, always ready to research census records and to help find and document a family. Her help extends much beyond just this single volume.

Julie LeBaron Garito, Radnor, Pennsylvania, who has provided much research on the Thomas Willett (1767-1828) family.

Joan Grabenstein, Wilmington, Delaware, who has provided much research on the Burgess Willett (1810-1870) family.

Marie Hempy, Riverside, California, who has provided much research on the Lewis F. Willet (1809-1865) family of Cumberland County, Pennsylvania.

Ruth Z. Lewis, Lansing, Michigan, one example of the level of her help is that she copied every mention of the Willett surname in the 1900 and 1910 Michigan census record. Copying literally hundreds of census records from microfilm is one of the most tedious chores of family history but the results of all that effort has been extremely helpful over the years and has contributed much to this volume.

ACKNOWLEDGEMENTS

David Alan Ohliger, Pittsburgh, Pennsylvania, who has provided much research on the William Willett (1775-1856) family of Pittsburgh.

David Willett, Wayne County, Michigan, who has provided much research on the Abraham Willett (1759-1822).

Douglas Willett, Plymouth, Michigan. He has proofread the chapter on Abraham Willett, provided photographs of the family and made available his own unpublished (at this date) manuscript, "Descendants of Abraham Willett", dated February 1, 1997. The Abraham Willett chapter is heavily indebted to his research.

James Willett, Newport News, Virginia, who is my computer expert. and son. On call at all hours to answer questions on how to keep the computer running.

Keith Willett, Plummer, Idaho, who has provided much research, help, proofreading, a multitude of early photographs, and most importantly encouragement to see this project to completion. His is the Samuel Willett (1768-1857) family of Fulton County, Pennsylvania..

George Willits, Ontario, Canada, who supplies more than encouragement and proofreading, both of which he has provided in abundance. His friendship, encouragement and help has been unceasing.

PREFACE

Just a few words about this work.

Two notable Willett families of Pennsylvania are not in this work. One is the family which is centered around Bucks County, Pennsylvania, and is exemplified by Colonel Augustine Willett of Revolutionary War fame. He is descended from a New York family and his story has already been covered in *The Willett Families of North America*, 1985. Also part of that family are Samuel and Walter Willett; two Loyalists who joined the British Legion, fought for the King throughout the Revolutionary War and became exiles to Nova Scotia because of their Loyalty to England. The other family not found in this volume is represented by Robert White Willett of Northumberland County. His background is found in Maryland as a descendant of Edward Willett, the colonial pewterer. Although he was not listed in *The Willett Families*, his ancestry has been firmly connected to the Maryland Willett family.

Expect errors. In a work of this size and with numerous sources for data there are bound to be mistakes. The editor does not apologize for doing the impossible but offers the following work as a reasonable outline of the Willett families who came from Pennsylvania Ever effort has been made to compare data and note discrepancies by commenting internally and by circulating the original drafts of the manuscript for proofreading to interest parties and by circulating sections to the main researchers of each family for review. As many census records have been consulted as was possible in the time allotted for researching this volume. Published works, whether newspaper articles, obituaries, or printed biographies, have been consulted and extracted. Every effort has been made to ascribe data taken from previous published sources but here again some of the items collected whether in the distant past or more recent present have been separated from their original citation by the fact that often a researcher copied only the page which was of interest, but failed to copy the complete citation. Again, it has been felt more important to present what data which has been collected than to exclude data because it was not fully documented or properly cited. The goal in this volume is to point anyone interested in particular line to the records or locale where further information can be found thus saving them time and effort to fully document their own line. In this respect, I believe the following work has been successful.

The index is not an every-name index. Those names highlighted in **bold** are indexed. This index will lead a researcher only to the names of adults, or their children cited in this volume and who are closely related by blood or marriage to the Willett family.

Accuracy: this work does not pretend to be perfect. At the same time, what is presented is not "plausible" genealogy, but the results of numerous contributions of various individuals who consider the resultant data to be accurate. Information has been gleaned from numerous printed, manuscript, Bible Record, and oral history sources and thus each source will have to be weighed to determine its degree of accuracy and trustworthiness.

Abbreviations: The only abbreviations used are:
b = born
m = married
d = died
REF = Reference
sic = Latin for "as it is written"

Conventions:
There is a "Heading" for each family. If a husband is married only once, both husband and wife are mentioned in the "Heading." If a man (or woman) has multiple marriages, only he (or she) is listed in the "Heading".

There is a "Narrative" section beneath each heading.

Sometimes there is a reference (REF) list; these references are general to the narrative and are usually not otherwise listed.

Other sources, usually of citations which are specific to one generation, are cited internally in the narrative section. These are usually either newspaper articles or "favor" biographies of the 1870s-1920s.

Citations are usually listed in the text immediately following a quotation or as a reference to the previous statement.

There is a "List of Children". The surname in the "List of Children: is capitalized.

"See next ..." refers reader to additional information on descendants.

Only names written in **Bold** are indexed.

Under lined words are spelled exactly as the original document.

Italic words are used to cite titles of books. Manuscripts or other records which are not known to be published are listed in "Quotation Marks".

Italics are also used when citing the 1790-1840 census records. These early census records only cite the name of the head of the household and children by gender and approximate age. Whenever other sources make it possible, the name of the wife and children are listed beside the age and gender groupings as listed in the 1790-1840 census.

Italics are also used when citing directly from a primary or published record, letter, or document.

NOTE: Self explanatory.

FOR THE RECORD: Self explanatory.

Indentation: used for NOTES, FOR THE RECORD, and direct quotation from documents.

Question mark (?) behind a date: Date is estimated.

Star (*) behind date: Date does not agree within year range as applied to certain census records. This is reserved for census records of 1790-1840.

Dates: Any year date which is not prefaced with a month and day can be expected to be correct within +/- one year. Do not expect all dates as recorded to agree with each other. Even tombstone dates are notorious for the errors graven into the stone. All records need to be balanced against the sum total of all known and available data.

TABLE OF CONTENTS

CHAPTER ONE
CHRISTOPHER WILLET (1730-1801)
OF PENNSYLVANIA

PA. 1
CHRISTOPHER WILLET and **CHRISTINA HAAS**
of York County, Pennsylvania

Christopher Willet was born on August 17, 1730, most likely in one of the old German provinces, but possibly in England. In 1749, at age 19, he immigrated to the American colonies.

The *Ships Records* from Rupp's *Collection of Thirty Thousand Names of German Immigrants* shows that on October 17, 1749, a Christopher Willet was on board the ship <u>Fane</u>, as well as the George Nichel Haas and John Kraft Haas families. The <u>Fane</u> sailed from Rotterdam, Holland, with a stop in Cowes, Isle of Wight, England, with 596 passengers, mostly Palatinates from Wirtemberg and Ritterheim.

> NOTE: Since Willet appears to be an English name, it is possible that Christopher Willet boarded the ship "Fane" at Cowes, England. Most likely, Christina Haas was probably already on board. But this conjecture needs to be balanced with the fact that German Willet/t families do exist and are known to have immigrated to the United States and Canada in the 1800s. It this Christopher Willet is German, then he is the earliest known German Willet to immigrate.

Christopher Willet and Christina Haas probably met on board the ship and were married in 1749 either on shipboard or shortly after arriving in Pennsylvania. The ship <u>Fane</u> arrived in Philadelphia on or about October 17, 1749.

Christopher Willet and Christina Haas lived in Bucks County, Pennsylvania, from at least 1749 until 1759, when they removed to Codorus Township, York County, Pennsylvania. They were residents of Manheim, York (now Adams), Pennsylvania.

Christopher Willet is mentioned in the York County tax records before 1772.

On September 16, 1774, <u>Stoffel</u> (Christopher) <u>Willett</u> of Manheim Township, York County, sold to Thomas Armor fifty acres of land in Codorus Township, which he had cleared and fenced and seeded, about 14 years before. The deed was signed in German.

In 1779 and 1780, <u>Stophel</u> (Christopher) <u>Willett</u> was assessed on one hundred and eighty (180) acres of land in Manheim Township, York County.

In 1781, 1782, and 1783, Christopher Willett was assessed on one hundred and eighty (180) acres of land in Manheim Township, York County.

Christopher Willet's sons, Anthony, George, Jacob, and Lawrence, appear in the York County tax records in 1783, and 1795. They were affiliated with the (Old German) Lutheran Church.

On April 11, 1784, at Zieler's (St. Paul) Lutheran Church, Christopher Willett and Christina were witnesses of the baptism of Christina Krebs, the daughter of Peter and Barbara Krebs (*Records of York County, Church Records of the 18th Century*, by Marlene S. Bates and F. Edward Wright).

In 1790, Christopher Willett and family were listed in the York County, Pennsylvania, census, page 284, as follows:

1 male	16-up	bef.-1774	*Christopher*	*age 70 b 1730*
1 female			*Christina*	

In 1790, York County, Pennsylvania, included all of present day York County and Adams County. By 1800, the York County had been subdivided and York and Adams counties as they are presently known were established. The Willet families in the earliest days lived in the western part of York County. The Willets became quite numerous in Hanover, Mainheim and Codorus Township in the southwestern part of York County, near the borough of Hanover. The Willet families were associated with the two pioneer churches of York County: St. Matthews Lutheran Church and the First Reformed Church in Hanover. The Christian Reformed Church was situated seven miles west of Hanover in the new Adams County. There was also a Lutheran Reformed Church six miles south of Hanover near the Maryland State line.

In 1800, it would appear that Christopher and Christina Willet were listed in the household of their son, Anthony Willet, Junior, and in the York County, Pennsylvania, census, page 1355, as follows:

1-1-0-1-1 1-0-0-1-1

1 male	45-up	bef.-1755	*Christoph*	*age 80 b 1720*
1 female	45-up	bef.-1755	*Christina*	*age 80?b 1720?*
1 male	26-45	1755-1774	*Anthony*	*age 39 b 1761*
1 female	26-45	1774-1784	*Elizabeth*	*age 39 b 1761*
1 male	10-16	1784-1790	*(Adam)*	*age 16?b 1784?*
1 male	0-10	1790-1800	*(Fred)*	*age 6? b 1794?*
1 female	0-10	1790-1800	*(Susan)*	*age 5? b 1795?*

Christopher Willet died on July 30, 1801, and is buried at the Stone Church Cemetery, Codorus Township, York County, Pennsylvania.

NOTE: There is no consistent way of spelling of the Willet/t surname in the records for the Christopher Willet family. Records when cited will appear as they are published. The Christopher Willet family surname is most often spelled with a single "t". But even sometimes in the very next record and sometimes within the same record the surname will be spelled with two "tt"s. Within this chapter, the Christopher Willet family surname will be spelled as **Willet** except when quoting a published or original record which has a different spelling.

(REF: "Willett House" Quarterly, Volume II, No. 1, March, 1985, page 209).

1. **Anna Elizabeth WILLET**: b October 4, 1750, Keelersville, Bedminster, Bucks County, Pennsylvania; chr. October 28, 1750, Tohichen Lutheran Reformed Church, Bucks County, Pennsylvania.

2. **Lawrence WILLET**: b abt 1752, Pennsylvania. Lawrence Willet is mentioned in the 1772 Hellam Township, York County, tax records, and again in the 1783 and 1795 York County, Pennsylvania, tax records.

3. **Elizabeth WILLET**: b May 24, 1755, Keelersville, Bucks County, Pennsylvania; chr. June 15, 1755, Tohichen Lutheran Reformed Church, Bucks County, Pennsylvania.

4. **Anna Barbara WILLET**: b August 13, 1757, Keelersville, Bucks County, Pennsylvania; chr. November 6, 1757, Tohichen Lutheran Reformed Church, Bucks County, Pennsylvania.

5. **P. Anthony WILLET**: b August 27, 1761, (York County) Pennsylvania; m abt 1781, Elizabeth (b February 16, 1761; d July 18, 1834, age 70 years, 5 months, 2 days); d September 8, 1828, at Manheim, York County, Pennsylvania. See next PA.1.5.

6. **George WILLET**: b 1763, Pennsylvania; m 1st at York, Hanover, St. Matthews Lutheran Church on November 16, 1790, Mary Magdalena Werking; m 2d Anna Maria (b November 24, 1768; d February 12, 1845, Manheim, Lancaster County, Pennsylvania); d June 30, 1835, Manheim, York County, Pennsylvania. See next PA.1.6.

7. **Jacob WILLET**: b July 4, 1759, Keelersville, Bed-minster, Bucks County, Pennsylvania; chr. August 26, 1759, Tohichen Lutheran Reformed Church, Bucks County, Pennsylvania; m abt 1783 Rosina Flinchbaugh (b 1765; d December 22, 1850, Union Township, Adams County, Pennsylvania); d 1806 Conewago Township, Adams County, Pennsylvania. See next PA.1.7.

8. **Barbara Christina WILLET**: b August, 1766; chr. September 7, 1766, York, West Manchester Township, St. Pauls Lutheran and Reformed Church, West Manchester Township, York County, Pennsylvania.

PA.1.5
P. ANTHONY WILLET and ELIZABETH
of York County, Pennsylvania

P. Anthony Willet was born on August 27, 1761, (in York County) Pennsylvania.

On April 20, 1799, at Ziegler's (St. Paul) Lutheran Church, Anthony Willet and Elizabeth Krebs were witnesses to the baptism of Catharine Krebs, the daughter of Peter and Barbara Krebs (*Records of York County, Church Records of the 18th Century*, by Marlene S. Bates and F. Edward Wright).

In 1783, Anthony Willet of Manheim Township was a single man and taxed 1 pound, 10 shillings.

P. Anthony Willet married about 1784, Elizabeth (b February 16, 1761; d July 18, 1834, age 70 years, 5 months, 2 days).

In 1790, Anthony Willett and family were listed in the York County, Pennsylvania, census, page 285, as follows:
1-1-2-0-0

1 male	16-up	bef. 1774	*Anthony*	*age 29 b 1761*
1 female			*Elizabeth*	*age 29 b 1761*
1 female			*(Eliza)*	*age 9? b 1781?*
1 male	0-15	1775-1790	*(Adam)*	*age 6? b 1784?*

On July 8, 1792, Anthony Willett and wife Elizabeth were sponsors of the baptism of Elizabeth Cramer, the daughter of Henry Cramer and Christina (*Records of York County, Church Records of the 18th Century*, by Marlene S. Bates and F. Edward Wright).

In 1795, Anthony Willet of Manheim Township owned 180 acres of land valued at 185 pounds and had 3 horned cattle and 1 horse.

On April 11, 1800, at the Emanuel Reformed Church of

Hanover, Anthon Willett and wife Elizabeth were witnesses to the baptism of Wilhelm Schmidt, the son of Daniel and Elizabeth Schmidt (*Records of York County, Church Records of the 18th Century*, by Marlene S. Bates and F. Edward Wright). In 1800, Anthony Willet, Junior, and family were listed in the York County, Pennsylvania, census, page 1355, as follows:

1-1-0-1-1 1-0-0-1-1

1 male	45-up	bef.-1755	Christoph	age 80 b 1720
1 female	45-up	bef.-1755	Christina	age 80? b 1720?
1 male	26-45	1755-1774	Anthony	age 39 b 1761
1 female	26-45	1774-1784	Elizabeth	age 39 b 1761
1 male	10-16	1784-1790	(Adam)	age 16? b 1784?
1 male	0-10	1790-1800	(Fred)	age 6? b 1794?
1 female	0-10	1790-1800	(Susan)	age 5? b 1795?

In 1810, Anthony Willet and family were listed in the Manheim, York County, Pennsylvania, census, page 139, as follows:

1 male	45-up	bef.-1765	Anthony	age 49 b 1761
1 female	26-45	1765-1784	Elizabeth	age 49*b 1761*
1 male	26-45	1765-1784	(Adam)	age 26? b 1784?
1 male	10-16	1794-1800	(Fred)	age 16? b 1794?
1 female	0-10	1800-1810		
1 female	0-10	1800-1810		

In 1820, Anthony Willet and family were listed in the Hopewell, York County, Pennsylvania, census, page 35, as follows:

0-1-0-1-0-1 1-0-0-1-1

1 male	45-up	bef.-1775	Anthony	age 59 b 1761
1 female	45-up	bef.-1775	Elizabeth	age 59 b 1761
1 female	26-45	1775-1794		
1 male	16-26	1794-1804	(Fred)	age 26? b 1794?
1 male	10-16	1804-1810		
1 female	0-10	1810-1820		

P. Anthony Willet died on September 8, 1828, in Manheim, York County, Pennsylvania, age 67 years, 13 days. Both he and his wife are buried at the Stone Church, Codorus Township, York County.

P. Anthony Willet will was probated on November 11, 1828, Manheim Township, York County, Pennsylvania, and mentioned his "foster children whom he had raised from infancy" (will 1828).

1. **Elizabeth WILLET** (stepdaughter): b abt 1781? m abt 1801, Jacob Keller.
2. **Adam WILLET** (stepson): b abt 1784? m Fishel.
3. **Frederick Stromel WILLET** (stepson): b abt 1794?
4. **Susannah WILLET** (stepdaughter): b abt 1797? m abt 1817, Shaffer.

PA. 1.6
GEORGE WILLET
of York County, Pennsylvania

George Willet was born in 1763, in Pennsylvania.

George Willet married 1st at York, Hanover, St. Matthews Lutheran Church on November 16, 1790, Mary Magdalena Werking (*Records of York County, Church Records of the 18th Century*, by Marlene S. Bates and F. Edward Wright).

George Willet married 2d Anna Maria (b November 24, 1768; d February 12, 1845, Manheim, Lancaster County, Pennsylvania).

In 1800, George Wellet and family were listed in York County, Pennsylvania, page 349, as follows:

1 male	26-45	1765-1774	*George*	*age 37 b 1763*
1 female	16-26	1774-1784	*Mary M*	
1 male	0-10	1790-1800		
1 female	0-10	1790-1800		

In 1810, George Willett and family were listed in Hopewell, York County, Pennsylvania, page 36, as follows:

1 male	45-up	bef.-1765	*George*	*age 47 b 1763*
1 female	45-up	bef.-1765		
1 female	0-10	1800-1810		

FOR THE RECORD: In 1830, a George Willet and family were listed in Germany, Adams County, Pennsylvania, page 68, as follows:

1 male	30-40	1790-1800
1 female	30-40	1790-1800
1 female	15-20	1810-1815
1 female	10-15	1815-1820
1 female	5-10	1820-1825
1 female	5-10	1820-1825
1 female	0-5	1825-1830

1 female   0-5   1825-1830

Evidently, the George Willett of 1830 is not this George Willett and family, but possibly an otherwise unknown "son" of George Willet as noted in the 1800 York County census record.

George Willet died on June 30, 1835, at Manheim, in York County, Pennsylvania.

1. **WILLET** (son): b abt 1793.
2. **WILLET** (daughter): b abt 1797.

PA.1.7
JACOB WILLET and ROSINA FLINCHBAUGH
of Bucks County and Adams County, Pennsylvania

Jacob Willet was born on July 4, 1759, at Keelersville, Bedminster, Bucks County, Pennsylvania.

Jacob Willet married about 1783, Rosina Flinchbaugh (b 1765; d December 22, 1850, Littlestown, Union Township, Adams County, Pennsylvania.

They lived near Littlestown, Adams County, Pennsylvania.

In 1790, Jacob Willet and family were listed in the York County, Pennsylvania, census, page 290, as follows:

1 male	16-up	bef. 1774	*Jacob*	*age 31*	*b 1759*
1 female			*Rosina*	*age 25*	*b 1765*
1 male	16-up	bef.1744			
1 female					
1 female			*Eva Cath.*	*age 5*	*b 1785*
1 male	0-16	1774-1790	*John*	*age 3*	*b 1787*

On December 25, 1795, Jacob Willett and Christina were sponsors of the baptism of Christina Cramer, the daughter of Henry Cramer and Christina (*Records of York County, Church Records of the 18th Century*, by Marlene S. Bates and F. Edward Wright). Christina Willett may have been Jacob's sister.

In 1800, Jacob Willet and family were listed in the York County, Pennsylvania, census, page 514, as follows:

1 male	45-up	bef. 1765	*Jacob*	*age 41*	*b 1759*
1 female	26-45	bef. 1765	*Rosina*	*age 35*	*b 1765*
1 female	10-16	1784-1790	*Eva Cath.*	*age 15*	*b 1785*
1 male	10-16	1784-1790	*John*	*age 13*	*b 1787*

1 male	0-10	1790-1800	*Anthony*	*age 8*	*b 1792*
1 male	0-10	1790-1800	*Henry*	*age 8*	*b 1792*
1 male	0-10	1790-1800	*George*	*age 5*	*b 1795*
1 female	0-10	1790-1800	*Christina*	*age 4*	*b 1796*
1 female	0-10	1790-1800	*Elizabeth*	*age 2*	*b 1798*
1 female	0-10	1790-1800	*Susannah*	*age 0*	*b 1800*

Jacob Willet died in 1806, at Union Township, Adams County, Pennsylvania. His will mentions his brother, Anthony. In 1810, Rosannah Willet is listed as the head of a household in Germany Township, Adams County, Pennsylvania, census, page 124, as follows:

1 female	26-45	1765-1784	*Rosina*	*age 45*	*b 1765*
1 male	10-16	1784-1790	*John*	*age 13*	*b 1787*
1 male	16-26	1784-1794	*Anthony*	*age 18*	*b 1792*
1 male	16-26	1784-1794	*Henry*	*age 18*	*b 1792*
1 male	16-26	1784-1794	*George*	*age 15**	*b 1795**
1 female	10-16	1794-1800	*Christina*	*age 14*	*b 1796*
1 female	10-16	1794-1800	*Elizabeth*	*age 12**	*b 1798*
1 female	10-16	1794-1800	*Susannah*	*age 10*	*b 1810*
1 male	0-10	1800-1810	*Jacob*	*age 8*	*b 1808*
1 female	0-10	1800-1810	*Mary*	*age 6*	*b 1804*

(REF: Adams County Court Records; St. John's Lutheran Church Records; "Willett House" Quarterly, page 210).

1. **Eva Catherine WILLET**: b February 13, 1785, birth recorded at St. Johns Evangelical Lutheran Church, Littlestown, Adams County, Pennsylvania; m John Scholl; made the overland trip from Adams County, Pennsylvania, to Montgomery County, Ohio, about 1830.

2. **John** ("Johan") **WILLET**: b February 20, 1787, birth recorded at St. Johns Evangelical Lutheran Church, Adams County, Pennsylvania; m abt 1815, Anna Mary (February 23, 1792; d February 16, 1877); d May 28, 1863, Adams County, Pennsylvania. See next PA.1.7.2.

3. **Anthony WILLET**: b May 29, 1792, birth recorded at St. Johns Evangelical Lutheran Church, Adams County, Pennsylvania; d December 12, 1801.

4. **Henry WILLET**: chr. February 26, 1792, at St. Johns Evangelical Lutheran Church, Adams County, Pennsylvania; m abt 1819, Rebecca (also reported as Margaret [Bahr]); d September 25, 1866. See next PA.1.7.4.

5. **George WILLET**: b January 2, 1795, birth recorded at St. Johns Evangelical Lutheran Church; m Elizabeth McKinney (b March 25, 1797; d August 16, 1877); d April 9, 1876,

Adams County, Pennsylvania. See next PA.1.7.5.

6. **Christina WILLET**: chr. June 6, 1796, at St. Johns Evangelical Lutheran Church, Adams County, Pennsylvania; m Jacob Bardt.

7. **Elizabeth WILLET**: b May 13, 1798, birth recorded at St. Johns Evangelical Lutheran Church, Adams County, Pennsylvania; m in Pennsylvania abt 1820, David Warner (b December 26, 1795; d June 7, 1830), the son of Philip and Susannah Warner; abt 1845, removed to Butler County, Ohio; d July 9, 1869, Montgomery County, Ohio, buried Old German Lutheran Cemetery, Butler Township, Ohio.

8. **Susannah WILLET**: b August 13, 1800, near Littlestown, Adams County, Pennsylvania; m Henry Earhart (b 1801; d 1852); abt 1845, removed to Ohio; d October 17, 1881, Miami, Ohio. See next PA.1.7.8.

9. **Jacob WILLET**: chr. October 24, 1802, at St. Johns Evangelical Lutheran Church, Adams County, Pennsylvania; m Sarah (b June 24, 1803, Pennsylvania; d May 24, 1888, Carroll County, Maryland); d February 11, 1852, Carroll County, Maryland. See next PA.1.7.9.

10. **Mary** ("Polly") **WILLET**: b 1804, Pennsylvania; m Frederic Motter; made the overland trip from Adams County, Pennsylvania, to Montgomery County, Ohio, about 1830; d Ohio.

PA.1.7.2
JOHN WILLET and ANNA MARY
of Adams County, Pennsylvania

John ("Johan") Willet was born on February 20, 1787, in Adams County, Pennsylvania.

John Willet married about 1815, Anna Mary (b February 23, 1792; d February 11, 1877, buried Christ Reformed Cemetery, Union Township, Adams County, Pennsylvania).

In 1820, John Willett and family were listed in the Germany, Adams County, Pennsylvania, census, page 68, as follows:

1 male	26-45	1775-1794	*John*	*age 33*	*b 1787*
1 female	26-45	1775-1794	*Anna Mary*	*age 28*	*b 1792*
1 male	16-26	1794-1804			
1 female	0-10	1810-1820	*Henrietta*	*age 5*	*b 1815*
1 female	0-10	1810-1820	*Lydia*	*age 4*	*b 1816*
1 female	0-10	1810-1820	*Sarah*	*age 2*	*b 1818*
1 female	0-10	1810-1820	*Mary Ann*	*age 0?*	*b 1820?*

In 1830, John <u>Willet</u> and family were listed in the Germany, Adams County, Pennsylvania, census, page 68, as follows:

1 male	40-50	1780-1790	John	*age 43 b 1787*
1 male	20-30	1800-1810		
1 female	20-30	1800-1810		
1 female	10-15	1815-1820	*Henrietta*	*age 15 b 1815*
1 female	10-15	1815-1820	*Lydia*	*age 14 b 1816*
1 female	5-10	1820-1825	*Mary Ann*	*age 10? b 1820?*

In 1840, John <u>Willet</u> and family were listed in the Germany Township, Adams County, Pennsylvania, census, page 62, as follows:

1 male	50-60	1780-1790	*John*	*age 53 b 1787*
1 female	40-50	1790-1800	Anna Mary	age 48 b 1792
1 female	20-30	1810-1820	*Mary Ann*	*age 20 b 1820*
1 female	20-30	1810-1820	*Elizabeth*	*age 18* b 1822**
1 male	20-30	1810-1820		

In 1850, John Willet and family are listed in the Union Township, Adams County, Pennsylvania, census, page 271, dwelling 98-101, as follows:

Willet	John	64	m	PA	farmer, $2,000
	Mary	54	f	PA	
	Elizabeth	28	f	PA	

John Willet died on May 26, 1863.

(REF: *The Willett Families*, page 245; "Willett House" Quarterly, page 211).

　　1. **Henrietta WILLET**: b May 5, 1815, chr. July 23, 1815, at York, Hanover, St. Mathews Lutheran Church; m March 23, 1837, Jacob Sell.

　　2. **Lydia WILLET**: b December 18, 1816, chr. on March 20, 1817, at York, Hanover, St. Mathews Lutheran Church; m April 26, 1840, Reuben Shanebrough.

　　3. **Sarah WILLET**: b 1818; d July 23, 183x.

　　4. **Mary Ann WILLET**: b abt 1820; m at York, Hanover, St. Mathews Lutheran Church on February 4, 1847, Daniel Palmer.

　　5. **Elizabeth WILLET**: b 1822; m at York, Hanover, St. Mathews Lutheran Church, on February 15, 1859, Isaac Rife.

PA.1.7.4
HENRY WILLET and REBECCA
of Adams County, Pennsylvania

Henry Willet was born on July 20, 1790, Adams County, Pennsylvania. He was christened on September 26, 1792, at Adams, Littlestown, St. Johns Evangelical Lutheran Church.

Henry Willet married about 1819, Rebecca (Rebecca is in the 1850 census; also reported as Margaret Bahr) (b 1799, Pennsylvania; d May 5, 1881, age 82 years, 1 month, 13 days, buried St. Bartholomew Cemetery, W. Manheim Township, Adams County, Pennsylvania).

In 1820, Henry <u>Willett</u> and family were listed in the Germany, York County, Pennsylvania, census, page 66, as follows:

1 male	26-45	1775-1794	*Henry*	*age 30*	*b 1790*
1 female	16-26	1794-1804	*Rebecca*	*age 21*	*b 1799*
1 male	0-10	1810-1820			

In 1830, Henry <u>Willett</u> and family were listed in the Germany, York County, Pennsylvania, census, page 68, as follows:

1 male	30-40	1790-1800	*Henry*	*age 40*	*b 1790*
1 female	30-40	1790-1800	*Rebecca*	*age 31*	*b 1799*
1 male	5-10	1820-1825	*Henry*	*age 5*	*b 1825*
1 female	0-5	1825-1830	*Louisa*	*age 2*	*b 1828*
1 male	0-5	1825-1830	*Emmanuel*	*age 0*	*b 1830*
1 male	0-5	1825-1830			

In 1840, Henry <u>Willett</u> and family were listed in the Germany, York County, Pennsylvania, census, page 64, as follows:

1 male	50-60	1780-1790	*Henry*	*age 50*	*b 1790*
1 female	40-50	1790-1800	*Rebecca*	*age 41*	*b 1799*
1 male	20-30	1810-1820			
1 male	15-20	1820-1825	*Henry*	*age 15*	*b 1825*
1 female	10-15	1825-1830	*Louisa*	*age 12*	*b 1828*
1 male	10-15	1825-1830	*Emmanuel*	*age 10*	*b 1830*
1 male	5-10	1830-1835			
1 male	0-5	1835-1840	*David*	*age 3*	*b 1837*
1 female	0-5	1835-1840	*Mary Ann*	*age 1*	*b 1839*

In 1850, Henry Willett and family were listed in the Union Township, Adams County, Pennsylvania, census, dwelling

115-117, page 272, as follows:

Willett	Henry, Sr.	62	m	PA	mason
	Rebecca	51	f	PA	
	Emmanuel	36	m	PA, shoemaker	
	David	13	m	PA	
	Mary A.	11	f	PA	

Henry Willet died on September 25, 1866.
(*The Willett Families*, page 245; "Willett House" Quarterly, page 211).

1. (male) **WILLET**: b abt 1820; possibly died young.
2. **Henry WILLET** (II): b 1825 in Pennsylvania; m on October 27, 1846, Elizabeth Palmer (b November 2, 1825, Pennsylvania; d September 29, 1865, buried Mt. Carmel Cemetery, Germany Township, Adams County); resided in Union Township, Adams County, Pennsylvania. See next PA.1.7.4.2.
3. **Louisa WILLET**: b January 27, 1828, chr. May 22, 1828, Adams, Littlestown, St. Johns Evangelical Lutheran Church; d May 22, 19--.
4. **Emmanuel WILLET**: b August 30, 1830 (1824), in Pennsylvania, chr. November 7, 1830, Adams, Littlestown, St. Johns Evangelical Lutheran Church (father Henrich Willet, mother Margretha); a shoemaker; d 1857.
5. **Maria Elizabeth WILLET**: chr. May 7, 1834, Adams, Littlestown, St. Johns Evangelical Lutheran Church.
6. **David WILLET**: b March 31, 1837, Pennsylvania, chr. July 2, 1837, Adams, Littlestown, St. Johns Evangelical Lutheran Church (father Henry, mother Margaret); m abt 1865, Lizzie (b 1838, Pennsylvania). See next PA.1.7.4.6
7. **Mary Ann** ("Marian") **WILLET**: b October 11, 1839, Pennsylvania, chr. March 15, 1840, Adams, Littlestown, St. Johns Evangelical Lutheran Church; d August 24, 1892, age 52 years, 10 months, 5 days, buried St. Bartholomew Cemetery, W. Manheim Township, Adams County, Pennsylvania.

PA.1.7.4.2
HENRY WILLET and ELIZABETH PALMER
of Union Township, Adams County, Pennsylvania

Henry Willet (II) was born in 1825 (1828) in Pennsylvania.
Henry Willet married on October 27, 1846, Elizabeth Palmer (b November 2, 1827, Pennsylvania; d September 29, 1865, buried Mt. Carmel Cemetery, Germany Township,

Adams County).

In 1850, Henry Willet and family are listed in the Union Township, Adams County, Pennsylvania, page 270, dwelling 79-80, as follows:

Willet	Henry	25	m	PA	laborer $400
	Elizabeth	25	f	PA	
	Unias	3	m	PA	
	Louisa	1	f	PA	
Palmer	Catherine	44	f	PA	

In 1860, Henry Willet and family are listed in the Germany Township, Adams County, Pennsylvania, no. 169, as follows:

Willet	Henry	32	m	PA	farmer
	Eliza	33	f	PA	
	Aarah	12	m	PA	
	Susannah	9	f	PA	
	Jacob	6	m	PA	
	Abbey	3	f	PA	
	Mary	2	f	PA	

(REF: *The Willett Families*, page 245; "Willett House" Quarterly, page 212).

    1. **Urias** ("Unias", "Uriah") **WILLET**: b May 8, 1847, York, Hanover, St. Mathews Lutheran Church; m abt 1870, Susan (b October 25, 1852, Pennsylvania; d June 17, 1923); d September 16, 1911. See next PA.1.7.4.2.1.

    2. **Louisa WILLET**: b 1849.

    3. **Susannah WILLET**: b 1851, Pennsylvania.

    4. **Jacob WILLET**: b July 16, 1852, chr. September 22, 1852, York, Hanover, St. Mathews Lutheran Church; m abt 1874, Amanda (b January 12, 1855, Pennsylvania; d November 3, 1928, Frederick County, Maryland); d January 16, 1935, buried Frederick County. See next PA.1.7.4.2.4.

    5. **Amos David WILLET**: b March 28, 1855, chr. May 15, 1855, York, Hanover, St. Mathews Lutheran Church; m abt 1877, Hattie (b April 24, 1857, Pennsylvania; d July 26, 1920, buried Mt. Carmel Cemetery, Germany Township). See next PA.1.7.4.2.5.

    7. **Mary Minerva WILLET**: chr. May 24, 1858, Adams, Littlestown, St. John Evangelical Lutheran Church.

PA.1.7.4.2.1
URIAS WILLET and SUSAN
of Adams County, Pennsylvania

Urias ("Unias", "Uriah") Willet was born on May 8, 1847, at York, Hanover, St. Mathews Lutheran Church record.

Urias Willet married about 1870, Susan (b October 25, 1852, Pennsylvania; d June 17, 1923, age 70 years, 7 months, 22 days).

In 1880, Uriah Willet and family are listed in the Germany Township, Adams County, Pennsylvania, as follows:

Willet	Uriah	33	m	PA
	Susan	28	f	PA
	Edward	9	f	MD
	William A.	7	m	MD
	Bertie E.	6	f	MD
	Henry J.	4	m	PA
	Laura B.	2	f	PA
	Frank	10/12	m	PA
Harner	J. P.	67	f	PA

Urias Willet died on September 16, 1911, age 64 years, 4 months, 8 days; both Urias and Susan are buried at St. John's Cemetery, Germany Township, Adams County, Pennsylvania.

1. **Edward WILLET**: b 1871, Maryland.

2. **William A. WILLET**: b 1873, Maryland; d December 23, 1893, age 21 years, 5 months, 8 days, buried St. John's Cemetery, Germany Township, Adams County, Pennsylvania.

3. **Bertie E. WILLET**: b 1874, Maryland.

4. **Henry J. WILLET**: b 1876, Pennsylvania; d March 1, 1894, age 17 years, 8 months, 25 days, buried at St. John's Cemetery, Germany Township, Adams County, Pennsylvania.

5. **Laura B. WILLET**: b 1878, Pennsylvania.

6. **Frank WILLET**: b late 1879 or early 1880.

7. **Ezra G. WILLET**: b 1884; d August 10, 1885, age 9 months, 14 days, buried at St. John's Cemetery, Germany Township, Adams County, Pennsylvania.

8, **Luella E. WILLET**: b 1892; d August 20, 1900, age 8 years, 3 months, 27 days, buried at St. John's Cemetery, Germany Township, Adams County, Pennsylvania.

PA.1.7.4.2.4
JACOB WILLET and AMANDA
of York County, Pennsylvania

Jacob Willet was christened on September 22, 1852 (1854), York, Hanover, St. Mathews Lutheran Church. Jacob Willet married about 1874 Amanda (b 1855, Pennsylvania).

In 1880, Jacob Willet and family are listed in the Adams County, Pennsylvania, as follows:

Willet	Jacob	27	m	PA
	Amanda	25	f	PA
	Ada	4	f	PA
	Harvey	3	m	PA
	Kate R.	3/12	f	PA

Jacob Willett died in 1924, leaving the following will:

I, Jacob Willet of Hanover Borough, York County, being of sound mind and memory and understanding, do make this my last will and testament in manner and form following:

I give and bequeath unto my beloved wife, Amanda Willet, her heirs and assigns, all my property, real, personal, and mixed.

I nominate, constitute, and appoint my said wife, sole Executrix of this my last will and testament.

In Witness Whereof, I have hereunto set my hand and seal this fifteenth day of September, A.D. 1924.

Jacob Willet

1. **Emma Ada WILLET**: b October 5, 1875, Pennsylvania; chr. March 6, 1876, at St. Matthews Lutheran Church, Hanover, Penn Township, York County, Pennsylvania.
2. **Howard** ("Harvey") **C. WILLET**: b October 8, 1877, Pennsylvania; chr. August 7, 1878, at St. Matthews Lutheran Church, Hanover, Penn Township, York County, Pennsylvania.
3. **Kate R. WILLET**: b 1880, Pennsylvania.
4. **Lulu Grace WILLET**: b February 20, 1888.
5. **J. Russell WILLET**: b April 18, 1894.

PA.1.7.4.2.5
AMOS DAVID WILLET and HATTIE
of Adams County, Pennsylvania

Amos David Willet was born on March 28, 1855. He was christened on May 15, 1855, at York, Hanover, St. Mathews Lutheran Church.

Amos Willet married about 1877, Hattie ("Hettie") (b April 24, 1857, Pennsylvania; d July 26, 1920, buried Mt. Carmel Cemetery, Germany Township).

In 1880, Amos Willet and family are listed in the Union Township, Adams County, Pennsylvania, as follows:

Willet	Amos	25	m	PA
	Hettie	23	f	PA
	Howard	2	m	PA
	Claretta	5/12	f	PA

1. **Howard WILLET**: b 1878, Pennsylvania.
2. **Claretta WILLET**: b 1880, Pennsylvania.
3. **George Henry WILLET**: b December 10, 1890, chr. May 17, 1891, Christ Reformed Church, Littlestown, Union Township, Adams County, Pennsylvania.

PA.1.7.4.6
DAVID WILLET and LIZZIE
of Union Township, Adams County, Pennsylvania

David Willet was born on March 31, 1837, Pennsylvania. He was chr. on July 2, 1837, at St. Matthews Lutheran Church, Hanover, Penn Township, York County, Pennsylvania, the son of Henry Willet and Margaret.

David Willet married about 1865, Lizzie (b 1838, Pennsylvania).

In 1880, David Willet and family are listed in the Union Township, Adams County, Pennsylvania, as follows:

Willet	David	42	m	PA
	Lizzie	42	f	PA
	Eliza	12	m	PA
	Sarah	10	f	PA
	Isaiah	5	m	PA

1. **Eliza WILLET**: b 1869, Pennsylvania.
2. **Sarah WILLET**: b 1870, Pennsylvania.
3. **Isaiah George WILLET**: b March 26, 1875, Pennsylvania; m at Hanover, York County, on November 21, 1897, Elsie A. Ernst.

PA.1.7.5
GEORGE WILLET and **ELIZABETH MCKINNEY**
of Adams County, Pennsylvania

George Willet was born on January 2, 1795 (July, 1794).

George Willet married about 1815, Elizabeth McKinney (b March 25, 1797, Maryland; d August 16, 1877).

In 1820, George <u>Willett</u> and family were listed in the Germany, Adams County, Pennsylvania, census, page 66, as follows:

1 male	26-45	1775-1794	*George*	*age 25*	*b 1795*
1 female	26-45	1775-1794	*Elizabeth*	*age 23*	*b 1797*
1 female	0-10	1810-1820			
1 female	0-10	1810-1820	*Dorothy*	*age 4?*	*b 1816?*
1 female	0-10	1810-1820	*Sally*	*age 2*	*b 1818*
1 female	0-10	1810-1820	*Lydia*	*age 0*	*b 1820*

In 1830, George <u>Willet</u> and family were listed in the Germany, Adams County, Pennsylvania, census, page 68, as follows:

1 male	30-40	1790-1800	*George*	*age 32*	*b 1798*
1 female	30-40	1790-1800	*Elizabeth*	*age 33*	*b 1797*
1 female	15-20	1810-1815	*Dorothy*	*age 15?*	*b 1815?*
1 female	10-15	1815-1820	*Sally*	*age 12*	*b 1818*
1 female	5-10	1820-1825	*Lydia*	*age 10*	*b 1820*
1 female	5-10	1820-1825	*Emilia*	*age 6*	*b 1824*
1 male	0-5	1825-1830	*David G*	*age 4*	*b 1826*
1 female	0-5	1825-1830	*Susannah*	*age 2*	*b 1828*

In 1840, George <u>Willet</u> and family were listed in the Germany, Adams County, Pennsylvania, census, page 64, as follows:

1 male	40-50	1790-1800	George	age 45	b 1795
1 female	40-50	1790-1800	Elizabeth	age 43	b 1797
1 female	20-30	1810-1820	Sally	age 22	b 1818
1 female	15-20	1820-1825	Lydia	age 20	b 1820
1 female	10-15	1825-1830	Emilia	age 16*	b 1824*
1 male	10-15	1825-1830	David G	age 14	b 1826
1 female	5-10	1830-1835	Lucinda	age 5	b 1835
1 male	0-5	1835-1840	George H	age 4	b 1836

In 1850, George Willet and family are listed in the Union Township, Adams County, Pennsylvania, census, page 273, dwelling 126-132, as follows:

Willet	George	56	m	PA	laborer
	Elizabeth	56	f	MD	
	Lucinda	15	f	PA	
	George	13	m	PA	

George Willet died on April 9, 1876, Adams County, Pennsylvania, and is buried in the Conewago Chapel, Conewago Township, Adams County.

(REF: *The Willett Families*, 1985, pages 245-246; "Willett House" Quarterly, page 212).

1. **Dorothy WILLET**: b abt 1815; m abt 1835, Mr. Kreps.
2. **Sally WILLET**: b July 20, 1818.
3. **Lydia WILLET**: b May 14, 1820, chr. August 13, 1820, Adams, Littlestown, Christ Reformed Church.
4. **Emilia WILLET**: b December 8, 1824, chr. March 20, 1825, at the Christ Reformed Church, Littlestown, Union Township, Adams County, Pennsylvania.
5. **David Gregory WILLET**: b December 4, 1826, Adams County, Pennsylvania, chr. March 11, 1827, at the Christ Reformed Church, Littlestown, Union Township, Adams County, Pennsylvania; m October 31, 1851, Mary A. Hott (b March 29, 1823, Berkeley County, (now West) Virginia; d March 21, 1905, age 82 years, 11 months, 21 days); d on November 11, 1916, and is buried in the Gerradstown Presbyterian Church Cemetery, Gerradstown, Berkeley County, West Virginia. See next PA.1.7.5.5.
6. **Susannah WILLET**: b 1828, Maryland; m October, 185x, John F. Krug (b December 28, 1849, Meyers District, Carroll County, Maryland) of Kingsdale, Hanover, York County, Pennsylvania.
7. **Lucinda WILLET**: b 1835, Pennsylvania.
8. **George H. WILLET**: b December 31, 1836, Pennsylvania; m at Conewago Chapel, Edge Grove, Pennsylvania, on April 28, 1861, Joanna Seigfried (b June 26, 1813; d June 28, 1865); d February 12, 1920, both are buried at the Conewago Chapel, Conewago Township, Adams County, Pennsylvania. See next PA.1.7.5.8.

PA.1.7.5.5
DAVID GREGORY WILLET and MARY A. HOTT
of Berkeley County, West Virginia

David Gregory Willet was born on December 3, 1826, Adams County, Pennsylvania, and was chr. on March 11, 1827.

David Willet married on October 31, 1851, Mary A. Hott (b March 29, 1823, Berkeley County, (now West) Virginia; don March 21, 1905, and is buried in the Gerradstown Presbyterian Church Cemetery, Gerradstown, Berkeley County, West Virginia, age 82 years, 11 months, 21 days), the daughter of Jacob and Anna (Frieze) Hott of Frederick County, Virginia.

In 1870, David <u>Willet</u>, age 44, born Pennsylvania, and family are listed in the Gerardtown Township, Berkeley County, (West) Virginia, census, page 186 (not copied).

David Willett was a miller in Mill Creek District, Berkeley County, West Virginia.

In 1880, David <u>Willet</u> and family are listed in the Mill Creek District, Township, Berkeley County, (West) Virginia, census, as follows:

Willet	David	m	52	PA
	Mary A.	f	55	VA
McKonn	Lydia	f	27	VA
Willet	Mary J.	f	22	VA
	Arthalinda	f	21	VA
	George	m	17	VA
	Jacob	m	15	VA
	Cana	m	10	VA

David Willet died on November 11, 1916, and is buried in the Gerradstown Presbyterian Church Cemetery, Gerradstown, Berkeley County, West Virginia (*Cemeteries of Martinsburg, and Berkeley County, West Virginia*, Berkeley County Historical Society, page 132).

(*Historical Hand Atlas*, "Personal History Department, Berkeley County, West Virginia," pages 2-3).

1. **Lydia A. WILLET**: b September 5, 1852, Virginia; m Braithwaith; resided (1934) Martinsburg, Berkeley County, West Virginia.

2. **David H. WILLET**: b February 5, 1854; d before 1934.

3. **John W. WILLET**: b July 2, 1855; d before 1934.

4. **Mary J. WILLET**: b January 14, 1857, Virginia.

5. **Arthalinda** ("Arthur L.") **Linda WILLET**: b February 16, 1859, Berkeley County, (West) Virginia, the daughter of

Dave and Mary Willett; m 1887, John Swimley; removed to Urbana, Champaign County, Ohio; d February 18, 1934, Urbana, Champaign County, Ohio. See next PA.1.7.5.5.5.

6. **Lucy E. WILLET**: b December 13, 1860.

7. **George W. WILLET**: b March 10, 1863, near Martinsburg, Berkeley County, West Virginia; George W. Wellet married in Champaign County, Ohio, on December 22, 1893, Laura Tarbutton (b 1871; d February 2, 1953, age 82, buried Maple Grove Cemetery, Mechanicsburg, Champaign County, Ohio), the daughter of James and Sara Given Tarbutton; d on September 12, 1926, age 63 years, 6 months, and 2 days, and is buried in the Mausoleum, Maple Grove Cemetery, Mechanicsburg, Champaign County, Ohio. See next PA.1.7.5.5.7.

8. **Jacob H. WILLET**: b February 3, 1865; d on June 14, 1911, and is buried in the Gerradstown Presbyterian Church Cemetery, Gerradstown, Berkeley County, West Virginia.

9. **Floyd C. WILLET**: b October 11, 1869; d before 1934.

PA.1.7.5.5.5
ARTHALINDA WILLETT and JOHN SWIMLEY

Arthalinda (Arthur L., Linda) Willett was born on February 16, 1859, Berkeley County, (West) Virginia, the daughter of Dave and Mary Willett.

Miss Arthalinda Willett married in 1887, John Swimley. They resided in Urbana, Champaign County, Ohio.

Mrs. Arthalinda (Willett) Swimley died on February 18, 1934, Urbana, Champaign County, Ohio.

1. **Bess SWIMLEY**: m Baker.

   1. **Virginia BAKER**:

PA.1.7.5.5.7
GEORGE W. WILLET and LAURA TARBUTTON
of Champaign County, Ohio

George W. Willet was born on March 10, 1863, near Martinsburg, Berkeley County, West Virginia. About 1890, he removed to Champaign County, Ohio. George W. Wellet married in Champaign County, Ohio, on December 22, 1893, Laura Tarbutton (b 1871; d February 2, 1953, age 82, buried Maple Grove Cemetery, Mechanicsburg, Champaign County, Ohio), the daughter of James and Sara Given Tarbutton.

George W. Willet died on September 12, 1926, age 63 years, 6 months, and 2 days, and is buried in the Mausoleum, Maple Grove Cemetery, Mechanicsburg, Champaign County, Ohio.

(REF: Obituary, 1926, Geo. Willett, Mechanicsburg, Champaign County, Ohio; Obituary, 1953, Mrs. Laura Willett, Mechanicsburg, Champaign County, Ohio).

1. **Edwin WILLETT** (adopted): September 10, 1910, Latty, Paulding County, Ohio; m 1st June, 1932, Elizabeth Dickey (b 1909; d October 23, 1933, age 24, buried Maple Grove Cemetery, Mechanicsburg, Champaign County, Ohio), the daughter of Harry Dickey; m 2d October 23, 1937, Charlotte Lavera Pullins (b May 10, 1919, West Alexandria, Ohio), the daughter of Dale Robinson and Vera Louise Holliday; resided (1953) Mechanicsburg, Champaign County, Ohio. (Obituary, 1933, Mrs. (Elizabeth Dickey) Willett, Mechanicsburg, Champaign County, Ohio; *Arvy A. Pullins and Eliza E. Spencer Pullins: Descendants and Ancestors*, 1988, Sauner, Candace Ann Tarpenning, pages 21-22).

1. **Linda Sue WILLETT**: b December 11, 1946, Champaign County, Ohio; m February 17, 1968, Steve Marion; resides (1988) Columbus, Franklin County, Ohio (*Arvy A. Pullins and Eliza E. Spencer Pullins: Descendants and Ancestors*, 1988, Sauner, Candace Ann Tarpenning, pages 21-22).

2. **William Edwin WILLETT**: b May 5, 1953, Champaign County, Ohio; works (1988) for Honda Motor Company; resides (1988) Urbana, Champaign County, Ohio (*Arvy A. Pullins and Eliza E. Spencer Pullins: Descendants and Ancestors*, 1988, Sauner, Candace Ann Tarpenning, pages 21-22).

PA.1.7.5.8
GEORGE H. WILLET and JOANNA SEIGFRIED
of Adams County, Pennsylvania

George H. Willett was born December 31, 1836, Pennsylvania.

George H. Willet married at Conewago Chapel, Edge Grove, Pennsylvania, on April 28, 1861, Joanna Seigfried (b June 26, 1813; d June 28, 1865).

George Willet died February 12, 1920, and both he and his wife are buried at the Conewago Chapel, Conewago Township, Adams County, Pennsylvania.

1. **Mary Ella Elizabeth WILLET**: b April 18, 1864; bp. April 24, 1864, Conewago Chapel, Conewago Township, Adams County, Pennsylvania.

PA.1.7.8
SUSANNAH WILLET and HENRY EARHART
of Miami, Ohio

Susannah Willet was born on August 13, 1800, near Littlestown, Adams County, Pennsylvania.

Miss Susannah Willet married about 1825, Henry Earhart (b 1801; d 1852).

About 1845, the Earharts removed to Ohio.

Mrs. Susannah (Willet) Earhart died on October 17, 1881, Miami, Ohio.

1. **George EARHART**: b February, 1836; m Elmira Esther Olwin (b February, 1842; d October 16, 1901); d 1900.

1. **Harry Leroy EARHART**: b December 25, 1878; m Orpha Leona Thomas (b June 24, 1879; d January 1, 1957); d January 22, 1935.

PA.1.7.9
JACOB WILLET and SARAH
of Carroll County, Maryland

Jacob Willet was christened on October 24, 1802, St. Johns Evangelical Lutheran Church, Adams County, Pennsylvania.

In 1819, Jacob Willet, of Adams County, Pennsylvania, had a county assessment of $1,619.99. He could not read or write (*History of Cumberland and Adams County, Pennsylvania*, page 265). Jacob Willet married about 1825, Sarah (b June 24, 1803, Pennsylvania; d May 24, 1888, aged 84 years, 11 months, buried at St. Mary's Cemetery (Old Section), Silver Run, Maryland).

In 1830, Jacob Willet and family were listed in the District 3, Carroll County, Maryland, census, page 2573, dwelling 210-218, as follows:

1 male	20-30	1800-1810	*Jacob*	*age 28 b 1802*
1 female	30-40	1790-1800	*Sarah*	*age 27* b 1803**
1 male	10-15	1815-1820		
1 female	0-5	1825-1830	*Miranda*	*age 1 b 1829*

In 1850, Jacob Willet and family are listed in the 3rd District, Carroll County, Maryland, census, page 257, dwelling 210-218, as follows:

Willet	Jacob	47	m	MD	farmer, $2,500
	Sarah	46	f	PA	
	Maranda F. C.,	20	f	PA	
	Rebecca	19	f	PA	
	Abraham	16	m	MD	farmer
	Caroline E.	13	f	MD	
	Susana	8	f	MD	
	Josephine A.	2	f	MD	

The Last Will and Testament of Jacob Willet of Carroll County, Maryland, as follows to wit:

I give and Bequeath to my wife Sarah Willet, such of my personal property as She may Select not to exceed one hundred dollars as its appraised value.

I give and Bequeath to my Son, Abraham Willet one horse Saddle and Bridle the choice of which to be left to my Said Son.

I give and Bequeath to my daughters, Amanda C. Willet, Rebecca Willet, each One Bed Bedstead and Bedding.

I order and direct authorize and empower my executor

hereinafter named to do the following Acts and things as Soon as may be convenient after my death to wit: To dispose of at Public Sale, the entire Residue of my Personal estate, Also to dispose of all my Real estate at Public or Private Sale, consisting of the Farm or Tract of Land upon which I now reside, lying and being in the county aforesaid, and containing One hundred and forty acres of land more or less. Also my wood lot containing Five acres of Land more or less, lying convenient to the Turnpike in the vicinity of Silver Run Church ...

First, to my wife Sarah Willet nine hundred dollars, Said Bequest to my Said wife to be Satisfaction in full of any Right of Dower which she may or might have of in and to my Said estate.

Secondly, I give and Bequeath the entire Residue of my whole estate to my Son Abraham Willet, and to my Daughters, Amanda, F. C. Willet, Rebecca Willet, Carolina Willet, Susannah Willet, and Josephine Willet, share and share alike.

Lastly, I constitute and appoint Benjamin Shunk Sole executor of this my Last Will and Testament ... Twenty seventh day of January, 1852.

Jacob Willet

(Carroll County, Maryland, Wills).

Jacob Willet died on February 11, 1852, aged 49 years, 6 months, 1 day, in Carroll County, Maryland, and is buried at St. Mary's Cemetery (Old Section), Silver Run, Maryland.

On May 16, 1853, Benjamin Shunk, Executor of Jacob Willet, late of Carroll County, Maryland, deceased, settled in the Orphans Court for Carroll County, an "Accountant" of the estate with a balance due for distribution of $2,018.84.

On November 6, 1854, Benjamin Shunk, Executor of Jacob Willet, late of Carroll County, Maryland, deceased, settled in the Orphans Court for Carroll County, an "Accountant" of the estate ... with a balance due for distribution of $1,489.53. The balance was equally distributed per the instructions in the will between Abraham, Amanda F. C., Rebecca, Carolina, Susanna, and Josephine Willet.

1. **Miranda** ("Marinda") **WILLET**: b April 3, 1828, Pennsylvania; chr. May 24, 1828, Littlestown, Christ Reformed Church.

2. **Rebecca WILLET**: b September 18, 1829, Pennsylvania; chr. October 27, 1829, Littlestown, Christ Reformed

Church; m in Carroll County, Maryland, on December 24, 1852, Jacob Wantz.

3. **Susanna** ("Susan") **WILLET**: b April 9, 1841, Carroll County, Maryland; m September 8, 1861, Jacob Lawyer.

4. **Abraham WILLET**: b October 15, 1833, Maryland; m in Carroll County, Maryland, on February 8, 1864, Elizabeth Myers (b 1831, Pennsylvania); resided Carroll County, Maryland (1880). See next PA.1.7.9.4.

5. **Caroline Elizabeth WILLET**: b July 23, 1836, Carroll County, Maryland.

6. **Josephine Agnes WILLET**: b March 8, 1848, Carroll County, Maryland.

PA.1.7.9.4
ABRAHAM WILLET and ELIZABETH MYERS
of Carroll County, Maryland

Abraham ("Abram") Willet (Villet) was born on October 15, 1833, in Maryland, and was chr. on November 17, 1833, at St. Mary's Lutheran Reformed Church, Silver Run, Carroll County, Maryland.

Abraham Willit married in Carroll County, Maryland, on February 8, 1864, Elizabeth Myers (b 1831, Pennsylvania) (*Carroll County, Maryland, Marriage Licenses 1837-1899*, page 128).

They resided Carroll County, Maryland (1880).

(1880 Frizzleburg, Carroll County census).

1. **Franklin A. WILLET**: b February 9, 1865, Carroll County, Maryland; m in Carroll County, Maryland, on October 24, 1892, Ella M. Wilt. (1880 Carroll County census).

2. **Flora V. WILLET**: b 1867, Maryland; m in Carroll County, Maryland, on December 22, 1886, Milton A. Myers. (1880 Carroll County census).

3. **Josephine E. WILLET**: b 1872, Maryland. (1880 Carroll County census).

CHAPTER TWO
ABRAHAM WILLETT (1759-1822)
OF PENNSYLVANIA

PA.O
ABRAHAM WILLETT
of Hunterdon County, New Jersey

Abraham Willett was born about 1730, possibly in New Jersey. This Abraham Willett, variously of the towns of Reading-ton, Tewksburg, New German Town, is well attested in the Court Records of Hunterdon County, Pennsylvania, as follows:

No. 31460 May 17, 1758
No. 7021 December 8, 1759
No. 34657 August 3, 1762 (1763)
No. 14592 November 26, 1763
No. 9755 May Term 1764
No. 7902 July 23, 1764
No. 33809 May 22, 1765 (1766)
No. 7617 July 26, 1765 (1766)
No. 28036 February Term 1768
No. 34956 October 27, 1768 (1769)
No. 6909 December 15, 1770
No. 33951 February 3, 1773 (1774)
No. 34379 August 3, 1773 (1774)

It is not proven that this Abraham Willet, of Readington (1765), Tewksbury (February, 1768), and New German Township (October, 1768, October, 1770) is the progenitor of the following Willett family. What is known, is that most of the Willett families living in Hunterdon County, New Jersey, can be accounted for, and none of those Willett families have ever claimed the following children as part of their heritage.

PA.2
WILLETT
family of Hunterdon County, New Jersey

There was a Willett family living at Tewksbury, Hunterdon County, New Jersey, in the 1740s.

In 1773-1774 New Jersey Ratable Tax List, the following Willett families were listed for Hunterdon County:

Willet	David	Hunterdon County, Amwell
	David	Hunterdon County, Lebanon
Willett	Cornelius	Hunterdon County, Tewksbury
	Samuel	Hunterdon County, Kingswood
Willit	Samuel	Hunterdon County, Tewksbury
	William	Hunterdon County, Kingswood

The 1800, and 1810 Federal Census records for New Jersey are lost, and so it is not possible to track which families remained in Hunterdon County, New Jersey, and which families removed from that county.

The most likely ancestor of Abraham Willett is William Willett of Hunterdon County, New Jersey (*The Willett Families*, pages 215-216). Bookstaver in his *Willet Genealogy*, 1907, page 66, lists as one of the children of this William Willett, an Abraham. However, this list has been found by later research to be much suspected, and this listing alone should not be sufficient to link the two families. Also, this Abraham, according to Bookstaver, is the one who married Betsey Bugsby, and appeared in Onondaga County, New York. However, Bookstaver correctly lists a birth date of 1800 for this Abraham, which effectively removes him from being a child of a William Willett who died in 1792!

At this time, all that can be definitely said is that the following 3 children (may) belong to the same Willett family of Hunterdon County, New Jersey.

In searching for the ancestry of this family, the notes made by Samuel Willett Comstock in 1927 and 1928 shed no light on the New Jersey background of this family.

(REF: *The Willett Families*, 1985, page 206).

1. **Peter WILLETT**: b abt 1757 in Hunterdon County, New Jersey. See next PA.2.1.

2. **Abraham WILLETT**: b December 15, 1759, at Hunterdon County, New Jersey; m abt 1783 Sarah Brittain (b November 7, 1764; d December 7, 1843, near Orangeville, Columbia County, Pennsylvania), the daughter of William and Mary

(Collins) Brittain; d August 13, 1822, near Bloomsburg, Columbia County, Pennsylvania. See next PA.2.2.

3. **Rachel WILLETT**: b abt 1761; m Moody; resided in New Jersey.

DISCUSSION OF THE WILLETT-BODINE CONNECTION:

The *Willett Genealogy*, 1906, by J. E. Bookstaver does not mention Abraham Willett or any of his family in either New Jersey, Pennsylvania or Michigan.

There is a persistent family tradition that the below listed children were orphaned by the death of their mother, (supposedly) Elizabeth (Bodine) Willett, the daughter of Jacob Bodine; and that her children were raised by the Bodine family of New Jersey. However, the only known Elizabeth (Bodine) Willett was married to Edward Willett (G.1.2.5.1.2). Vida Miller Pursel in her *Genealogy of the Miller and Pursel Families*, 1939, proposed the "theory" that these were the children of Edward and Elizabeth (Bodine) Willett. This Edward Willett of Lebanon, Hunterdon County, New Jersey, married on June 18, 1752, Elizabeth Bodine. However, Edward Willett and Elizabeth Bodine are known to have had Elbert (b 1753, bp Trinity Church, New York City), Jacob (b 1755; d March 11, 1757, buried Basking Presbyterian Churchyard, Somerset County, New Jersey), Aletta (b 1756), and Edward (b about 1757) (see *The Willett Families*, page 115). This would make it unlikely that Peter (b about 1758), Abraham (b December 15, 1759, Hunterdon County, New Jersey), and Rachel (b abt 1761) were the children of this Edward and Elizabeth Willett.

Also, it is not known that these children (Peter, Abraham, and Rachel) have ever been ascribed to this Edward Willett by any other researcher besides Vida Miller Pursel. However, Edward Willett of New Jersey, did marry a second time, and it could be possible that young children of his first wife were left with their grandparents (*Genealogy of the Miller and Pursel Families*, 1939, pages 150-157).

NOTE: There is no Willett-Bodine marriage mentioned in the *Annals of the Sinott, Rogers, Coffin, Corlies, Reeves, Bodine, and Allied Families*, Mary Elizabeth Sinnott, 1945. The family tradition ascribes Elizabeth Bodine as the daughter of Jacob Bodine. However, Jacob Bodine (b about 1690, or earlier; d 1748) with wife Elizabeth had the following children:

1. **Mary BODINE**: bp April 25, 1711.
2. **John BODINE**: bp October 4, 1714; died young.
3. **St. Jantien BODINE**: bp August 22, 1716.
4. **Jacob BODINE**: bp April 5, 1719.
5. **Catherine BODINE**: bp April 2, 1721.
6. **Cornelius BODINE**: bp September 29, 1723.
7. **Antje BODINE**: bp August 27, 1726.

Noticeably absent is any mention of a daughter, Elizabeth (*Bodine*, page 158).

However, Abraham Bodine (b about 1690; d after 1752) and Adriantje (Janse) had the following children:

1. **Catherine BODINE**: bp April 14, 1723, Readington, Hunterdon County, New Jersey.
2. **Peter BODINE**: bp December 11, 1726, Readington, Hunterdon County, New Jersey.
3. **Elizabeth BODINE**: bp September 23, 1728, New Brunswick, Hunterdon County, New Jersey.
4. **John BODINE**: bp September 6, 1730, Readington, Hunterdon County, New Jersey; m Catherine Brittain.
5. **Abraham BODINE**: bp April 15, 1733, Somerville, Somerset County, New Jersey.
6. **Judick BODINE**: bp March 17, 1735, Somerville, Somerset County, New Jersey.
7. **Isaac BODINE**: bp July 10, 1737, Somerville, Somerset County, New Jersey.
8. **Oken BODINE**: bp November 18, 1739, Somerville, Somerset County, New Jersey.
9. **Arriantje BODINE**: bp November 18, 1741, Somerville, Somerset County, New Jersey.
10. **Maria BODINE**: bp June 10, 1741.

The above Elizabeth Bodine (b 1728) is the only Elizabeth Bodine who is known to be of the correct approximate age and living in Hunterdon County, New Jersey (*Bodine*, page 162). This also agrees with Vida Miller Pursel, page 151, 153.

PA.2.1
PETER WILLETT
of Hunterdon County, New Jersey

Peter Willett was born about 1757 in Hunterdon County, New Jersey.

It is reputed, but not proven, that this Peter Willett removed to Albany, Albany County, New York, after the Revolutionary War, possibly as early as 1780.

A Peter Willett did marry at Albany, Albany County, New York, on October 30, 1808, Helen Van Tassel. This Peter Willett was a cabinet-maker in Troy, New York, in 1808. It is unknown who his parents were, but the Peter of 1757 is not the 1808 Peter Willett of Albany, New York (See penciled notes of Samuel Willett Comstock in *Genealogy of the Miller and Pursel Families*, 1939).

The 1790, 1800, and 1810 Federal Census records, do not list a Peter Willett as the head of a household anywhere in the state of New York.

PA.2.2
ABRAHAM WILLETT and **SARAH BRITTAIN**
of Bloomsburg, Columbia County, Pennsylvania

Abraham Willett was born on December 15, 1759, in Hunderton County, New Jersey, possibly at Tewksbury.

The Revolutionary War caused a lot of uncertainty, and division of loyalties. Perhaps, the uncertainty of being so exposed to forays by either the British Army, Loyalist sympathizers, or the Continental Army caused both the Brittain family and the Willett family to removed into the interior where they would be more safe from the armed conflict. Just as likely, a true pioneering spirit could have motivated them to remove into a new country were land was cash cheap and a person could make a fresh start and a new home for himself and his family through his own hard work.

If the following record belongs to this Abraham Willett, he may have been a Continental soldier.

> In the MSS Ref. No. 2224 (Received Indent.) No. 274 (in 1784, for the depreciation of his Continental pay in the Sussex County Militia); amount 2 pounds, 6 shillings, 2 pence (which indent. was given by Abram's order to Frederick Cramer) being apprenticed to said Cramer.
>
> Name: Abram Willet; Rank Private, Captain Mackay's Company.
>
> *Genealogical Society Revolutionary War Slips* (Microfilm New Jersey State Archives).

About 1783, Abraham Willett married Sarah Brittain (b November 7, 1764; d December 7, 1843, at Orangeville, Columbia County, Pennsylvania), the daughter of William Brittain and Mary Collins of Kingwood Township, Hunterdon County, New Jersey. The date of this marriage is estimated from the birth date of their earliest known child, Mary Willett, born 1785. This marriage should have taken place in New Jersey, but no New Jersey record of this marriage has yet been found. Perhaps, Abraham Willett crossed into Pennsylvania for his marriage, even though he was usually a resident of New Jersey.

Miss Sarah Brittain reputedly saw General George Washington when her brothers, Nathaniel Brittain, Zebedee Brittain, and Samuel Brittain, joined the Northampton County, Pennsylvania, Militia. This was possibly on August 1, 1775, at Plumsted Township, Bucks County, Pennsylvania (Purcell, page 15). Reputedly, on the same date, her brothers, James Brittain, William Brittain and Joseph Brittain, joined the British Army (Purcell, page 14). James, William, and Joseph Brittain, left

America after the war and settled in New Brunswick, Canada, where they died (*Loyalists of New Brunswick*, Sabine; *Royalists of New Jersey*, Stryker).

Mrs. Sarah (Brittain) Willett also is reputed to have seen General Washington after the war when he passed through Trenton.

In 1787, Abraham Kline and family came to Northumberland County, Pennsylvania. They "lived in covered wagons till they had cleared enough ground to raise grain and build a log house. Later, they built more substantial homes" (Pursel, page 60). The Kline family would provide a son-in-law to Abraham Willett. Abraham Willett probably came about the same time (1787 or 1788) as the Kline family and most likely endured similar hardships.

Most previous researchers state that all of Abraham Willett's children were born in New Jersey. This has been misleading the search for Abraham Willett's ancestry. Actually, a check of several different censuses show that the following children were born in Pennsylvania: William, 1793, Peter, 1795, Abraham, 1801, Sarah, 1803. Therefore, other children in the family are also likely to have been born in Pennsylvania and at this date it seems certain that only the first three children were born in New Jersey.

No mention of an Abraham Willet(s) has been found in the 1790 Federal Census for New Jersey or Pennsylvania; nor has an Abraham Willet(s) been found in any other 1790 census. However, one indicator that Abraham Willett and family were in Northumberland County, Pennsylvania, earlier than previously thought, is that in the 1790 census, an Abraham <u>Villet</u> and family were listed in the Northumberland County, Pennsylvania, as follows:

1 male	16-up	bef. 1774	*Abraham*	*age 31*	*b 1759*
1 female			*Sarah*	*age 26*	*b 1764*
1 female			*Mary*	*age 5*	*b 1785*
1 female			*Catherine*	*age 3*	*b 1787*
1 female			*Rachel*	*age 0*	*b 1790*

This census could very well belong to the Abraham Willett family. The original Northumberland County census has been checked to see if this was just a transcription error (it was not: the surname is clearly spelled Villet), but the coincidence is striking and it is most likely the entry for "our" Abraham Willett of Hunterdon County, and now of Northumberland County, Pennsylvania. The William Brittain family was listed next in the 1790 Upper Bethel Township, Northumberland County, Pennsylvania, census; thus the father-in-law of Abraham Willett lived nearby.   William Brittain had previously lived at Kingswood Township, Hunterdon County, New Jersey, and had married on November 30, 1743, Mary Collins of Middletown, Monmouth County, New Jersey.

Abraham Willett and Sarah settled and cleared a farm three miles east of Bloomsburg, Northumberland (now Columbia) County, Pennsylvania.   A deed of purchase was written in Northumberland (now Columbia) County, Pennsylvania, on May 28, 1798, for Abraham Willets (sic) and recorded on June 14, 1809 (*Northumberland County, Pennsylvania, Grantor-Grantee Book Index*, Courthouse, Sunbury).

> *"This Indenture made the twenty eight day of May in the year of Our Lord One Thousand seven hundred and Ninety eight, Between Jeremiah Jackson of the Borough of Sunbury in the County of Northumberland and Commonwealth of Pennsylvania, Gentleman of the one part, and Abraham <u>Willets</u> of Fishing Creek Township in the County aforesaid, Yeoman, of the other part. Witnesseth that the said Jeremiah Jackson for and in Consideration of the sum of Five hundred and seventy five pounds in Gold and Silver Specie to him in hand paid by the said Abraham <u>Willets</u> at and before the ensealing and Delivery hereof the Receipt whereof is hereby Acknowledged have granted ... A certain tract or parcel of land situate in Fishing Creek Township aforesaid Bounded and described as follows:*
>
> *Beginning at a Marked pine thence North sixteen degrees west along a line of Land of George Miller, Junr. Ninety six perches and five tenths to a post thence by land Surveyed for John Bright North seventy four degrees East one hundred and seventy six perches to a post thence by other land of the said Jeremiah Jackson south sixteen degrees West Ninety six perches and five tenths to a post thence by land of Andrew Curling south seventy four Degrees West one hundred and seventy six perches to the place of Beginning, Containing one hundred acres and one tenth and the usual allowance of six percent for Roads, and highways.*
>
> *It is part of the same tract of Land which John Brady Esquire, the then High Sheriff of the County of Northumberland had seized and taken by Execution by virtue of a writ of "Lavari Facias" issued out of the Court of Common Pleas at Sunbury as the late estate of Dennis Perry and was commanded to expose the same to sale, And whereas the said Sheriff after having given due and public notice of the time and the place of its sale of the said Tract of Land did expose the same to sale by public vendue or outcry on Saturday the fifth day of August 1797 and sold the same to the said Jeremiah Jackson party hereto, he*

being the highest bidder at the said Vendue, as in and by the Sheriffs Deed Recorded in the Office for Recording of Deeds in and for the County of Northumberland in Book K, page 106 Relation being hereto had may fully appear.

Together with all and singular the Houses and outhouses, Barns, Stables, Orchards, Gardens, Woods, Waters, Watercourses, Right, Liberties, Privileges, Hereditiments, and appurtences whatsoever ...

Received the day of this date of the within written Indenture of the above named Abraham <u>Willets</u> the sum of Two hundred and Seventy five pounds it being the Consideration Money within mentioned in full."

In the above deed, Abraham Willets (sic) was already noted as being "of" Fishing Creek, Northumberland County, Pennsylvania. Also to be noted is the fact that Abraham's surname is clearly and repeatedly spelled "Willets."

Presumably Abraham Willets/Willett had removed to Pennsylvania before 1798, and most likely he had left New Jersey at an earlier date, and at least in 1793 and possibly as early as 1788 or 1789. Also, it is most likely that Jeremiah Jackson held the deed as security for the payment of the purchase price as he had to sue in 1800 for money due him (perhaps a colonial mortgage payment), and in 1804 his estate had to sue Abraham Willet for additional money due. Also considering that the deed was not recorded in Northumberland County until 1809 leaves the impression that Abraham Willets made the original payment of the purchase in installments.

Thus, Abraham Willett is presumably in Pennsylvania in 1793 and 1798, yet (previously) his children were reportedly born in New Jersey in 1785, 1787, 1790, 1793 (now known to actually having been born in Pennsylvania), 1795 (actually born in Pennsylvania), and 1798. This Abraham Willet(s) has not been found in the 1800 New Jersey or Pennsylvania census, nor has he been found in any other state census for 1800. The 1800 censuses need to be closely checked for alternative and alliterative spellings of the Willett surname.

FOR THE RECORD: An Abraham Willet(t) was living at Cumberland County, New Jersey, in 1800 with the following family listed:

1 male	45-up	bef.-1755
1 female	45-up	bef.-1755
1 male	26-45	1755-1775
1 male	10-16	1785-1790
1 male	10-16	1785-1790

1 female	10-16	1785-1790
1 female	0-10	1790-1800

The above census record is listed "For the Record". The children in this list do not "match" the ages of the children of Abraham Willett and Sarah Brittain who would have had two sons under the age of ten in 1800, so this Abraham Willet(t) is discounted as being the same as the Abraham Willets who purchased land in Northumberland County, Pennsylvania, in 1798.

On April 28, 1800, Abraham Willet was overdue 66 pounds and 13 shillings and 4 pence, owed to Jeremiah Jackson.

Again on January 24, 1804, Abraham Willet was summoned: "Northumberland County Court: The Commonwealth of Pennsylvania to the Sheriff of Northumberland County --- Greeting --- We command you, that you summon Abraham Willits, late of your County yeoman ...

so that he be and appear before our Justices at Sunbury, at our County Court of Common Pleas, there to be held for the County of Northumberland fourth Monday of April next to answer Henry Vanderslie, Administrator de bonis Non of Jeremiah Jackson, deceased, of a plea that he render unto him the sum of sixty-eight pounds, 13/4 lawful money of Pennsylvania which to the Estate of the said deceased he owes and unjustly detains." Documented as 83 pounds 6/8 on the face of the document, the difference evidentially being accrued interest and court cost" (Northumberland County Court record).

In 1810, Abraham Willet (sic) was residing in Bloom Township, Northumberland (now Columbia) County. At that time the Northumberland County, Pennsylvania, census record on page 192 shows:

1 male	45-up	bef.1765	*Abraham*	*age 51*	*b 1759*
1 female	26-45	1765-1785	*Sarah*	*age 46*	*b 1764*
1 female	16-26	1785-1795	*Rachel*	*age 20*	*b 1790*
1 male	16-26	1785-1795	*William*	*age 17*	*b 1793*
1 male	10-16	1795-1800	*Peter*	*age 15*	*b 1795*
1 female	10-16	1795-1800	*Hannah*	*age 12*	*b 1798*
1 male	0-10	1800-1810	*Abraham*	*age 9*	*b 1801*
1 female	0-10	1800-1810	*Sarah*	*age 7*	*b 1803*
1 female	0-10	1800-1810	*Elizabeth*	*age 3*	*b 1807*

On March 19, 1819, Abraham Willet and wife sold to his son William Willet part of the original Willet homestead of 100 acres.

This INDENTURE made the nineteenth day of March in the year of Our Lord one thousand Eight hundred and Nineteen. Between Abraham Willet of Blooms township in the County of Columbia and the State of Pennsylvania and Sarah his wife the one part, And William Willet of the same place, Tanner of the other part.

Witnesseth That the said Abraham Willet and Sarah his wife for and in consideration of Forty five Dollars lawful money of the State of Pennsylvania ...

(sell) Beginning above ... land belonging to Casper Christman thence by the same ... thence by land of the said Abraham Willet North ... to a stone corner ... one acre and sixty two perches and a half.

It being part of the same tract of land (from) John Brady Esquire (the then) high Sheriff of the county of Northumberland ... out of the estate of Dennis Leary ... (Book K, page 106) ... Indenture dated May, 1798.

   Seal: Abraham Willet   Seal: Sarah Willet

Personally appeared before me, Isaac Kline, Justice of Peace.
   Dower release by Sarah Willet
   Recorded April 6, 1819.

In 1820, Abraham Willit (sic) was residing in Bloom Township, Columbia County. At that time the Columbia County, Pennsylvania, census record on page 10 shows:

1 male	45-up	bef. 1775	*Abraham*	age 61	b 1759
1 female	45-up	bef. 1775	*Sarah*	age 56	b 1764
1 male	16-26	1795-1805	*Abraham*	age 19	b 1801
1 female	16-26	1795-1805	*Sarah*	age 17	b 1803
1 female	10-16	1805-1810	*Elizabeth*	age 13	b 1807

Abraham's son, William Willit (sic), is listed as a separate head of a household in Columbia County. Missing in this 1820 census is Abraham's son, Peter Willett, age 25, born 1795.

Abraham Willett died near Bloomsburg, Columbia County, Pennsylvania, on August 13, 1822, age 63.

Abraham's will was probated September 4, 1822 (Book 1, page 146; Book W, page 53) (Pursel, pages 153-154).

NOTE: Underlined words are spelled as in the original document.

Abraham Willet, Dec.d's Will:

No. 6 will

A small accout to my wife and children giving them to un-
derstand the please is not to be sold till the youngest comes of
age and is to ceap the please in her care till hur death without
they consult to sel in the time of the youngest coming of age -
they to make vandue and sel to pay of the debt. Abraham to
work the said place till all paid of and he is to have the incum
of a mare and as such graine as will git him his sundy close
and must provide him self a share Equal to the others boys
wen married - the wife is for her part to have two cows, six
Sheep and a five hogs, and graine as much as she will want
for the while she lives - the children are all to have an Equal
share - June 22, 1822.

These five lines from your Coind father in the sixty three
years of his age, Abraham Willet. Sarah Willet.

Witnesses present: Joseph Garrison, Robert Gadnere.

Having choseing in my small will my wife and Isic Kline in
order to settle my affairs, Columbia County.

Be it remembered that on the fourth day of September,
Anno Domini Eighteen hundred and twenty two - Personally
appeared before me Ellis Hughes, Register, etc., in and for the
said County of Columbia, Joseph Garrison and Robert Gard-
ner, the subscribing witnesses to the forgoing will, who being
duly qualified according to law, did depose and say that they
were personally present at the dwelling house of the within
named Abraham Willet (sic), the testator, in Bloom Township,
and heard him the said testator, acknowledge that he signed
the foregoing instrument of writing as and for his last will and
testament, that at the time of his doing, he the said testator
was of sound and disposing mind, memory, and understand-
ing according to the best of their knowledge, observation and
belief: that at the request of the testator and in his presence
and in the presence of each other, they signed their names, as
witnesses, thereto ...

Be it remembered that on the 4th day of September Anno
Domini 1822, before me Ellis Hughes, Register for the probate
of wills, etc., in and for the county of Columbia, was proven
and approved the last will and testament of Abraham Willet,
late of Bloom Township, in the said county ...

The executor, Isaac Kline, was Abraham Willet's eldest
son-in-law. This will keeps the Abraham Willet farm from being
sold before 1828 when the youngest daughter, Elizabeth would
become 21 and of legal age.

The *Orphan Court Docket 1814-1827*, Columbia County
Courthouse, Sunbury, Pennsylvania, was checked for orphan

records of Abraham Willett's minor children (Sarah and Elizabeth were under 21 in 1822), but no record was found.

In the 1830 census, Abraham Willet and Peter Willet, sons of Abraham Willet, deceased, are listed as heads of their own household. Missing in the 1830 census are William Willet and family, and the widow, Sarah Willett. However, Mrs. Sarah Willett, widow, could have been living with one of her married daughters at this time.

The petition of Sarah Willets and Isaac Kline Esquire, Executors of Abraham Willets, late of Bloom Township, in said county deceased, was preferred to the Court. Humbly sheweth that the said testator did not leave personal estate sufficient for the payment of his debt as by the account hereto annexed appears that the said testator died seized in his demense of fee and in a certain plantation and tract of land situate in Bloom Township aforesaid,

Containing sixty-eight and a half acres more or less adjoining lands of John Bright, Peter Melick, John Robinson, and others, and of no other real estate.   Your Petitioners hu-mbly pray your honors to grant them an order to make sale of the said Plantation and tract of land ... for the payment of the debts of the said estate.

Whereupon August 20, 1833, petition and sale ordered and ... (bond?) to be given in the sum of two thousand dollars.

By the Court

No. 1, Petition for confirmation of the sale of Abraham Willets estate:

The petition of Sarah Willets and Isaac Kline Esquire, Executors of Abraham Willets deceased was preferred to the Court Respectfully. Report that in pursuance of an order of this Honorable Court granted at last term they did on the 25th day of September 1835 expose a certain tract of land situate in Bloom township Containing Sixty-eight acres and one half more or less adjoining lands of John Bright, Peter Mellick, John Robinson, and others ... The estate of said deceased ... sale by public vendue or out cry upon the premises and Sold the same on same day to William Willets in the sum of sixteen hundred dollars, he being the highest bidder and that the highest and best price bidden for the same which sale was aforesaid made, we pray your honrs to confirm thereupon. November 19, 1833. Report and was confirmed.

By the Court

(Columbia County, Petition, Pennsylvania)

NOTE: The above two petitions were very faint on microfilm and difficult to read; they would not reproduce in a readable photocopy. However, the surname was clearly spelled "Willets" both for Abraham Willets, deceased, and his wife Sarah Willets (Albert J. Willett, January, 1990).

In 1831, and 1833, Abraham Willet's estate debts at his decease were greater than his personal estate, so on November 19, 1833, his executor sold, for $1700.00, the remaining sixty-eight and one-half acres to Abraham Willett's eldest son, William Willett. Abraham Willett's son, William Willett, keeps this land for only six months, selling it on April 12, 1834, to Nicholas Grover for $2,500.00; a profit of $800.00 in only six months. (REF: Purcell, pages 153-154; *The Willett Families*, 1985, pages 206-207).

    1. **Mary WILLETT**: b November 27, 1785, in New Jersey; m on February 9, 18(03), Isaac Kline (b March 15, 1779, Kingwood, Hunterdon County, New Jersey; d April 19, 1846, buried at Hidlays Cemetery, Columbia County, Pennsylvania), the son of Abraham Kline and Charity Ann Kramer of Kingwood, Hunterdon County, New Jersey; d June 15, 1854, Fishing Creek Township, Columbia County, Pennsylvania, buried at Hidlays Cemetery, Jamestown, Columbia County, Pennsylvania.
    2. **Catherine WILLETT**: b July 3, 1787, in New Jersey; m in 1810 William Robbins (b February 15, 1786; d January 18, 1867, at Fishing Creek Township, buried Jamestown, Columbia County, Pennsylvania), the son of Thomas Robbins and Elizabeth Kline of Hunterdon County, New Jersey; d October 1, 1828, Fishing Creek Township, Columbia County, buried Jamestown, Hidlays Cemetery, Columbia County, Pennsylvania.
    3. **Rachel B. WILLETT**: b July 11, 1790, in New Jersey; m January 1, 1812, Eli Thornton (b May 10, 1786; d November 19, 1852); d May 19, 1826, at Bloomsburg, Columbia County, Pennsylvania. See next PA.2.2.3.
    4. **William WILLETT**: b May 24, 1793, in Pennsylvania (according to 1850 Richland County, Ohio, census); m January 29, 1818, Hannah Webb (b May 5, 1797, Columbia County, Ohio; d 1882, Plymouth, Richland County, Ohio); d June 30, 1858, near Plymouth, Richland County, Ohio, buried Pioneer Rest Cemetery, Richland County, Ohio. See next PA.2.2.4.
    5. **Peter WILLETT**: b August 1, 1795, in Pennsylvania (according to 1850 Huron County, Ohio, census); m 1st abt 1819 Catherine Sidle (b February 5, 1799; d January 1, 1843); m 2d before 1850, Mrs. Rebecca Webb (b 1811, Pennsylvania; d abt December, 1874, Blissfield, Lenawee County, Michigan); d April

10, 1869, near Blissfield, Lenawee County, Michigan. See next PA.2.2.5.

6. **Hannah WILLETT**: b May 27, 1798 (family tradition in New Jersey); m abt 1818 John Hidley; removed to Richland County, Ohio; d February 28, 1847, near Plymouth, Richland County, Ohio.

7. **Abraham WILLETT**: b March 1, 1801, in Northumberland (now Columbia) County, Pennsylvania (according to 1850 Richland County, Ohio, census); m 1st abt 1821, Esther Aikman (b 1802; d September 20, 1826, age 24) of Columbia County, Pennsylvania; m 2d abt 1828, Catherine Hazlett (d 1843) of Columbia County, Pennsylvania; he removed to Ohio about 1825; m 3d Miss Leah Bevier of Richland County, Ohio; d December 14, 1887, near Plymouth, Richland County, Ohio. See next PA.2.2.7.

8. **Sarah WILLETT**: b November 3, 1803, in Pennsylvania (according to 1850 Columbia County, Pennsylvania, census); m abt 1825, Alexander Hughes (a Friend, of Catawissa); d November 16, 1891, at Shickshinny, Luzerne County (adjacent to Columbia County), Pennsylvania. See next PA.2.2.8.

9. **Elizabeth WILLETT**: b August 27, 1807 (family tradition in New Jersey, but more likely in Pennsylvania); m abt 1830, Jacob Melick of Monmouth County, New Jersey; d March 1, 1889, at Light Street, Columbia County, Pennsylvania. See next PA.2.2.9.

PA.2.2.3
RACHEL B. WILLETT and ELI THORNTON
of Bloomsburg, Columbia County, Pennsylvania

Rachel Willett was born on July 11, 1790, in New Jersey.

Miss Rachel Willett married on January 1, 1812, Eli Thornton (b May 10, 1786; d November 19, 1852) ("Republican Argus," January 1, 1812). "All of Bloomsburg."

Mrs. Rachel (Willett) Thornton died on May 19, 1826, at Bloomsburg, Columbia County, Pennsylvania.

(REF: Pursel, page 157; *The Willett Families*, 1985, page 207).

    1. **Hiram Willett THORNTON**: b October 16, 1812, near Bloomsburg, Columbia County, Pennsylvania; m February 25, 1839, Elizabeth Frick Norbury (b December 19, 1816, Philadelphia, Pennsylvania; d April 21, 1886), in Danville, Montour County, Pennsylvania; d April 21, 1886, Danville, Montour County, Pennsylvania. See next PA.2.2.3.1.

    2. **Washington THORNTON**: b October 22, 1814; d September 6, 1829.

    3. **Sarah THORNTON**: b November 1, 1818; m October 6, 1841, at Mt. Pleasant, Dr. Wellington Bird.

    4. **Lavina THORNTON**: b December 24, 1820; m May 4, 1841, in Bloomsburg, Pennsylvania, Benjamin Hagenbuch; d April 29, 1886, near Mt. Pleasant, Iowa.

    5. **Rachel Willett THORNTON**: b May 15, 1826, in Bloomsburg, Columbia County, Pennsylvania; m in Millersburg, Illinois, on March 29, 1846, Charles Gossard Willits; d March 21, 1862.

    1. **Charlotte Rebecca WILLITS**: b December 29, 1846; m on June 15, 1863, William Hendrix; d January 1, 1923.

PA.2.2.3.1
HIRAM WILLETT THORNTON
and ELIZABETH FRICK NORBURY
of Danville, Montour County, Pennsylvania

Hiram Willett Thornton was born on October 16, 1812, near Bloomsburg, Columbia County, Pennsylvania.

Hiram Willett Thornton married on February 25, 1839, Elizabeth Frick Norbury (b December 19, 1816, Philadelphia, Pennsylvania; d April 21, 1886), in Danville, Montour County, Pennsylvania by D. M. Halliday.

Hiram Willett Thornton died on April 21, 1886, Danville, Montour County, Pennsylvania.

(REF: *The Willett Families*, 1985, page 207).

    1. **Martha Norbury THORNTON**: b June 3, 1841; m May 11, 1869, John S. Lutz (b October 18, 1837; d May 3, 1918); d September 20, 1918. See next PA.2.2.3.1.1.

    2. **Sarah Elizabeth THORNTON**: b August 30, 1843.

    3. **Rebecca Rachel THORNTON**: b November 30, 1845; d January 3, 1846.

    4. **Susan Britt THORNTON**: b September 25, 1847; d January 12, 1869.

    5. **Lavina Willett THORNTON**: b May 5, 1850.

    6. **Norbury Willett THORNTON**: b November 20, 1852.

    7. **George Eli THORNTON**: b March 23, 1856.

PA.2.2.3.1.1
MARTHA NORBURY THORNTON and JOHN S. LUTZ

Martha Norbury Thornton was born on June 3, 1841.

Miss Martha Thornton married on May 11, 1869, John S. Lutz (b October 18, 1837; d May 3, 1918).

Mrs. Martha (Thornton) Lutz died on September 20, 1918.

    1. **Martha LUTZ**: m John Sipes Price.

        1. **Mary Eleanor PRICE**: m Beverly Horace Scott.

            1. **Charlene Ann SCOTT**: m Roy ("Joe") Kramer.

            2. **John David SCOTT**: m Phyllis Irene Keenan.

PA.2.2.4
WILLIAM WILLETT and HANNAH WEBB
of Columbia County, Pennsylvania,
and Richland County, Ohio

William Willett was born on May 24, 1793, in (Northumberland County) Pennsylvania (born Pennsylvania according to the 1850 Richland County, Ohio census; born New Jersey according to family tradition).

William Willet married in Northumberland (now Columbia) County, Pennsylvania, on January 29, 1818, Hannah Webb (b May 5, 1797, in Northumberland, now Columbia County, Pennsylvania; d 1882 in Plymouth, Richland County, Ohio, buried at the Plymouth Pioneer Rest Cemetery in Plymouth, Ohio).

William Willett learned the trade of tanning in Bloomsburg, Columbia County, Pennsylvania, and continued in that trade (1819 deed, 1834, 1836) when he removed to Ohio.

On March 19, 1819, William Willet purchased a little over an acre of his father's homestead.

This INDENTURE made the nineteenth day of March in the year of Our Lord one thousand Eight hundred and Nineteen. Between Abraham Willet of Blooms township in the County of Columbia and the State of Pennsylvania and Sarah his wife the one part, And William Willet of the same place, Tanner of the other part.

Witnesseth That the said Abraham Willet and Sarah his wife for and in consideration of Forty five Dollars lawful money of the State of Pennsylvania ...

(sell) Beginning above ... land belonging to Casper Christman thence by the same ... thence by land of the said Abraham Willet North ... to a stone corner ... one acre and sixty two perches and a half.

It being part of the same tract of land (from) John Brady Esquire (the then) high Sheriff of the county of Northumberland ... out of the estate of Dennis Leary ... (Book K, page 106) ... Indenture dated May, 1798.

Seal: Abraham Willet   Seal: Sarah Willet

Personally appeared before me, Isaac Kline, Justice of Peace.

Dower release by Sarah Willet

Recorded April 6, 1819.

In 1820, William Willit was listed as the head of a household in Bloom Township, Columbia County, Pennsylvania, page 10, next to his father Abraham Willit. His family consisted of:

1 male	26-45	1775-1795	*William*	*age 27 b 1793*
1 female	16-26	1795-1805	*Hannah*	*age 23 b 1797*
1 male	0-10	1810-1820	*Thomas*	*age 1 b 1819*

On November 19, 1833, the executor (Isaac Kline - also William's brother-in-law) of the estate of his father, Abraham Willett, deceased, sold to William Willet for $1700.00 the 68 1/2 acres in the Abraham Willett estate.

On April 12, 1834, William Willett and Hannah sold this family farm acreage for $2,500.00; a profit of $800.00 in less than six months.

> *This INDENTURE made the twelfth day of April in the year of Our Lord one thousand eight hundred and thirty four.*
>
> *Between William Willet of Bloom township in the County of Columbia and State of Pennsylvania and Hannah his wife of the one part and Nicholas Grover of the same place of the other part.*
>
> *Witnesseth ... for and in consideration of the sum of two thousand five hundred dollars lawfully money ...*
>
> *(sell) Beginning at a marked pine thence by land of Peter Melick North sixteen degrees West ninety six and a half perches to a post thence by land of John Bright North seventy four degrees East one hundred and twenty three perches to a stone, thence by land of Alem Marr South sixteen degrees East ninety six perches and a half to a corner in the line of land belonging to John Robison and thence by the same South seventy four degrees West one hundred and twenty three perches to the place of Beginning containing Seventy acres and allowance be the same more or less.*
>
> *It being part of the same tract of land (from) Jeremiah Jackson to Abraham Willet ... Northumberland in Book P, pages 187 and 188 ... situated in Bloom township aforesaid ...*
>
> *And the said Abraham Willet with Sarah his wife by Indenture bearing date of 19th day of March A.D. 1819 conveyed one acre sixty perches and a half part of the same ... Columbia Deed Book D, pages 240 and 241 ...*

(the remaining to William Willet from) Sarah Willet and Isaac Kline by Indenture ... 6 November ... (forms one tract).

The other tract of land is situated in Mifflin Township

in the County of Columbia (purchased) 24th March 1831 (by) William Willet containing eight acres and sixteen perches ...

William Willett and Hannah removed to Plymouth, Richland County, Ohio, in 1834, in two covered wagons, where he turned his attention to farming and tanning. They brought along two square pianos, one for Sarah and one for Hannah.

In 1836, William Willett built a tannery on his farm in Cass Township, Richland County, Ohio.

"They came from Pennsylvania (1834) in a covered wagon before railroads were introduced into this part of the country and located in the woods. Here William Willett built the tanyard which he conducted for so long and at the time of his death he also owned three farms" (Graham A. A., *History of Richland County, Ohio, from 1808 to 1908*, 1908, page 728).

In 1840, William Willet (sic) and family were listed in the Plymouth Township, Richland County, Ohio, census, as follows:

1 male	40-50	1790-1800	*William*	*age 47*	*b 1793*
1 female	40-50	1790-1800	*Hannah*	*age 43*	*b 1797*
1 male	20-30	1810-1820	*Thomas*	*age 21*	*b 1819*
1 male	15-20	1820-1825	*Abraham*	*age 17*	*b 1823*
1 female	15-20	1820-1825	*Rebecca*	*age 15*	*b 1825*
1 female	10-15	1825-1830	*Hannah*	*age 10*	*b 1830*
1 female	5-10	1830-1835	*Sarah*	*age 6*	*b 1834*

In 1850, William Willett and family were listed in the Cass Township, Richland County, Ohio, census, page 210, No. 229, as follows:

Willett	William	54	m	PA	farmer
	Hannah	51	f	PA	
	Abraham	25	m	PA	
	Rebecca	25	f	PA	
	Hannah	19	f	PA	
	Sarah	15	f	PA	

William Willett died on June 30, 1858, at age of 66, near Plymouth, Richland County, Ohio, and is buried at the Plymouth Pioneer Rest Cemetery in Plymouth, Richland County, Ohio, along with his wife and several of his children.

In 1860, Hannah Willet and family were listed in the Cass

Township, Richland County, Ohio, census, No. 1407, as follows:

Willet	Hannah	62	f	PA	(mother)
	Abraham	38	m	PA	(son)
	Hannah	29	f	PA	(daughter)
	Sarah	21	f	PA	(daughter)

(REF: Graham, A. A., *History of Richland County, Ohio* (1880), "Willett, Hannah, Mrs.", pages 783-784; Purcell, page 154; *The Willett Families*, pages 208-209; 1850 Cass Township, Richland County, Ohio, census, dwelling 229; 1860 Cass Township, Richland County, Ohio, dwelling 1407).

1. **Thomas WILLETT**: b May 13, 1819, in Columbia County, Pennsylvania; m in Cass Township, Richland County, Ohio, on March 26, 1846, in Cass Township, Richland County, Ohio, Rachel Be Vier (Bevier) (b January 26, 1827, Ohio; d December 12, 1897); d May 30, 1906, Mansfield, Richland County, Ohio. See next PA.2.2.4.1.

2. **Rebecca WILLETT**: b October 1, 1821, Columbia County, Pennsylvania; died an infant about late 1821 or early1822.

3. **Abram ("Abraham") WILLETT**: b December 23, 1823, Columbia County, Pennsylvania (born July, 1830; born 1825 according to the 1850 census; born 1822 according to the 1860 census); a bachelor; d August 23, 1900, age 76 years, 8 months, buried in the Plymouth Pioneer Rest Cemetery in Plymouth, Ohio. See next PA.2.2.4.3.

4. **Rebecca WILLETT**: b 1825, Pennsylvania (named for deceased sister); m abt 1852, Abraham Beaver.

5. **Margaret WILLETT**: b October 10, 1826, Columbia County, Pennsylvania; d August 17, 1830, age 3 years, 10 months, 7 days.

6. **Hannah WILLETT**: b November 21, 1829, Columbia County, Pennsylvania; unmarried; d October 30, 1901, age 71 years, 11 months, 1 day, buried at the Plymouth Pioneer Rest Cemetery, Plymouth, Richland County, Ohio.

7. **Sarah WILLETT**: b April 9, 1833, Columbia County, Pennsylvania (born 1835 according to the 1850 census; born 1839 according to the 1860 census); unmarried. She was a maiden aunt, her nephew Franklin Pierce Willett administered her 600 acre estate. Miss Sarah Willett died in 1915, Plymouth, Ohio.

8. **Mary WILLETT**: b April 9, 1833, Columbia County, Pennsylvania; d April 21, 1833, age 12 days, Columbia County, Pennsylvania.

PA.2.2.4.1
THOMAS WILLETT and RACHEL BE VIER
of Cass Township, Richland County, Ohio

Thomas Willett was born on May 13, 1819, in Columbia County, Pennsylvania. In 1834, as a youth of 15, he was bought to Richland County, Ohio, by his parents.

Thomas Willett married in Cass Township, Richland County, Ohio, on March 26, 1846, to Rachel Be Vier (Bevier) (b January 26, 1827, Richland County, Ohio; d December 12, 1897, Plymouth, Ohio, buried Plymouth Green Lawn Cemetery, Plymouth Township, Richland County, Ohio), the daughter of Andries ("Andrus") and Elizabeth Be Vier.

THOMAS WILLETT   RACHEL BEVIER WILLETT

In 1850, Thomas <u>Willett</u> and family were listed in the Cass Township, Richland County, Ohio, census, page 210, No. 228, as follows:

Willett	Thomas	31	m	OH (sic)	farmer
	Rachel	24	f	OH	
	Andrew B	1	m	PA (sic)	

"Thomas Willett was a stalwart Democrat and held many local offices, the most important of which was that of county treasurer, to which he was continuously elected in 1858. Up to this time, he had resided continuously on the farm, but on being elected to this office, he removed to Mansfield and resided there during his two years' term of service.

It was at this period that he bought the Jacob Cribb's farm of one hundred acres, adjoining the old home place of one hundred and sixty acres. In 1860, he resumed his farming operations, which involved the cultivation of about three hundred acres of land at this time, though he later disposed of some of his holdings" (*History of Richland County, Ohio, from 1808-1908*, 1908, page 728).

In 1860, Thomas <u>Willet</u> and family were listed in the 1st Ward, Mansfield City, Richland County, Ohio, census, page 6, No. 76-76, as follows:

Willet	Thos	(sic) 21	m	PA (sic) farmer
Willitt	Rachel	33	f	O (sic)
	Wm	8	m	
	Hiram	6	m	
	Franklin	6	m	
	Ann Regina	4	f	
	Baby	2m	f	
Brier	Mary	22	f	domestic

In 1870, Thomas <u>Willet</u> and family were listed in the Plymouth Township, Richland County, Ohio, census, page 279, No. 56-54, as follows:

Willet	Thos	51	m	PA 2,000
	Rachel	44	f	OH
	Frank	16	m	OH
	Hiram	16	m	OH
	Ervin	14	f	OH (sic = female)
	Kate	11	f	OH
	Edward	6	m	OH
	Peter	2	m	OH

"Mrs. Thomas Willett of Plymouth, wife of ex-county Treasurer, died Saturday night at her home, age about 68 years. Her maiden name was Rachel Bevier. Leaves husband, sons, Hiram, Frank, and Edward, and daughters, Mrs. Kate Hills, and Mrs. Clarence Bevier" ("Shelby News," Friday, September 17, 1897, Shelby, Richland County, Ohio).

"At the time of his death he owned, however, two hundred, sixty-nine and one-half acres of land. In 1864, he removed to the village of Plymouth, where he resided for some time. He was the administrator for some estates. He died in Mansfield, May 30, 1906, having been afflicted with total blindness for fourteen years prior to his death" (History *of Richland County, Ohio, from 1808-1908*, 1908, page 728).

In 1900, Abraham Willett, age 81, was enumerated the household of his son, Hiram Willett, in Plymouth Village, Richland County, Ohio.

Thomas Willett died on May 30, 1906, at age 87, and is buried in the Plymouth Greenlawn Cemetery, Richland County, Ohio.

(REF: *The Willett Families*, 1985, page 209).

1. **Andries ("Andrew") Be Vier WILLETT**: b May 13, 1848, Richland County, Ohio (born Pennsylvania according to 1850 census); d August 21, 1852, buried Plymouth Greenlawn Cemetery, Richland County, Ohio. His tombstone is inscribed "Child of T. and R. Willett.".

2. **William WILLETT**: b May 6, 1852, Richland County, Ohio; d July 2, 1863, buried Plymouth Greenlawn Cemetery, Richland County, Ohio. His tombstone is inscribed "Child of T. and R. Willett.

3. **Franklin Pierce WILLETT** (twin): b May 15, 1854, Richland County, Ohio; m in Richland County, Ohio, on April 3, 1879, Mrs. Amanda J. (Saviers) Kirkland (b April 14, 1846, Plymouth Township, Richland, County, Ohio; d 1919, buried Plymouth Greenlawn Cemetery), the daughter of Henry Saviers, Sr; d May 30, 1906. See next PA.2.2.4.1.3.

4. **Hiram WILLETT** (twin): b May 15, 1854, Richland County, Ohio; m in Huron County, Ohio, on October 19, 1875, Jennie Ione Wheeler (Whiller) (b February, 1852, Ohio; d August, 1922, buried Plymouth Greenlawn Cemetery); d August 22, 1922, buried Plymouth Greenlawn Cemetery, Richland County, Ohio. (1880 Cass Township, Richland Count, Ohio, census). See next PA.2.2.4.1.4.

5. **Anna Rachel WILLETT**: b May 13, 1856, Richland County, Ohio; m Clarence Be Vier; d November, 1930.

6. (child) **WILLETT**: b abt 1858, Richland County, Ohio; died infant before 1860.

7. **Kate WILLETT**: b March 26, 1860, Richland County, Ohio; m in Richland County, Ohio, on December 30, 1885, James Hills; resided Seattle, Washington.

8. **Abram Edward WILLETT**: b April 25, 1864, Plymouth Township, Richland County, Ohio; m abt 1890 Alice Grace Kelser (b 1869; d June 20, 1935); d March 12, 1940. See next PA.2.2.4.1.8.

9. **Peter WILLETT**: b 1868; d 1889 at age 22, buried Plymouth Greenlawn Cemetery, Richland County, Ohio.

PA.2.2.4.1.3
FRANKLIN PIERCE WILLETT
and AMANDA SAVIERS KIRKLAND
of Richland County, Ohio

Franklin Pierce Willett, twin to Hiram, was born on May 15, 1854, in Ohio.

Franklin P. Willett married in Richland County, Ohio, on April 3, 1879, Mrs. Amanda J. (Saviers) Kirkland (b April 14, 1846; d 1919, buried Plymouth Greenlawn Cemetery), the daughter of Henry Saviers, Sr.

In 1880, Franklin Willett and family were listed in the Plymouth Township, Richland County, Ohio, census, as follows:

Willett	Franklin	26	m	OH	
	Amanda	34	f	OH	(wife)
Kirkland	Emila	10	f	OH	(stepdaughter)

In 1900, Frank P. Willett is the head of a household in the Shelby Village, Richland County, Ohio, census, Sheet 1, location 57-12-15, as follows:

Willett	Frank P.	head	May 1854	46	m 20	
	Amanda	wife	Apr 1846	54	m 20	1-0

In 1900, Amanda was listed as the "boarding house keeper" with 11 residents, while Frank was listed as a "day laborer."

> "Following his marriage, Mr. Willett located on one of his father's farms, and engaged in farming for the next eight years. In 1887, he removed to Shelby and took charge of the old Park House, which hotel he conducted for four years. From there he went to Bucyrus, where he engaged in the hotel business for two years, and then went to Mansfield, where he lived for one year, at the expiration of which time he went to Shelby, where he conducted a boarding-house for six years, a portion of his time being employed with the Shelby Tube Works there.
>
> Seven years ago (1900), he returned to his birthplace, on which farm he now resides. He finds ample opportunity for the expenditure of his time in the duties now devolving upon him as, in conjunction with his brother Edward, he has charge of the estate of his maiden aunt, Sarah Willett, which consists of something over six hundred acres of land" (History of Richland County, Ohio, page 729).

Franklin Willett died on May 30, 1906.

1. **Emila KIRKLAND** (stepdaughter): b 1870, Ohio.

PA.2.2.4.1.4
HIRAM WILLETT and JENNY IONE WHEELER
of Plymouth, Richland County, Ohio

Hiram Willett (twin) was born on May 15, 1854, at Plymouth, in Richland County, Ohio.

Hiram Willett married in Huron County, Ohio, on October 19, 1875, Jenny Ione Wheeler (Whiller) (b February, 1852, Ohio; d August, 1922, buried Plymouth Greenlawn Cemetery, Richland County, Ohio).

In 1880, H. Willet and family are listed in the Cass Township, Richland County, Ohio, census, as follows:

Willet	H.	26	m	OH	
	J.	28	f	OH	wife
	W.	3	m	OH	son
	F.	2	NR	OH	
Lyon	R.	18	m	OH	Bo.

In 1900, Hiram Willett is the head of a household in the Plymouth Township, Richland County, Ohio, census, Sheet 1, dwelling 21-21, as follows:

Willett	Hiram	head	May 1854	46	m 25
	Jennie	wife	Feb 1852	48	m 25 2-2
	Thomas	father	May 1819	81	wd

Hiram Willett died on August 22, 1922, and is buried in the Plymouth Greenlawn Cemetery, Richland County, Ohio.

1. **B. Wheeler WILLETT**: b 1877, Ohio; d 1922.

　　1. **Joan WILLETT**:
　　2. **Virginia WILLETT**:

2. **Thomas WILLETT**: b April, 1878, Ohio; m in 1896, Dora Kockenderfer (b June 26, 1872); d February, 1905. See next PA.2.2.4.1.4.2.

PA.2.2.4.1.4.2
THOMAS WILLETT and DORA KOCKENDERFER
of Plymouth, Richland County, Ohio

Thomas Willett was born in April, 1878, in Ohio.

Thomas Willett married in 1896, Dora Kockenderfer (b June 26, 1872, Ohio). They resided in Plymouth, Richland County, Ohio.

In 1900, Thomas Willett and family are listed in the Cass Township, Richland County, Ohio, census, Sheet 11, dwelling 274-274, as follows:

Willett	Thomas	head	Apr 1878	22	m 4
	Dora	wife	Jun 1872	27	m 4 2-2
	Lillian M.	daughter	Oct 1896	3	
	Louise	daughter	Jun 1898	1	
Wheeler,	Fred C.	uncle	Feb 1845	55	

Thomas Willett died in February, 1905.

1. **Lillian M. WILLETT**: b October, 1896, Ohio; m Andrews; d before 1991.

2. **Louise WILLETT**: b June, 1898, Ohio; m Martin; d before 1991.

3. **Horace M. WILLETT**: b May 24, 1902, Plymouth, Richland County, Ohio; m Helen Limbird (b January 28, 1903; d October 29, 1994); d at Bellevue, Plymouth County, Ohio, on January 31, 1995, age 92. See next PA.2.2.4.1.4.2.3.

4. **Myron WILLETT**: b abt 1903; d before 1991.

5. **Lucille WILLETT**: b abt 1904; died infant.

6. **Josephine WILLETT**: b September 29, 1905, Plymouth, Richland County, Ohio; m Otto Albert Curpen. She was formerly employed by Shelby Business Forms, formerly Shelby Sales Book. She was a member of the First Lutheran Church, Plymouth, Richland County, Ohio; resided Plymouth Street, Plymouth, Richland County, Ohio; d 1991, buried Greenlawn Cemetery, Plymouth, Richland County, Ohio.

PA.2.2.4.1.4.2.3
HORACE M. WILLETT and **HELEN LIMBIRD**
of Plymouth, Richland County, Ohio

Horace M. Willett was born on May 24, 1902, Plymouth, Richland County, Ohio.

Horace M. Willett married Helen Limbird (b January 28, 1903; d October 29, 1994). He worked for the Railway Express Company, owned a fruit farm and was a carpenter. They resided (1991) at Clyde, Ohio.

Horace M. Willett died at Bellevue, Plymouth County, Ohio, on January 31, 1995, age 92 (Obituary, "Horace Willett").

1. **Douglas WILLETT**: d before 1995.

2. **Thomas P. WILLETT**: b 1942; resides (1995) Stuart, Florida 34996.

PA.2.2.4.1.8
ABRAM EDWARD WILLETT and ALICE GRACE KELSER
of Richland County, Ohio

Abram Edward Willett was born on April 25, 1864, in Richland County, Ohio. Abram E. Willett married about 1890, Alice Grace Kelser (b 1869; d June 20, 1935). Abram Edward Willett died on March 12, 1940.

1. **Grace WILLETT**: b abt 1893.
2. **Florence WILLETT**: b abt 1895.
3. **Phillip WILLETT**: b abt 1897.
4. **Gertrude Lois WILLETT**: b October 12, 1899, at 183 Sandusky Street, Plymouth, Richland County, Ohio; m Theodore August Wagner, U.S.N; resided Canton, Ohio, and Brooklyn Heights, New York. See next PA.2.2.4.1.8.4.
5. **Albert Edward WILLETT**: b 1914; resided Salinas, California.

PA.2.2.4.1.8.4
GERTRUDE LOIS WILLETT
and THEODORE AUGUST WAGNER
of Canton, Ohio, and Brooklyn Heights, New York

Gertrude Lois Willett was born on October 12, 1899, 183 Sandusky Street, Plymouth, Richland County, Ohio. She was a 1917 graduate Plymouth High School, Plymouth, Ohio. She attended Wittemberg College for one year and later went on to Columbia University, New York. A friend introduced her to Theodore Wagner, the with the U.S. Navy.

"I only met my husband nine times before we married. But we wrote each other a lot."

Miss Gertrude Lois Willett married Theodore August Wagner, U.S.N. They resided at Canton, Ohio, and Brooklyn Heights, New York.

"They lived for many years in Canton. After Pearl Harbor, her husband went back to his first love, the sea, by joining the Merchant Marine. Gertrude moved to Brooklyn Heights so she could be close when his ship came to port.
When he died many years later, his body was buried at sea. His first son and namesake died young. A Navy pilot, Theodore, Jr., suffered a heart attack during take-off at the age of 47 (from an undated, unknown Plymouth area newspaper article).

1. **Theodore August WAGNER**, Jr: d age 47 of a heart attack.
2. **Walter WAGNER** (twin): died young.
3. **Edward WAGNER** (twin): Korean Language teacher and scholar at Harvard University.
4. **John WAGNER**: folk dance instructor; resides Brooklyn Heights, New York.
5. **Rachel Be Vier WAGNER**: police and fire dispatcher, Fort Lauderdale, Florida; genealogist.

PA.2.2.4.3
ABRAHAM WILLETT
of Plymouth, Richland County, Ohio

Abraham ("Abram") Willett was born on December 23, 1823, Columbia County, Pennsylvania. His birth year is given variously in different records: born July, 1830; born 1825 according to the 1850 census; born 1822 according to the 1860 census.

Abraham Willett was a bachelor. He took over the tannery that his father had built when the family first moved to Cass Township, Ohio.

In 1850, William Willett (father) and family were listed in the Cass Township, Richland County, Ohio, census, page 210, No. 229, as follows:

Willett	William	54	m	PA	farmer
	Hannah	51	f	PA	
	Abraham	25	m	PA	
	Rebecca	25	f	PA	
	Hannah	19	f	PA	
	Sarah	15	f	PA	

In 1860, (Mrs.) Hannah Willet (widow) and family were listed in the Cass Township, Richland County, Ohio, census, No. 1407, as follows:

Willet	Hannah	62	f	PA	
	Abraham	38	m	PA	(son)
	Hannah	29	f	PA	(daughter)
	Sarah	21	f	PA	(daughter)

In 1870, Abraham Willett was listed as the head of his own household. His real estate was valued at $35,000 at this time.

In 1900, Abraham Willett was the head of a household in Cass Township, Richland County, Ohio, Sheet 10, dwelling 269-269, as follows:

Willett	Abraham	head	Dec 1823	76 s PA NJ PA
	Hannah	sister	Nov 1829	70 s PA NJ PA
	Sarah	sister	Apr 1833	67 s PA NJ PA

Abraham Willett died on August 23, 1900, age 76 years, 8 months, and is buried in the Plymouth Pioneer Rest Cemetery in Plymouth, Ohio.

PA.2.2.5
PETER WILLETT
of Columbia County, Pennsylvania
and Huron County, Ohio

Peter Willett was born on August 1, 1795, in Pennsylvania (born Pennsylvania according to the 1850 Huron County, Ohio, census; born New Jersey by family tradition).

Peter Willett married 1st abt 1819, Catherine Sidle (b February 5, 1799, New Jersey; d January 1, 1843, Cass County, Ohio).

Peter Willett resided at Berwick, Columbia County, where he was an Innkeeper (1823 deed) and a farmer.

On October 14, 1822, Peter Willet and Catharine purchased two water front lots in Berwick which fronted on the Susquehanna River.

> *This INDENTURE made the twenty ninth day of April in the year of our Lord one thousand eight hundred and twenty three,*
> *Between Peter Willet of the Borough of Berwick, County of Columbia and State of Pennsylvania, Innkeeper, and Catharine his wife of the one part;*
> *And ... managers of the company for erecting a Bridge over river Susquehanna at the falls of Nescopick of the other part ...*
> *for three hundred dollars lawful money of the state of Pennsylvania;*
> *(sell) Water Lot No. Ten situate lying and being in the Borough of Berwick, aforesaid ... bounded at the corner of Canal and Chestnut Street, thence by Canal Street to the River Susquehanna, thence along the river Susquehanna to the corner of Water lot number nine ...*
> *(sell) Water Lot No. Nine ...*
> *Being the same two Water Lots which was granted conveyed to the said Peter Willett in fee by Indenture of the Reverend William B. Sloan and Ann his wife ... dated October 24, 1822 ...*
> Peter Willet signed his name
> Catharine Willet made her mark.

Berwick is on the Susquehanna River in Columbia County, Pennsylvania, while East Berwick and Nescopeck are slightly northeast but in Luzerne County, Pennsylvania.

In the 1830, Bloom Township, Columbia County, Pennsylvania, census, Peter Willet (sic) is listed as the head of a household which consisted of:

1 male	30-40	1790-1800	*Peter*	*age 35*	*b 1795*
1 female	30-40	1790-1800	*Catherine*	*age 31*	*b 1799*
1 male	10-15	1815-1820	*Abram*	*age 10*	*b 1820*
1 female	10-15	1815-1820	*(unknown)*		
1 male	5-10	1820-1825	*Enos*	*age 8*	*b 1822*
1 male	5-10	1820-1825	*Phillips*	*age 6*	*b 1824*
1 male	0-5	1825-1830	*William*	*age 4*	*b 1826*
1 male	0-5	1825-1830	*Benjamin*	*age 2*	*b 1828*

Peter Willett resided in Pennsylvania from at least 1821 until 1836.

Peter Willett is mentioned in Columbia County deeds for land located in Berwick, Columbia County, Pennsylvania, on December 20, 1830 (Deed Book 6, page 76) and on April 8, 1833 (Deed Book 6, page 417).

On April 8, 1833, Peter Willett sold for $60.00 the two waterfront lots (No. 39 and No. 40) in Berwick, on the Susquehanna River, Columbia County, Pennsylvania.

About 1836, Peter Willett removed to Ohio, evidently following in the wake of his brother, William Willett, who had removed to Ohio in 1834.

On August 16, 1836, Peter Willett was a witness to the will of Elizabeth Sealey of Plymouth Township, Cass County, Ohio.

Mrs. Catherine (Sidle) Willett died in 1843 when she was about 44 years old.

About 1845, Peter Willett married 2d Mrs. Rebecca (Rebecah) Webb (b 1811, Pennsylvania; d abt 1874, Blissfield, Lenawee County, Michigan).

On October 20, 1845, Peter and Rebecca Willett purchased 203 acres of land from Sabin K. Smith for $2,250 in Section 4 of Lyme Township, Erie County, Ohio. This land was located west of Section Line Road and just north of what is now (1994) Highway 547.

In 1850, Peter <u>Willett</u> and family were listed in the Lyme Township, Huron County, Ohio, census, page 92, No. 1219, as follows:

Willett	Peter	53	m	PA	farmer
	Rebeccah	39	f	PA	
	William	21	m	PA	
	Benjamin	19	m	PA	
	Peter	17	m	PA	
	John	14	m	PA	

Huron County adjoins Erie County, Ohio, to the north and Richland County, Ohio, to the south.

About 1858, Peter Willett removed to Lenawee County, Michigan.

In 1860, Peter Willett and family are listed in the Ogden Township, Lewanee County, Michigan, census, page 451, dwelling 1537-1580, as follows:

Willett	Peter	head	63	m	PA	farmer
	Rebecca	wife	49	f	PA	
	William		32	m	PA	farmer
	Elizabeth		24	f	PA	
	Benjamin		28	m	PA	farmer
	John		24	m	OH	farmer
	John		4	m	OH	
Wilver	Clinton		10	m	PA	

On October 9, 1861, Peter and Rebecca Willett sold 218 and 8/10 acres of land in the town of Ogden, Lenawee County, Michigan, to Daniel S. Giles of Blissfield for $3,600. At this time they were residents of Blissfield, Lenawee County, Michigan.

In 1863, Abram Willett, Peter Willett's son, removed to Michigan (*Pioneer Collections, Report of the Pioneer Society of the State of Michigan*, Vol. 32, page 599, 1902. Also about 1863, another son, Enos Willett, removed to Michigan.

Peter Willett died on April 10, 1869, near Blissfield, Lenawee County, Michigan, and is buried in the Pleasant View Cemetery, Blissfield, Lenawee County, Michigan. Peter Willett's tombstone is inscribed, "Peter Willett, died April 10, 1869, age 72 years, 8 months, 10 days." He is buried with his sons, William Willett and John Willett, along with William Willett's family in Block E, Lot 291, Pleasant View Cemetery, Blissfield, Lenawee County, Michigan.

After Peter Willett' death, Rebecca went to live with her son-in-law, William Willett and family in Blissfield, Lenawee County, Michigan.

Mrs. Rebecca (Webb) Willet's will is abstracted:

> *In the name of God Amen. I Rebecca Willet of Blissfield, Lenawee County, Michigan, widow of the late Peter Willet ...*
> *1st, I give and bequeath to my daughter, Louisa, wife of Daniel F. Owen, and to her heirs the sum of $500 dollars. She was last heard from of Denver, Colorado Territory and her children reside in Luzerne County, Pennsylvania.*
> *2nd: To Peter Willet, seventh son of my late husband and*

residing at Elmore, Ohio, the sum of $300 dollars.

3rd: To William Willet, husband of my daughter, Elizabeth J., and fourth son of my late husband ... (remission) of his mortgage.

4th: To Wellington J. Willet, son of William and Elizabeth J. Willett, the sum of $500 dollars.

5th: The balance to Benjamin and John Willet, sons of my late husband, the balance ... share and share alike ...

Rebecca Willet

dated March of 1875 by Francis Brown

NOTE: Birth and death dates (as listed below) of Peter Willett and his children are taken from the family Bible of Peter Willett, Sr., published 1941, property of Dr. R. A. Willett, of Elmore, Ohio.

(REF: *The Willett Families*, 1985 page 207; Comstock penciled notes in Pursel).

1. **Abram WILLETT**: b September 6, 1820, Berwick, Columbia County, Pennsylvania; m in Monroeville, Erie County, Ohio, on December 13, 1858, Alma Depuy (Depuey) (b March 13, 1834, Shamokin, Pennsylvania; d January 2, 1936, Adrian, Lenawee County, Michigan), the daughter of Joseph Depuy (b 1795, Pennsylvania); d November 27, 1900, age 80, buried Pleasant View Cemetery, Blissfield, Lenawee County, Ohio. See next PA.2.2.5.1.

2. **Enos WILLETT**: b April 13, 1822, Espy, Columbia County, Pennsylvania; m in Margaretta Township, Erie County, Pennsylvania, on May 20, 1852, Beulah Depuy (b March 24, 1832, Sunbury, Pennsylvania; d May 31, 1917, Adrian, Michigan), the sister to Alma Depuy; d in Adrian on February 2, 1897, and is buried in the Oakwood Cemetery, Adrian, Lenawee County, Michigan. See next PA.2.2.5.2.

3. **Phillip Sidle WILLETT**: b January 28, 1824, Bloomsburg, Columbia County, Pennsylvania; m in Huron County, Ohio, on January 20, 1844, Margaret Ann Easter (b December 25, 1823, Greenfield, Highland County, Ohio; d October 31, 1889, Burlington, Coffey County, Kansas, buried Graceland Cemetery, Burlington, Kansas); d December 17, 1886, Burlington, Coffey County, Kansas. See next PA.2.2.5.3.

4. **William WILLETT**: b June 6, 1826, Columbia County, Pennsylvania; m December 12, 1854, Elizabeth J. Welliver (b September 1, 1833, Pennsylvania; d September 4, 1912, Petersburg, Monroe County, Michigan, buried Pleasant View

Cemetery, Blissfield, Michigan); d October 27, 1914, in Petersburg, Monroe County, Michigan, and is buried in the "Pleasant View" Cemetery, Blissfield, Lenawee County, Michigan. See next PA.2.2.5.4.

5. **Benjamin S. WILLETT**: b February 1, 1828, Danville, Columbia County, Pennsylvania; m in Hudson, Lenawee County, Michigan, in July, 1877, Rachel Calista Marr (b May 29, 1852, Hudson, Michigan; d September 12, 1921, Adrian, buried Pleasant View Cemetery, Blissfield, Lenawee County, Michigan); d November 6, 1894, Petersburg, Monroe County, Michigan, buried Pleasant View Cemetery, Blissfield, Michigan. See next PA.2.2.5.5.

6. **Peter WILLETT**: b October 8, 1833, Columbia County, Pennsylvania; m at Bucyrus, in Crawford County, Ohio, on July 22, 1858, Maria Augenstein (Augustine) (b March, 1837, Pennsylvania; d May, 1915, Elmore, Ottawa County, Ohio); d January 2, 1913, Elmore, Ottawa County, Ohio, buried Elmore Union Cemetery, Ottawa County, Ohio. See next PA.2.2.5.6.

7. **John WILLETT**: b June 1, 1836, Pennsylvania (this is only of various dates which is mentioned in various records); d June 19, 1916, buried Pleasant View Cemetery, Blissfield, Lenawee County, Michigan. See next PA.2.2.5.7.

PA.2.2.5.1
ABRAM WILLETT and **ALMA DEPUY**
of Erie County, Ohio, and Lenawee County, Michigan

Abram Willett was born in September 6, 1820, Berwick, Columbia County, Pennsylvania.

About 1836, Abram's father, Peter Willett, removed to Ohio, evidently following in the wake of Abram's uncle, William Willett, who had removed to Ohio in 1834. Evidently, Abram came along at this time. At the age of 14, he started working in a store in Plymouth, Richland County, Ohio. He worked here for 7 years, and then wanted to become a minister of the gospel. He took the theological course in a seminary at Milan, Ohio, and upon finishing it, he entered upon duties as a member of the Northern Ohio Methodist Episcopal Conference.

"He served in this capacity for several years. One day, he had a crisis and learned he must either drop his studies and seek outdoor employment or lose his life. He took a western trip in the hope of restoring his health but it did not suffice, so he was forced to lay down his mission he had selected and sought employment of the farm" (unpublished notes, no date, no ascription).

On October 2, 1848, Abram, Phillip, and Enos Willett purchased 50 acres of land in Groton Township, Erie County, Ohio, from Bourdett Wood for $520. The land was described as the north half of the east half of Lot 5, Section 1, Range 24, Town 5.

On December 20, 1848, Abram, Phillip, and Enos Willett purchased 170 acres of land in Groton Township and Oxford Townships, Erie County, Ohio, from Nathan Strong for $3000. This land included Lots 33 and 34 in Oxford as well as a large section of land just across the street in Groton.

In 1850, Abram Willet, age 30, and his brother Enos Willet, age 28, were enumerated with their brother Phillip Willet in Erie County, Ohio.

Abram Willett married in Monroeville, Erie County, Ohio, on December 13, 1858, Alma Depuy (Depuey) (b March 13, 1834, Shamokin, Northumberland County, Pennsylvania; d January 2, 1936, Adrian, Lenawee County, Michigan), the daughter of Joseph Depuy (b 1795, Pennsylvania; living 1880, age 85), and the sister of Beulah Depuy who married Enos Willett. Abram was 38 years old, his bride, 23.

On February 5, 1860, Abram and Phillip Willett sold their 222 acres of land in Groton and Oxford Townships to Moses Fox for $10,000.

In 1860, Abram <u>Willet</u> and his new wife were listed in the Oxford Township, Erie County, Ohio, census, No. 1826, household of his brother, E. Willet, as follows:

Willet	E.	38	m	PA	farmer
	Beulah	28	f	PA	
	Wesley	7	m	OH	
	<u>Abram</u>	39	m	PA	
	<u>Alma</u>	23	f	PA	

Abram Willett and Alma resided in Ohio from at least 1860 until 1870. However, according to the *Pioneer Collections, Report of the Pioneer Society of the State of Michigan*, Vol. 32, page 599, 1902, they "removed to Michigan in 1863."

On October 4, 1866, Abram Willett bought some land just north east of the village in Section 29. This was purchased from Timothy L. Goff for $1250. He continued to buy adjacent land over several years until he owned 72 acres on the Raisin River, Lenawee County, Michigan.

ABRAHAM WILLETT
(Photograph courtesy of Douglas Willett)

In 1870, Abram <u>Willett</u> and family were listed in the Bliss-field Township, Lenawee County, Michigan, census, as follows:

Willett	Abram	49	m	PA	farmer
	Alma	35	f	PA	
	Grace	10	f	OH	
	Aggie	3	f	OH	
	Eva	1	f	OH	

In 1880, Abram <u>Willit</u> and family were listed in the Bliss-field Township, Lenawee County, Michigan, census, as follows:

Willit	Abram	58	m	PA	
	Alma	46	f	OH	
	Grace	17	f	OH	
	Katie	13	f	OH	
	Eva	10	f	OH	
Dupay	Joseph	85	m	PA	father-in-law

CIRCA 1920
MRS. ALMA (DEPUY) WILLETT
(Photograph courtesy of Douglas Willett)

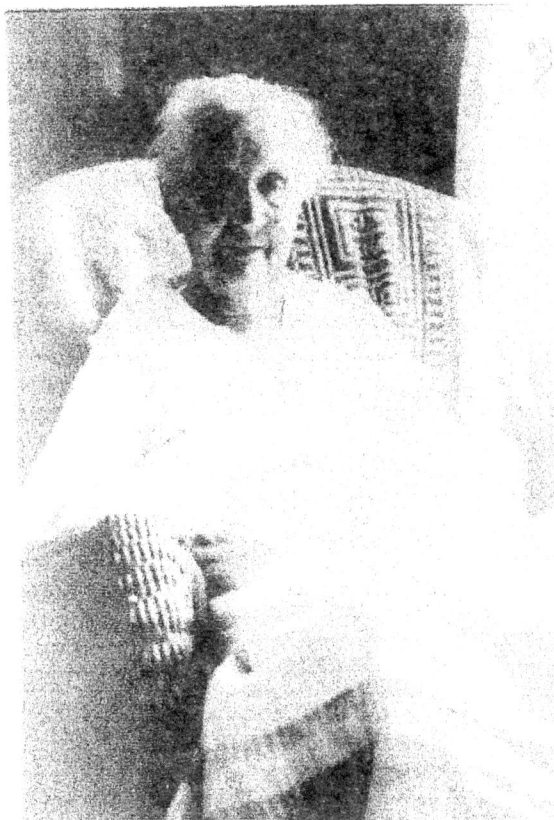

Abram was mentioned in the local newspaper on April 18, 1884 ("Descendants of Abraham Willet", unpublished manuscript, page 15):

> *"We understand Mr. A. Willett has purchased back the farm sold by him last spring and intends moving back at once. City life doesn't agree with Mr. Willett."*

In 1900, Abram <u>Willett</u> and family were listed in the Blissfield Township, Lenawee County, Michigan, census, as follows:

Willett	Abram	79	Sep 1820	PA
	Alma	65	Mar 1835	PA

Abram Willett died on November 27, 1900, age 80, in Blissfield, Lenawee County, Michigan, of a capillary pneumonia and general decline and is buried in the Pleasant View Cemetery, Blissfield, Lenawee County, Michigan.

1. **Sarah Grace WILLETT**: b 1860, Ohio; m George E. Miller (b May 1, 1858, Beavertown, Pennsylvania; d January 14, 1934, Mexico City, Mexico, buried Roseland Park Cemetery, Berkley, Michigan); d June 30, 1909, Washington, D. C., and is buried in the Pleasant View Cemetery, Blissfield, Lenawee County, Michigan. See next <u>PA.2.2.5.1.1</u>.

2. **Agnes** ("Aggie") **I. WILLETT**: b 1863, Ohio; m in Blissfield, Lenawee County, Michigan, in January, 1885, Henry C. Wilson (b February, 1853, Michigan); d 1938, buried Pleasant View Cemetery, Blissfield, Lenawee County, Michigan. See next <u>PA.2.2.5.1.2</u>.

3. **Katherine** ("Katie") **WILLETT**: b 1867, Ohio; m George M. VanEvera; resided (1900; 1936) Des Moines, Iowa. See next <u>PA.2.2.5.1.3</u>.

4. **Evelyn** ("Eva") **Moisselle WILLETT**: b June 24, 1871, Blissfield, Lenawee County, Michigan; m in Detroit, Wayne County, Michigan, on February 28, 1901, Ora James Mulford (b September 8, 1868, Monroe, Ohio; d August 2, 1943, Detroit, Wayne County, Michigan); d April 6, 1943, age 71, Detroit, Wayne County, Michigan, buried Roseland Park Cemetery, Berkley, Michigan. See next <u>PA.2.2.5.1.4</u>.

CIRCA 1867
AGNES AND SARAH GRACE WILLETT
(Photograph courtesy of Douglas Willett)

PA.2.2.5.1.1
SARAH GRACE WILLETT and **GEORGE E. MILLER**
of Washington, D. C., and Lenawee County, Michigan

Sarah Grace Willett was born in 1860, Ohio.
She was a teacher.
Miss Sarah Grace Willett married George E. Miller (b May 1, 1858, Beavertown, Pennsylvania; d January 14, 1934, Mexico City, Mexico, buried Roseland Park Cemetery, Berkley, Michigan) (he was a press correspondent).   They lived in Washington, D. C., for a number of years, where her mother would visit her.
Mrs. Sarah Grace (Willett) Miller died on June 30, 1909, in Washington, D. C., and is buried in the Pleasant View Cemetery, Blissfield, Lenawee County, Michigan.

1. **Tom Applegate MILLER**: b February 2, 1892, Detroit, Wayne County, Michigan; m Helen Catherine Youngbluth; d July 19, 1948, Hibbin, Michigan, buried at Ishpeming, Marquette County, Michigan. See next PA.2.2.5.1.1.1.
2. **Karl Willett MILLER**: b 1894; member (1934) of the staff of the Washington Bureau of the Detroit News; buried Roseland Park Cemetery, Berkley, Michigan; m Edna Gates; d abt 1960.
3. **Alma E. MILLER**: b 1904; m Stephen J. Carey; resided Wayne County, Michigan; d 1987.
4. **Helen MILLER**: b 1906; m Hal Smith; d 1991.

MISS SARAH GRACE WILLETT
(Photograph courtesy of Douglas Willett)

STANDING: ROBERT WILSON AND HELEN MILLER
SEATED: KARL WILLETT MILLER
(Photograph courtesy of Douglas Willett)

TOM APPLEGATE MILLER
(Photograph courtesy of Douglas Willett)

PA.2.2.5.1.1.1
TOM APPLEGATE MILLER and
HELEN CATHERINE YOUNGBLUTH

Tom Applegate Miller was born on February 2, 1892, Detroit, Wayne County, Michigan.

Tom Applegate Miller married Helen Catherine Youngbluth.

Tom Applegate Miller died on July 19, 1948, Hibbin, Michigan, buried at Ishpeming, Marquette County, Michigan.

1. **Grace MILLER**: b March 20, 1920, Ishpemimg, Marquette County, Michigan; m in Alaska in 1943, Robert Collins (b June 13, 1920, Mt. Vernon, New York; d 1992). See next PA.2.2.5.1.1.1.1.

2. **George Willett MILLER**: b November 25, 1924, Ishpeming, Marquette County, Michigan; m in Greece, New York, on June 21, 1947, Phyllis Poray (b July 7, 1926, Williamson, New York). See next PA.2.2.5.1.1.1.2.

3. **Mary Claire MILLER**: b March 26, 1931, Ishpemimg, Marquette County, Michigan; m in Hibbing, Minnesota, in 1952, Charles Stepan (b June 30, 1931, Chisholm, Minnesota). See next PA.2.2.5.1.1.1.3

PA.2.2.5.1.1.1.1
GRACE MILLER and ROBERT COLLINS
of Ohio and Michigan

Grace Miller was born on March 20, 1920, at Ishpemimg, Marquette County, Michigan.

Miss Grace Miller married in Alaska in 1943, Robert Collins (b June 13, 1920, Mt. Vernon, New York; d 1992).

1. **Susan Margaret COLLINS**: b November 4, 1945, Columbus, Ohio.
2. **Gordon Thomas COLLINS**: b February 15, 1948, Cleveland, Ohio.
3. **Jeffrey Craig COLLINS**: b December 20, 1949, Detroit, Wayne County, Michigan.
4. **David COLLINS**: b 1951, Detroit, Wayne County, Michigan.

PA.2.2.5.1.1.1.2
GEORGE WILLETT MILLER and PHYLLIS PORAY

George Willett Miller was born on November 25, 1924, Ishpeming, Marquette County, Michigan.

George Willett Miller married in Greece, New York, on June 21, 1947, Phyllis Poray (b July 7, 1926, Williamson, New York).

1. **Thomas Harmon MILLER**: b July 27, 1949.
2. **Timothy Randall MILLER**: b January 1, 1951.
3. **Charles Gregory MILLER**: b June 10, 1953.
4. **Richard Willett MILLER**: b January 19, 1956.

PA.2.2.5.1.1.1.3
MARY CLAIRE MILLER and CHARLES STEPAN
of Minneapolis, Minnesota

Mary Claire Miller was born on March 26, 1931, Ishpemimg, Marquette County, Michigan.

Miss Mary Claire Miller married in Hibbing, Minnesota, in 1952, Charles Stepan (b June 30, 1931, Chisholm, Minnesota).

1. **Mark Charles STEPAN**: b July 6, 1953, Minneapolis, Minnesota.
2. **Constance STEPAN**: b May 28, 1955, Minneapolis, Minnesota.
3. **Bruce Martin STEPAN**: b July 29, 1957, Minneapolis, Minnesota.
4. **Thomas Joseph STEPAN**: b April 11, 1960.
5. **Laura Helen STEPAN**: b April 25, 1962.
6. **Alison Jo STEPAN**: b December 28, 1964.
7. **Michael STEPAN**: b June 3, 1970 .

PA.2.2.5.1.2
AGNES I. WILLETT and HENRY C. WILSON

Agnes I. Willett was born in 1863, Ohio.

Miss Agnes I. Willett married in Blissfield, Lenawee County, Michigan, in January, 1885, Henry C. Wilson (b February, 1853, Michigan).

Mrs. Agnes (Willett) Wilson died in 1938, and is buried in the Pleasant View Cemetery, Blissfield, Lenawee County, Michigan.

1. **Robert Willett WILSON**: b July 10, 1895, Paw Paw, Michigan; m Nan McAllister (d February 1, 1981); d May 23, 1983. See next PA.2.2.5.1.2.1.

PA.2.2.5.1.2.1
ROBERT WILLETT WILSON and NAN MCALLISTER

Robert Willett Wilson was born on July 10, 1895, at Paw Paw, Michigan.

Robert Willett Wilson married Nan McAllister (d February 1, 1981).

Robert Willett Wilson died on May 23, 1983.

1. **Robert McAllister WILSON**: b September 1, 1925, Detroit, Wayne County, Michigan; m Christine Jane Crouse (b Phoenix, Arizona, on February 18, 1930).

1. **Lawrence Boyd WILSON**: b November 21, 1953, Evanston, Illinois.
2. **Lindsay McAllister WILSON**: b October 12, 1956, Evanston, Illinois.

ROBERT WILLETT WILSON
(Photograph courtesy of Douglas Willett)

PA.2.2.5.1.3
KATHERINE WILLETT and GEORGE M. VANEVERA
of Des Moines, Iowa

Katherine ("Katie") Willett was born in 1867, Ohio.

Miss Katherine Willett married George M. VanEvera. They resided (1900; 1936) Des Moines, Iowa.

1. **Grace VANEVERA:** m in Des Moines, Iowa, to George Dale Willard; removed to Minneapolis, Minnesota; d abt 1929, Chicago, Illinois.

2. **Katherine VANEVERA:** m Richard W. Redfield; resided Pasadena, California; d July 10, 1983, Weston, Massachusetts, at the home of her son-in-law.

PA.2.2.5.1.4
EVELYN MOISSELLE WILLETT and ORA JAMES MULFORD
of Detroit, Wayne County, Michigan

Evelyn ("Eva") Moisselle Willett was born on June 24, 1871, Blissfield, Lenawee County, Michigan.

Miss Evelyn M. Willett married in Detroit, Wayne County, Michigan, on February 28, 1901, Ora James Mulford (b September 8, 1868, Monroe, Ohio; d August 2, 1943, Detroit, Wayne County, Michigan).

Mrs. Evelyn (Willett) Mulford died on April 6, 1943, age 71, Detroit, Wayne County, Michigan, and is buried in the Roseland Park Cemetery, Berkley, Michigan.

1. **John Willett MULFORD:** b November 12, 1902, Detroit, Wayne County, Michigan; m Andrea Burks (b April 26, 1905; d September 16, 1980); organized the Mulford Advertising and Printing Company which he operated for 35 years before selling it in 1953; d June 2, 1964, Detroit, Wayne County, Michigan, and is buried in the Roseland Park Cemetery, Berkley, Michigan.

    1. **Joan MULFORD:**
    2. **Mary MULFORD:** m Sterling Graham.
    3. **Susan MULFORD:** m Thomas Little.

PA.2.2.5.2
ENOS WILLETT and BEULAH DEPUY
of Erie County, Ohio,
and Adrian, Lenawee County, Michigan

Enos Willett was born on April 13, 1822, at Espy, Columbia County, in Pennsylvania.

About 1836, Enos Willett's father, Peter Willett, removed to Ohio, evidently following in the wake of his brother, William Willett, who had removed to Ohio in 1834.

In 1850, Enos Willet, age 28, and his brother Abram Willet, age 30, were enumerated in the household of their brother Philip Willet in Erie County, Ohio.

Enos Willett, age 30, married in Margaretta Township, Erie County, Pennsylvania, on May 20, 1852, Beulah DePuy (age 20, born May 24, 1832, Sunbury, Pennsylvania; d May 31, 1917, Adrian, Michigan, buried Oakwood Cemetery, Adrian, Lenawee County, Michigan), the daughter of Joseph Depuy and Sarah Woolverton, and sister to Alma Depuy. The marriage took place at the bride's home (farm).

In 1860, E. <u>Willet</u> and family were listed in the Oxford Township, Erie County, Ohio, census, No. 1826, as follows:

Willet	E.	38	m	PA	farmer
	Bulah	28	f	PA	
	Wesley	7	m	OH	
	Abram	39	m	PA	
	Alma	23	f	PA	

In the spring of 1868, they removed to Blissfield, Lenawee County, Michigan, where they lived for one year. In 1869 or 1870, they moved again to Adrian, Lenawee County, Michigan. He started a grocery business in 1872 with Benjamin Laing as partner. This partnership only lasted a year and a half; then Enos operated the grocery store for the next 25 years, until the time of his death. In the 1874-1875 Adrian City directory, the store was listed as "Willett and Son" groceries, provisions, flour, feed, etc. His son Wesley and his brother Benjamin were listed as clerks in the store. The address of the store was 91 North Main. Enos was listed as residing at South Hunt between Main and Broad. The store later relocated to the downtown Adrian area, and was located at 8 North Main Street and renamed "E. Willett and Company," groceries and provisions store. It was across the street from the Fox Confectionery and the Hays Shoe Store.

Enos Willett died at his home on 10 Hunt Street, on February 2, 1897, age 73, as the result of a stroke he had suffered earlier in the week. He is buried at the Oakwood Cemetery, Adrian, Lenawee County, Michigan.

In 1900, Beulah <u>Willets</u> (sic) age 68, born 1832, Pennsylvania, mother, is enumerated in the household of her son-in-law, Ashley D. Walker (1900 Lenawee County census).

ENOS WILLETT (1822-1897)
CIRCA 1890
(Photograph courtesy of Gaillard P. Willett)

In 1910, Beulah <u>Willat</u> (sic), age 78, born Pennsylvania, mother-in-law, is enumerated in the household of her son-in-law, Winfield Tudor (1910 Lenawee County census).

CIRCA 1920
MRS. BEULAH (DEPUY) WILLETT
(Photograph courtesy of Douglas Willett)

1. **Wesley John WILLETT**: b April 18, 1853, at Oxford Township, Erie County, Ohio; m at Adrian, Lenawee County, Michigan, on November 20, 1878, Josephine Laing (b June 15, 1859, Michigan; d February 20, 1939, Detroit, Wayne County, Michigan); d December 9, 1902, Hot Springs, Arkansas, while on a visit to restore his health, buried Oakwood Cemetery, Adrian, Lenawee County, Ohio. (1860 Erie County census). See next PA.2.2.5.2.1.

2. **Orlando WILLETT**: b March 21, 1856, at Oxford Township, Erie County, Ohio; d September 18, 1856, at Oxford Township, Erie County, Ohio, and is buried in the Sand Hill Cemetery, Margaretta, Groton Township, Erie County, Ohio, with his brother Harmon Willett and his grandparents Joseph and Sarah DePuy.

3. **Harmon WILLETT**: b August 6, 1859; "Harmy" Willett died on July 2, 1860 and is buried in the Sand Hill Cemetery, Margaretta, Groton Township, Erie County, Ohio, with his brother Orlando Willett and his grandparents Joseph and Sarah DePuy. He was named after his uncle Harmon Depuy who was a Colonel in the Union Army during the Civil War.

4. **Julia Bell WILLETT**: b October 30, 1863, Goshen, Indiana (possibly while the family was visiting relatives); m November 15, 1887, Winfield Scott Tudor (b March 2, 1862, Indiana; d November 4, 1940, buried Oakwood Cemetery, Adrian, Michigan); d March 9, 1964, Adrian, Michigan, and is buried in the Oakwood Cemetery, Adrian, Lenawee County, Michigan.

5. **Martha May WILLETT**: b August 11, 1866, at Cooks Corner, North Monroeville, Ohio; m at Adrian, Lenawee County, Michigan, on March 26, 1889, Ashley Dexter Walker (b October 15, 1858, Lapeer, Michigan; d September 29, 1917, Adrian, Lenawee County, Michigan); d December 5, 1956, Adrian, Lenawee County, Michigan. See next PA.2.2.5.2.5.

PA.2.2.5.2.1
WESLEY JOHN WILLETT and JOSEPHINE E. LAING
of Adrian, Lenawee County, Michigan

Wesley John Willett was born at Oxford Township, Erie County, Ohio, on April 18, 1853. Erie County, Ohio, is on the western most tip of Lake Erie. The move from Erie County, Ohio, to Lenawee County, Michigan, was a short trip across two other counties. In the 1870 Adrian City Directory, he is listed as a college student.

When his father and Benjamin Laing started the Willett and Laing Grocery Store around 1872, Wesley began working there as a clerk. The store was at 91 North Main Street, Adrian, Michigan. Wesley was living with his parents at Hunt Street about this time. In 1874, Wesley was living on McKenzie Street in Adrian near the West Branch School. When his father's partnership with Mr. Laing ended, the grocery became "Willett and Son" Groceries and Provisions.

Wesley John Willett married at Adrian, Lenawee County, Michigan, on November 20, 1878, Josephine E. Laing (b June 15, 1859, Michigan; d February 20, 1939, Detroit, Wayne County, Michigan), the daughter of Joseph S. Laing and Jennette.

Wesley Willett was a member of the Knights of the Maccabees. This group met every second and fourth Monday of each month at Maccabee Hall over 14 and 16 South Main Street, Adrian.

In 1900, Wesley Willett and family were listed in the Adrian Township, Lenawee County, Michigan, census, as follows:

Willett	Wesley	39	Apr 1855	OH
	Josephine	39	Jun 1860	MI
	Fred W	18	May 1882	MI
	Louis J	15	Sep 1884	MI

At one time, he owned a billiard hall for a few years, but after that period, he was in the grocery business with his father, Enos Willett, for about 25 years. After the death of Enos, in February, 1897, Wesley John Willett continued to operated the store until February, 1902, when he sold out due to health reasons. He was suffering from rheumatism.

In 1900, he made the trip to Hot Springs, Arkansas, and when he returned, he was greatly improved. In the fall of 1902, he became worse again, and returned to Hot Springs with his wife. He began to improved, and was considering relocating to Hot Springs when he took a hard cold followed by pneumonia which led to his death. His body was returned to Adrian for burial.

WESLEY JOHN WILLETT (1853-1902)
CIRCA 1900
(Photograph courtesy of Gaillard P. Willett)

Wesley J. Willett died on December 9, 1902, at Hot Springs, Arkansas, age 49, and was buried in the Oakwood Cemetery, Adrian, Lenawee County, Michigan.

In 1910, Josephine Willett, age 49, born Michigan, was listed in the household of her father, Joseph Laing, along with her son, Louis J. Willett, age 26.

1. **Bessie WILLETT**: b January 8, 1880, Adrian, Lenawee County, Michigan; d August 6, 1880, age 7 months, of infant cholera, at Adrian, Lenawee County, buried Oakwood Cemetery, Adrian, Lenawee County, Michigan.

2. **Fred Wesley WILLETT**: b May 27, 1882, Adrian, Lenawee County, Michigan; m in the Methodist Church, at Windsor, Ontario, Canada on November 12, 1902, Ella Louise Knowles (b February 19, 1884, Adrian, Lenawee County, Michigan, the daughter of Cullen Knowles and Emma Cook; d February 26, 1949, Detroit, Wayne County, Michigan); d April 17, 1977, Adrian, Michigan, and is buried in the Oakwood Cemetery, Adrian, Lenawee County, Michigan.   See next PA.2.2.5.2.1.2.

3. **Louis John WILLETT**: b September 25, 1884, Adrian, Lenawee County, Michigan; he was a taylor; never married; d September 20, 1932, Eloise, Westland, Wayne County, buried Oakwood Cemetery, Adrian, Lenawee County, Michigan.

CIRCA 1902
JOSEPHINE (LAING) AND WESLEY JOHN WILLETT
(Photograph courtesy of Douglas Willett)

PA.2.2.5.2.1.2
FRED WESLEY WILLETT and **ELLA LOUISE KNOWLES**
of Adrian, Lenawee County, Michigan

Fred Wesley Willett was born on May 27, 1882, at Adrian,
Lenawee County, Michigan.   Lenawee County, Michigan, is
adjacent to the Ohio state border, and is surrounded by the
Michigan counties of Hillsdale, Jackson, Washtenaw and
Monroe, and Fulton, Williams, and Lucas counties in Ohio are
just to the south.

Fred Wesley Willett, salesman, age 21 of Adrian, Michigan,
married in a Methodist Church in Windsor, Canada on
November 12, 1902, Ella Louise Knowles, age 19 (b February
19, 1884, Adrian, Lenawee County, Michigan; d February 26,
1949, Detroit, Wayne County, Michigan), the daughter of
Cullen Knowles and Emma Cook (Ontario Vital Statistics
Index, No. 007111).

FRED WESLEY ("POPS") WILLETT ORCHESTRA,
ADRIAN, MICHIGAN
Fred Wesley Willett is the young man seated on the far right
CIRCA 1910
(Photograph courtesy of Gaillard P. Willett)

During his early years in Adrian, he played the violin and the piano at the historic Croswell Opera House, and with his own orchestra. He was listed as the director of the "Willett Orchestra." Fred was very musically inclined and played the violin, piano, drums, base fiddle, and xylophone. He also had an orchestra booking agency which would furnish orchestra, big or small, for special occasions. Christmas and New Year were always busy seasons.

CIRCA 1915
WESLEY FRED EDWIN WILLETT (standing center)
FRED WESLEY ("POPS") WILLETT - ELLA (KNOWLES) WILLETT
(Photograph courtesy of Gaillard P. Willett)

Fred Willett worked as a salesman for Grinnells for a few years. He then entered into partnership to sell pianos with Ora ("Web") Calhoun, Henry Knoblaugh, his uncle Carroll Knowles, and a Mr. Goodrich. In 1911, he and Web Calhoun soon bought out the other partners and started "Willett and Calhoun Piano Store" in Adrian. The piano store was located at 39 South Main Street. In 1917, the city of Adrian changed their address system, and the store was listed as at 145 South Main.

In December 1920, he was manager of the Kurtz Oakland Company in Adrian. This company sold Oakland and Cadillac motor cars and GMC trucks. In 1923, he was co-owner with Clifford A. Kurtz in the "Willett Motor Sales and Kurtz Oakland Company." The dealership was located at 201-203 Maumee Street. Later, Mr. Willett owned a Chevrolet dealership which was eventually merged with an Oldsmobile agency.

In 1926, Fred moved his family to Detroit where he entered the real estate business. In the beginning he was selling lots for B. E. Taylor. In 1929, the family were residing at 4025 W. Philadelphia, Detroit. He worked as a salesman for Dan J. Harrison selling improved property. Later, he became active in construction during the height of the depression. He was a partner in the firm of "Willett and Gregory" with George E. Gregory and Ralph W. Stevens from Adrian who was their financier. A few of the houses that where constructed were on Coyle Avenue in the Inglewood Park Subdivision of Detroit. His son, Wesley, purchased one of these homes and lived at 18516 Coyle with his family.

On January 15, 1943, Fred Willett and his son, Wesley, entered into partnership to operate the Riveria Recreation Center, Detroit, which business he managed for 30 years. It was during this time that he invented the first electric bowling ball cleaner while working at the alley. The bowling alley was located on the Grand River near Joy road.

He was a musician with the Detroit News Studio Orchestra. He and son played with many Detroit area orchestras. He was the oldest living member of the Detroit Federation of Musicians at the time of his death in 1977. He enjoyed teaching bowling to those area residents who wanted to learn the game.

He spent his summers on Sand Lake in Onsted, Michigan, where his father had built the family cottage with his grandpa Laing, when he was a young boy.

Fred Wesley Willett died on April 17, 1977, in Adrian, Lenawee County, Michigan, and is buried in the Oakwood Cemetery, Adrian, Lenawee County, Michigan.

CIRCA 1940
FRED WESLEY WILLETT
(Photograph courtesy of Douglas Willett)

1. **Wesley Fred Edwin WILLETT**: b August 10, 1903, Adrian, Lenawee County; m in Monroe, Michigan, on June 16, 1934, Mildred Rose Remdt (b June 14, 1913, Findlay, Ohio; d December 22, 1993, Plymouth, Wayne County, Michigan), the daughter of Lyle Carl Remdt and Hazel Dana Morrison; newspaper publisher; d December 7, 1975, at Garden City, Wayne County, Michigan, buried Oakwood Cemetery, Adrian, Michigan. See next PA.2.2.5.2.1.2.1.

CIRCA 1940
MRS. ELLA (KNOWLES) WILLETT
(Photograph courtesy of Douglas Willett)

PA.2.2.5.2.1.2.1
WESLEY FRED EDWIN WILLETT
and **MILDRED ROSE REMDT**
of Michigan

Wesley Fred Edwin Willett was born August 10, 1903, Adrian, Lenawee County, Michigan, the only child of Fred and Ella Willett.

In 1926, Wesley removed to Detroit, Michigan, with his parents, and in 1929, he was employed by the Times Publishing Company. He met Mildred Remdt while staying at the family cottage at Sand Lake, Onsted, Michigan.

Wesley Fred Willett married in Monroe, Michigan, on June 16, 1934, Mildred Rose Remdt (b June 14, 1913, Findlay, Ohio; d December 22, 1993, Plymouth, Wayne County, Michigan), the daughter of Lyle Carl Remdt and Hazel Dana Morrison.

In 1939, Wes was a salesman for the Beard Newspaper Publishing Company and was boarding at 18516 Coyle Avenue.

Wesley became a newspaper publisher. Wes was a past member of the Michigan Press Association, the Suburban Press Foundation, and the Accredited Home Newspapers of America. He was a member of the National Newspapers Association. He was the pass president of the Wayne State University Press Club, the Detroit Press Club, a 20 year member of the Adcraft Club and a former staff member of the Detroit Times.

Wesley Fred Edwin Willett died on December 7, 1975, at Garden City, and is buried in the Oakwood Cemetery, Adrian, Michigan.

1. **Marilynn Joanne WILLETT**: b February 20, 1935, Toledo, Ohio; m 1st March 31, 1953, Alan Dean Lawrence (b April 20, 1933, Santa Monica, California; d November 15, 1969, buried Lambs Cemetery, Port Huron, Michigan); m 2nd at Plymouth, Ohio, on June 18, 1977, Wesley Dean Gardner. See next PA.2.2.5.2.1.2.1.1.

2. **Barbara Ann WILLETT**: b July 29, 1936, Detroit, Wayne County; m June 16, 1957, Dale Ward Larkin (b February 25, 1937, Detroit, Wayne County, Michigan). See next PA.2.2.5.2.1.2.1.2.

3. **Ronald Wesley WILLETT**: b April 4, 1939, Highland Park, Wayne County, Michigan; m at St. John's Episcopal Church, Wayne, Michigan, on September 1, 1962, Nina Mae Kates (b June 5, 1941, Oklahoma City, Oklahoma). See next PA.2.2.5.2.1.2.1.3.

4. **David John Lyle WILLETT**: b May 1, 1943, Wayne County, Michigan; m 1st in the First Methodist Church, Wayne, Michigan, September 28, 1963, Donna Jean Glenn (b October 14, 1943, Tecumseh, Lenawee County, Michigan), the daughter of Joseph Frank Glenn and Donna Jean Kopke; m 2d at Mackinaw Island, July 18, 1986, Susan Carol Bachand (b May 1, 1943); resides Westland, Michigan; newspaper publisher. See next PA.2.2.5.2.1.2.1.4.

CIRCA 1940
MRS. MILDRED ROSE (REMDT) WILLETT
(Photograph courtesy of Douglas Willett)

WESLEY FRED WILLETT (1903-1975)
(Photograph courtesy of Douglas Willett)

MRS. MILDRED ROSE (REMDT) WILLETT (1913-1993)
(Photograph courtesy of Douglas Willett)

PA.2.2.5.2.1.2.1.1
MARILYNN JOANNE WILLETT

Marilynn Joanne Willett was born on February 20, 1935, at Toledo, Ohio, at St. Vincent's Hospital. Her mother went into labor while she was visiting her Grandma. That is why she was born at Toledo.

Miss Marilynn Joanne Willett married 1st on March 31, 1953, Alan Dean Lawrence (b April 20, 1933, Santa Monica, California; d November 15, 1969, buried Lambs Cemetery, Port Huron, Michigan).

Mrs. Marilynn Joanne (Willett) Lawrence married 2nd at the courthouse in Plymouth, Ohio, on June 18, 1977, Wesley Dean Gardner.

1. **Lynn Elaine LAWRENCE**: b November 13, 1953; m December 4, 1971, Paul Anton Simcheck, Sr. (b October 25, 1952). See next PA.2.2.5.2.1.2.1.1.1.

2. **Cynthia Ann LAWRENCE**: b May 1, 1958; m December 23, 1977, Steven Reed. See next PA.2.2.5.2.1.2.1.1.2.

3. **Leslie Carol LAWRENCE**: b December 15, 1961; m Joey Wayne Nye. See next PA.2.2.5.2.1.2.1.1.3.

4 **Nancy Joanne LAWRENCE**: b April 20, 1963; m Jeffrey Carl Sparks. See next PA.2.2.5.2.1.2.1.1.4.

5. **Janice Michelle LAWRENCE**: b July 28, 1967.

6. **Julie Deanne LAWRENCE**: b March 31, 1970; m November 15, 1991, David James Menzel. See next PA.2.2.5.2.1.2.1.1.6.

PA.2.2.5.2.1.2.1.1.1
LYNN ELAINE LAWRENCE and PAUL ANTON SIMCHECK

Lynn Elaine Lawrence was born on November 13, 1953.

Miss Lynn Elaine Lawrence married on December 4, 1971, Paul Anton Simcheck, Sr. (b October 25, 1952).

1. **Brandi Lynn SIMCHECK**: b May 19, 1972; d June 30, 1991.
2. **Jamison Alan SIMCHECK**: b July 16, 1974; m at South Lyon, Oakland County, Michigan, on January 23, 1993, Jessie Virginia Hummecky. See next PA.2.2.5.2.1.2.1.1.1.2
3. **Paul Anton SIMCHECK**, Jr: b November 1, 1977; m on October 15, 1994, Julie Diane Gonzales.
4. **Candice April SIMCHECK**: b August 15, 1980.
5. **Nicholas Ryan SIMCHECK**: b April 16, 1987.

PA.2.2.5.2.1.2.1.1.1.2
JAMISON ALAN SIMCHECK
and JESSIE VIRGINIA HUMMECKY

Jamison Alan Simcheck was born on July 16, 1974.

Jamison Alan Simcheck married at South Lyon, Oakland County, Michigan, on January 23, 1993, Jessie Virginia Hummecky

1. **Victoria Brandi SIMCHECK**: b March 17, 1994.
2. **Valerie Morgan SIMCHECK**: b January 12, 1997.

PA.2.2.5.2.1.2.1.1.2
CYNTHIA ANN LAWRENCE and STEVE REED

Cynthia Ann Willett was born on May 1, 1958;
Miss Cynthia Ann Willett married on December 23, 1977, Steven Reed.

1. **Steven Alan REED**: b April 29, 1978.
2. **Michael Ryan REED**: b June 29, 1981.
3 **Andrew Bradley REED**: b September 22, 1987.

PA.2.2.5.2.1.2.1.1.3
LESLIE CAROL LAWRENCE and JOEY WAYNE NYE

Leslie Carol Lawrence was born on December 15, 1961.
Miss Leslie Carol Lawrence married Joey Wayne Nye.

1. **Krystle Carol NYE**: b July 20, 1987.
2. **Justin Wayne Alan NYE**: b June 1, 1994.

PA.2.2.5.2.1.2.1.1.4
NANCY JOANNE LAWRENCE and JEFFREY CARL SPARKS

Nancy Joanne Lawrence was born on April 20, 1963.
Miss Nancy Joanne Lawrence married Jeffrey Carl Sparks.

1. **Amanda Rose SPARKS**: b May 3, 1989.

PA.2.2.5.2.1.1.6
JULIE DEANNE LAWRENCE and DAVID JAMES MENZEL

Julie Deanne Lawrence was born on March 31, 1970.
Miss Julie Deanne Lawrence married on November 15, 1991, David James Menzel.

1. **Brittany Lynn MENZEL**: b January 28, 1994.

PA.2.2.5.2.1.2.1.2

BARBARA ANN WILLETT and **DALE WARD LARKIN**

of Detroit, Wayne County, Michigan

Barbara Ann Willett was born on July 29, 1936, Detroit, Wayne County, Michigan.

Miss Barbara Ann Willett married on June 16, 1957, Dale Ward Larkin (b February 25, 1937, Detroit, Wayne County, Michigan) (separated 1975).

1. **Jeff LARKIN**: b October 30, 1958, Detroit, Wayne County, Michigan.

2, **Phillip LARKIN**: b March 15, 1961, Detroit, Wayne County, Michigan.

3. **Dawn LARKIN**: b June 12, 1963, Detroit, Wayne County, Michigan; at Fort Lauderdale, Florida, on February 11, 1995, Stuart E. Hyden.

PA.2.2.5.2.1.2.1.3

RONALD WESLEY WILLETT and **NINA MAE KATES**

of Michigan

Ronald Wesley Willett was born April 4, 1939, Highland Park, Detroit, Wayne County, Michigan. He attended Redford High School and Wilbur Wright Vocational School where he graduated in 1959.

Ronald Wesley Willett married at St. John's Episcopal Church, Wayne, Michigan, on September 1, 1962, Nina Mae Kates (b June 5, 1941, Oklahoma City, Oklahoma).

He is an insurance agent.

1. **Dean Gregory WILLETT**: b August 27, 1965, Wayne, Wayne County, Michigan.

2. **Christian Alan WILLETT**: b September 30, 1970, Wayne, Wayne County, Michigan.

PA.2.2.5.2.1.2.1.4
DAVID JOHN LYLE WILLETT
of Wayne, Michigan

David John Lyle Willett was born May 1, 1943, Wayne County, Michigan.

David Willett married 1st in the First Methodist Church, Wayne, Michigan, September 28, 1963, Donna Jean Glenn (b October 14, 1943, Tecumseh, Lenawee County, Michigan), the daughter of Joseph Frank Glenn and Donna Jean Kopke.

David Willett married 2d at Mackinaw Island, July 18, 1986, Susan Carol Bachand (b May 1, 1943).

They reside in Westland, Michigan, where he is a newspaper publisher.

1. **Douglas John WILLETT**: b December 15, 1966, Howell, Livingston County, Michigan; attended George Washington Elementary School and Adams, Jr. High School, in Westland, Michigan; graduated 1990 with a Bachelor of Science degree in Computer Science, Central Michigan University; m at the First United Methodist Church, Wayne, Michigan, on July 18, 1992, Theresa Lynn Raymond (b March 25, 1969, Detroit, Michigan); works for EDS. See next PA.2.2.5.2.1.2.1.4.1.

2. **Deborah** ("Debbie") **Jean WILLETT**: b April 6, 1969, Howell, Livingston County, Michigan; graduated from Wayne Memorial High School (1987); completed two years of technical training at the William D. Ford Vocational Technical Center. She works with the family owned company for the past 10 years. She has been a member of the Michigan Jaycees for 6 years and has held 5 board positions in the local Jaycee Chapter.

PA.2.2.5.2.1.2.1.4.1
DOUGLAS JOHN WILLETT and THERESA LYNN RAYMOND

Douglas John Willett was born on December 15, 1966, Howell, Livingston County, Michigan. He attended George Washington Elementary School and Adams, Jr. High School, in Westland, Michigan. Doug graduated in 1990, with a Bachelor of Science degree in Computer Science, from Central Michigan University.

Douglas John Willett married at the First United Methodist Church, Wayne, Michigan, on July 18, 1992, Theresa Lynn Raymond (b March 25, 1969, Detroit, Michigan). He works for EDS.

1. **Ashley Rose Jean WILLETT**: b September 20, 1995, Garden City, Michigan.
2. **Adam Joseph WILLETT**: b May 11, 1996, Royal Oak, Michigan.

ASHLEY ROSE WILLETT
(Photograph Courtesy of Douglas Willett)

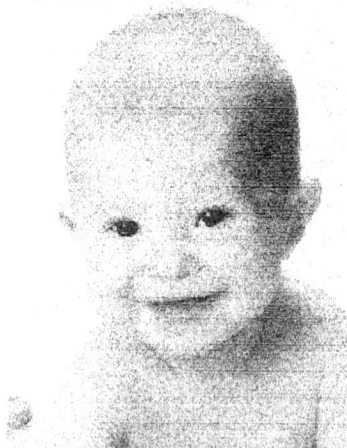

PA.2.2.5.3.5
MARTHA MAY WILLETT and ASHLEY DEXTER WALKER
of Adrian, Lenawee County, Michigan

Martha May Willett was born on August 11, 1866, at Cooks Corner, North Monroeville, Ohio.

Miss Martha May Willett married at Adrian, Lenawee County, Michigan, on March 26, 1889, Ashley Dexter Walker (b October 15, 1858, Lapeer, Michigan; d September 29, 1917, Adrian, Lenawee County, Michigan).

Mrs. Martha May (Willett) Walker died on December 5, 1956, Adrian, Lenawee County, Michigan.

MARTHA MAY WILLETT and ASHLEY DEXTER WALKER
(Photograph Courtesy of Douglas Willett)

1. **Charles Willett WALKER**: b March 16, 1890, Adrian, Lenawee County, Michigan; m Pearl A. Stadler; d December 4, 1971, buried Oakwood Cemetery, Adrian, Michigan.

2. **Harold Enos WALKER**: b July 5, 1893, Adrian, Lenawee County, Michigan; m in Penrose, Colorado, in July, 1922, Marguerite Bell Gearhart; d March 12, 1970, Pueblo, Colorado. See next PA.2.2.5.3.5.2.

3. **Lawrence Ashley WALKER**: b February 9, 1895, Adrian, Lenawee County, Michigan; m in Adrian, Lenawee County, Michigan, on January 24, 1921, Mildred Caroline Stadler (d February 7, 1968); d August 19, 1964. See next PA.2.2.5.3.5.3.

4. **Bruce Dexter WALKER**: b November 29, 1897, Adrian, Lenawee County, Michigan; d May 27, 1908, at the age of 10, in Adrian, Michigan, after a severe attack of tonsillitis and a mastoid abscess complicated by blood poisoning, buried Oakwood Cemetery, Adrian.

5. **Leslie Winfield WALKER**: b July 6, 1901, Adrian, Lenawee County, Michigan; m at Zanesville, Muskingum County, Ohio, on October 14, 1927, Elizabeth Beall; d 1980, buried Oakwood Cemetery, Adrian, Michigan.

6. **Richard Douglas WALKER**: b May 28, 1911, Adrian, Lenawee County, Michigan; m at Ann Arbor, Michigan, on July 21, 1939, Cornelia Moll. See next PA.2.2.5.3.5.6.

PA.2.2.5.3.5.2
HAROLD ENOS WALKER
and **MARGUERITE BELL GEARHART**

Harold Enos Walker was born on July 5, 1893, Adrian, Lenawee County, Michigan.

Harold Enos Walker married in Penrose, Colorado, in July, 1922, Marguerite Bell Gearhart.

Harold Enos Walker died on March 12, 1970, at Pueblo, Colorado.

1. **Leslie Richard WALKER**: b July, 1923, Penrose, Colorado; Lieutenant bombardier during World War II; went missing in action on his seventh raid over Germany on April 29, 1944, soon after declared dead by the War Department; d April 29, 1944.

PA.2.2.5.3.5.3
LAWRENCE ASHLEY WALKER
and MILDRED CAROLINE STADLER

Lawrence Ashley Walker was born on February 9, 1895, Adrian, Lenawee County, Michigan.

Lawrence Ashley Walker married in Adrian, Lenawee County, Michigan, on January 24, 1921, Mildred Caroline Stadler (b April 5, 1899, Adrian, Michigan; d February 7, 1968, Adrian).

Lawrence Ashley Walker died on August 19, 1964.

1. **Robert Bruce WALKER**: b August 6, 1925, Adrian, Michigan; m Sandra Snyder; resides (1995) Toledo, Ohio.

2. **John Stadler WALKER**: b October 17, 1928, Adrian, Michigan; m on April 6, 1959, Barbara Pasternacki (b August 20, 1932; d October 6, 1987); resides Adrian, Michigan.

    1. **Leslie Elizabeth WALKER**: b March 7, 1960.
    2. **Catherine WALKER**: b November 21, 1961.
    3. **Barbara Ann WALKER**: b May 7, 1963.
    4. **John Stadler WALKER**: b July 9, 1965.

3. **Ralph Eugene WALKER**: b July 13, 1932, Adrian, Michigan; m on January 24, 1953, Lorena Nizzardi (b June 24, 1953).

    1. **Martha Ann WALKER**: b December 30, 1953.
    2. **Michelle Maria WALKER**: b March 20, 1956.

PA.2.2.5.3.5.6
RICHARD DOUGLAS WALKER and CORNELIA MOLL

Richard Douglas Walker was born on May 28, 1911, Adrian, Lenawee County, Michigan.

Richard Douglas Walker at Ann Arbor, Michigan, on July 21, 1939, Cornelia Moll.

1. **Karen Joan WALKER**: b June 7, 1942; m on November 30, 1963, Bradley Bruce; he is a taxidermist.

2. **Winfield Joseph WALKER**: b August 14, 1944.

PA.2.2.5.3
PHILLIP SIDLE WILLETT and **MARGARET ANN EASTER**
of Erie County, Ohio, and Coffey County, Kansas

Phillip Sidle Willett was born on January 28, 1824, at Bloomsburg, in Columbia County, Pennsylvania.

Phillip S. Willett married in Huron County, Ohio, on January 20, 1844, Margaret Ann Easter (b December 25, 1823, Greenfield, Highland County, Ohio; d October 31, 1889, Burlington, Coffey County, Kansas). He was a farmer (1850).

In 1850, his brother, Enos, age 28, and William, age 23 (sic, as recorded in the Erie County census record), were enumerated in his household. William Willett, age 21 (sic, as recorded in the Huron County census record), may have also been enumerated in his father's, Peter Willett, household in the same census year in Huron County, Ohio. It is not that unusual for a person to be enumerated in two different census records.

In 1850, Phillip <u>Willet</u> and family were listed in the Oxford Township, Erie County, Ohio, census, page 383, No. 9, as follows:

Willet	Phillip	26	m	PA	farmer
	Margaret	25	f	OH	
	Catherine A	5	f	OH	
	John H	3	m	OH	
	Frances E	1	f	OH	
	William	23	m	PA	laborer (bro.)
	Enos	28	m	PA	laborer (bro.)

In 1870, they were in St. Joseph County, Michigan; in 1880, they were living in Burlington, Coffey County, Kansas.

Phillip Sidle Willett died December 17 1886, age 63 years. 10 months, 19 days, at Burlington, Coffey County, Kansas, and is buried in the Graceland Cemetery, Burlington, Kansas.

1. **Catherine Ann WILLETT**: b December 19, 1844, Milan, Erie County, Ohio; m at White Pigeon, St. Joseph County, Michigan, on January 8, 1867, Martin Luther Gortner (b June 10, 1844, Muncy, Pennsylvania; d November 10, 1928, Burlington, Coffey County, Kansas); d March 9, 1925, Burlington, Coffey County, Kansas, buried Graceland Cemetery, Burlington. See next <u>PA.2.2.5.3.1</u>.

2. **Hamilton John WILLETT**: b January, 1848 (1846), Milan, Erie County, Ohio; m at Blissfield, Lenawee County, Michigan, January 23, 1872, Emma Gage Worth (b June 10, 1851, New York; d June 28, 1932, Emporia, Kansas, buried

Graceland Cemetery, Burlington, Kansas); residing (1880) St. Lawrence Street, Burlington, Coffey County, Kansas; d October 6, 1921, Burlington, Coffey County, Kansas, buried Graceland Cemetery, Burlington, Kansas.

3. **Frances Elvin WILLETT**: b April 22, 1848, Milan Township, Erie County, Ohio; m at Burlington, Coffey County, Kansas, on September 12, 1871, Henry Wagoner (b 1848; d March 11, 1915, Sedalia, Missouri); d November 24, 1919, Los Angeles, California, buried Graceland Cemetery, Burlington, Kansas.

4. **Harriet WILLETT**: b 1854, Milan Township, Erie County, Ohio; m at Burlington, Coffey County, Kansas, on September 14, 1876, A. C. Majors; d October 16, 1919, Raton, New Mexico. See next PA.2.2.5.3.4.

5. **Belle B. WILLETT**: b 1856, Ohio; m at Burlington, Coffey County, Kansas, on February 1, 1876, George G. Hall (b abt 1855). See next PA.2.2.5.3.5.

PA.2.2.5.3.1
CATHERINE ANN WILLETT
and **MARTIN LUTHER GORTNER**
of Coffey County, Kansas

Catherine Ann Willett was born on December 19, 1844, Milan, Erie County, Ohio.

Miss Catherine Ann Willett married at White Pigeon, St. Joseph County, Michigan, on January 8, 1867, Martin Luther Gortner (b June 10, 1844, Muncy, Pennsylvania; d November 10, 1928, Burlington, Coffey County, Kansas).

Mrs. Catherine Ann (Willett) Gortner died on March 9, 1925, Burlington, Coffey County, Kansas, and is buried in the Graceland Cemetery, Burlington.

1. **George Alvin GORTNER**: b December 17, 1867, White Pigeon, St. Joseph County, Michigan; m October 5, 1892, Vannie T. Sanders; d April 25, 1939, Wichita, Kansas, buried Graceland Cemetery, Burlington, Kansas.

2. **Harriet E. GORTNER**: b June 24, 1874, White Pigeon, St. Joseph County, Michigan; m 1st at Burlington, Coffey County, Kansas, on October 7, 1893, Charles Edgar Riley; m 2d at Burlington, Coffey County, Kansas, on February 21, 1899, Charles A. Pratte; m 3rd at Burlington, Coffey County, Kansas, on July 22, 1908, Edward N. Farris; d June 22, 1954, Burlington, Coffey County, Kansas, buried Graceland Cemetery, Burlington, Kansas.

3. **Grace M. GORTNER**: m at Burlington, Coffey County,

Kansas, on October 5, 1903, Charles Edward South (b November 7, 1873, Marysville, Union County, Ohio; d May 13, 1948, St. Louis, Missouri).

PA.2.2.5.3.4
HARRIET WILLETT and A. C. MAJORS

Harriet Willett was born 1854, Milan Township, Erie County, Ohio.

Miss Harriet Willett married at Burlington, Coffey County, Kansas, on September 14, 1876, A. C. Majors.

Mrs. Harriet (Willett) Majors died on October 16, 1919, Raton, New Mexico.

1. **Leigh W. MAJORS**: b 1877; d October 15, 1909, San Francisco, California, buried Graceland Cemetery Burlington, Coffey County, Kansas.
2. **Jessie MAJORS**:
3. **John MAJORS**:

PA.2.2.5.3.5
BELLE B. WILLETT and GEORGE G. HALL

Belle B. Willett was born 1857, in Ohio.

Miss Belle B. Willett married at Burlington, Coffey County, Kansas, on February 1, 1876, George G. Hall (b abt 1855).

1. **Franklin HALL**: b February, 1878; d April 2, 1885, buried Graceland Cemetery, Burlington, Kansas.
2. **Phil HALL**:
3. **Max HALL**:

PA.2.2.5.4
WILLIAM WILLETT and ELIZABETH J. WELLIVER
of Monroe County, Michigan

William Willett was born June 6, 1826, Columbia County, Pennsylvania. He removed to Ohio with his parents when he was young.

William Willett married in Huron County, Ohio, on December 12, 1854, Elizabeth J. Welliver (b September 1, 1833, Pennsylvania; d September 4, 1912, Petersburg, Monroe County, Michigan, buried Pleasant View Cemetery, Blissfield, Michigan).

In 1859, they removed to Lenawee County, Michigan.

In 1860, William Willett and his family are enumerated in the household of his parents in Ogden Township, Lewanee County, Michigan, census, page 451, dwelling 1537-1580, as follows:

Willett	Peter	head	63	m	PA	farmer
	Rebecca	wife	49	f	PA	
	William		32	m	PA	farmer
	Elizabeth		24	f	PA	
	Benjamin		28	m	PA	farmer
	John		24	m	OH	farmer
	John		4	m	OH	
Wilver	Clinton		10	m	PA	

On October 20, 1866, William Willett purchased 58 and 1/2 acres of land in Blissfield, Lenawee County, Michigan.

In 1870, William Willett and family are listed in the Blissfield, Lenawee County, census, page 139, as follows:

Willett	William	head	41	m	PA	farmer
	Elizabeth	wife	38	f	PA	
	John	son	13	m	OH	at school
	Clinton	son	18	m	PA	R. R. employee
	John	(brother)	36	m	OH	farm laborer
	Rebecca	mother	68	f	PA	no occupation

In 1880, a large barn belonging to William Willett caught fire and was destroyed.

In 1900, William <u>Willetts</u>, and family were listed in the Monroe County, Michigan, census, as follows:

<u>Willetts</u>	William	84	PA
	Elizabeth	75	PA
	Clinton	55	OH

William Willett died on October 27, 1914, in Petersburg, Monroe County, Michigan, and is buried in the "Pleasant View" Cemetery, Blissfield, Lenawee County, Michigan.

1. **Clinton D. WILLETT**: b March, 1854, Pennsylvania; m abt 1880 H. B. (most likely died before 1900); Clinton was living (1907) in Petersburg, Monroe County, Michigan; d after 1912. See next <u>PA.2.2.5.4.1</u>.

2. **John Wellington WILLETT**: b 1856, Ohio; railroad worker; d October 10, 1881, buried Pleasant View Cemetery, Blissfield, Lenawee County, Michigan. His death was the result of a railway accident when he was coupling cars near Topeka, Kansas.

PA.2.2.5.4.1

CLINTON D. WILLETT and H. B.

Clinton D. Willett was born in March, 1854, Pennsylvania.

Clinton D. Willett married about 1880 H. B. (most likely died before 1900).

Clinton D. Willett lived in Blissfield, Lenawee County, and later (1907) in Petersburg, Monroe County, Michigan.

Clinton was still living as late as October 11, 1907, when he was mentioned in the Petersburg local newspaper.

Clinton D. Willett died after December, 1915, Petersburg, Monroe County, Michigan.

1. **Mary WILLETT** (twin): b February 25, 1881; d March 2, 1881, buried Pleasant View Cemetery, Blissfield, Lenawee County, Michigan.

2. **Ina WILLETT** (twin): b February 25, 1881; d March 2, 1881, buried Pleasant View Cemetery, Blissfield, Lenawee County, Michigan.

PA.2.2.5.5
BENJAMIN S. WILLETT and **RACHEL CALISTA MARR**
of Lenawee County, Michigan

Benjamin S. Willett was born February 1, 1828, at Danville, Columbia County, Pennsylvania.

On October 26, 1854, Benjamin Willett paid for a marriage license in Norwalk, Huron County, Ohio. The marriage license was made out to Benjamin S. Willett and Sarah Hollis. A week later, Benjamin Willett returned the license to the Probate Judge, stating that he could not use it.

Benjamin S. Willett married in Hudson, Lenawee County, Michigan, in 1877, Rachel Calista Marr (b May 29, 1852, Hudson, Lenawee County, Michigan; d September 12, 1921, buried Pleasant View Cemetery, Blissfield, Lenawee County, Michigan). He was 43, she was 25. He was a grocer.

In 1880, Benjamin Willett, and family were listed at 1 Hunt Street, Adrian City, Lenawee County, Michigan, as follows:

Willett	Benj.	45	m	PA	
	Calista	28	f	MI	wife
	Allice	4	f	MI	daughter

Benjamin Willett died on November 6, 1894, and is buried in the Pleasant View Cemetery, Blissfield, Lenawee County, Michigan.

1. **Allice WILLETT**: b 1876, Michigan; m Huntington; resided (1921) Jackson, Michigan.

2. **Nelson Marr WILLETT**: b August 19, 1878; d January 24, 1880, age 1 year, 5 months, 4 days, of cholera, Adrian, Lenawee County, Michigan, buried Pleasant View Cemetery, Blissfield, Lenawee County, Michigan.

3. **Ruth Calista WILLETT**: b August 2, 1890, Blissfield, Michigan; m in Hudson, Michigan, on June 26, 1906, Ernest L. Frye (d February 5, 1956, buried Adrian, Lenawee County, Michigan); d April 26, 1954, Adrian, Lenawee County, Michigan. See next PA.2.2.5.5.3.

PA.2.2.5.5.3
RUTH CALISTA WILLETT and **ERNEST L. FRYE**
of Lenawee County, Michigan

Ruth Calista Willett was born on August 2, 1890, Blissfield, Lenawee County, Michigan.

Miss Ruth C. Willett married in Hudson, Michigan, on June 26, 1906, Ernest L. Frye (d February 5, 1956, buried Adrian, Lenawee County, Michigan.

Mrs. Ruth Calista (Willett) Frye died on April 26, 1954, Adrian, Lenawee County, Michigan.

1. **Dorothy Marie FRYE**: b February 27, 1907; d 1923, Adrian, Lenawee County, Michigan.

2. **Kenneth Willett FRYE**: b February 25, 1908; resided (1954) Los Angeles, California.

3. **Richard Douglas FRYE**: b July 10, 1910, Adrian, Lenawee County, Michigan; resided (1954) Erie, Michigan.

4. **Ernest Homer FRYE**:: b May 28, 1913; d December 7, 1942,

5. **Elwood FRYE:**

6. **Robert Wayne FRYE**: b March 18, 1915; resided (1954) Toledo, Ohio.

PA.2.2.5.6
PETER WILLETT and **MARIA AUGENSTEIN**
of Ottawa County, Ohio

Peter Willett was born on October 8, 1833, in Columbia County, Pennsylvania.

He began his work as a teacher in Milan, Erie County, Ohio.

Peter Willett married in Bucyrus, Crawford County, Ohio, on July 22, 1858, Maria Augenstein (Augustine) (b March, 1835, Pennsylvania; d May, 1915, Elmore, Ottawa County, Ohio, buried Union Cemetery, Ottawa County, Ohio).

In 1859, and 1860, he attended the University of Michigan studying anatomy and medicine. He attended the Cleveland Medical College (matriculation ticket session) in 1863 and 1864, and became a doctor.

PETER WILLETT
(Photograph courtesy of Douglas Willett)

Peter Willett served in the 182th Ohio Infantry were he was assistant surgeon, serving from December, 1864, until March, 1865.

He first began civilian practice in Genoa, Ottawa County, Ohio, then in 1865, he removed to Fremont, Sandusky County, Ohio.

In 1867, they removed to Elmore, Ottawa County, Ohio.

He was also a Methodist traveling preacher who resided in Elmore, Ottawa County, Ohio, but traveled by horse into Michigan.

In 1900, Peter Willett, Maria, Roland, and servant Tracy Jake were living on E. Clinton Street, Elmore, Harris Township, Ottawa County, Ohio.

In 1910, Peter Willett, Maria, Roland, and servant Jennie Witty were living on E. Clinton Street, Elmore, Harris Township, Ottawa County, Ohio.

Peter Willett died January 2, 1913, age 79, at Elmore, Ottawa County, Ohio, and is buried in the Elmore Union Cemetery.

1. **Roland A. WILLETT**: b April 14, 1866, Fremont, Sandusky County, Ohio; m 1st in Elmore, Ottawa County, Ohio, October 22, 1890, Miss Mamie Guinke (d September 20, 1899, Toledo, Ohio, buried Elmore Union Cemetery, Ottawa County, Ohio); m 2d after 1907 Emily V. Bullimer; d February 26, 1942, age 75 years, 10 months, 12 days. See next PA.2.2.5.6.1.

PA.2.2.5.6.1
ROLAND A. WILLETT
of Ottawa County, Ohio

Roland A. Willett was born on April 14, 1866, Fremont, Sandusky County, Ohio. He went to public school in Elmore, Ottawa County, Ohio.

He was a graduate of Oberlin College and University of Michigan, Medicine, and in 1888, of Bellevue Hospital Medical College, New York City, where he took his degree and became a doctor.

MAMIE GUINKE
(Photograph courtesy of Douglas Willett)

Roland Willett married 1st in Elmore, Ottawa County, Ohio, October 22, 1890, Miss Mamie Guinke (Quincke) (d September 20, 1899, Toledo, Ohio, buried Elmore Union Cemetery, Ottawa County, Ohio).   Among the wedding gifts that they received was a set of solid silver spoons that were more than 200 years old.   This was a gift from Marie's father and mother.   The Willett's went "out west" for their honeymoon.

In August, 1898, Roland Willett was at a display of fireworks after a Saturday evening peace jubilee meeting, when he met with an accident.   He was engaged in exploding a large dynamite firecracker, when one exploded in the air immediately after leaving his hand.   The third finger on his left hand was torn off at the first joint, and his thumb was nearly torn out of the socket.   His father, Peter Willett, and L. J. Gahn succeeded in dressing the wound so there would be no further damage.

RUDOLF WILLETT AND GAILLARD WILLETT
(Photograph courtesy of Douglas Willett)

Roland Willett married after 1907 2d Emily V. Bullimer (b 1874; d 1947, buried Elmore Union Cemetery, Ottawa County, Ohio).

At the time of his death, he was the head of the Ottawa County Medical Society and president of the Ottawa County Board of Health.

Roland Willett died on February 26, 1942, age 75 years, 10 months, 12 days, after suffering from an illness for three years, and being confined to his home for the previous three months.

ROLAND A. WILLETT WITH
HIS GRANDSON, GAILLARD PETER WILLETT, JR.
(Photograph courtesy of Douglas Willett)

Children of Roland A. Willett and his 1st wife, Marie Guinke:

1. **Marie WILLETT**: b July 2, 1891, Elmore, Ottawa County, Ohio; d July 20, 1891, age 18 days, buried Elmore Union Cemetery, Ottawa County, Ohio.
2. **Gaillard Peter WILLETT**: b July 25, 1892, Ohio; m 1924 Margaret (d 1990, Elmore, Ottawa County, Ohio, buried Elmore Union Cemetery, Ottawa County, Ohio); graduate of University of Michigan; interned at Toledo Hospital, Toledo, Ohio; a doctor of Elmore, Ohio; d October 11, 1957, buried Elmore Union Cemetery, Ottawa County, Ohio. See next PA.2.2.5.6.1.2.
3. **Rudolf Edward WILLETT**: b February 19, 1897, Elmore, Ottawa County, Ohio; m Edith A. Fleckner (b 1899; d 1973, Elmore, Ottawa County, Ohio, buried Elmore Union Cemetery); d July 13, 1978, buried Elmore, Ottawa County, Ohio. See next PA.2.2.5.6.1.3.
4. **Florence Hathaway VOLGEMAN** (foster daughter): of Shaker Heights near Cleveland, Cuyahoga County, Ohio.

PA.2.2.5.6.1.2
GAILLARD PETER WILLETT and **MARGARET**
of Toledo, Ohio

Gaillard Peter Willett was born July 25, 1892, Ohio. After his mother's death in 1899, Gaillard and his brother Rudolf lived with their Quincke grandparents for a short while. Gaillard Willett interned at St. Vincent's hospital, in Toledo, Ohio, and then served as house surgeon at the Toledo Hospital for one year where he met Margaret. She was a nurse at Toledo Hospital when she married. Margaret was very much involved with the Girl Scouts and was a Brownie leader for several years.

Gaillard Peter Willett married 1924 Margaret (d 1990, Elmore, Ottawa County, Ohio). He was a graduate of University of Michigan; and interned at Toledo Hospital, Toledo, Ohio.

He became a doctor and had a general practice at Elmore, Ohio.

Gaillard Peter Willett died on October 11, 1957, and is buried in the Elmore Union Cemetery, Ottawa County, Ohio.

1. **Gaillard Peter WILLETT**, Jr: b January 31, 1932, Elmore, Ottawa County, Ohio; m on December 31, 1958, Sharon Ann Sitcler (b June 23, 1936, Fort Wayne, Indiana). See next PA.2.2.5.6.1.2.1.

2. **Jeannene WILLETT**: m Shemeth.

1932
MARGARET WILLETT - GAILLARD PETER WILLETT, SR.
GAILLARD PETER WILLETT. JR.
(Photograph courtesy of Douglas Willett)

GAILLARD PETER WILLETT

PA.2.2.5.6.1.2.1
GAILLARD PETER WILLETT and SHARON ANN SITCLER

Gaillard Peter Willett, Jr., was born on January 31, 1932, Elmore, Ottawa County, Ohio.

Gaillard Peter Willett, Jr: married on December 31, 1958, Sharon Ann Sitcler (b June 23, 1936, Fort Wayne, Indiana).

1. **Laurie WILLETT**: January 26, 1962, Lucas County, Oregon.
2. **Nina WILLETT**: July 17, 1963, Lucas County, Oregon.

GAILLARD PETER WILLETT,. JR.
(Photograph courtesy of Douglas Willett)

SECOND FROM LEFT: MRS. MARGARET WILLETT
FAR RIGHT: GAILLARD PETER WILLETT, JR. AND HIS WIFE
(Photograph courtesy of Douglas Willett)

PA.2.2.5.6.1.3
RUDOLF EDWARD WILLETT and **EDITH A. FLECKNER**
of Ottawa County, Ohio

Rudolf Edward Willett was born February 19, 1897, Elmore, Ottawa County, Ohio.

Rudolf Edward Willett married Edith A. Fleckner (b 1899; d 1973, Elmore, Ottawa County, Ohio, buried Elmore Union Cemetery).

Rudolf Edward Willett died July 13, 1978, and is buried in the Elmore, Union Cemetery, Ottawa County, Ohio.

1.   **Carolyn WILLETT**: m Thober.
2.   **Annette WILLETT**: m Troutman.

PA.2.2.5.7
JOHN WILLETT
of Blissfield, Lenawee County, Michigan

John Willett was born on June 1, 1836, in Pennsylvania (also listed as born Ohio).

In the 1880 census, John Willett is listed in his brother's William Willett's household as a laborer, age 35 (sic). This age does not agree with his tombstone which reads, "1835-1916."

In 1890, John Willett was living in Deerfield, Lenawee County, Michigan.

On March 4, 1890, John Willett and his brother Benjamin issued a quitclaim to Benjamin's wife, Rachel, for the remainder of their land located in Blissfield, Lenawee County, Michigan.

John Willett died on June 19, 1916, age 81 years 14 days, of old age and gangrene. He is buried in the Pleasant View Cemetery, Blissfield, Lenawee County, Michigan.

John Willett's will was executed on June 7, 1917; he left an estate of 54 acres of land.

PA.2.2.7
ABRAHAM WILLETT
of Columbia County, Pennsylvania,
and Richland County, Ohio

Abraham (Abram) Willett was born on March 1, 1801, in Northumberland (now Columbia) County, Pennsylvania.

In 1820, Abraham Willett, age 19, was living at home with his parents (Columbia County, Pennsylvania, census, male 16-26).

Abraham Willett married 1st in Pennsylvania about 1821 Esther Aikman (b 1802; d September 30, 1826, age 24 years, 22 days, buried Plymouth Greenlawn Cemetery) of Columbia County, Pennsylvania, the daughter of Levi Aikman, Sr. (b 1776) and Margaret Hutchinson of Columbia County (*Twelve Families, An American Experience*, William F. O'dell, page 428). He was a tanner and farmer.

Abraham Willett rented a farm in Columbia County, Pennsylvania for one year, and then after the death of his wife, went back to his mother's farm, remaining there for three years.

Abraham Willett married 2d in Pennsylvania about 1828 Catherine Hazlett (b May 7, 1802; d May 27, 1842, age 40 years, 3 months, and 20 days, buried Plymouth Green Lawn Cemetery, Richland County, Ohio) of Columbia County, Pennsylvania.

The 1830 Fishing Creek, Columbia County, Pennsylvania, census, list Abraham Willet (sic) and family as follows:

1 male	20-30	1800-1810	*Abraham*	*age 29 b 1801*
1 female	20-30	1800-1810	*Catherine*	*age 28 b 1802*
1 male	10-15	1815-1820	*(unknown)*	
1 male	0-5	1825-1830	*(infant who died young)?*	

Abraham Willett rented a farm in Columbia County, Pennsylvania, for one year, then removed to Bloomsburg, Pennsylvania, for three years.

"Hearing favorable reports of the then new country of Ohio, and wishing to obtain for himself a farm and to gain a competence for his declining years, he sold his farming implements, and bidding adieu to friends and neighbors of his native county, he started with his family in a two horse wagon, coming via Pittsburgh, settling in Richland County, Ohio; he brought an improvement right of a 50 acre tract in Plymouth, now Cass; he paid all the money he had except $28.00; the improvements were of the kind usually in a new country, consisting of a log house and stable; he went to

*work with characteristic energy of the most class of pio-
neers, to carve for himself a home and competence"*
(Graham A. A., *History of Richland County, Ohio, from 1808
to 1908*, 1908, page 783).

In 1835, Abram Willet came to Richland County, Ohio. He
was a tanner and farmer who had been born in Columbia
County, Pennsylvania. He purchased Section 16, Cass
Township, Richland County, Ohio.

The 1840 Plymouth Township, Richland County, Ohio,
census, list Abraham Willet (sic) and family as follows:

1 male	30-40	1800-1810	*Abraham*	*age 39*	*b 1801*
1 female	20-30	1800-1810	*Catherine*	*age 38? b 1802?*	
1 male	10-15	1825-1830	*William*	*age 9?*	*b 1831?*
1 female	5-10	1830-1835	*Mary E*	*age 7*	*b 1833*
1 male	5-10	1830-1835	*John*	*age 5*	*b 1835*
1 female	0-5	1835-1840			

Abraham Willett married 3d in Richland County, Ohio, on
June 17, 1843, Miss Leah Bevier (b 1820, New York) of
Richland County, Ohio. He was 42 years old; she was 23.

He worked on a railroad (1850), and was a farmer (1860).

In 1850, Abram Willet and family were listed in the Cass
Township, Richland County, Ohio, census, page 207, No. 192,
as follows:

Willet	Abram	45	m	OH (sic)	farmer
	Leah	40	f	NY	
	William	20	m	PA	
	Mary	17	f	PA	
	John	15	m	OH	
	Sarah	11	f	OH	
Bevier	Jacob	84	m	NY	

In 1860, Abraham Willett and family were listed in the
Cass Township, Richland County, Ohio, census, No. ---, as
follows:

Willett	Abraham	59	m	PA
	Leah	59	f	
	Wm	29	m	PA
	John	24?	m	OH
	Sarah	21	f	OH
	Ransom	9	m	OH

In 1870, Abram Willett and family were listed in the Cass

Township, Richland County, Ohio, census, No. 175, as follows:

Willett	Abram	69	m	PA
	Leah	61	f	NY
	Sarah	31	f	OH
	Ransom	19	m	OH
Bevier	Catherine	76	f	NY

Abraham Willett died on December 14, 1887, age 86 years, 9 months, and 14 days, near Plymouth, Richland County, Ohio, and is buried in the Greenlawn Cemetery, Richland County, Ohio, along with all three of his wives. There are two other tombstones in the Willett family plot. They are simply marked "L. B." and "A. W." and are possibly simply foot-stones, instead of tombstone markers.

(Purcell, page 155; *The Willett Families*, page 207).

Children of Abraham Willett and his 1st wife, Esther Aikman:

1. **Margaret WILLETT**: b abt 1823.

Children of Abraham Willett and his 2d wife, Catherine Hazlett:

2. (infant) **WILLETT**: b abt 1829; died young.
3. **William WILLETT**: b July 10, 1830, Columbia County, Pennsylvania; m in Cass Township, Richland County, Ohio, on February 4, 1862, Christina Sheckler (b December 30, 1830, Auburn Township, Crawford County, Ohio; d November 26, 1912, age 81 years, 1 months, 5 days); d November 19, 1907, buried Plymouth Greenlawn Cemetery, Plymouth, Ohio. See next PA.2.2.7.3.
4. **Mary E. WILLETT**: b 1833, Pennsylvania; m in Richland County, Ohio, on February 20, 1855, Zachus J. Clark. See next PA.2.2.7.4.
5. **John H. WILLETT**: b 1835, Ohio; m in Richland County, Ohio, on February 12, 1862 Alice F. Marsh (b October 27, 1845, Ohio; d January 31, 1915); resident of Cass Township, Richland County, Ohio; d June 30, 1913, buried Plymouth Green Lawn Cemetery, Richland County, Ohio. See next PA.2.2.7.5.

Children of Abraham Willett and his 3d wife, Leah Bevier:

6. **Sarah WILLETT**: b 1849, Ohio; unmarried 1870.
7. **Ransom WILLETT**: b 1851, Ohio; d January 22, 1877, age 26 years, 4 months, 13 days, buried Plymouth Greenlawn Cemetery, Richland County, Ohio.

PA.2.2.7.3
WILLIAM WILLET and CHRISTINA SHECKLER
of Richland County, Ohio

William Willet was born on July 10, 1830, (most likely in Columbia County), in Pennsylvania.

NOTE: At some point this branch of the Willett family began to consistently use Willet as their surname.

John D. Bevier of Cass Township, Richland County, Ohio, wrote his will on October 19, 1861 (probate December 29, 1871), and mentioned that "Friends James Jones and William Willet to superintend the farming after the decease of the testator and until the sale of the farm" (*Abstracts of Wills, Richland County, Ohio*, page 200).

William Willet married in Richland County, Ohio, on February 4, 1862, Christina Sheckler (b December 30, 1830, Auburn Township, Crawford County, Ohio; d November 26, 1912, age 81 years, 11 months, 5 days) (Bible Record).

Peter Broch of Cass Township, Richland County, Ohio, wrote his will on May 28, 1870 (probate March 13, 1872), and mentioned that Christeen, wife of William Willet, was to receive $1,000 paid by Meriott Pettet, and that the executor of his will was to be William Willett (*Abstracts of Wills, Richland County, Ohio*, page 202).

In 1870, Wm. Willett, and family were listed in the Cass Township, Richland County, Ohio, census, No. 180, as follows:

Willett	Wm	40	PA
	Christina	39	OH
	Geo. O.	7	OH
	Peter	4	OH
	Abraham J.	2	OH
Perkins	Cora A.	14	OH

In 1880, W. Willet, and family were listed in the Cass Township, Richland County, Ohio, census, as follows:

Willet	W.		49	PA
	C.	wife	49	OH
	G. O.	son	17	OH
	P. L. N.	son	14	OH
	A. J.	son	12	OH
	S. C.	daughter	11	OH
	J. R.	son	5	OH

In 1900, William Willet was the head of a household   in Cass Township, Richland County, Ohio, Sheet 13, dwelling 322-322, as follows:

Willet	William	head	Jul 1830	69 m 39
	Christina	wife	Dec 1830	60 m 39 5-5
	Abraham	son	Apr 1868	32 s

William Willet died on November 19, 1907, age 77 years, 4 months, 10 days, buried Mount Hope Cemetery, Cass Township, Richland County, Ohio (Bible Record).
(Bible Record, William Willett 1830-1907).

1. **George Ornan WILLET**: b (Monday) April 6, 1863, Cass Township, Richland County, Ohio (Bible Record); m September 14, 1899, Bertha B. Hunter (Bible Record); d November 18, 1925, age 62 years, 7 months, 12 days, North Olmstead, Ohio (Bible Record). No issue.

2. **Peter La Norman WILLET**: b (Friday) December 8, 1865, Cass Township, Richland County, Ohio (Bible Record); m March 12, 1890, Harriet ("Hattie") E. Gedney (b October 21, 1870; d December, 1957) (Bible Record); d August 22, 1938, age 72 years, 8 months, 14 days, Shiloh, Richland County, Ohio (Bible Record), buried Mount Hope Cemetery, Cass Township, Richland County, Ohio. See next PA.2.2.7.3.2.

3. **Abraham John WILLET**: b (Tuesday) April 14, 1868, Cass Township, Richland County, Ohio (Bible Record); d July 17, 1945, age 77 years, 3 months, 3 days, Shiloh, Richland County, Ohio (Bible Record), buried Plymouth Greenlawn Cemetery, Richland County, Ohio. Never married.

4. **Sarah Catherine WILLET**: b (Monday) March 27, 1870, Ohio (Bible Record); m November 29, 1899, Tully A. Barnes (d 1945) (Bible Record); resided Shiloh, Ohio; d July 8, 1967, age 96 years, 2 months, 11 days (Bible Record). See next PA.2.2.7.3.4.

5. **James Ransom WILLET**: b (Thursday) July 30, 1874, Ohio (Bible Record); m January 17, 1899, Dessie F. May (b June 5, 1874 (Bible Record); d December 29, 1951, buried Plymouth Greenlawn Cemetery, Plymouth, Ohio); d January 4,

1920, age 45 years, 5 months, 5 days, buried Plymouth Greenlawn Cemetery, Plymouth, Ohio (Bible Record). See next PA.2.2.7.3.5.

PA.2.2.7.3.2
PETER LA NORMAN WILLET and **HARRIET E. GEDNEY**
of Plymouth, Richland County, Ohio

Peter La Norman Willet was born on Friday, December 8, 1865, Cass Township, Richland County, Ohio, on his father's farm which was two miles southwest of Shiloh, Richland County, Ohio (Bible Record).

Peter Willet married on March 12, 1890, Harriet ("Hattie") E. Gadney (b October 21, 1870; d December, 1957) (Bible Record). He spent 24 years teaching in Richland County and retired at the age of 66.

In 1900, Peter Willett and family are listed in the Cass Township, Richland County, Ohio, census, Sheet 11, dwelling 281-281, as follows:

Willett	Peter	head	Dec 1865	34	m	10	
	Hattie	wife	Oct 1870	29	m	10	3-2
	Beatrice	daughter	Apr 1893	7			
	William R	son	May 1896	4			
Gedney,	Alice L.	m-i-l	Oct 1843	56	wd		
	Ray	b-i-l	Jun 1881	18			

Peter <u>Willet</u> died on August 22, 1938, at the age of 72 years, 8 months, 14 days, buried Mount Hope Cemetery, Cass Township, Richland County, Ohio.

(Bible Record, William Willett 1830-1907).

1. **Ada Marie WILLET**: b August 20, 1891 (Bible Record); Ada Marie <u>Willet</u> died on June, 1892 (Bible Record), buried Mount Hope Cemetery, Cass Township, Richland County, Ohio.

2. **Beatrice WILLET**: b April 19, 1893 (Bible Record); m Roy Black (b December 7, 1887); d August 12, 1981.

3. **William Roscoe WILLET**: b May 28, 1896 (Bible Record); m Esther Richards; resided (1938) Olmstead Falls, Cuyahoga County, Ohio; d 1938. See next PA.2.2.7.3.2.3.

4. **Gladys Lucille WILLET**: b August 30, 1902 (Bible Record); m November 29, 1929, Lloyd Joseph Bouffard (b June 23, 1904); resided (1938) Pittsburgh; d February 28, 1977.

5. **Arlo Gedney WILLET**: b July 31, 1905 (Bible Record);

m July 14, 1928, Dorcas Haun (b November 15, 1907); resided (1938) Shiloh Township, Ohio, and Shelbyville, Ohio; d July 24, 1970, age 64, buried Mount Hope Cemetery, Cass Township, Richland County, Ohio. See next <u>PA.2.2.7.3.2.5</u>.

PA.2.2.7.3.2.3
WILLIAM ROSCOE WILLET and ESTHER RICHARDS

William Roscoe Willet was born on May 28, 1896 (Bible Record).

William Roscoe Willet married Esther Richards. They resided (1938) Olmstead Falls, Cuyahoga County, Ohio.

William Roscoe Willet died in 1938.

1. **Richard WILLET**:
2. **Bernadine WILLET**:

PA.2.2.7.3.2.5
ARLO GEDNEY WILLET and DORCAS HAUN

Arlo Gedney Willet was born on July 31, 1905 (Bible Record).

Arlo Gedney Willet married on July 14, 1928, Dorcas Haun (b November 15, 1907). They resided (1938) Shiloh Township, Ohio, and resided Shelbyville, Ohio.

Arlo Gedney Willet died on July 24, 1970, age 64, and is buried in the Mount Hope Cemetery, Cass Township, Richland County, Ohio.

1. **Shirley Ann WILLET**: b May 31, 1930; m Donald Heller (b January 17, 1931); d October 17, 1989.

2. **Mary Lou WILLET**: b July 31, 1936; m Thomas Olsen (b June 10, 1931).

PA.2.2.7.3.4
SARAH CATHERINE WILLET and TULLY A. BARNES
Richland County, Ohio

Sarah Catherine Willet was born on (Monday) March 27, 1870, Ohio (Bible Record).

Miss Sarah Catherine Willet married on November 29, 1899, Tully A. Barnes (d 1945) (Bible Record). They resided at Shiloh, Richland County, Ohio.

Mrs. Sarah (Willet) Barnes died on July 8, 1967, age 96 years, 2 months, 11 days (Bible Record).

1. **Christine BARNES**: m Howard Long.
2. **Ralph BARNES**: m Alice Anderson.

PA.2.2.7.3.5
JAMES RANSOM WILLET and DESSIE F. MAY

James Ransom Willet was born on Thursday, July 30, 1874, Ohio (Bible Record).

James Ransom Willet married January 17, 1899, Dessie F. May (b June 5, 1874; d December 29, 1951, buried Plymouth Greenlawn Cemetery, Plymouth, Ohio) (Bible Record).

In 1900, James Willett and family are listed in the Cass Township, Richland County, Ohio, census, Sheet 11, dwelling 277-277, as follows:

```
Willett  James      head      Jul 1874   25  m1
         Dessie F   wife      Jun 1874   25  m1
```

James Ransom Willet died January 4, 1920, age 45 years, 5 months, 5 days, buried Plymouth Greenlawn Cemetery, Plymouth, Ohio (Bible Record).

(Bible Record, William Willett 1830-1907).

1. **Aiden Ralph WILLET**: b January 21, 1902 (Bible Record); m December 2, 1923, Esther Esbenshade (b 1899; d 1957); d 1983. See next PA.2.2.7.3.5.1.

2. **Thelma C. WILLET**: b January 26, 1903 (Bible Record).

3. **Donald J. WILLET**: b July 3, 1905.

4. **William Elden WILLET**: b October 21, 1911 (Bible Record); m March 21, 1936, Ellen McConneghy; d March 21, 1936, buried Plymouth Greenlawn Cemetery, Richland County, Ohio. See next PA.2.2.7.3.5.4.

5. **Ethel Eva WILLET**: b February 20, 1913; m April 24, 1943, George Morgan Ireland (b October 19, 1913). See next PA.2.2.7.3.5.5.

PA.2.2.7.3.5.1
AIDEN RALPH WILLET and ESTHER ESBENSHADE

Aiden Ralph Willet was born January 21, 1902 (Bible Record).

Aiden Ralph Willet married December 2, 1923, Esther Esbenshade (b 1899; d 1957). He was a farmer.

Aiden Ralph Willet died in 1983.

1. **Ralph WILLET**: b November 16, 1924; m Maxine Dininger. See next PA.2.2.7.3.5.1.1.
2. **Jessie Raymond WILLET**: b September 26, 1926; m Agnes Roberts. See next PA.2.2.7.3.5.1.21.
3. **Ethel Ruth WILLET**: b January 20, 1928; m William Wright.
4. **Alice Joanne WILLET**: b April 8, 1933.
5. **Phyllis Arlene WILLET**: b April 15, 1935; m John Kleman.

PA.2.2.7.3.5.1.1
RALPH WILLET and MAXINE DINIGER

Ralph Willet was born on November 16, 1924.
Ralph Willet married Maxine Dininger. He was a farmer.

1. **Judy WILLET**: m Long.
2. **Diana WILLET**:
3. **Grace WILLET**:

PA.2.2.7.3.5.1.2
JESSIE RAYMOND WILLET and AGNES ROBERTS

Jessie Raymond Willet was born on September 26, 1926.
Jessie Raymond Willet married Agnes Roberts. He was a truck driver.

1. **Gerald Ray WILLET**: b August 3, 1948.
2. **Cathy Irene WILLET**: b November 4, 1949.
3. **Timothy Allen WILLET**: b September 10, 1951.

PA.2.2.7.3.5.4
WILLIAM ELDEN WILLET and ELLEN MCCONNEGHY
of Richland County, Ohio

William Elden Willet was born on October 21, 1911.

William Elden Willet married on March 21, 1936, Ellen McConneghy.

William E. Willet died on March 21, 1936, and is buried in the Plymouth Greenlawn Cemetery, Richland County, Ohio.

1. **William WILLET**: b January 19, 1936 (Bible Record); d January 31, 1936, infant.

2. **Mary Ellen WILLET**: b November 27, 1938 (Bible Record); m John Nolder.

3. **Kay Ann WILLET**: b July 29, 1941 (Bible Record); m Jack Hemperley.

4. **James A. WILLET**: b April 3, 1943 (Bible Record).

5. **Linda Sue WILLET**: b February 20, 1945 (Bible Record); m Gary Spigar.

    1. **Geoffrey SPIGAR**:

PA.2.2.7.3.5.5
ETHEL EVA WILLET and GEORGE MORGAN IRELAND

Ethel Eva Willet was born on February 20, 1913.

Miss Ethel Eva Willet married on April 24, 1943, George Ireland (b October 19, 1913).

1. **Anita Lynne IRELAND**: b November, 1944 (Bible Record).

2. **David IRELAND**: b July 10, 1948 (Bible Record).

PA.2.2.7.4
MARY E. WILLETT and ZACHUS J. CLARK

Mary E. Willett was born in 1833, Pennsylvania.

Miss Mary E. Willett married in Richland County, Ohio, on February 20, 1855, Zachus J. Clark.

1. **Ellie CLARK**:
2. **Lucy CLARK**: b February 3, 1856; d July 27, 1922.

PA.2.2.7.5
JOHN H. WILLETT and ALICE F. MARSH
of Richland County, Ohio

John H. Willett was born in 1836, in Ohio.

John H. Willett married in Richland County, Ohio, on February 12, 1862 Alice F. Marsh (b October 27, 1845, Ohio; d January 31, 1915, buried Plymouth Greenlawn Cemetery, Richland County, Ohio).

They were residents of Cass Township, Richland County, Ohio (1870).

In 1870, John Willett, and family were listed in the Cass Township, Richland County, Ohio, census, No. 176, as follows:

Willett	John	34	OH
	Allice	24	OH
	Sarepta	8	OH
	Wm	4	OH
	Samuel	4/12	OH
Marsh	Oliver	71	VT

In 1880, John Willet, and family were listed in the Cass Township, Richland County, Ohio, census, as follows:

Willet	John	44	OH	
	A. (sic)	34	OH	wife
	S. J.	17	OH	daughter
	W. J.	13	OH	son
	S.	10	OH	son
	S. L.	5	OH	daughter

In 1900, John Willett and family are listed in the Cass Township, Richland County, Ohio, census, Sheet 11, dwelling 280-280, as follows:

Willett	John	head	Oct 1835	64	m37

Alice F.	wife	Oct 1845	54	m	37	4-3
Samuel M	son	Jan 1870	29	m	6	
Gertrude	d-i-l	Jun 1874	25	m	6	0-0

John Willett died June 30, 1913, and is buried in the Plymouth Greenlawn Cemetery, Richland County, Ohio.

   1. **Sarepta June WILLETT**: b June 23, 1862, Ohio; m in Richland County, Ohio, on November 26, 1884, Philip Burnett; d September 4, 1897. See next PA.2.2.7.5.1.
   2. **William John WILLETT**: b June 25, 1868, Ohio; m in 1894 Mary ("Mamie E.") Ellen (b December, 1870, Ohio; d 1936, buried Plymouth Green Lawn Cemetery); d 1944, buried Plymouth Greenlawn Cemetery, Richland County, Ohio. As of the 1900 Richland County, Ohio census, they had had one child who died as an infant before 1900.
   3. **Samuel Martin WILLETT**: b January 24, 1870, Ohio; m in 1896, Gertrude Taylor (b June 6, 1873, Ohio; d July 10, 1956, buried Plymouth Green Lawn Cemetery, Richland County, Ohio); d October 6, 1946, buried Plymouth Green Lawn Cemetery, Richland County, Ohio. See next PA.2.2.7.5.3.
   4. **Sarah Lucy WILLETT**: b September 2, 1874, Ohio; m Myron Gilger. See next PA.2.2.7.5.4.

PA.2.2.7.5.1
SAREPTA JUNE WILLETT and PHILIP BURNETT

Sarepta June Willett was born on June 23, 1862, Ohio.
Miss Sarepta June Willett married in Richland County, Ohio, on November 26, 1884, Philip Burnett.
Mrs. Sarepta June (Willett) Burnett died on September 4, 1897.

   1. **Hazel BURNETT**: m Clarence Fair.
   2. **Aiden BURNETT**:

PA.2.2.7.5.3
SAMUEL MARTIN WILLETT and GERTRUDE TAYLOR
of Richland County, Ohio

Samuel Martin Willett was born on January 24, 1870, Ohio.

Samuel Martin Willett married in 1896, Gertrude Taylor (b June 6, 1873, Ohio; d July 10, 1956, buried Plymouth Green Lawn Cemetery, Richland County, Ohio).

Samuel Martin Willett died on October 6, 1946, and is buried in the Plymouth Green Lawn Cemetery, Richland County, Ohio.

1. **Lois A. WILLETT**: b March 25, 1906; buried Plymouth Green Lawn Cemetery, Richland County, Ohio.

PA.2.2.7.5.4
SARAH LUCY WILLETT and MYRON GILGER

Sarah Lucy Willett was born on September 2, 1874, Ohio. Miss Sarah Lucy Willett married Myron Gilger.

1. **Grace GILGER**: m Percy Dininger.
2. **John Earl GILGER**:

PA.2.2.8
SARAH WILLETT and ALEXANDER HUGHES
of Bloom Township, Columbia County, Pennsylvania

Sarah Willett was born on November 16, 1803, in Pennsylvania (born in Pennsylvania according to the 1850 Columbia County, Pennsylvania, census).

Miss Sarah Willett married about 1825 Alexander Hughes (b 1800, Pennsylvania; a Friend) of Catawissa Township, Columbia County, Pennsylvania.

Mrs. Sarah (Willett) Hughes died on December 16, 1891, at Shickshinny, Luzerne County, Pennsylvania.

(1850 Bloom Township, Columbia County, Pennsylvania, dwelling 327-339; Purcell, page 155).

1. **Joseph C. HUGHES**: b 1829, Pennsylvania; m Florence. (1850 Columbia County census).

2. **Alex Willett HUGHES**: b 1836, Pennsylvania; possibly died young. (1850 Columbia County census).

3. **Hannah Lavina HUGHES**: b 1838, Pennsylvania; m Low. (1850 Columbia County census).

4. **Mason Beach HUGHES**: b 1842, Pennsylvania; m Katherine Patterson. (1850 Columbia County census).

5. **Alex HUGHES** (sic): b 1846, Pennsylvania. (1850 Columbia County census).

6. **Mary HUGHES**:

7. **Elizabeth HUGHES**: died young.

8. **William HUGHES**: m Eugene.

PA.2.2.9
ELIZABETH WILLETT and JACOB MELICK
of Columbia County, Pennsylvania

Elizabeth Willett was born on August 27, 1807 (family tradition has birth occurring in New Jersey).

Miss Elizabeth Willett married about 1830 Jacob Melick of Monmouth County, New Jersey.

Mrs. Elizabeth (Willett) Melick died on March 1, 1889, at Light Street, Columbia County, Pennsylvania.

1. **Annetta MELICK**: m William Boyd.
2. **Pasey MELICK**:
3. **Sadie MELICK**: m Smucker.
4. **Samantha MELICK**: m Brown.
5. **Pulaski MELICK**:
6. **Oran MELICK**:
7. **Leone MELICK**:

CHAPTER THREE
SAMUEL WILLETT (1768-1822)
OF FULTON COUNTY, PENNSYLVANIA

PA.3
WILLETT
family of Bedford County, Pennsylvania

About the summer of 1789, this Willett family reputedly removed from Anne Arundel County, Maryland, to Bedford County, Pennsylvania. They came about the same time as the Andersons, both families being associated with a group of settlers called the Duvall Colonists, followers of Dr. and Methodist Minister, Jeremiah Duvall.

FOR THE RECORD: Ann ("Anna") Rigbie, born March 1, 1735 (St. Georges Parish, Hartford County, Register and Vestry Proceedings), was admitted a member of the Deer Creek Friends Meeting on November 2, 1762. Miss Ann Rigbie married in 1768, Samuel Willits (sic) (Deer Creek Records).

There are no Willett families living in Anne Arundel County, Maryland, listed in the 1790 Maryland census. However, Edward, Ninian, and William Willet are heads of households in adjacent Prince George County, Maryland.

Who was this William Willett? Could be an ancestor or near relation to Samuel? In looking for the Samuel Willett family, the following records need to be kept in mind:

During the War of 1812, a Samuel Willet and a William Willet were Privates in Captain Jacob Hammel's Company, Lieutenant Colonel George Weirick, Regiment (payroll records of 11/10/1814) (*History of Susquehanna and Juniata Valley, Pennsylvania*, Union, Snyder, Mifflin, and Juniata Counties).

January 6, 1824. Mullen Sheriff to Thomas Allender, 75 acres in Hopewell Township, adjoining William Willett.

There was a Willett family living in Pennsylvania in the early 1800s. The following two children, Elizabeth and

Samuel, are from the same family.

(*True Stories of Broad Top Mountain and the Surrounding Valleys*, David Foster Horton).

1. **Elizabeth WILLETT:** b abt 1765; m in Anne Arundel County, Maryland, by license on January 11, 1785, William Anderson (b 1765, Prince Georges County, Maryland; d 1842, Pennsylvania); resided in Wells Valley, Fulton County, Pennsylvania. See next PA.3.1.

2. **Samuel WILLETT:** b August 15, 1768, Maryland (or in one record Massachusetts); m 1st abt 1788 (wife's name unknown); m 2d abt 1799, Rachel Edwards (b April, 1778; d August 2, 1851); d May 1, 1857, Wells Township, Fulton County, Pennsylvania. See next PA.3.2.

PA.3.1
ELIZABETH WILLETT and WILLIAM ANDERSON

Elizabeth Willett was born about 1765?

Miss Elizabeth Willett married in Anne Arundel County, Maryland, by license on January 11, 1785, William Anderson (b 1765, Prince George County, Maryland; d 1842, Pennsylvania).

About 1789, they removed to Wells Valley, Fulton County, Pennsylvania.

1. **Samuel ANDERSON:** b October 6, 1785, Maryland.

2. **Thomas ANDERSON:** b June 13, 1787, Maryland.

3. **William ANDERSON** (twin): b June 2, 1790, Bedford County, Pennsylvania.

4. **Sarah ANDERSON** (twin): b June 2, 1790, Bedford County, Pennsylvania.

5. **Elizabeth ANDERSON:** b November 20, 1792, Bedford County, Pennsylvania.

6. **Mary ANDERSON:** b November 6, 1794, Bedford County, Pennsylvania.

7. **James ANDERSON:** b about 1795, Bedford County, Pennsylvania.

8. **Edward ANDERSON:** b October 6, 1798, Bedford County, Pennsylvania.

9. **Susanna ANDERSON:** b May 6, 1801, Bedford County, Pennsylvania.

10. **Jemima ANDERSON:** b May 20, 1803, Bedford County, Pennsylvania.

11. **Jonathan ANDERSON:** b March 6, 1805, Bedford County, Pennsylvania.

PA.3.2
SAMUEL WILLETT
of Wells Valley, Bedford County, Pennsylvania

Samuel Willett was born on August 15, 1768, in Maryland (or occasionally listed as Massachusetts; however, all his children always put on the Federal Census records that their father was born in Maryland).

On July 9, 1787, Samuel Willet applied for 50 acres in the forks of Six Mile Run in Hopewell Township, Bedford County, Pennsylvania. The price was 10 pounds per 100 acres with interest to commence from July 9, 1787. The warrant was granted on July 9, 1787 (*Early Land Applications, Warrant Book II, Bedford County*, Pennsylvania, page 338).

Samuel Willett reputedly married 1st about 1788, Mary Fenner. His 1st wife must have died young probably about 1795, possibly earlier. Mary is given as the Christian name by a Mrs. Annette Patterson (no substantiation). Fenner is assumed as the surname of Samuel Willett's first wife from the 1799 will of Stephen Fenner which mentions a grandson, Stephan Willot, but no surviving married daughter.

Samuel Willett, along with John Cheney, among others, were early settlers of Wells Valley Bedford (now Fulton) County, Pennsylvania. Fulton County was created from Bedford County sometime about 1840-1850.

In 1790, Samuel Willett and family were listed in the Bedford County, Pennsylvania, census, page 21, as follows:

1 male	16-up	*Samuel*	*age 22*	*b 1768*
1 female		*Mary*	*age 20?*	*b 1770?*

Samuel Willett married, most likely in Pennsylvania, his 2d wife about 1799, Rachel Edwards (b 1778 in Massachusetts; d August 2, 1851, aged 73 years, 5 months, and 2 days), the daughter of Robert Edwards (b 1745, England; d 1831, Pennsylvania).

Joseph Edwards, Samuel Willett, and Nathan Green, were among the earliest members of the Methodist Episcopal Church. Before 1790 and until about 1800, it is believed that they worshipped in private houses. A class was formed about 1800.

On December 1, 1799, the will of Stephen Fenner, late of Union Township, Bedford County, Pennsylvania, mentions grandson, Stephan Willot. No married (Fenner) Willett/Willot granddaughter is mentioned, and it is presumed that Stephan Willot's wife had predeceased her father. Stephen Fenner's will was probated January 8, 1800 (Huntington County,

Pennsylvania, Will Book 1, page 154).

In 1800, Samuel Willett and family were listed in the Hopewell Township, Wells Valley area of Bedford (now Fulton) County, Pennsylvania, census, page 438, as follows:

1 male	26-45	1755-1774	*Samuel*	*age 32 b 1768*
1 female	26-45	1755-1774	*Rachel*	*age 22* b 1778**
1 male	0-10	1790-1800	*Stephen*	*age 11* b 1789**

In 1808, Samuel Willet paid a tax of $1.60 to the Hopewell Township, Bedford County, Pennsylvania.

In 1810, Samuel Willet and family were residing in Hopewell Township, Bedford County, Pennsylvania, census, page 48, as follows:

1 male	26-45	1755-1774	*Samuel*	*age 42 b 1768*
1 female	45-up	bef.-1775	*Rachel*	*age 32* b 1778**
1 male	10-16	1794-1800	*Elisha*	*age 19* b 1791**
1 female	0-10	1800-1810	*Mary*	*age 9 b 1801*
1 male	0-10	1800-1810		
1 male	0-10	1800-1810		
1 male	0-10	1800-1810	*John*	*age 4 b 1804*
1 female	0-10	1800-1810	*Rachel*	*age 3? b 1807?*
1 male	0-10	1800-1810	*Thomas*	*age 0 b 1810*

On January 6, 1812, there is a deed between Samuel Willet and wife, Rachel, who sell 75 acres, 51 perches of land on Broad Top, Wells Valley, Hopewell Township, Bedford County, Pennsylvania, to William Anderson (presumed to be married to Samuel Willett's sister, Elizabeth). The description of the land does not state who conveyed the land to Samuel Willett (*Bedford County Deed Book I*, page 439). The deed was not recorded until October 10, 1814. The location is at Wells Tannery (village) located at the head of Wells Valley, Fulton County. The deed does not state where (or when) Samuel Willett obtained the land.

During the War of 1812, a Samuel Willet and a William Willet were Privates in Captain Jacob Hammel's Company, Lieutenant Colonel George Weirick, Regiment (payroll records of 11/10/1814) (*History of Susquehanna and Juniata Valley, Pennsylvania*, Union, Snyder, Mifflin, and Juniata Counties).

In 1817, Samuel Willet was listed as residing in Hopewell Township, Bedford County, Pennsylvania.

In 1820, Samuel Willot and family were listed as residing in Hopewell Township, Bedford County, Pennsylvania, census, page 49, as follows:

1 male	26-45	1755-1775	*Samuel*	*age 52* b 1768**
1 female	26-45	1755-1775	*Rachel*	*age 42 b 1778*
1 female	16-26	1794-1804	*Mary*	*age 19 b 1801*
1 male	16-18	1802-1804		
1 male	10-16	1804-1810	*John*	*age 14 b 1804*
1 female	10-16	1800-1810	*Rachel*	*age 13?b 1807?*
1 male	10-16	1804-1810	*Thomas*	*age 10 b 1810*
1 male	10-16	1804-1810	*Allen*	*age 10 b 1810*
1 male	0-10	1810-1820	*Samuel*	*age 0 b 1820*

On December 29, 1821, Samuel Willet, and wife Rachel, donated one half acre to help establish the Wells Valley Methodist Church, Hopewell Township. The deed description does not state how Samuel Willett acquired the land (*Bedford County Deed Book P*, page 564). A log church was constructed in that year. The description of the land does not state where (or when) Samuel Willett obtained the land.

In the September 13, 1825, will of John Edwards, there is a mention of his daughter Rachael Willit (Huntington County, Pennsylvania, Wills, page 356).

Samuel Willett, Sr., operated a mill and a farm, at (present day) Wells Tannery, Fulton County, at the head of the Wells Valley.

Samuel Willett was a member of the old Whig Party and Methodist Episcopalian.

In 1830, Samuel Willet and family were residing at Hopewell, Bedford County, Pennsylvania, census, page 79 (not copied).

1 male	50-60	1770-1780	*Samuel*	*age 62* b 1768**
1 female	50-60	1770-1780	*Rachel*	*age 52 b 1778*
1 male	20-30	1800-1810	*Allen*	*age 20 b 1810*
1 female	15-20	1810-1815	*Elizabeth*	*age 12?b 1818?*
1 male	5-10	1820-1825	*Samuel*	*age 10 b 1820*

In 1840, Samuel Willet and family were residing at Hopewell, Bedford County, Pennsylvania, census, page 296, as follows:

1 male	70-80	1760-1770	*Samuel*	*age 72 b 1768*
1 female	60-70	1770-1780	*Rachel*	*age 62 b 1778*
1 female	20-30	1810-1820	*Anne*	*age 19?b 1821?*

In 1850, Samuel Willet and family are listed in the 1850 Wells Township, Fulton County, Pennsylvania, census, dwelling 35, as follows:

Willet	Samuel	82	no occupation	b MD
	Rachel	73		b MD
Green	Sarah J	10		

NOTE: The 1850 census taker had a quirk of making a "curly Q" at the end of most names; most transcribers rendered this as an "S" to form "Willets." However, an examination of the original census shows clearly that the census taker meant to spell "Willet."

Samuel Willett's will is dated January 23, 1845; probated June 2, 1857, Fulton County, Pennsylvania: wife Rachel (probated in Fulton County, Pennsylvania, Volume 1, page 110).

> *To: Samuel, Jr., the farm;*
> *To: Allen, $1.00;*
> *To: Thomas, $1.00;*
> *To: John, $1.00;*
> *To: Stephen, $1.00;*
> *To: Elisha, $1.00;*
> *To: Mary Woodcock, and her husband Joseph, 7 or 8 acres which included the mill and saw mill;*
> *To: Rachel French, (called Sarah in the will), $50.00, and Samuel, Jr., was to pay her an additional $50.00 within the year;*
> *After all the expenses were paid, the balance of the estate was to go to Samuel, Jr.*

Samuel Willett, Senior, died on May 1, 1857, aged 89 years, 9 months, and 15 days. Both he and his wife, Rachel, are buried in the Wells Valley Methodist Cemetery, Wells Tannery, Bedford County, Pennsylvania. The tombstone of Mrs. Rachel Willett reads, "Rachel, wife of Samuel Willett, died August 2, 1851. Aged 73 years, 5 mo. 2 days." Their tombstones survive.

(*Commemorative Biographical Encyclopedia of the Juniata Valley .... Pennsylvania*, page 844; *History of Susquehanna and Juniata Valley, Pennsylvania*, David Foster Horton; *The Willett Families*, 1985, pages 241-242).

Children of Samuel Willett and his 1st wife, Mary Fenner:

1. **Stephen WILLETT**: b July 19, 1789, Bedford County, Pennsylvania; m in Highland County, Ohio, January 10, 1817, Sarah A. Chaney (b 1794, Bedford County, Pennsylvania; d June 4, 1875, Highland County, Ohio), the daughter of Gabriel Chaney of Liberty Township, Highland County, Ohio; d

October 28, 1882, Highland County, Ohio. See next PA.3.2.1.

2. **Elisha WILLETT**: b 1791, Pennsylvania. In 1820, Elijah Willett and family were residing at Athens, Bedford County, Pennsylvania, census, page 110. See next PA.3.2.2.

Children of Samuel Willett and his 2d wife, Rachel Edwards:

3. **Mary WILLETT**: b August 21, 1801, Pennsylvania; m March 27, 1821, Joseph P. Woodcock (b 1797, Maryland; d October 12, 1875, age 77 years, 10 months, 2 days, buried Wells Valley United Methodist Cemetery, Fulton County, Pennsylvania); d 1881. See next PA.3.2.3.

4. **John WILLETT**: b 1804, Pennsylvania; m 1st Highland County, Ohio, October 15, 1828, Catherine Miller (d before 1841), the daughter of John Miller; February 2, 1841, Nancy Landis (b 1815, Ohio); d 1882, age 78, Iola, Allen County, Kansas. See next PA.3.2.4.

5. **Rachel WILLETT**: b abt 1807, Pennsylvania; m abt 1830, Mr. French.

6. **Thomas WILLETT**: b March 1, 1805 (1810) in Pennsylvania (Bible Record); m abt 1830, Rachel (b March 1, 1805 [1812] in Pennsylvania) (Bible Record); resided in Wells Valley, evidently on land purchased from his father (or perhaps his father made a deed of gift); d after 1870 in Fulton County, Pennsylvania. See next PA.3.2.6.

7. **Allen WILLETT**: b November 20, 1810, Fulton County, Pennsylvania; m 1st February 16, 1832, Sarah Ann Green (b November 27, 1813, in Pennsylvania; d January 31, 1851); m 2d after September, 1865, Mrs. Margaret Henry Woodcock (b 1822), the widow of Jesse Woodcock (d September, 1865); d January 12, 1892, Arbisonia, Pennsylvania. See next PA.3.2.7.

8. **Elizabeth** ("Betsey", "Betty") **WILLETT**: b abt 1818, Pennsylvania; m abt 1838, Mr. Green; will dated August 4, 1843, probated September 22, 1843. See next PA.3.2.8.

9. **Samuel WILLETT** (II): b 1820, Pennsylvania; m 1st abt 1840, Elizabeth Lockard (b 1821 in Pennsylvania; d June 15, 1875, buried Wells Valley E.U.B. Cemetery, Fulton County); resided in Wells Valley, Fulton County, Pennsylvania; m 2d in 1879, Maggie Edwards (b 1841, Pennsylvania); d 1894. See next PA.3.2.9.

10. **Anne WILLETT**: b abt 1821, Pennsylvania; m abt 1845, Mr. Smith

11. **David WILLETT**: (reputedly). Most likely grandchild.

12. **Ur WILLETT**: (reputedly). Most likely grandchild.

NOTE: Mrs. Annette Patterson believes that Stephen Willet is the son of Samuel and Mary (Ferner/Fenner) Willett of Massachusetts.

NOTE: Stephen Willett, Elisha Willett and John Willett are identified as sons of Samuel Willett solely on the basis of the similarity of Christian names in their respective families and on the fact that the known children of Samuel Willett mentioned in Samuel Willett's will of 1845 have the same names as the three who appear in Highland County, Ohio, on or after 1814.

PA.3.2.1
STEPHEN WILLETT and SARAH A. CHANEY
of Liberty Township, Highland County, Ohio

Stephen Willett was born on July 19, 1789, in Bedford County, Pennsylvania.

In 1814, Stephen Willett removed to Liberty Township, Highland County, Ohio.

> NOTE: In 1784, The Virginia Military District of Ohio was opened to white settlers. Highland County was formed out of the Virginia Military District; Pike and Ross Counties are adjacent. The Northwest Territory was formed in 1787, from land previously claimed by England. However, native American Indian tribes still controlled the majority of the land being claimed by the new American Republic. The Northwest Territory includes the present states of Ohio, Indiana, Illinois, Michigan, Wisconsin, and part of Minnesota.

Stephen Willett married in Highland County, Ohio, on January 10, 1817, Sarah ("Sally") A. Chaney (b 1794, Bedford County, Pennsylvania; d June 4, 1875, Highland County, Ohio, buried Hillsboro Cemetery), the daughter of Gabriel Chaney, of Liberty Township.

The 1820 Liberty Township, Highland County, Ohio, census, lists Stephen Willets (sic) and family as follows:

1 male	16-26	1794-1804	*Stephen*	*age 31? b 1789?*
1 female	16-26	1794-1804	*Sarah*	*age 26 b 1794*
1 male	10-16	1804-1810	*Samuel*	*age 3? b 1817?*
1 male	10-16	1804-1810	*James*	*age 0? b 1820?*

The ages given in the 1820 census do not agree with what is known of the Stephen Willett family, and they are noted for the record until such time as they can be rechecked.

The 1830 Liberty Township, Highland County, Ohio, census, lists Stephen Willett (sic) and family as follows:

1 male	30-40	1790-1800	*Stephen*	*age 41* b 1789**
1 female	40-50	1780-1790	*Sarah*	*age 36* b 1794**
1 female	20-30	1800-1810		
1 male	10-15	1815-1820	*Samuel*	*age 13 b 1817*
1 male	10-15	1815-1820	*James*	*age 10 b 1820*
1 female	10-15	1815-1820		
1 female	10-15	1815-1820		
1 male	5-10	1820-1825	*Moses*	*age 6 b 1824*

1 male	5-10	1820-1825	*Thomas*	*age 6*	*b 1824*
1 female	5-10	1825-1830			
1 male	5-10	1825-1830	*John*	*age 4*	*b 1826*

"He worked by the month on farms about three years and purchased a farm on the Chillicothe Pike, three miles from Hillsborough. This farm was sold and one bought between Rocky fork and Clear creek, on which he lived until 1836, when he purchased a farm of one hundred and thirty acres located on the Belfast pike, adjoining the town, where he has lived ever since" (*History of Ross and Highland Counties, Ohio, with Illustrations and Biographical Sketches*, 1880, page 358.

The 1840 Liberty Township, Highland County, Ohio, census, page 11, lists Stephen Willet (sic) and family as follows:

1 male	50-60	1790-1800	*Stephen*	*age 51 b 1789*
1 female	40-50	1780-1790	*Sarah*	*age 46 b 1794*
1 male	30-40	1800-1810		
1 male	30-40	1800-1810		
1 male	20-30	1810-1820	*Samuel*	*age 23 b 1817*
1 male	15-20	1820-1825	*James*	*age 20 b 1820*
1 male	10-15	1825-1830	*John*	*age 14 b 1826*
1 female	10-15	1820-1825	*Mary E.*	*age 11 b 1829*
1 male	5-10	1830-1835	*Nathan*	*age 5 b 1835*
1 male	0-5	1835-1840	*Gabriel*	*age 3 b 1837*

The 1850 Liberty Township, Highland County, Ohio, census, page 74, No. 406, lists the Stephen Willett family, as follows:

Willett	Stephen	60	m	PA	farmer
	Sarah	54	f	PA	
	John	24	m	OH	
	Nathan	15	m	OH	
	Gabriel C	13	m	OH	

In 1870, Stephen <u>Willetts</u> and family are listed in the Hillsborough, Highland County, Ohio, census, No. 317, as follows:

| Willetts Stephen | 80 | PA |
| Sarah | 75 | PA |

Stephen Willett died on October 28, 1882, and is buried in the Hillsboro Cemetery, Highland County, Ohio.

(*The Willett Families*, 1985, page 919).

1. **Samuel WILLETT**: b 1817, Highland County, Ohio; m in Highland County, Ohio, January 7, 1841, Elizabeth Chaney (b January 15, 1818, New Market Township, Ohio; d March 14, 1898, buried Salem Township Cemetery), the daughter of Amos Chaney and Rachel Mitchell; d April 14, 1893, age 75 years, 6 months, 4 days, buried Salem Township Cemetery. See next PA.3.2.1.1.

2. **James WILLETT**: b February 20, 1820, Highland County, in Ohio; m 1st in Highland County, Ohio, March 28, 1844, Eliza Miller (d May 30, 1856, Highland County, Ohio); m 2d in Highland County, Ohio, September 13, 1855, Elmira Houp (Eliza Almira Harett); settled in Iowa before 1880; d October 16, 1902, Villisca, Montgomery County, Iowa. See next PA.3.2.1.2.

3. **Moses WILLETT**: b 1822, Highland County, Ohio; m in Highland County, Ohio, May 11, 1848, Catherine Cress (b 1828, Germany; d May 1, 1906); living in Highland County, Ohio, in 1880; d November 11, 1906. See next PA.3.2.1.3.

4. **Thomas WILLETT**: b 1824, Highland County, Ohio; m in Highland County, Ohio, on December 28, 1848, Mary B. Haggett (b 1833, Virginia); living Highland County, Ohio, in 1880. See next PA.3.2.1.4.

5. **John F. WILLETT**: b May 7, 1826, Highland County, Ohio; m abt 1860 Serena Holmes (b 1834, Ohio; d October 25, 1910); d July 20, 1901. See next PA.3.2.1.5.

6. **Mary Elizabeth WILLETT**: b January 18, 1829, Highland County, Ohio; m in Highland County, Ohio, on October 17, 1848, John Adair Long (b October 19, 1824; d February 9, 1897); living in Ross or Highland County, Ohio, in 1880; d March 22, 1910, in Hillsboro, Highland County, Ohio. See next PA.3.2.1.6.

7. **Nathan** ("Nate") **WILLETT**: b abt 1835, Highland County, Ohio; m in Highland County, Ohio, November 20, 1856, Elizabeth Bishir (b July 11, 1837, Ohio; d February 28, 1885); living in Highland County, Ohio, in 1880; d October 28, 1885. See next PA.3.2.1.7.

8. **Gabriel Chaney WILLETT**: b April 1, 1837, Highland County, Ohio; m in Highland County, Ohio, June 21, 1859, Mary Ann Bishir (b July 4, 1839, Ohio; d October 24, 1911); living in Highland County, Ohio, in 1880; d March 27, 1901. See next PA.3.2.1.8.

PA.3.2.1.1
SAMUEL WILLETT and ELIZABETH CHANEY
of Highland County, Ohio

Samuel Willett was born in 1817 in Highland County in Ohio.

Samuel Willett married in Highland County, Ohio, January 7, 1841, Elizabeth Chaney (b January 15, 1818, New Market Township, Ohio; d March 14, 1898, buried Salem Township Cemetery), the daughter of Amos Chaney and Rachel Mitchell.

They resided (1850-1870) in Salem Township, Highland County, Ohio.

In 1850, Samuel Willett and family were listed in the Salem Township, Highland County, Ohio, census, page 299, dwelling 93, as follows:

Willett	Samuel	33	OH	farmer
	Elizabeth	33	OH	
	Sarah	8	OH	
	Rachel	6	OH	
	Amos W.	4	OH	
	Stephen	2	OH	

In 1860, Samuel Willet and family were listed in the Salem Township, Highland County, Ohio, census, page 958, as follows:

Willet	Samuel	45	OH	farmer
	Elizabeth	43	OH	
	Sarah	19	OH	
	Rachel	16	OH	
	Amos	15	OH	
	Stephen	13	OH	
	Barbara	7	OH	
	Elizabeth	3	OH	

In 1870 Samuel Willett and family were listed in the Salem Township, Highland County, Ohio, census, dwelling 128, as follows:

Willet	Samuel	52	OH	farmer
	Elizabeth	52	OH	
	Stephen	22	OH	
	Dora	16	OH	
	Elizabeth	12	OH	

Samuel Willett died on April 14, 1893, at age 75 years, 6

months, 4 days, and is buried in the Salem Township Cemetery.

1. **Sarah A. WILLETT**: b 1841, Highland County, Ohio; m October 6, 1864, William Thomas Duvall (b c 1843; d May 18, 1903), the son of James Duvall and Mary Ann Gossett. See next PA.3.2.1.1.1.

2. **Rachel WILLETT**: b 1844, Highland County, Ohio; possibly the same Rachel Willett who married on February 15, 1866, Charles F. Sanders.

3. **Amos M. WILLETT**: b August 11, 1845, Highland County, Ohio; m in Highland County, Ohio, on October 10, 1867, Nancy Jane Sanders (b April 18, 1847; d February 20, 1904, buried Salem Township Cemetery); d June 2, 1928, buried Salem Township Cemetery. See next PA.3.2.1.1.3.

4. **Stephen WILLETT**: b 1848, Highland County, Ohio; m in Highland County on September 21, 1872, Barbara Ann Mount (b August 2, 1851, Ohio; d May 9, 1931); d August 28, 1929. See next PA.3.2.1.1.4.

5. **Mary WILLETT**: b November, 1850, Highland County; d January 10, 1854, buried Salem Township Cemetery.

6. **Dora Barbara WILLETT**: b February, 1853, Highland County, Ohio; d March 10, 1871, age 18 years, 1 month, and 3 days, buried Salem Township Cemetery.

7. **Catherine WILLETT**: b June, 1855, Highland County; d August 12, 1855, buried Salem Township Cemetery.

8. **Reuben WILLETT**: b June, 1855, Highland County; d August 11, 1855, buried Salem Township Cemetery.

9. **Laura WILLETT**: b July, 1856, Highland County; d August 7, 1856, age 18 days, buried Salem Township Cemetery.

10. **Elizabeth WILLETT**: b 1857, Highland County, Ohio; m December 25, 1874, Sylvester Smith; resided (1893) Clermont County, Ohio.

PA.3.2.1.1.1
SARAH A. WILLETT and WILLIAM THOMAS DUVALL
of Highland County, Ohio

Sarah A. Willett was born in 1841, Highland County, in Ohio.

Miss Sarah A. Willett married on October 6, 1864, William Thomas Duvall (b c 1843; d May 18, 1903), the son of James Duvall and Mary Ann Gossett.

1. **Henry C. DUVALL**: b circa 1866.
2. **Lenna DUVALL**: b circa 1868.
3. **Charles E. DUVALL**: b circa 1870.
4. **James W. DUVALL**: b circa 1875.
5. **Albert E. DUVALL**: b March, 1880.

PA.3.2.1.1.3
AMOS M. WILLETT and NANCY JANE SAUNDERS
of Highland County, Ohio

Amos M. ("N. W.") Willett was born in 1846 Highland County in Ohio.

Amos M. Willett married in Highland County on October 10, 1867, Nancy Jane Sanders (b April 18, 1847; d February 20, 1904, buried Salem Township Cemetery).

In 1880, they were residents of Hamer Township, Highland County, Ohio.

Amos M. Willett died June 2, 1928, and is buried in the Salem Township Cemetery.

1. **Charles C. WILLETT**: b September 9, 1872, Highland County, Ohio; m Margaret Knupp (b August 27, 1870, Hamer Township, Highland County, Ohio; d September 20, 1958, Coldwater, Ohio), the daughter of Jonathan A. Knupp and Mary Ellen Pence; d March 26, 1936, and is buried in the Greenlawn Cemetery, Greenwich, Ohio.

    1. **Ray WILLETT**: b August 30, 1900; m on June 12, 1922, Charlotte M. Childs (b November 27, 1899; d August 5, 1989, Greenwich, Ohio); d June 26, 1985.

    2. **Earl WILLETT**: b June 9, 1902; d June 12, 1972, Fort Myers, Florida.

2. **Samuel WILLETT**: b 1875, Highland County, Ohio.
3. **Henry WILLETT**: b January, 1880, Highland County, Ohio.

PA.3.2.1.1.4

STEPHEN WILLETT and **BARBARA ANN MOUNT**

of Highland County, Ohio

Stephen Willett was born in 1848 (1842) Highland County in Ohio.

Stephen Willett married in Highland County, Ohio, on September 21, 1872, Barbara Ann Mount (b August 2, 1851, Ohio; d May 9, 1931).

In 1880, Stephen Willett and family are listed in the Salem Township, Highland County, Ohio, census, as follows:

Willett	Stephen	head	38	OH
	Barbara A.	wife	24	OH
	Callie L.	daughter	3	OH
	Dora A.	daughter	1/12	OH

Stephen Willett died August 28, 1929.

1. **Callie L. WILLETT**: b 1877, Highland County, Ohio.
2. **Dora A. WILLETT**: b 1880, Highland County, Ohio.
3. **William S. WILLETT**: b January 4, 1884, Highland County; d July 18, 1950.

PA.3.2.1.2
JAMES WILLETT
of Highland County, Ohio, and Adams County, Iowa

James Willett was born on February 20, 1822 (1820), Highland County, Ohio.

James Willett married 1st in Highland County, Ohio, on March 28, 1844, Eliza Miller (b 1827, Ohio; d May 30, 1856, Highland County, Ohio), the daughter of William H. Miller.

The 1850 Liberty Township, Highland County, Ohio, census, page 62, No. 240, lists the James Willett family, as follows:

Willett	James	28	m	OH	farmer
	Eliza	23	f	OH	
	William	54	m	OH	
	Sally M	1	f	OH	

James Willett married 2d in Highland County, Ohio, September 13, 1855, Elizabeth Elmira Houp (Eliza Almira Harett) (b December 22, 1836; d May 26, 1865), the daughter of John Houp (b 1811, Pennsylvania) and Mahala Kehaugh (b 1815, Ohio).

> *"January 24, 1857: James Willett appointed Guardian of William Harvey, aged 12 years on January 6, 1857; Sally Ann Willett, aged 8 years on January 6, 1857; John, aged 5 years on December 12, 1856; Martha D., aged 4 years on January 1, 1857; and Nathan Willett, aged 2 years on February 16, 1856; minor children of said James Willett and heirs and legal representatives of William H. Miller, deceased. Surety: Stephen Willett"* (Wills, Administrations, Guardianships, and Adoptions of Highland County, Ohio [1805-1880], Southern Ohio Genealogical Society, 1981, page 203).

In 1860, James Willett and family are listed in the Highland County, Ohio, census, page 40 (not copied).

In 1870, James Willett, age 54, born Ohio, was living with his son-in-law, David Hill. James Willett's three youngest children were living with their maternal grandparents, John and Mahala Houp, (Liberty Township, Highland County, Ohio, census, No. 359), as follows:

Houp	John	59	m	PA	farmer
	Mahala	55	f	OH	
	Maxwell	24	m	OH	
	Martha	18	f	OH	

Willett	Annie M	13	f	OH
	Ida Bell	11	f	OH
	Elizabeth A	5	f	OH

James Willett removed to Iowa about late 1879 or early 1880.

In 1880, James Willett, age 56 (sic), born Ohio, is the head of a Nodaway Township, Adams County, Iowa, household, as follows:

Willett	James	head	56	OH
	Ida	daughter	19	OH
	Bertie	grandson	8/12,	OH

James Willett died on October 16, 1902, age 82, at Villisca, Montgomery County, Iowa, and is buried in the Villisca Cemetery, Villisca, Iowa.

(*The Willett Families*, 1985, page 920; 1880 Nodaway Township, Adams County, Iowa, census).

Children of James Willett and his 1st wife, Eliza Miller:

1. **William Harvey** ("Harve") **WILLETT**: b January 6, 1845, Hillsboro, Highland County, Ohio; m in Hillsboro, Ohio, Samantha Jane Beard (b 1848, Hillsboro, Highland County, Ohio); removed to Iowa after 1873. See next PA.3.2.1.2.1.

2. **Sarah** ("Sally") **M. WILLETT**: b January 6, 1849, Hillsboro, Highland County, Ohio; m in Highland County, Ohio, on July 23, 1868, David H. Hill (b February 15, 1846, Ohio; d November 12, 1914), the son of Samuel Hill and Harriet Shoemaker; d April 3, 1927. (1870 Hillsborough, Highland County, Ohio, census, No. 151). See next PA.3.2.1.2.2.

3. **John WILLETT**: b December 12, 1850, Hillsboro, Highland County, Ohio; d January 19, 1907, Iowa, buried Villisca Cemetery, Villisca, Montgomery County, Iowa.

4. **Martha L. WILLETT**: b January 1, 1852, Hillsboro, Highland County, Ohio; unmarried at the time her twins were born in Highland County, Ohio; m in Iowa Lewis Higgins. See next PA.3.2.1.2.4.

5. **Richard Nathaniel** ("Nathan") **WILLETT**: b February 12, 1854, Hillsboro, Highland County, Ohio; removed to Iowa; m June 2, 1886, Josephine Gibbs (b July 8, 1866; d March 21, 1915, Nodaway, Adams County, Iowa); d September 7, 1927, Nodaway, Adams County, Iowa. See next PA.3.2.1.2.5.

Children of James Willett and his 2d wife, Elmira Houp:

6. **Annie** ("Annie M."; "Millie") **Melissa WILLETT**: b April 30, 1857, Hillsboro, Highland County, Ohio; m September 29, 1881, George Rice (b March 27, 1857; d November 22, 1940), the son of Paul Rice and Elizabeth K. Funk. See next PA.3.2.1.2.6.

7. **Ida Bell WILLETT**: b December 6, 1858, Hillsboro, Highland County, Ohio; m Julius Bean. (1880 Adams County, Iowa, census). See next PA.3.2.1.2.7.

8. **Harriet L. WILLETT**: b February 6, 1861, Highland County.

9. **Ollie Jane WILLETT**: b January 25, 1863, Highland County.

10. **Elizabeth A.** ("Sallie") **WILLETT**: b April 9, 1865, Highland County, Ohio. (1870 Highland County census).

11. **James WILLETT**, Jr: b abt 1869, Hillsboro, Highland County, Ohio.

PA.3.2.1.2.1

WILLIAM HARVEY WILLETT and **SAMANTHA JANE BEARD**
of Montgomery County, Iowa

William Harvey ("Harve") Willett was born on January 6, 1845, Hillsboro, Highland County, Ohio.

William Harvey Willett married in Hillsboro, Ohio, Samantha Jane Beard (b 1848, Hillsboro, Highland County, Ohio).

They removed to Montgomery County, Iowa, after 1873.

In 1880, W. H. Willett and family are listed in the Scott Township, Montgomery County, Iowa, census, as follows:

Willett	W. H.	head	35	OH
	S. J.	wife	32	OH
	E. M.	daughter	10	IL
	O. B.	daughter	6	IL

("Richard Nathaniel Willett 1852-1927"; 1880 Scott Township, Montgomery County, Iowa, census).

1. **Effie Marie WILLETT**: b 1870, Illinois; m Lee Penton. See next PA.3.2.1.2.1.1.

2. **Ollie Bell WILLETT**: b 1874, Illinois; m Omer Day. See next PA.3.2.1.2.1.2.

3. **Ivy May WILLETT**: b abt 1877, died in infancy.

PA.3.2.1.2.1.1
EFFIE MARIE WILLETT and LEE PENTON

Effie Marie Willett was born in 1870, Illinois.
Miss Effie Marie Willett married Lee Penton.

1. **Gladys PENTON**: m Walter Nelson.
2. **Waldo PENTON**: m Elzene Gourley.

PA.3.2.1.2.1.2
OLLIE BELL WILLETT and OMER DAY

Ollie Bell Willett was born in 1874, Illinois.
Miss Ollie Bell Willett married Omer Day.

1. **Elwin Willett DAY**: m Lillian Froyd.
2. **Mary Opal DAY**: m Lawrence Focht.

PA.3.2.1.2.2
SARAH M. WILLETT and DAVID H. HILL
of Highland County, Ohio

Sarah ("Sally") M. Willett was born on January 6, 1849, Hillsboro, Highland County, Ohio.

Miss Sarah M. Willett married in Highland County, Ohio, on July 23, 1868, David H. Hill (b February 15, 1846, Ohio; d November 12, 1914), the son of Samuel Hill and Harriet Shoemaker.

Mrs. Sarah M. (Willett) Hill died on April 3, 1927.

(1870 Hillsborough, Highland County, Ohio, census, No. 151).

1. **James Frank HILL**: b March 3, 1869, Highland County, Ohio; d September 26, 1870. (1870 Highland County census).

2. **Harry** (Harvey) **S. HILL**: b May 19, 1870, Highland County, Ohio; d January 9, 1909. (1870 Highland County census).

PA.3.2.1.2.4
MARTHA L. WILLETT and LEWIS HIGGINS
of Montgomery County, Iowa

Martha L. Willett was born on January 1, 1852, Hillsboro, Highland County, Ohio.

Miss Martha L. Willett was unmarried at the time her twins were born in Highland County, Ohio.

Miss Martha L. Willett married in Iowa Lewis Higgins.

1. **Mary WILLETT** (twin): b May 9, 1873, Hillsboro, Highland County, Ohio; m in Villisca, Montgomery County, Iowa, on November 2, 1890, William Henry Wade, witnesses were Katie Wade and Henrietta Dean; d April 21, 1935, at Villisca, Montgomery County, Iowa; d March 16, 1946, Moorhead, Monona County, Iowa.

2. **Lewis WILLETT** (twin): b May 9, 1873, Hillsboro, Highland County, Ohio.

PA.3.2.1.2.5
RICHARD NATHANIEL WILLETT and **JOSEPHINE GIBBS**
of Adams County, Iowa

Richard Nathaniel ("Nathan") Willett was born on February 12, 1854, Hillsboro, Highland County, Ohio.

Richard Nathaniel Willett married on June 2, 1886, Josephine Gibbs (b July 8, 1866; d March 21, 1915, Nodaway, Adams County, Iowa).

They made their home in Adams County, Iowa.

Richard Willett died on September 7, 1927, Nodaway, Adams County, Iowa, and is buried in the Nodaway Cemetery. ("Richard Nathaniel Willett 1852-1927").

1. **Mary WILLETT**: b abt 1887, Adelph, Iowa.

2. **Eber James WILLETT**: b September 7, 1888, Adelph, Iowa; m January 7, 1914, Faye Houck (b September 30, 1894; d July 4, 1980, Manchester, Iowa); d May 22, 1926, Corning, Adams County, Iowa, buried in the Nodaway Cemetery, Adams County, Iowa. See next PA.3.2.1.2.5.2.

3. **Blanche Winnifred WILLETT**: b December 11, 1890, Adelphi, Iowa; m March 9, 1916, Edward Lamb Hoyt (b August 12, 1884, Corning, Iowa; d December 10, 1970); d April 22, 1981, Red Oak, Montgomery County, Iowa, and is buried in the, Nodaway Cemetery, Adams County, Iowa.

4. **Olin Norwood WILLETT**: b March 4, 1894, Corning (Douglas Township), Adams County, Iowa; m March 7, 1916, Evelyn Jane Arthur (b November 19, 1892; d September 17, 1982). See next PA.3.2.1.2.5.4.

5. **Clyde Richard WILLETT**: b August 30, 1898, Corning, Adams County, Iowa; m Emma Hunstad (b February 16, 1903); d April 16, 1945, San Diego, California. See next PA.3.2.1.2.5.5.

6. **Beulah WILLETT**: b August 28, 1903, Corning, Adams County, Iowa; m June 2, 1928, Parke W. Bowers (b March 19, 1904, Whitfield, Iowa); d July 121, 1981, Ottumwa, Wapello County, Iowa.

7. **Bernice Leah WILLETT**: b March 30, 1907, Corning, Adams County, Iowa; m Paul P. Turner (b March 2, 1908, Centerville, Appanoose County, Iowa; d July 2, 1965).

PA.3.2.1.2.5.2
EBER JAMES WILLETT and FAYE HOUCK
of Corning, Adams County, Iowa

Eber James Willett was born on September 7, 1888, Adelph, Iowa.

Eber James Willett married on January 7, 1914, Faye Houck (b September 30, 1894; d July 4, 1980, Manchester, Iowa).

Eber James Willett died on May 22, 1926, Corning, Adams County, Iowa, and is buried in the Nodaway Cemetery, Adams County, Iowa.

("Richard Nathaniel Willett 1852-1927").

1. **Wilton James WILLETT**: b February 5, 1915, Corning, Adams County, Iowa; m December 30, 1941, Ella Sahs (b March 8, 1913, Salem, McCook County, South Dakota; d December 17, 1968). See next PA.3.2.1.2.5.2.1.

2. **Helen Lucille WILLETT**: b January 6, 1917, Corning, Adams County, Iowa; m October 28, 1943, Arnold Everett Sorum (b November 30, 1918, Hillsboro, Henry County, North Dakota).

3. **Marvin Houck WILLETT**: b July 15, 1918, Corning, Adams County, Iowa; m February 2, 1935, Lois Mae Austin (b October 1, 1915, Albion, Boone County, Nebraska. See next PA.3.2.1.2.5.2.3.

PA.3.2.1.2.5.2.1
WILTON JAMES WILLETT and ELLA SAHS
of Delaware County, Iowa

Wilton James Willett was born on February 5, 1915, at Corning, Adams County, Iowa.

Wilton James Willett married on December 30, 1941, Ella Sahs (b March 8, 1913, Salem, McCook County, South Dakota; d December 17, 1968).

("Richard Nathaniel Willett 1852-1927").

1. **Bruce Douglas WILLETT**: b August 31, 1942, Ft. Smith, Arkansas; m August 8, 1963, Carolyn Hamasake (b January 29, 1945, Hilo, Hawaii). See next PA.3.2.1.2.5.2.1.1.

2. **Brian Ernest WILLETT**: b October 10, 1944, Manchester, Delaware County, Iowa; m August 3, 1968, Katherine ("Kitty") Lorraine Nunn (b July 26, 1946, Montgomery, Alabama). See next PA.3.2.1.2.5.2.1.2.

3. **Nancy Ellen WILLETT**: b April 21, 1947, Manchester,

Delaware County, Iowa; m November 16, 1974, Jeffrey Hugh Maynard (b February 6, 1949, Waukegan, Illinois).

4. **Mary Helen WILLETT**: b May 31, 1952, Manchester, Delaware County, Iowa; m June 21, 1975, Mark Kline (b November 21, 1950, Manchester, Delaware County, Iowa..

PA.3.2.1.2.5.2.1.1.
BRUCE DOUGLAS WILLETT and CAROLYN HAMAAKE
of California

Bruce Douglas Willett was born on August 31, 1942, at Ft. Smith, Arkansas.

Bruce Douglas Willett married on August 8, 1963, Carolyn Hamasake (b January 29, 1945, Hilo, Hawaii).

1. **Kristin WILLETT**: b February 12, 1967, Torrance, California.

PA.3.2.1.2.5.2.1.2
BRIAN ERNEST WILLETT
and **KATHERINE LORRAINE NUNN**

Brian Ernest Willett was born on October 10, 1944, Manchester, Delaware County, Iowa.

Brian Ernest Willett married in August 3, 1968, Katherine ("Kitty") Lorraine Nunn (b July 26, 1946, Montgomery, Alabama).

1. **Katherine Brent WILLETT**: b November 1, 1972, Arlington Heights, Illinois.
2. **Terrill WILLETT**: b June 17, 1977, Montgomery, Alabama.

PA.3.2.1.2.5.2.3
MARVIN HOUCK WILLETT and **LOIS MAE KLINE**
of Carbon, Adams County, Iowa

Marvin Houck Willett was born on July 15, 1918, at Corning, Adams County, Iowa.

Marvin Houck Willett married on February 2, 1935, Lois Mae Austin (b October 1, 1915, Albion, Boone County, Nebraska.

("Richard Nathaniel Willett 1852-1927").

1. **James Robert WILLETT**: b June 21, 1936, Morton Mills, Montgomery County, Iowa; m October 23, 1955, Carolyn Joan Rash (b May 11, 1937, Chariton, Lucas County, Iowa). See next PA.3.2.1.2.5.2.3.1.

2. **Janis Kay WILLETT**: b October 2, 1940, Carbon, Adams County, Iowa; m June 5, 1960, Allan Robert Gurnsey (b May 20, 1937, Des Moines, Polk County, Iowa.

3. **Gary Lee WILLETT**: b July 20, 1942, Carbon, Adams County, Iowa; m October 14, 1966, Sue Ann Shortley (b June 26, 1945, Des Moines, Polk County, Iowa. See next PA.3.2.1.2-.5.2.3.3.

PA.3.2.1.2.5.2.3.1
JAMES ROBERT WILLETT and **CAROLYN JOAN RASH**
of Adams County, Iowa

James Robert Willett was born on June 21, 1936, Morton Mills, Montgomery County, Iowa.

James Robert Willett married on October 23, 1955, Carolyn Joan Rash (b May 11, 1937, Chariton, Iowa).

1. **James Allan WILLETT**: b July 22, 1957, Des Moines, Polk County, Iowa; m May 16, 1981, Susan Marie McEntee (b May 27, 1958, Des Moines, Iowa.   See next PA.3.2.1.2.5.-2.3.1.1.

2. **Marvin Forest WILLETT**: b July 31, 1959, Des Moines, Polk County, Iowa; m September 30, 1978, Ann Marie Haroldson (b March 5, 1958; divorced 1983).   See next PA.3.2.1.2.5.2.3.1.2.

3. **Diana Joan WILLETT**: b January 4, 1964, Des Moines, Polk County, Iowa; m October 1, 1983, Gregory Freemen (b February 12, 1962).

PA.3.2.1.2.5.2.3.1.1
JAMES ALLAN WILLETT and **SUSAN MARIE MCENTEE**
of Polk County, Iowa

James Allan Willett was born on July 22, 1957, Des Moines, Polk County, Iowa.

James Allan Willett married on May 16, 1981, Susan Marie McEntee (b May 27, 1958, Des Moines, Iowa.

1. **Ryan James WILLETT**: b October 1, 1983, Des Moines, Polk County, Iowa.

PA.3.2.1.2.5.2.3.1.2
MARVIN FOREST WILLETT and **ANN MARIE HAROLDSON**
of Polk County, Iowa

Marvin Forest Willett was born on July 31, 1959, Des Moines, Polk County, Iowa.

Marvin Forest Willett married on September 30, 1978, Ann Marie Haroldson (b March 5, 1958; divorced 1983).

1. **Dustin Forest WILLETT**: b October 25, 1979, Des Moines, Polk County, Iowa.

PA.3.2.1.2.5.2.3.3
GARY LEE WILLETT and **SUE ANN SHORTLEY**
of Des Moines, Iowa

Gary Lee Willett was born on July 20, 1942, Carbon, Adams County, Iowa.

Gary Lee Willett married on October 14, 1966, Sue Ann Shortley (b June 26, 1945, Des Moines, Polk County, Iowa.

1. **Donald Lee WILLETT**: b June 17, 1967, Des Moines, Iowa.

2. **David Shortley WILLETT**: b January 11, 1969, Des Moines, Iowa.

PA.3.2.1.2.5.4
OLIN NORWOOD WILLETT and EVELYN JANE ARTHUR
of Corning, Adams County, Iowa

Olin Norwood Willett was born on March 4, 1894, Corning (Douglas Township), Adams County, Iowa.

Olin Norwood Willett married on March 7, 1916, Evelyn Jane Arthur (b November 19, 1892, Adams County, Iowa; d September 17, 1982, Corning, Iowa).

Olin N. Willett died after 1982.

("Richard Nathaniel Willett 1852-1927").

1. **Charles Richard WILLETT**: b April 28, 1917, Corning, Adams County, Iowa; m in Parkersburg, Iowa, on December 22, 1937, Dolores Ella Olds (b March 24, 1916, Adams County, Iowa). See next PA.3.2.1.2.5.4.1.

2. **Richard Olin WILLETT**: b March 23, 1920, Corning, Adams County, Iowa.

3. **Dorothy Jane WILLETT**: b June 29, 1922, Corning, Adams County, Iowa; m June 29, 1922, Max Peterson (b September 22, 1918; d August 29, 1947).

PA.3.2.1.2.5.4.1
CHARLES RICHARD WILLETT and DOLORES ELLA OLDS
of Adams County, Iowa

Charles Richard Willett was born on April 28, 1917, Corning, Adams County, Iowa.

Charles Richard Willett married in Parkersburg, Iowa, on December 22, 1937, Dolores Ella Olds (b March 24, 1916, Adams County, Iowa).

1. **Donald Dean WILLETT**: b March 1, 1941, Corning, Adams County, Iowa; m in Corning, Adams County, Iowa, on December 31, 1961, Janice Joy Jackson (b July 26, 1943, Adams County, Iowa). See next PA.3.2.1.2.5.4.1.1.

2. **Donnis Ann WILLETT**: b May 15, 1944; m August 28, 1964, Samuel Richey.

PA.3.2.1.2.5.4.1.1
DONALD DEAN WILLETT and JANICE JOY JACKSON
of Iowa

Donald Dean Willett was born on March 1, 1941, Corning, Adams County, Iowa.

Donald Dean Willett married in Corning, Adams County, Iowa, on December 31, 1961, Janice Joy Jackson (b July 26, 1943, Adams County, Iowa).

1.   **Dawn Rochelle WILLETT**: b November 27, 1962; m September 11, 1962, Donald Ashenfelter (b December 30, 1959, Corning, Adams County, Iowa).

2.   **David Charles WILLETT**: b July 9, 1966.

PA.3.2.1.2.5.5
CLYDE RICHARD WILLETT and EMMA HUNSTAD
of California

Clyde Richard Willett was born on August 30, 1898, Corning, Adams County, Iowa.
Clyde Richard Willett married Emma Hunstad (b February 16, 1903); d April 16, 1945, San Diego, California. ("Richard Nathaniel Willett 1852-1927").

1. **Robert Nathaniel WILLETT**: b April 25, 1927, Charles City, Floyd County, Iowa; m Barbara Barnes (b March 25, 1936). See next PA.3.2.1.2.5.5.1.
2. **Barbara Ann WILLETT**: b October 2, 1937, San Diego, California; m Lawrence Burke Fletcher (b August 10, 1936, San Diego, California. See next PA.3.2.1.2.5.5.2.

PA.3.2.1.2.5.5.1
ROBERT NATHANIEL WILLETT and BARBARA BARNES
of San Diego, California

Robert Nathaniel Willett was born on April 25, 1927, at Charles City, Floyd County, Iowa.
Robert Nathaniel Willett married Barbara Barnes (b March 25, 1936).

1. **Brian Nathaniel WILLETT**: b January 16, 1957, San Diego, California; m Lucy Conners. See next PA.3.2.1.2.5.-5.1.1.
2. **Tamra WILLETT**: b January 5, 1959, San Diego, California; Associate Degree in Chemical Dependency Counseling, and a Bachelor of Science Degree in Addiction Studies; m in 1983, William Craig (divorced 1991). See next PA.3.2.1.2.-5.5.1.2.
3. **Brad Richard WILLETT**: b October 10, 1961, Lincoln, Nebraska; m Maryanne. See next PA.3.2.1.2.5.5.1.3.
4. **Amy Kathleen WILLETT**: b June 19, 1965, Las Crues, New Mexico; m David Muller.

PA.3.2.1.2.5.5.1.1.
BRIAN NATHANIEL WILLETT and **LUCY CONNERS**

Brian Nathaniel Willett was born on January 16, 1957, San Diego, California.

Brian Nathaniel Willett married Lucy Conners.

1. **Brian Nathaniel WILLETT** (II):
2. **Christopher WILLETT**:

PA.3.2.1.2.5.5.1.2
TAMRA WILLETT

Tamra Willett was born on January 5, 1959, San Diego, California.

Miss Tamra Willett joined the Air Force in 1980, serving until 1984, with the Armed Forces Radio and Television (AFRN), Elmendorf Air Force Base, Alaska; E-4 at discharge. Tamra has an Associate Degree in Chemical Dependency Counseling, and a Bachelor of Science Degree in Addiction Studies.

Miss Tamra Willett married in 1983, William Craig (divorced 1991). No children.

She works as a counselor to chemical dependent adolescents.

PA.3.2.1.2.5.5.1.3
BRAD RICHARD WILLETT and **MARYANNE**

Brad Richard Willett was born on October 10, 1961, Lincoln, Nebraska.

Brad Richard Willett married Maryanne.

1. **Sarah WILLETT**:
2. **Emma Pauline WILLETT**:
3. **Matthew Richard WILLETT**:

PA.3.2.1.2.5.5.2
BARBARA ANN WILLETT
and **LAWRENCE BURKE FLETCHER**
of San Diego, California

Barbara Ann Willett was born on October 2, 1937, San Diego, California.

Miss Barbara Ann Willett married Lawrence Burke Fletcher (b August 10, 1936, San Diego, California.

1. **Russell Lawrence FLETCHER**: b June 22, 1960, San Diego, California.

2. **Bonnie Martina FLETCHER**: b July 31, 1961, San Diego, California.

3. **Ronald Richard FLETCHER**: b March 19, 1963, San Diego, California.

4. **Gary Neil FLETCHER**: b June 19, 1964, San Diego, California.

PA.3.2.1.2.6
ANNIE MELISSA WILLETT and GEORGE RICE

Annie ("Annie M."; "Millie") Melissa Willett was born on April 30, 1857, Hillsboro, Highland County, Ohio.

Miss Annie Melissa Willett married on September 29, 1881, George Rice (b March 27, 1857; d November 22, 1940), the son of Paul Rice and Elizabeth K. Funk.

1. **Helen RICE**: b September, 1883; m Raymond Sheldon (b August 10, 1882; d March, 1911); d February 1, 1920.

PA.3.2.1.2.7
IDA BELL WILLETT and JULIUS BEAN
of Adams County, Iowa

Ida Bell Willett was born on December 6, 1858, Hillsboro, Highland County, Ohio.

Miss Ida Bell Willett married Julius Bean.

In 1880, James Willett, age 56 (sic), born Ohio, is the head of a Nodaway Township, Adams County, Iowa, household, which includes his daughter and grandson, as follows:

Willett	James	head	56	OH
	Ida	daughter	19	OH
	Bertie	grandson	8/12,	OH

1. **Bertie BEAN**: b 1879, Ohio.

PA.3.2.1.3
MOSES WILLETT and CATHERINE CRESS
of Highland County, Ohio

Moses Willett was born in 1822, in Ohio.

Moses Willett married in Highland County, Ohio, May 11, 1848, Catherine Cress (b 1828, Germany; d May 1, 1906).

They resided in Highland County, Ohio.

The 1850 Liberty Township, Highland County, Ohio, census, page 48, No. 43, lists the Moses Willett family, as follows:

Willett	Moses	26	m	OH	carpenter
	Catherine	23	f	Germany	
	Albert	1	m	OH	

The 1860 Liberty Township, Highland County, Ohio, census, No. 325, lists the Moses Willett family, as follows:

Willett	Moses	38	m	OH	carpenter
	Catherine	30	f	Germany	
	Albert	18	m	OH	
	Ella	20?	F	OH	

The 1870 Liberty Township, Highland County, Ohio, census, No. 231, lists the Moses Willett family, as follows:

Willett	Moses	48	m	OH	carpenter
	Catherine	43	f	Germany	
	Albert G	21	m	OH	
	Lizzie E.	14	f	OH	

Moses Willett died November 18, 1906.

1. **Albert G. WILLETT**: b 1849, Ohio.
2. **Lizzie E. ("Ella") WILLETT**: b 1856, Ohio.

PA.3.2.1.4
THOMAS WILLETT and MARY B. HAGGETT
of Highland County, Ohio

Thomas Willett was born in 1824, in Ohio.

Thomas Willett married in Highland County, Ohio, on December 28, 1848, Mary B. Haggett (Hogsett) (b 1833, Virginia).

The 1850 Liberty Township, Highland County, Ohio, census, page 62, No. 242, lists the Thomas Willett family, as follows:

Willett	Thomas	26	m	OH	farmer
	Martha B.	22	f	VA	
	Harriet E.	7/12	f	OH	

In 1860, Thomas Willett and family are listed in the Highland County, Ohio, census, page 39 (not copied).

The 1870 Liberty Township, Highland County, Ohio, census, No. 363, lists the Thomas Willett family, as follows:

Willett	Mary M. B.	42	f	VA
	Thomas	45	m	OH
	Josiah H.	18	m	OH
	Cary W.	14	m	OH
	Lizzie M.	7	f	OH

In 1880, the Liberty Township, Highland County, Ohio, census, lists <u>Thom</u> Willett and family as follows:

Willett	Thom	53	OH	
	Mary B.	47	VA	wife
	Elizabeth	17	OH	daughter
	Newton	28	OH	son
	Elisa	11	OH	granddaughter

1. **Harriet E. WILLETT**: b 1849, Ohio.

2. **Josiah Newton WILLETT**: b February 20, 1851, Ohio; m 1st in Highland County, Ohio, on December 28, 1871, Mary Jane Miller (d circa 1873 in childbirth of Elva); m 2d c1878 Mary Jane Weaver (b March 12, 1858; d February 14, 1941), the daughter of James Frederick Weaver and Mary Aiken; d February 6, 1918, Iowa. See next PA.3.2.1.4.2.

3. **Carey Wilson WILLETT**: b 1856, Ohio; m in Highland County, Ohio, on August 10, 1876, Martha E. Garman (b 1862, Ohio). See next PA.3.2.1.4.3.

4. **Elizabeth** ("Lizzie") **M. WILLETT**: b 1863, Ohio.

PA.3.2.1.4.2
JOSIAH NEWTON WILLETT
of Iowa

Josiah Newton Willett was born February 20, 1851, Ohio.

Josiah N. Willett married 1st in Highland County, Ohio, on December 28, 1871, Mary Jane Miller (d circa 1873 in childbirth of daughter, Elva).

Josiah N. Willett married 2d circa 1878, Mary Jane Weaver (b March 12, 1858; d February 14, 1941), the daughter of James Frederick Weaver and Mary Aiken.

Josiah N. Willett died on February 6, 1918, Iowa.

(1880 Highland County census).

1. **Elva D. WILLETT**: b circa 1873, Ohio; m William McConnaughey; resided Sheridan, Wyoming. (1880 Highland County census).

2. **Bessie Inez WILLETT**: b January 5, 1882; m Edward Fenton.

3. **George Walter WILLETT**: b February 4, 1884; m June 21, 1910, Evelyn Lowery.

4. **Lawrence Roscoe WILLETT**: b April 25, 1889; m 1st Irma Mathais (divorced); m 2d Sarah Durland (no issue); m 3d Ella Swatek (no issue).

5. **Vernon Perry WILLETT**: b October 24, 1896; m Esther Suthers.

PA.3.2.1.4.3
CAREY WILSON WILLETT and MARTHA E. GARMAN
of Highland County, Ohio

Carey Wilson Willett was born in 1856, in Ohio.

Carey Wilson Willett married in Highland County, Ohio, on August 10, 1876, Martha E. Garman (Gormand) (b 1862, Ohio), the daughter of Amy Garman (b 1838, Ohio).

In1880, C. Wilson Willett and family are listed in the Liberty Township, Highland County, Ohio, census, as follows:

Willett	C. Wilson	head	24	OH
	Martha E.	wife	18	OH
	Chas H.	son	8/12	OH

1. **Charles H. WILLETT**: b 1879, Ohio.

PA.3.2.1.5
JOHN F. WILLETT and SERENA HOLMES
of Highland County, Ohio

John F. Willett was born in 1826, in Ohio.

In 1850, John Willett, age 24, was living with his parents.

John Willett married about 1860, Serena Holmes (b 1834, Ohio; d October 25, 1910). They resided in Liberty Township, Highland County, Ohio.

He was a farmer (1850).

The 1860 Liberty Township, Highland County, Ohio, census, No. 534, lists the John <u>Willetts</u> family, as follows:

Willetts	John	30	m	OH	farmer
	Susana (sic)	35	f	OH	
	Sarah	8	f	OH	
	William	5	m	OH	
	Nancy	2	f	OH	

The 1870 Liberty Township, Highland County, Ohio, census, No. 367, lists the John <u>Willett</u> family, as follows:

Willett	John	44	m	OH	farmer
	Serena	38	f	OH	
	Sarah M.	18	f	OH	
	Stephen W.	7	m	OH	
	Samuel C.	5	m	OH	
	Cary A.	3	m	OH	
	Anna M.	1	f	OH	

The 1880 Liberty Township, Highland County, Ohio, census, lists the John <u>Willett</u> family, as follows:

Willett	John	54	m	OH	farmer
	Serena	46	f	OH	
	Stephen	17	m	OH	
	Samuel	15	m	OH	
	Allen	16	m	OH	
	Annie	11	f	OH	
	Cora	7	f	OH	

John F. Willett died July 20, 1901.

Only 4 of his children survived him (1901 Obit), while the 1910 obituary for Mrs. Serena Willett states that 2 sons and 2 daughters survived her.

1. **Sarah M. WILLETT:** b 1852, Ohio; probably died as a young adult.
2. **William WILLETT:** b 1855, Ohio; probably died young before 1870.
3. **Nancy WILLETT:** b 1858, Ohio; probably died young before 1870.
4. **Stephen W. WILLETT:** b 1863, Ohio.
5. **Samuel C. WILLETT:** b 1865, Ohio.
6. **Carey Allen WILLETT:** b 1867, Ohio.
7. **Annie M. WILLETT:** b 1869, Ohio.
8. **Cora WILLETT:** b 1873, Ohio.

PA.3.2.1.6
MARY ELIZABETH WILLETT and JOHN ADAIR LONG
of Highland County, Ohio

Mary Elizabeth Willett was born on January 18, 1829, in Ohio (reputedly born in Pennsylvania).

Miss Mary Elizabeth Willett married in Highland County, Ohio, on October 17, 1848, John Adair (Adam) Long (b February 18, 1824; d February 9, 1897), the son of William R. Long and Matilda Harper.

They lived in Ross or Highland County, Ohio, in 1880.

Mrs. Mary (Willett) Long died on March 22, 1910, in Hillsboro, Highland County, Ohio.

1. **William Allen LONG:** b October 4, 1849; m in Highland County, Ohio, August 19, 1873, Susannah Frump (b April 2, 1847; d June 6, 1935); d August 6, 1939, buried North Bradley, Midland County, Ohio.
2. **Henry Harper LONG:** b May 14, 1851; d December 28, 1851, buried Kelley Cemetery, Highland County, Ohio (Bible Reference).
3. **Sarah Catherine LONG:** b December 21, 1852; m William Paley (b 1852; d 1932); d May, 1932, buried Hillsboro Cemetery (Bible Reference).
4. **Matilda Leona LONG:** b March 31, 1854; m February 15, 1877, Joseph A. Butters (b 1854; d 1936), the son of William Butters and Elizabeth Frump; d August 5, 1878, buried Union Chapel Cemetery (Bible Reference).
5. **Mary Laverne LONG:** b March 31, 1856; m September 16, 1875, Zeri M. Sutters (b 1856), the son of William Sutters and Elizabeth Frump; d February 27, 1924, Whiting, Kansas.
6. **Martha Kansas LONG:** b April 6, 1858; m Samuel Davis; no issue.
7. **Ida Mae LONG:** b May 7, 1860; m August 28, 1886,

William Henry Hopkins (b September 9, 1861; d December 7, 1923), the son of Jarret Hopkins and Mary Palmer; d August 23, 1953, Barberton, Ohio, buried Lakewood Cemetery, Akron, Ohio.

8. **John Amos LONG**: b March 2, 1862; m Eva Walker (buried Sugar Tree Ridge Cemetery); he was a minister; d July 30, 1939, buried Sugar Tree Ridge Cemetery.

9. **Thomas R. LONG**: b May 31, 1863; d January 21, 1864, buried Union Chapel Cemetery (Bible Reference).

10. **Clara Bell LONG**: b February 4, 1865; d November 30, 1866, buried Union Chapel Cemetery (Bible Reference).

11. **Ollie Elizabeth LONG**: b February 2, 1868; m July 28, 1892, Jesse Norris Rhodes (b October 6, 1868; d November 6, 1949, buried Hillsboro Cemetery), the son of Isaac Boone Rhodes and Elizabeth Martha Walters; d November 4, 1936, buried Union Chapel, Hillsboro, Highland County, Ohio. See next PA.3.2.1.6.11.

12. **Anna Mariah LONG**: b October 1, 1871; m 1st Aaron Stewart (b 1868; d 1897, buried Union Chapel Cemetery); m 2d John Robinson (b 1878; d 1917, buried New Market); m 3d Frank Stanforth (b 1852; d 1943, buried IOOF Cemetery, Nevada); m 4th August 15, 1946, Charles Anders (b 1870; d 1951, buried Hillsboro Cemetery).

PA.3.2.1.6.11
OLLIE ELIZABETH LONG and JESSE NORRIS RHODES
of Highland County, Ohio

Ollie Elizabeth Long was born February 2, 1868.

Miss Ollie Elizabeth Long married July 28, 1892, Jesse Norris Rhodes (b October 6, 1868; d November 6, 1949, buried Hillsboro Cemetery), the son of Isaac Boone Rhodes and Elizabeth Martha Walters.

Mrs. Ollie Elizabeth (Long) Rhodes died November 4, 1936, buried Union Chapel, Hillsboro, Highland County, Ohio.

1. **Earl Austin RHODES**: b May 23, 1893, Highland County, Ohio; m at Wilmington, Ohio, on January 1, 1932, Dorothy Bess Shaper (b June 14, 1902); d December 23, 1970, Highland County, Ohio, buried Lynchburg Cemetery.

2. **Leora Esther RHODES**: b July 28, 1905, Highland County, Ohio; m 1st September 2, 1926, Firman Dunham Corwin (b June 25, 1901, Warren County, Ohio; d March 1, 1936, Hamilton County, Ohio, buried Lebanon); m 2d in New York City, New York, June 4, 1947, William B. Spindler (b September 9, 1892, Highland County, Ohio; d April 29, 1967, Highland County, Ohio, buried Lebanon); resides (1987) 4635 Swallow Court, Lebanon, OH 45036.

PA.3.2.1.7
NATHAN WILLETT and ELIZABETH BISHIR
of Highland County, Ohio

Nathan ("Nate") Willett was born in 1835 in Ohio.

Nathan Willett married in Highland County, Ohio, November 20, 1856, Elizabeth Bishir (b July 11, 1837, Ohio; d February 28, 1885), the daughter of Jacob Bishir (b October 17, 1796, Pennsylvania; d January 30, 1868, of dropsy) and Elizabeth Corrington (b November 30, 1797, Warren County, Ohio; d January 23, 1875, of dyspepsia). She was a sister to Mary Bishir who married Gabriel Willett.

In the January 9, 1868, will of Jacob Bishir is mentioned "Jacob Willitt, son of Nathan Willitt" three hundred dollars (1868 will of Jacob Bishir, Highland County, Ohio) and if he dies, to his mother "Elizabeth Willitt."

NOTE: It is unknown why Jacob Bishir did not bequeath to his other grandchildren.

Nathan Willett was a farmer (1870).

In 1870, Nathan Willet and family were listed in the Liberty Township, Highland County, Ohio, census, No. 385, as follows:

Willet	Nathan	37	OH	farmer
	Elizabeth	32	OH	
	Charles F	12	OH	
	William W	11	OH	
	Ida May	8	OH	
	Mary E	7	OH	

They resided in Highland County, Ohio (1870).
Nathan Willett died on October 28, 1885.

1. **Charles F(rank) WILLETT**: b 1858, Ohio.
2. **William W. WILLETT**: b 1859, Ohio; m in Highland County, Ohio, on October 11, 1877, Sarah A. Garman. See next PA.3.2.1.7.2.
3. **Stella WILLETT**: b 1880, Ohio.
4. **Ida May WILLETT**: b 1862, Ohio; m in Highland County, Ohio, on October 1885, Salon L. Jackson.
5. **Mary E. WILLETT**: b 1863, Ohio.
6. **Jacob Wesley WILLETT**: b February 18, 1866, Hillsborough, Highland County, Ohio; married May Carr; d July 6, 1928 (Bible Record). See next PA.3.2.1.7.6.

PA.3.2.1.7.2
WILLIAM W. WILLETT and SARAH A. GARMAN
of Highland County, Ohio

William W. Willett was born in 1859, Ohio.

William W. Willett married in Highland County, Ohio, on October 11, 1877, Sarah A. Garman.

In 1880, William Willett and family were listed in the Liberty Township, Highland County, Ohio, census, as follows:

Willett	William	head	41	OH	
	Sarah	wife	21	OH	
	Harley	daughter	2	OH	(sic)
	Stella	daughter	5/12	OH	

1. **Harley** (daughter) **WILLETT**: b 1878, Ohio.
2. **Stella WILLETT**: b 1880, Ohio.

PA.3.2.1.7.6
JACOB WESLEY WILLETT and MAY CARR
of Highland County, Ohio

Jacob Wesley Willett was born on February 18, 1866, in Hillsborough, Highland County, Ohio.

In the January 9, 1868, will of Jacob Bishir is mentioned "Jacob <u>Willitt</u>, son of Nathan <u>Willitt</u>" three hundred dollars (1868 will of Jacob Bishir, Highland County, Ohio) and if he dies, to his mother "Elizabeth <u>Willitt</u>."

On March 6, 1871, his uncle, Gabriel Willett was appointed guardian of Jacob W. Willett, age 5 on February 18, 1871, in order to administer a legacy from the Estate of Jacob Bisher, grandfather (*Application for Appointment of Guardian, The State of Ohio*, March 6, 1871).

Jacob Wesley Willett married May Carr (b January 18, 1871; d April 22, 1947, buried Baptist Cemetery, New Market), the daughter of Aaron Carr (divorced).

Jacob W. Willett died July 6, 1928 (Bible Record).

1. **Beatrice WILLETT**: b September 6, 1904; m September 20, 1934, Walter Waites.

PA.3.2.1.8
GABRIEL CHANEY WILLETT and **MARY ANN BISHIR**
of Highland County, Ohio

Gabriel Chaney Willett was born April 1, 1837, in Ohio.
Gabriel Chaney Willett married in Highland County, Ohio,
June 21, 1859, Mary Ann Bishir (b July 4, 1839, Ohio; d
October 24, 1911), the daughter of Jacob Bishir (b October 17,
1796, Pennsylvania; d January 30, 1868, of dropsy) and
Elizabeth Corrington (b November 30, 1797, Warren County,
Ohio; d January 23, 1875, of dyspepsia).

In 1860, Gabriel Willett and family are listed in the
Highland County, Ohio, census, page 36 (not copied).

In the January 9, 1868, will of Jacob Bishir is mentioned
"daughter Mary Ann <u>Willitt</u>, wife of Gabriel <u>Willitt</u> my house
and lot in Highsborough, Highland County, Ohio" (1868 will of
Jacob Bishir, Highland County, Ohio).

They were living in Liberty Township, Highland County,
Ohio, in 1880.

In 1880, Gabriel <u>Willett</u> and family were listed in the
Liberty Township, Highland County, Ohio, census, 33-46-50-
36, as follows:

Willett	Gabriel	43	OH	
	Mary	40	OH	wife
	Edward L	19	OH	son
	Francis E	18	OH	daughter
	Jacob W	14	OH	son
	Lizzie	9	OH	daughter
	Mary C	6	OH	daughter
	Ira E	4	OH	son
	Sarah	1	OH	daughter
	Stephen	31	OH	Bo(arder)

Gabriel C. Willett died March 27, 1901.

(Typed page of Bible Record from Bedford County Histori-
cal Society listing "Children of Gabriel and Mary A. Willett"
filed as "Bible Record Gabriel Willett [1837-1901]").

1. **Edward Lyman WILLETT**: b November 30, 1859,
Ohio; m in Highland County, Ohio, on September 15, 1885,
Ida B. Griffith; d August 21, 1901. See next <u>PA.3.2.1.8.1</u>.

2. **Francis Ellen WILLETT**: b August 30, 1861, Ohio
(Bible Record); m Duckwall; d March 10, 1932 (Bible Record).

3. **Jacob Wesley WILLETT**: b February 16, 1866,
Hillsborough, Highland County, Ohio; d February 18, 1871,
age 5 years. His father is appointment administrator of his

estate March 6, 1871.

4. **Clara Elizabeth** ("Lizzie") **WILLETT**: b April 30, 1871, Ohio, Hillsborough, Highland County, Ohio (Bible Record), daughter of Gabriel Chaney Willett and Mary Ann Bishir (IGI); m DeHaas; d January 10, 1942 (Bible Record).

5. **Mary** ("Mollie") **Cecilia WILLETT**: b July 6, 1873, Ohio (Bible Record); died 1895, as "a young woman" (Bible Record), buried Prospect Cemetery.

6. **Ira Ernest WILLETT**: b December 23, 1875, Hillsborough, Highland County, Ohio, son of Gabriel Chaney Willett and Mary Ann Bishir (IGI); d March 12, 1962, buried Hamer Cemetery.

7. **Sarah** ("Sallie") **Alice WILLETT**: b April 1, 1879, Ohio (Bible Record); m Green; d May 9, 1944 (Bible Record).

PA.3.2.1.8.1

EDWARD LYMAN WILLETT and IDA B. GRIFFITH
of Highland County, Ohio

Edward Lyman Willett was born on November 30, 1859, Ohio (Bible Record).

Edward Lyman Willett married in Highland County, Ohio, on September 15, 1885, Ida B. Griffith (IGI); d August 21, 1901 (Bible Record).

1. **Ezra WILLETT**: b circa 1897; d February 18, 1899, age 1 year, 5 months, 2 days, buried F. and A. M. Cemetery, L'burg.

PA.3.2.2
ELISHA WILLETT of Bedford County, Pennsylvania

Elisha Willett was born in 1791, in Pennsylvania.

In 1820, <u>Elijah</u> <u>Willett</u> and family were residing at Athens, Bedford County, Pennsylvania, census, page 110, as follows:

1 male	26-45	1775-1794	Elijah age 29 b 1791
1 female	26-45	1775-1794	
1 female	10-16	1804-1810	
1 male	10-16	1804-1810	
1 male	0-10	1810-1820	
1 male	0-10	1810-1820	
1 male	0-10	1810-1820	
1 male	0-10	1810-1820	
1 female	0-10	1810-1820	
1 female	0-10	1810-1820	

PA.3.2.3
MARY WILLETT and JOSEPH P. WOODCOCK
of Fulton County, Pennsylvania

Mary Willett was born on August 21, 1801, Pennsylvania.

Miss Mary Willett married on March 27, 1821, Joseph P. Woodcock (b 1797, Maryland; d October 12, 1875, age 77 years, 10 months, 2 days, buried Wells Valley United Methodist Cemetery, Fulton County, Pennsylvania).

Mrs. Mary (Willett) Woodcock died in 1881.

(1850 Wells Township, Fulton County, Pennsylvania, census, dwelling 31).

1. **Rachel WOODCOCK**: b November 10, 1828. (1850 Fulton County census).

2. **Oliver WOODCOCK**: b December 18, 1833. (1850 Fulton County census).

3. **Susan WOODCOCK**: b December 5, 1836; m abt 1860 Joseph C. Alexander. (1850 Fulton County census).

4. **William W. WOODCOCK**: b September 18, 1840. (1850 Fulton County census).

5. **Emaline WOODCOCK**: b August 10, 1842; m abt 1865 William Beavens. (1850 Fulton County census).

PA.3.2.4
JOHN WILLETT of Highland County, Ohio

John Willett was born in 1804, Pennsylvania. He was reared in the state of Pennsylvania.

John Willett married 1st in Highland County, Ohio, on October 15, 1828, Catherine Miller, the daughter of John Miller. In 1830, John Willett and family were listed in the Highland County, Ohio, census, as follows:

1 male	20-30	1800-1810 John	age 26 b 1804
1 female	20-30	1800-1810 Catherine	
1 female	0-5	1825-1830 Rachel	age 0 b 1830

Mrs. Catherine Willett died about 1840.

John Willett married 2d in Highland County, Ohio, February 2, 1841, Nancy Landis (Landoss) (b 1815, Ohio).

The 1850 Union Township, Highland County, Ohio, census, page 193, No. 2085, lists the John Willett family, as follows:

Willett	John	46	m	PA	farmer
	Nancy	35	f	OH	
	Rachel	20	f	OH	
	Amey	15	m	OH	
	James	12	f	OH	
	John W.	8	m	OH	
	Louisa	4	f	OH	
	Samuel	2	m	OH	
	Mary	1	f	OH	

John Miller, in his will dated December 11, 1852, mentions the "children of my daughter Catherine Miller, deceased" (*Wills, Administrations, Guardianships, and Adoptions, of Highland County, Ohio 1805-1880*, page 87).

The John Willett family removed first to Illinois, then to Missouri, and finally, in 1868, to Iola, Allen County, Kansas.

In 1870, John Willett and family are listed in the Iola Township, Allen County, Kansas, census, page 61, dwelling 13-13, as follows:

Willett	John	head	64	PA farmer
	Nancy	wife	52	OH
	Samuel	son	22	OH works on farm
	Cynthia	daughter	16	IL attending sch.
	Ezra	son	14	IL works on farm
	Ira	son	11	MO attending sch.

John Willett died in 1882, at the age of 78 years, in Iola, Allen County, Kansas.

In 1900, Mrs. Nancy (Landis) Willett, age 82, born Ohio, was residing with her son, Ezra N. Willett, in Moran, Allen County, Kansas.

(Duncan, Lew Wallace, *History of Allen and Woodson Counties*, Kansas, 1901, page 221, "Ezra N. Willett;" *The Willett Families*, 1985, page 920).

Children of John Willett and his 1st wife, Catherine Miller:

1. **Rachel WILLETT:** b 1830, Ohio.
2. **Amy WILLETT:** b 1835, Ohio.
3. **James** (A.) **WILLETT:** b 1838, Ohio.

Children of John Willett and his 2d wife, Nancy Landoss:

4. **John Wesley WILLETT:** b April, 1843, Ohio; m abt 1882, Mary A. (b June, 1848, Wisconsin); of Seattle, Washington (1901). See next PA.3.2.4.4.
5. **Louisa** ("Lew") **E. WILLETT:** b 1846, Ohio; m C. A Sensor, of Denver, Colorado.
6. **Samuel E. WILLETT:** b 1848, Ohio; residing (1870) Allen County, Kansas; of Malone, New York (1901). (1870 Allen County, Kansas, census).
7. **Mary WILLETT:** b 1849, Ohio; m Jacob Fitzpatrick, of Wichita, Kansas (1901).
8. **Cynthia E. WILLETT:** b 1854, Illinois; of Denver, Colorado (1901). (1870 Allen County, Kansas, census).
9. **Ezra N. WILLETT:** b January 20, 1856, Pike County, Illinois; removed to Kansas (1868); m in Kansas on February 28, 1878, Amy McNaught (b July, 1857, Indiana); resided Moran, Allen County, Kansas. See next PA.3.2.4.9.
10. **Ira WILLETT:** b 1859, Missouri; of Miami, Florida (1901). (1870 Allen County, Kansas, census).
11. **Clay C. WILLETT:** b 1861, Missouri. (1870 Allen County, Kansas, census).

PA.3.2.4.4

JOHN WESLEY WILLETT and MARY A.
of King County, Washington

John Wesley Willett was born in April, 1843, in Ohio.

John Wesley Willett married about 1882 Mary A. (b June, 1848, Wisconsin).

In 1900, John W. Willett and family were listed in the Duwamish Precinct, King County, Washington, family census, as follows:

Willett	John W.	head	Apr 1843	57	OH
	Mary A.	wife	Jun 1848	52	WI
	Laura M.	Ad.	Apr 1889	11	NE

1. **Laura M. WILLETT** (adopted): b April, 1889, Nebraska.

PA.3.2.4.9

EZRA N. WILLETT and AMY MCNAUGHT
of Allen County, Kansas

Ezra N. Willett was born on January 20, 1856, in Pike County, Illinois.

In 1868, he came to Allen County, Kansas, with his parents.

Ezra N. Willett married on February 28, 1878, to Amy McNaught (b July, 1857, Indiana), the daughter of James R. McNaught of Moran, Allen County, Kansas.

In 1900, Mrs. Nancy (Landis) Willett, age 82, born Ohio, was residing with her son, Ezra N. Willett, in Moran, Allen County, Kansas.

(1900 Marmaton Township, Allen County, Kansas, census; Duncan, Lew Wallace, *History of Allen and Woodson Counties*, Kansas, 1901, page 221, "Ezra N. Willett).

1. **Zella P. WILLETT**: b August, 1884, Kansas. (1900 Allen County census).

2. **Ethel WILLETT**: b October, 1889, Kansas. (1900 Allen County census).

PA.3.2.6
THOMAS WILLETT and **RACHEL**
of Wells Valley, Fulton County, Pennsylvania

Thomas Willett was born September 4, 1802 (1810), in Pennsylvania (Bible Record).

Thomas Willett married about 1823 Rachel (b March 1, 1805 [1812, 1807] in Pennsylvania) (Bible Record).

In 1830, Thomas <u>Willet</u> and family were residing at Hopewell, Bedford County, Pennsylvania, census, page 79, as follows:

1 male	20-30	1800-1810 Thomas	age 28	b 1802
1 female	20-30	1800-1810 Rachel	age 25	b 1805
1 female	5-10	1820-1825 Sarah Ann	age 6	b 1824
1 male	0-5	1825-1830 Er	age 4	b 1826
1 male	0-5	1825-1830 David	age 0?	b 1830?

In 1840, Thomas <u>Willet</u> and family were listed in the Broad Township, Bedford County, Pennsylvania, census, page 296, as follows:

1 male	40-50	1790-1800 Thomas	age 38*	b 1802*
1 female	40-50	1790-1800 Rachel	age 35*	b 1805*
1 female	15-20	1820-1825 Sarah Ann	age 16	b 1824
1 female	15-20	1820-1825		
1 male	10-15	1825-1830 Er	age 14	b 1826
1 male	5-10	1830-1835 David	age 10	b 1830
1 female	5-10	1830-1835 Elizabeth	age 8	b 1832
1 female	0-5	1835-1840		
1 male	0-5	1835-1840 Elisha	age 6	b 1834
1male	0-5	1835-1840 William W	age 2	b 1838

In 1850, Thomas and Rachel, were in Fulton County, Pennsylvania. The 1850 census taker had a quirk of making a "curly Q" at the end of most names; most transcribers rendered this as an "S" to form "Willets." However, an examination of the original census shows clearly that the census taker meant to spell "Willet."

Willet	Thomas	40	m	PA	farmer $400
	Rachel	38	f	PA	
	David	19	m	PA	
	Elizabeth	17	f	PA	
	Elisha	15	m	PA	
	Demanst	14	m	PA	
	William W	12	m	PA	

Rachel	8	f	PA
Nancy J	7	f	PA
Allen B	5	m	PA

They resided in Wells Valley, evidently on land purchased from his father (or perhaps his father made a deed of gift).

In 1860, Thomas and Rachel Willett were listed in the Wells Township, Fulton County, Pennsylvania, census, No. 38, as follows:

Willet	Thomas	58	m	PA	farmer
	Rachel	53	f	PA	
	William	21	m	PA	
	Rachel	19	f	PA	
	Nancy	17	f	PA	
	Allan B	15	m	PA	

In 1870, Thomas Willett, age 68, was residing in the household of Walter McLain, age 25, and Nancy S. McLain, age 27 (his daughter) (1870 Wells Township, Fulton County, Pennsylvania, census, page 7, dwelling 42-42, taken June 8, 1870).

CIRCA 1870   CIRCA 1875
THOMAS WILLETT   THOMAS WILLETT

Thomas Willett died after 1870 in Fulton County, Pennsylvania.

(*The Willett Families*, 1985, page 242; 1850 Wells Township, Fulton County, Pennsylvania, census, page 94, dwelling 11-11; 1860 Wells Township, Fulton County, Pennsylvania, census, page 220, dwelling 22-23).

1. **Sarah Ann WILLETT**: b February 19, 1824 (Bible Record) (Fulton County), Pennsylvania.

2. **Er WILLETT**: b January 28, 1826 (Bible Record) (Fulton County), Pennsylvania.

3. **Elvirah WILLETT**: b December 28, 1828 (Bible Record), (Fulton County), Pennsylvania; of Wells Valley, Fulton County (1854). Miss Elvira Willett of Wells Valley, Fulton County, Pennsylvania, married in Cambria County, Pennsylvania, on Monday July 17, 1854, William Layton of Cambria County, Pennsylvania (*Marriages and Deaths, Cambria County, Pennsylvania, 1853-1858*).

4. **David WILLETT**: b January 18, 1831 (Bible Record), (Fulton County) Pennsylvania; a laborer. (1850 Wells Township, Fulton County, census).

5. **Elizabeth** ("Lizzie") **WILLETT**: b November 14, 1832 (Bible Record), (Fulton County) Pennsylvania; m Lockhard. (1850 Wells Township, Fulton County, census).

6. **Elisha S. WILLETT**: b August 25, 1834 (Bible Record), (Fulton County) Pennsylvania; m abt 1860 Mercy (b 1849, Iowa); in 1882, removed to Broadwater County, Montana; d after 1883. (1850 Wells Township, Fulton County, census). See next PA.3.2.6.6.

7. **Demaras** ("Demarest"; "Demaris") **WILLETT**: b August 22, 1836 (Bible Record), (Fulton County) Pennsylvania. (1850 Wells Township, Fulton County, census).

8. **William Washington** ("Wash") **WILLETT**: b November 29, 1838 (Bible Record), New Grenada, Fulton County, Pennsylvania; m in Chariton County, Missouri, November 22, 1870, Anna Earl (b August 18, 1846, New Salem, Pike County, Illinois; d May 14, 1907, Linn County, Missouri); d May 22, 1921, Marceline, Linn County, Missouri. (1850, 1860 Wells Township, Fulton County, census). See next PA.3.2.6.8.

9. **Rachel WILLETT**: b October 23, 1840 (Bible Record), (Fulton County) Pennsylvania. (1850, 1860 Wells Township, Fulton County, census).

10. **Nancy J. WILLETT**: b March 10, 1843 (Bible Record), (Fulton County) Pennsylvania; m abt 1865, Walter McLain (b 1845, Pennsylvania); resided (1921), Twin Falls, Idaho. (1850, 1860 Wells Township, Fulton County, census).

11. **Alleh** ("Allan") **Benjamin WILLETT**: b April 21, 1845

(Bible Record), (Fulton County) Pennsylvania; m at Mt. Sterling, Brown County, Illinois, on January 15, 187(4) Mary ("Mollie") Elizabeth Greenleaf (b 1845, Illinois; d 1921, Colville, Stevens County, Washington); d in 1924, Colville, Stevens County, Washington. See next PA.3.2.6.11.

CIRCA 1880
MRS. ELVIRA (WILLETT)
LAYTON

CIRCA 1880
MRS. "LIZZIE" (WILLETT)
LOCKHARD

PA.3.2.6.6
ELISHA S. WILLIT and MERCY
of Labette County, Kansas,
and Broadwater County, Montana

Elisha S. Willit was born on August 24, 1834 (Bible Record), in Pennsylvania.

In 1850, Elisha Willett was enumerated in his parents household in Fulton County, Pennsylvania.

It must have been soon afterwards that he began his westward journeying which led to the Iowa Territory. In the 1850s every-thing west of the Missouri River was still Indian country, wild and unsettled "frontier". White men only traversed the great plains and Rocky Mountains in great wagon trains in order to reach California or Oregon. And at this time period, the Mormons had only just begun settling in Utah.

The only white men to the west of the Missouri River were a few French-Canadian employees of the American Fur Company, some Rocky Mountain trappers, and a few of the hardest of buffalo hunters. Fort Laramie in Wyoming was a fort in name only. It was a "company" fort and seven hundred miles from the nearest American military outpost. In 1850, this expanse in the northwest was controlled by the Dakota Sioux nation, Snakes further westward to the Rockies; Arapaho, Comanche and Apache controlled the western deserts. Yet, by 1860, Kansas and Nebraska had become Territories, as had Utah and Arizona. It was into this forward edge of frontier civilization that Elisha Willett came, settled down and married.

Elisha Willett married about 1860, Mercy (b 1849, Iowa).

In 1860, Elisha Willit (Willet/Willett) and family are not listed in any of the census indexes for Iowa. Neither is he listed by name in the index in Missouri, Illinois, Minnesota. The closest possible name combination is an Eli L. Willitt at Millbrook Township, Peoria County, Illinois, page 809 (not copied).

Elisha Willett was living in Iowa from 1861 (birth of first child), and presumably would have been there at least a few years earlier in order to meet and court his future wife. They remained until about 1864 when they removed to Kansas.

In 1870, Elisha Willet and family are listed in the Sarcoxie Township, Jefferson County, Kansas, census, page 491 (not copied).

In 1880, Elisha <u>Willit</u> and family are listed in the Parsons, Labette County, Kansas, census, as follows:

Willit	Elisha	45	PA	
	Mercy	31	IA	wife
	Maggie	19	IA	daughter
	Clara	17	IA	daughter
	Phillip	15	KS	son
	Emma	12	KS	daughter
	Mimi	7	KS	daughter
	Kirby	5	KS	son

In June, 1882, Elisha Willett and family removed first to Radersburg, Broadwater County, Montana, and then in 1883 to Townsend, Broadwater County, Montana. Helena, Montana, is only 40 miles northwest of these towns, while Bozeman is about 40 miles southeast.

On July 3, 1890, Elisha S. Willett, wife Mercy W., of Montana, applied for and received a Civil War Military Pension, Certificate No. 409,024, for his service in Company D, 28th Iowa Infantry ("Civil War Pension Applications").

1. **Margaret** ("Maggie") **WILLETT**: b 1861, Iowa; m 1905 as his 2d wife, James Edgar Kanouse (b December 18, 1843, Woodstock, New Jersey; 1930), Montana Pioneer Jurist and State G.A.R. Commander; resided (1937) Townsend, Montana. (1880 Labette County, Kansas, census) (Obit 1930: "J. E. Kanouse, Montana Pioneer Jurist, and State G. A. R. Commander dies").

2. **Clara WILLETT**: b 1863, Iowa.

3. **Phillip WILLETT**: b 1865, Kansas; resided (1937) Townsend, Montana.

4. **Ulysses R. WILLETT**: b June, 1866, Kansas; living (1900) Billings, Yellowstone County, Montana. In 1902, <u>Uulysses P.</u> Willett is noted as having removed to Baldwin, Montana ("Billings City Directory, 1902, page 150).

5. **Emma WILLETT**: b 1868, Kansas.

6. **Mimi WILLETT**: b 1873, Kansas.

7. **Kirby Allen WILLETT**: b May 3, 1875 (November, 1876), Parsons, Labette County, Kansas; m abt 1898 Lillian E. (b April, 1882, Montana); d September 15, 1937, Baker, California. See next <u>PA.3.2.6.6.7.</u>

PA.3.2.6.6.7
KIRBY ALLEN WILLETT and **LILLIAN E.**
of Montana

Kirby ("Kirley") Allen Willett was born on May 3, 1875 (November, 1876), Parsons, Labette County, Kansas.

> "*He was born in Parsons, Kansas, May 3, 1875, and came to Radersburg in June, 1882 and to Townsend in 1883 when he started working for the Northern Pacific wiping engines when a very small boy. When 15 he went to work for the Southern Pacific and for a short time helped build the W. A. Clark road between Salt Lake and Los Angeles*" (Obituary, Kirley Allen Willett, 1937).

Kirby Allen Willett married about 1898 Lillian E. (b April, 1882, Montana).

In 1900 Kirby A. Willett and family are listed in the Billings, Yellowstone County, Montana, census, as follows:

Willett Kirby A. Nov 1876 KS 25 Northern Pac. RR
         Lillian E. Apr 1882 MT 18 wife
         Ulysses R. Jun 1866 KS 34 brother

In 1900-1901, K. C. Willett is noted as working at N. P. (Northern Pacific) roundhouse, with his residence at 34th Street and 1st Avenue South ("Billings City Directory, 1900-1901, page 101).

> "*Mr. Willett, an expert railway engineer was one of the first to operate the new fast streamline trains for the Southern Pacific and had reached the top passenger run from Las Vegas, Nevada, to Yermo, California, which run he was still to take when he was killed in an automobile accident*" (Obituary, Kirley Allen Willett, 1937).

Kirby Allen Willett died on September 15, 1937, in Baker, California.

1. (daughter) **WILLETT**: m O. E. Larson; resided (1937) Los Angeles, California.
2. **Lucille WILLETT**: m Wells; (1937) resided Visalia, California.

PA.3.2.6.8
WILLIAM WASHINGTON WILLETT and **ANNA M. EARL**
of Chariton County, and Linn County, Missouri

William Washington ("Wash") Willett was born November 29, 1838 (Bible Record), New Grenada, Fulton County, Pennsylvania.

William ("Wash") Willett mustered on August 17, 1861, Company B, 147th Pennsylvania Volunteers. He was promoted to 1st Sergeant on March 1, 1863. He was in the three days fighting of July 1st, 2nd, and 3rd, 1863, at Gettysburg, Pennsylvania, and later marched with General Sherman to the sea. He was promoted to 2d Lieutenant Company B, 147th Pennsylvania Volunteers. On May 25, 1864, he was wounded at New Hope Church, Georgia. He was demobilized on April 7, 1865. He is also reported as serving as a Lieutenant in Company O, 28th Pennsylvania Volunteers.

CIRCA 1865
LIEUTENANT WILLIAM "WASH" WILLETT

William Willett married in Chariton County, Missouri, November 22, 1870, Miss Anna M. Earl (b August 18, 1846, New Salem, Pike County, Illinois; d May 14, 1907, Linn County, Missouri).

In 1880, W. W. Willett and family are listed in the Clark Township, Chariton County, Missouri, census, as follows:

Willett	W. W.	head	41	PA
	Ann M.	wife	34	IL
	Albert G	son	7	MO
	Nora L	dau	2	MO

On June 21, 1880, William W. Willett applied for and received a Civil War Military Pension, Certificate No. 375,157, for his service in Company B, 147th Pennsylvania Infantry ("Civil War Pension Applications").

CIRCA 1900
SITTING:
MRS. ANN WILLETT
WILLIAM W. WILLETT
STANDING:
ALBERT G. WILLETT
NORA LEE WILLETT

In 1913, Washington Willett visited the Grand Army of the Republic (G.A.R.) reunion in 1913 in Gettysburg.

William Willett died May 22, 1921, age 82 years, 5 months, 23 days, in Marceline, Linn County, Missouri, at the home of his son, A. G. Willett. William Willett is buried in the Mt. Olivet Cemetery (1921 Obituary, William Washington Willett, Linn County, Missouri).

CIRCA 1915
WILLIAM "WASH" WILLETT

1. **Myrtle A. WILLETT**: d infant age 11 months.

2. **Albert G. WILLETT**: b 1873, Missouri; of Marceline, Linn County, Missouri; m Una May (b 1872; d 1952); resides (1921) Marceline; d 1955, Linn County, Missouri. See next PA.3.2.6.8.2.

3. **Nora Lee WILLETT**: b January 19, 1878, Chariton County, Missouri; m June 16, 1908, Charles D. Williams (d 1948, Linn County, Missouri); resides (1921) Missouri; d 1924, age 48 years, 3 months, 24 days, buried Mt. Olivet Cemetery, Linn County, Missouri. See next PA.3.2.6.8.3.

PA.3.2.6.8.2
ALBERT G. WILLETT and **UNA MAY**
of Linn County, Missouri

Albert G. Willett was born in 1873, in Missouri.
He resided at Marceline, Linn County, Missouri.
Albert G. Willett married about 1895, Una May (b 1872; d 1952).

SEATED: BERT WILLETT AND UNA MAY
STANDING: BEULAH, RALPH, HELEN

OCTOBER 6, 1947, 50TH WEDDING ANNIVERSARY
UNA MAY AND BERT WILLETT

Albert G. Willett died in 1955, Linn County, Missouri.

1. **Beulah WILLETT:** b 1900; d 1979.
2. **Ralph L. WILLETT:** b 1906; d 19--.
3. **Helen WILLETT:** b abt 1911.

PA.3.2.6.8.3
NORA LEE WILLETT and CHARLES D. WILLIAMS
of Linn County, Missouri

Nora Lee Willett was born on January 19, 1878, Chariton County, Missouri.

Miss Nora Lee Willett married in June 16, 1908, Charles D. Williams (d 1948, Linn County, Missouri) of Marceline, Linn County, Missouri; resides (1921) Missouri.

CIRCA 1909
NORA WILLETT WILLIAMS, CHARLES D. WILLIAMS
VIRGINIA WILLIAMS

Mrs. Nora Lee (Willett) Williams died in 1924, age 48 years, 3 months, 24 days, and is buried in the Mt. Olivet Cemetery, Linn County, Missouri.

1. **Virginia Lee WILLIAMS**: b 1908; m Byars; resided (1948) Fort Worth, Texas.
2. **Dempsey Willett WILLIAMS**: b 1909; resided (1948) Argentine.
3. **Marguerite Ann WILLIAMS**: b 1911; m Knox; resided (1948) Monet, Missouri.

PA.3.2.6.11
ALLEN BENJAMIN WILLETT
and MARY ELIZABETH GREENLEAF
of Altamont, Effingham County, Illinois, and
Colville, Stevens County, Washington

Allen Benjamin Willett was born in April 21, 1845 (Bible Record), in Arbisonia, Pennsylvania.

Allen B. Willett married at Mt. Sterling, Brown County, Illinois, on January 15, 187(4), Mary ("Mollie") Elizabeth Greenleaf (b 1845, Illinois; d 1921, Colville, Stevens County, Washington, and is buried in the Highland Cemetery, Colville).

CIRCA 1875

A. B. WILLETT   ALLEN WILLETT AND FRIEND

They resided at Altamont, Effingham County, Illinois.

In 1880, Allen B. <u>Willitt</u> and family were enumerated in the Altamont, Effingham County, Illinois, census, as follows:

Willitt	Allen B.	35	PA	
	Mollie E.	35	IL	wife
	Maude	5	IL	daughter
	Lola	4	IL	daughter
	Dan	2	IL	son
	Ralph	6/12	IL	son

CIRCA 1880

MARY GREENLIEF WILLETT   ALLEN BENJAMIN WILLETT

CIRCA 1880
MARY WILLETT
ALLEN WILLETT

CIRCA 1885
THE ALLEN BENJAMIN WILLETT FAMILY
ALLEN WILLETT, DON, RALPH, ROLLA
MAUD, LOLA, MRS. MARY WILLETT

CIRCA 1895
BACK ROW: MAUD, RALPH, ROLLA, LOLA
FRONT ROW: ALLEN, MARY, DON

LOLA WILLETT   MAUD WILLETT

The Allen Willett family was supposed to be related to wealthy Chicago, Illinois, and California Willett families. They were related to the Humphrey W. Willett (see PA.3.2.7.3), of Kern County, California, and Cambridge W. Willett (see PA.3.2.7.7) of Los Angeles, California, and George Howard Willett (see PA.3.2.9.4.5) of Detroit, Michigan. Whether or not these are the "wealthy" Willett families of family tradition is unknown at this time (1994).

About 1908, or 1909, Allen Benjamin and Mary Willett came to Colville, Stevens County, Washington, Washington, where their three sons, Don, Ralph, and Rolla, had opened a bicycle shop.

They owned a vacation lake resort at Lake Thomas, Pend Oreille Lakes, Washington. Their advertisement stated, "Furnished cottages, floating bathing dock, steel boats, bathing suits to rent, meals served". They were Methodist.

CIRCA 1917
THE ALLEN BENJAMIN WILLETT FAMILY OF WASHINGTON

BACK ROW:
MAUD, ROLLA AND WIFE ROXIE, RALPH
VIOLET STOUT, NOVA AND DON WILLETT

FRONT ROW:
VERA, ALLEN B. WILLETT, LOLA, GERALD,
AND MARY ELIZABETH (GREENLEAF) WILLETT

Allen B. Willett died in April, 1924, at Colville, Stevens County, Washington, and is buried in the Highland Cemetery, Colville.

CIRCA 1920
ALLEN B. AND MARY E. WILLETT
AT THE LAKES

1. **Maud** ("Maude") **A. WILLETT**: b April 23, 1875, Altamont, Effingham County, Illinois; spinster; she was an office secretary at Willett Brothers, Inc; d February 4, 1959, Colville, Stevens County, Washington, and is buried in the Highland Cemetery, Colville. (1880 Effingham County census).

2. **Lola I. WILLETT**: b March 16, 1876, Altamont, Effingham County, Illinois; spinster; d June 18, 1959, Colville, Stevens County, Washington, and is buried in the Highland Cemetery, Colville, Stevens County, Washington. (1880 Effingham County census).

3. **Don Roy WILLETT**: b September 4, 1877, Altamont, Effingham County, Illinois; m Nova Feely (b 1886; d 1957, buried in the Colville Cemetery); worked at power plant at Colville; d March 19, 1945, and is buried in the Colville Cemetery. (1880 Effingham County census). See next PA.3.2.6.11.3.

4. **Ralph Volney WILLETT**: b October 5, 1880, Altamont, Effingham County, Illinois; m June 9, 1918, Wanda Margaret Bell (b August 16, 1895, Vanwert, Ohio; d May 19, 1962, Vanwert, Van Wert County, Ohio); d June 25, 1961, Clarkson, Asotin County, Washington. (1880 Effingham County census). See next PA.3.2.6.11.4.

5. **Rolla Abraham WILLETT**: b June 3, 1882, Altamont, Effingham County, Illinois; m June 17, 1916, Roxie Rosalind Gilbert (b October 21, 1896, Meredosia, Illinois; d August 29, 1986, Colville, Stevens County, Washington); d September 30, 1951, Colville, Stevens County, Washington, buried Seattle, Washington. See next PA.3.2.6.11.5.

PA.3.2.6.11.3
DON ROY WILLETT and NOVA FEELY
of Colville, Stevens County, Washington

Don Roy Willett was born September 4, 1877, Altamont, Effingham County, Illinois.

In March, 1908, Don Roy Willett removed to Colville, Stevens County, Washington, with his brothers, Ralph and Rolla A. Willett, as the following Colville "Examiner" newspaper item attests:

> "*Ralph, Don and Rolla Willett of Anderson, Indiana, arrived here this week and have purchased the Gilliland tract of five acres at the north end of Main Street. They will erect a residence and bring their parents here from Indiana.*"

Don Roy Willett married Nova Feely (b 1886; d 1957, and is buried in the Colville Cemetery).

He worked at the power plant at Colville, Stevens County, Washington.

Don Willett died March 19, 1945, and is buried in the Colville Cemetery, Stevens County, Washington.

1. **Vera WILLETT**: b June 13, 1907; school teacher; m Blye; d 1987, and is buried in the Highland Cemetery, Colville, Stevens County, Washington.

2. **Gerald M. WILLETT**: b August 17, 1910, Myers Falls, Washington; m Lillian Beardsley. See next PA.3.2.6.11.3.2.

PA.3.2.6.11.3.2
GERALD M. WILLETT and **LILLIAN BEARDSLEY**
of Stevens County, Washington

Gerald M. Willett was born August 17, 1910, Myers Falls, Washington.
Gerald M. Willett married Lillian Beardsley.
He is an insurance agent.

    1. **Nova Dawn WILLETT**: b March 18, 1947, Colville, Stevens County, Washington; m Greg Beaman (b November 27, 1947). See next PA.3.2.6.11.3.2.1.
    2. **Rex WILLETT**: b June 22, 1949, Colville, Stevens County, Washington; m Linda Raska (b February 16, 1954, Colville, Stevens County, Washington). See next PA.3.2.6.-11.3.2.2.

PA.3.2.6.11.3.2.1
NOVA DAWN WILLETT and **GREG BEAMAN**

Nova Dawn Willett was born on March 18, 1947, Colville, Stevens County, Washington.
Miss Nova Dawn Willett married Greg Beaman (b November 27, 1947).

    1. **Cole BEAMAN**: b March 22, 1972.
    2. **Katie BEAMAN**: b November 12, 1981.

PA.3.2.6.11.3.2.2
REX WILLETT and **LINDA RASKA**
of Spokane, Washington

Rex Willett was born on June 22, 1949, Colville, Stevens County, Washington.
Rex Willett married Linda Raska (b February 16, 1954, Colville, Stevens County, Washington).

    1. **Jeff WILLETT**: b December 27, 1978.
    2. **Keelan WILLETT**: b December 28, 1983.

PA.3.2.6.11.4
RALPH VOLNEY WILLETT and **WANDA MARGARET BELL**
of Lewiston, Nez Perce County, Idaho

Ralph Volney Willett was born on October 5, 1880, at Alta-
mont, Effingham County, Illinois.
He removed with his parents to Anderson, Madison
County, Indiana.
From the fall of 1903 until March 28, 1904, he worked as
a salesman for Morrell and Campbell, Groceries, Queensware,
Shoes, Hosiery, and Notions, at Blockton, Iowa.
From March 15, 1906, until February 1, 1907, he worked
at the Philadelphia Quartz Company in Anderson, Madison
County, Indiana where he received a letter of recommendation
stating "that Ralph V. Willett worked for this Company as
Fireman, using automatic chain grate stokers under water-
tube boiler ..."
In March, 1908, Ralph V. Willett removed to Colville,
Stevens County, Washington, with his brothers, Don Roy and
Rolla A. Willett, as the following Colville "Examiner" newspaper
items attests:

> *"Ralph, Don and Rolla Willett of Anderson, Indiana,*
> *arrived here this week and have purchased the Gilliland*
> *tract of five acres at the north end of Main Street. They will*
> *erect a residence and bring their parents her from Indiana."*

On February, 1929, the following newspaper article
documents the Willett family:

> *"One of the few business firms which has shared in the*
> *life of Colville and Stevens County for two decades is Willett*
> *Bros. For 21 years Rolla A. Willett and Ralph V. Willett*
> *have carried on their business in Colville as a partnership.*
> *The two boys arrived in Colville in March, 1908, from*
> *Anderson, Indiana, when bicycles were all the go. In look-*
> *ing around town they decided that Colville needed a bicycle*
> *and repair shop, so they rented the basement of the build-*
> *ing now occupied by the Smith Studio on Main and First,*
> *and opened up, repairing anything that came along from the*
> *family teapot to the family carriage.*
> *Electricity was then coming into general use and T. A.*
> *Winter persuaded the boys to buy an electric lighting and*
> *supply business and to move to the light company substa-*
> *tion location where John Carlin's residence now stands ...*
> *In December, 1912, Willett Bros. signed their first con-*
> *tract with Henry Ford to sell ten of his "Lizzies" during*
> *1913. It looked like ten would glut the market but they*
> *were all sold and the market cried for more. J. A. Roch-ford*

bought the first Ford. Ralph went to Spokane and drove it up through the mud and rain, and the next day Mr. Rochford took delivery in all its shining brassy splendor with the stains of the country road washed away.

There were five cars in town. Dr. L. B. Harvey, Jack Mohney, Bell and McFarland had Maxwells; T. A. Winter had a car, and Dr. Peck had a little white Buick which wound up on the side, and made its home in the rear of Willett Bros. shop on First Avenue, and were all its many eccentricities were attended" (The Colville Examiner, Saturday, February 9, 1929, page 8).

Ralph Volney Willett married in Colville, Stevens County, Washington, on June 9, 1918, Wanda Margaret Bell (b August 16, 1895, Vanwert, Ohio; d May 19, 1962, Spokane, Washington, and is buried in the Lewiston Normal Hill Cemetery).

Continuing the 1929 newspaper article:

"In 1913, Willett Bros. were sold on automobiles and moved the shop to Main Street, occupying the building where the City garage now does business, and a growing business necessitated two additions in quick succession.

The day of the automobile was here and Willett Bros. found their quarters cramped. The early cars needed many attentions and tires were good if they went 2,000 miles. They looked for larger space and no buildings being available in 1917 they purchased the Hofstetter two story frame and two lots on the corner of Main and Beech, razed the frame building and erected the one-story brick of their present Colville establishment ...

Two branch service stations were opened in 1925 at Addy and Kettle Falls, and in 1928, Ralph Willett removed to Lewiston, Idaho, where a wholesale branch was established and during the same year the firm opened a wholesale and retail store in Spokane on Second Avenue in charge of Guy S. Jameson.

The Ford contract was given up in 1926, and for two years the firm sold Willys Overland and Knight cars, but in 1928 devoted all of its energy and attentions to car service, accessories, repair and storage. At one time the firm sold over 50% of all cars registered in the county, and sold as many as 150 cars in a year.

In January, 1921, 21 years after the establishment of the bicycle repair shop, the firm incorporated under the name of Willett Bros., Inc., to continue the same policy of service that prospered the business of Willett Bros., the partnership. Officers in the new company are R. A. Willett, president and general manger; R. V. Willett, vice president; G. S. Jameson, secretary; Willett, treasurer and assistant secretary. The company also includes Don R. Willett, manager in charge of equipment and gasoline and oil distribu-

tion" (The Colville Examiner, Saturday, February 9, 1929, page 8).

RALPH WILLETT

They resided at Lewiston, Nez Perce County, Idaho.

In 1956, Ralph V. Willett retired from Willett Bros., Inc., and the business was continued in the family by his sons, Robert J., Keith V., and Fred A. Willett.

Ralph Volney Willett died on June 25, 1961, at Clarkson, Asotin County, Washington, and is buried in the Lewiston Normal Hill Cemetery.

Clarkson, Washington, and Lewiston, Idaho, are twin cities separated by the Snake River.

WANDA BELL WILLETT

1. **Robert** ("Bob") **John WILLETT**: b November 28, 1920, Colville, Stevens County, Washington; m in Lewiston, Idaho, June 26, 1948, Margaret Evelyn Zettle (b June 26, 1919, Mitchell, South Dakota; d January 20, 1988, Port Townsend, Washington), the daughter of John W. Zettle and Rose Atherton; d January 20, 1988, Port Ludlow, Washington. See next PA.3.2.6.11.4.1.

2. **Keith Volney WILLETT**: b November 25, 1922, Colville, Stevens County, Washington; m Spokane, Washington, on March 7, 1950, Loretta ("Laura") Marie Sand (b July 7, 1927, Greenwald, Minnesota), the daughter of Peter Sand and Ida Vornbrock. See next PA.3.2.6.11.4.2.

3. **Frederick** ("Fred") **Allen WILLETT**: b May 10, 1924, Colville, Stevens County, Washington; m 1st in Lewiston, Idaho, on March 27, 1955, Rita Lee McCracken (divorced), the daughter of Virgil McCracken; m 2d Linda Smith. See next PA.3.2.6.11.4.3.

PA.3.2.11.4.1
ROBERT JOHN WILLETT and MARGARET EVELYN ZETTLE

Robert ("Bob") John Willett was born November 28, 1920, Colville, Stevens County, Washington. He graduated from Lewiston High School.

BOB
KEITH - FRED

Robert John Willett married in Lewiston, Idaho, June 26, 1948, Margaret Evelyn Zettle (b June 26, 1919, Mitchell, South Dakota; d January 20, 1988, Port Townsend, Washington), the daughter of John W. Zettle and Rose Atherton.

He was a part owner of an auto parts store.

Robert John Willett died January 20, 1988, at Port Ludlow, Washington.

MAY, 1968
MARGARET - SHARON - ROBERT

1. **Sharon WILLETT**: b October 27, 1950, Lewiston, Idaho; m Rodney Edwards. See next <u>PA.3.2.11.4.1</u>.

2. **John William WILLETT** (adopted): b April 4, 1951, Nuremberg, Germany; graduated Lewiston High School; m June 22, 1974, Pamela Jean Willoughby (divorced).

PA.3.2.11.4.1
SHARON WILLETT and **RODNEY EDWARDS**

Sharon Willett was born on October 27, 1950, Lewiston, Idaho.

Miss Sharon Willett married Rodney Edwards.

1. **Melissa Ann EDWARDS:**
2. **James Robert EDWARDS:**
3. **Fred Russell EDWARDS:**
4. **Amanda Kay EDWARDS:**

RODNEY EDWARDS and SHARON (WILLETT) EDWARDS

PA.3.2.6.11.4.2
KEITH VOLNEY WILLETT and **LORETTA MARIE SAND**
of Plummer, Benewah County, Idaho

Keith Volney Willett was born November 25, 1922, Colville, Stevens County, Washington.   In 1928, his parents moved from Colville to Lewiston, Idaho.   At the time, his father, Ralph Willett, and uncle Rolla Willett divided the business which was located in Colville, Washington.   Rolla kept the shell bulk plant operation and Ralph invested in the Lewiston Automotive Parts business.   In 1934, Ralph Willett branched out with a store in Moscow, Idaho.

BOB
KEITH - FRED

In 1941, Keith Willett graduated from Lewiston High School. He attended the Northern Idaho College (LCSC today) for one year before going into the service during World War II. He served in the South Pacific as a Staff Sergeant in the Signal Corps, and was one of the first troops in Japan after the surrender. He was stationed at Nagoya, Japan, and then Kyoto, before being discharged.

Keith then returned to the family business. In 1948, Willett Bros., was incorporated with his father, and brothers, Robert ("Bob"), and Fred Willett. Bob was in sales, Fred was credit manager, and Keith was store manager and did the purchasing.

Keith Volney Willett married in Spokane, Washington, on March 7, 1950, Loretta ("Laura") Marie Sand (b July 7, 1927, Greenwald, Minnesota), the daughter of Peter Sand and Ida Vornbrock.

In 1975, Fred and Keith purchased Bob's share of the business. In 1978, a store was opened in Grangeville, Idaho. In 1986, Laura and Keith purchased Fred's share. They have lived in the same house at 309 3rd Street, Lewiston, Idaho, all their married life (only 43 years to date). They were involved in school activities and scouting programs for 25 years. Laura and Keith both advanced to adult scouting and became the first couple in the United States to receive the Silver Beaver Award together. Keith has sung in the First United Methodist Church choir for over 50 years and was on the Church Board for many years. He was a board member of the Tri-State Hospital, Clarkson, Washington, for nine years, and on the Board of Independent Welding Distributors was nine years ending his service there in 1993.

Keith is semi-retired after surgery. Lately, he has been remodeling the Lake Cabin on Lake Chatcolet in Benewah County, Idaho. This was begun in 1983, and finished in 1988. It is winterized, and Keith and Laura live there most of the year. Laura is still credit manager in the Willett family business, traveling to Lewiston regularly to help with the store.

Keith and Laura are involved in the city of Chatcolet. It is the largest Idaho city in area, but only has 72 residents. It is also a city within a state park, Heyburn State Park. Chatcolet has a city council, Laura is city clerk, and Keith is one of the 14 councilmen.

DAN - DEBRA - LAURA - KEITH - STEVE

CHRISTMAS, 1992
DEBRA ANN, STEVE, KEITH WILLETT
DAN, LAURA, MIKE

1. **Steven John WILLETT**: b July 16, 1950, Lewiston, Idaho; m December 31, 1989, Theresa Beavert (b November 23, 1954, Lewiston, Idaho), the daughter of Alvin Beavert and Louise. See next PA.3.2.6.11.4.2.1.

2. **Daniel** ("Dan") **Mark WILLETT**: b March 3, 1954; m Debbie Spence (divorced February, 1994); m May, 1995, Dona Pogue (divorced, 1996).

3. **Debra Ann WILLETT**: b March 12, 1953, Lewiston, Idaho; m 1st in Redland, California, May 3, 1974, Robert Simmons (b June 6, 1950, South Carolina) (divorced); m 2d in June, 1997, Dale Shell. See next PA.3.2.6.11.4.2.3.

4. **Michael James WILLETT**: b July 8, 1963, Clarkson, Washington; m in Lewiston, Idaho, June 8, 199x, Tina K. Grant (b September 7, 1962, Grangeville, Idaho), the daughter of Larry F. Grant and Sandra. See next PA.3.2.6.11.4.2.4.

KEITH V. WILLETT - LORETTA MARIE (SAND) WILLETT
1994
At our wedding meeting in Coeur d'Alene, Idaho

PA.3.2.6.11.4.2.1
STEVEN JOHN WILLETT and THERESA BEAVERT
of Idaho

Steven John Willett was born on July 16, 1950, at Lewiston, Idaho. He graduated University of Idaho.

Steven J. Willett married on December 31, 1989, Theresa Beavert (b November 23, 1954, Lewiston, Idaho), the daughter of Alvin Beavert and Louise.

Steven Willett spent all his life in Lewiston. In 1968, he graduated from Lewiston High School. He then spent one year at the University of Idaho. He then enlisted in the Air Force and after basic training he graduated in Entomology and spent two years at Norton Air Force Base. He was on the U.S.A.F. alpine ski team, a member of the Air Force Chess Team, and captain of the Norton Air Force Base Golf team. He then was assigned to Guam for one and one-half years. When he completed his Air Force tour of duty, he entered and graduated from the Lewis-Clark State College (1978) with a degree in business and accounting. He was on the Dean's lists during his college days.

Steven Willett went to work for Willett Bros., Inc., and has worked in all the jobs including the outside sales. He, along with his brother Mike Willett, are now the General Managers of the Lewiston Warehouse store of Willett Brothers, Inc.

Theresa was raised in Lewiston and graduated from Lewiston High School (1973). She then went to Phoenix, Arizona, graduating from Arizona State University in 1981. During her collegiate days, Theresa worked various jobs including waitressing, clerical, A. A. A., secretary to the President of the Mercedes dealership. She started in night school, and taking one class at a time completed half her requirements. Then she completed the last two years going full time completing her last semester on the Dean's List with a major in Elementary Education. She met Steve Willett on a trip to Lewiston during the Christmas season.

1. **Joshua WILLETT**: b September 17, 1988.
2. **Joseph Ryan WILLETT**: b March 6, 1994.

PA.3.2.6.11.4.2.3
DEBRA ANN WILLETT
of Lewiston, Idaho

Debra ("Debbie") Ann Willett was born March 12, 1953, at Lewiston, Idaho.

Miss Debra Ann Willett married 1st in Redland, California, May 3, 1974, Robert Simmons (b June 6, 1950, South Carolina) (divorced).

She is a school teacher, Lewiston, Idaho.

Mrs, Debra (Willett) Simmons married 2nd in June, 1997, Dale Shell.

1. **Stacey SIMMONS**: b August 15, 1977, Georgetown, South Carolina.
2. **Jennifer SIMMONS**: b May 4, 1981, Lewiston, Idaho.

STACY AND JENNIFER SIMMONS

PA.3.2.6.11.4.3
MICHAEL JAMES WILLETT and TINA K. GRANT

Michael ("Mike") James Willett was born on July 8, 1963, Clarkson, Washington.

Michael James Willett married in Lewiston, Idaho, June 8, 199x, Tina K. Grant (b September 7, 1962, Grangeville, Idaho), the daughter of Larry F. Grant and Sandra. He is a purchasing agent for Willett Brothers, Inc., and she is a computer expert for Willett Brothers, Inc.

TINA AND MIKE WILLETT

PA.3.2.6.11.4.3
FREDERICK ALLEN WILLETT
of Lewiston, Idaho

Frederick ("Fred") Allen Willett was born May 10, 1924, Colville, Stevens County, Washington. He graduated from Lewiston High School and in 1952 from the University of Idaho.

Frederick Allen Willett married 1st in Lewiston, Idaho, on March 27, 1955, Rita Lee McCracken (divorced), the daughter of Virgil McCracken.

Frederick A. Willett married 2d Linda Smith.

He retired as President of Willett Brothers, Inc.

1. **Paul WILLETT**: b January 18, 1957, Lewiston, Idaho; m Mary Louise, graduated University of Idaho; attorney. See next PA.3.2.6.11.4.3.

2. **Kent WILLETT**: b May 26, 1958, Lewiston, Idaho; graduated Lewiston High School.

3. **Stacey WILLETT**: b September 16, 1961, Lewiston, Idaho; graduated Lewiston High School.

PA.3.2.6.11.4.3
PAUL WILLETT and MARY LOUISE

Paul Willett was born on January 18, 1957, Lewiston, Idaho.

Paul Willett married Mary Louise, graduated University of Idaho; attorney.

1. **Paul McCracken** ("Mac") **WILLETT**: b March, 1990.

PA.3.2.6.11.5
ROLLA ABRAHAM WILLETT
and **ROXIE ROSALIND GILBERT**
of Colville, Stevens County, Washington

Rolla Abraham Willett was born June 3, 1882, in Alta-mont, Effingham County, Illinois.

In March, 1908, Rolla A. Willett removed to Colville, Stevens County, Washington, with his brothers, Ralph and Don Roy Willett, as the following Colville "Examiner" newspaper items attests:

> *"Ralph, Don and Rolla Willett of Anderson, Indiana, arrived here this week and have purchased the Gilliland tract of five acres at the north end of Main Street. They will erect a residence and bring their parents here from Indiana."*

Rolla Abraham Willett married June 17, 1916, Roxie Resilient Gilbert (b October 21, 1896, Meredosia, Illinois; d August 29, 1986, Colville, Stevens County, Washington, buried in the Acacia Mausoleum, Seattle, Washington).

He owned an automobile dealership and gas distributor company.

Rolla A. Willett died September 30, 1951, Colville, Stevens County, Washington, buried Seattle, Washington, in the Acacia Mausoleum.

1. **Betty Jean WILLETT**: b October 25, 1918, Colville, Stevens County, Washington; m July 4, 1943, Willis N. Collins (b January 17, 1917, Palermo, New York). See next PA.3.2.6.11.5.1.

2. **Neva Adelle WILLETT**: b December 3, 1922, Colville, Stevens County, Washington; m September 8, 1945, John Harrison Craig (b January 23, 1920, Memphis, Tennessee). See next PA.3.2.6.11.5.2.

PA.3.2.6.11.5.1
BETTY JEAN WILLETT and **WILLIS N. COLLINS**
of Mt. Vernon, Washington

Betty Jean Willett was born October 25, 1918, Colville, Stevens County, Washington.

Miss Betty Jean Willett married on July 4, 1943, Willis N. Collins (b January 17, 1917, Palermo, New York). She owns her own office supply business.

1. **Kevin Rolla COLLINS**: b April 24, 1952, Mt. Vernon, Washington; m September 13, 1975, Joan Ellen Bullard (b August 1, 1953, Tacoma, Washington); d December 12, 1991, Bellview, Washington, buried Acacia Mausoleum. See next PA.3.2.6.11.5.1.1.

PA.3.2.6.11.5.1.1
KEVIN ROLLA COLLINS and JOAN ELLEN BULLARD

Kevin Rolla Collins was born on April 24, 1952, Mt. Vernon, Washington.

Kevin Rolla Collins married on September 13, 1975, Joan Ellen Bullard (b August 1, 1953, Tacoma, Washington).

Kevin Rolla Collins died on December 12, 1991, Bellview, Washington, and is buried at the Acacia Mausoleum.

1. **Meredith Ann COLLINS**: b October 14, 1985, Bellview, Washington.
2. **Cheryl Elsie COLLINS**: b April 20, 1988, Bellview, Washington.

NEVA, GARY, BETTY JEAN, AND KEITH

PA.3.2.6.11.5.2
NEVA ADELLE WILLETT and JOHN HARRISON CRAIG
of The Dalles, Oregon

Neva Adelle Willett was born December 3, 1922, Colville, Stevens County, Washington.

Miss Neva Adelle Willett married September 8, 1945, John Harrison Craig (b January 23, 1920, Memphis, Tennessee).

1. **James Willett CRAIG**: b August 19, 1949, The Dalles, Oregon; m Colleen McKay. See next PA.3.2.6.11.5.2.1.

2. **Jeanie Ellen CRAIG**: b October 2, 1959, The Dalles, Oregon; m September 5, 197x, Danton Kraig Baggy. See next PA.3.2.6.11.5.2.2.

PA.3.2.6.11.5.2.1
JAMES WILLETT CRAIG and COLLEEN MCKAY

James Willett Craig was born on August 19, 1949, The Dalles, Oregon.

James Willett Craig married Colleen McKay.

1. **Carmen CRAIG**: b December 1, 1975, The Dalles, Oregon.

2. **Curtis CRAIG**: b March 6, 1979, The Dalles, Oregon.

PA.3.2.6.11.5.2.2
JEANIE ELLEN CRAIG and DANTON KRAIG BAGGY

Jeanie Ellen Craig was born on October 2, 1959, at The Dalles, Oregon.

Miss Jeanie Ellen Craig married on September 5, 197x, Danton Kraig Baggy.

1. **Danton Craig Connor BAGGY**: b April 26, 1993, The Dalles, Oregon.

PA.3.2.7
ALLEN WILLETT and SARAH ANN GREEN
of Wells Valley, Fulton County, Pennsylvania

Allen Willett was born on November 20, 1810, in Fulton County, Pennsylvania.

Allen Willett married on February 16, 1832, Sarah Ann Green (b November 27, 1813, in Wells Township, Bedford, now Fulton, County, Pennsylvania; d January 31, 1851, age 37 years, 8 months, 4 days), the daughter of Nathaniel Green (b December 25, 1776, Frederick County, Maryland).

On June 24, 1839, Allen Willett, Lewis Foster, and John Miller, witnesses the will of Joseph Edwards, late of Broad Top Township (*Bedford County Wills*, page 152).

In 1840, Allen Willet and family were residing at Broad Top, Bedford County, Pennsylvania, census, page 294, as follows:

1 male	20-30	1810-1820	Allen	age 30	b 1810
1 female	20-30	1810-1820	Sarah Ann	age 27	b 1813
1 female	15-20	1815-1820			
1 male	5-10	1830-1835	Oliver	age 6	b 1834
1 male	5-10	1830-1835	Humphrey	age 5	b 1835
1 female	0-5	1835-1840	Cordelia	age 1	b 1839

On December 8, 1841, Letters of Administration were granted to Allen Willett and Nelson Green, on the (estate? of) Benjamin Green of Broad Top Township; the bond was $1,000; the sureties were Thomas Speer and Charles McLaughlin (*Administration Abstracts, Register's Docket, Bedford County*, page 108).

They resided in Wells Valley, Fulton County, Pennsylvania, evidently on land purchased from his father (or perhaps his father made a deed of gift).

In 1850, Allen and Sarah J., were listed in the Fulton County census, dwelling 37, as follows:

Willet	Allen	39	m	PA	farmer
	Sarah J	36	f	PA	
	Oliver	16	m	PA	laborer
	Humphrey	14	m	PA	
	Cordila A	19	f	PA	
	William K H	9	m	PA	
	Elizabeth T	6	f	PA	
	George A	4	m	PA	
	Cambridge G	2	m	PA	

Allen Willett was a farmer. His wife Sarah died on January 31, 1851, age 37 years, 8 months, 4 days in Fulton County, Pennsylvania.

In 1860, Allen Willett and family were listed in the Fulton County census, page 221, dwelling 97-97, as follows:

Willet	Allen	50	m	PA	farmer
	Cordelia	21	f	PA	
	William H	19	m	PA	
	Frances	16	f	PA	
	George A	14	m	PA	
	Cambridge G	12	m	PA	

Allen Willett married 2d after September, 1865, Mrs. Margaret Henry Woodcock (b 1824, Pennsylvania), widow of Jesse Woodcock (d September, 1865). Allen Willett was a Republican and a steward in the Methodist Episcopal church.

Allen Willett died on January 12, 1892, age 81 years, and is buried in the Wells Valley Methodist Cemetery, Fulton County, Pennsylvania. He left a will which was probated in 1892 in Fulton County, Pennsylvania, Volume 2, page 493.

(*Commemorative Biographical Encyclopedia of the Juniata Valley .... Pennsylvania*, page 844; *The Willett Families*, 1985, pages 242-243; 1870 Wells Township, Fulton County, Pennsylvania, census, page 7, dwelling 43-43, taken on June 8, 1870; 1880 Wells Township, Fulton County, Pennsylvania, census, page 3, dwelling 41-42).

1. **Cordelia A. WILLETT**: b 1839 (1831) in Pennsylvania; m abt 1855 Alexander B. Boyd; resided in Topeka, Kansas; attended George A. Willett's (her brother) funeral in 1914.

2. **Oliver P. WILLETT**: b 1834 in Pennsylvania; a soldier in the Civil War; d Barren Fork, in the Indian Territory, December 18, 1863. See next PA.3.2.7.2.

3. **Humphrey W.** (B.) **WILLETT**: b August 29, 1835, Fulton County, Pennsylvania; was a soldier in the Civil War; removed to Lawrence County, Kansas; m May 28, 1866, Susanna ("Samantha") E. Sparr (b May 10, 1843, Ohio); removed to California. See next PA.3.2.7.3.

4. **William Henry WILLETT**: b February 4, 1841, Wells Township, Fulton County, Pennsylvania; m at Newton, Hamilton, Pennsylvania, on December 21, 1865, Mary E. Askin, the daughter of George and Matilda (Morrison) Askin. See next PA.3.2.7.4.

5. **Elizabeth J.** ("Frances", "Fannie") **WILLETT**: b 1844 in Pennsylvania; m abt 1865 H. L. Layton; resided in Emporia, Kansas.

6. **George A. WILLETT**: b March 30, 1846, in Fulton County, Pennsylvania; m in 1871 Mary J. Grove (b June 10, 1954, Pennsylvania; d March 26, 1938, buried Blackwell I.O.O.F. Cemetery, Blackwell, Kay County, Oklahoma); removed to Peabody, Marion County, Kansas; d January 21, 1914, buried Blackwell I.O.O.F. Cemetery, Blackwell, Kay County, Oklahoma. (1870 Wells Township, Fulton County, census). See next PA.3.2.7.6.

7. **Cambridge W.** (G.) **WILLETT**: b May, 1848, in Pennsylvania; removed to Topeka, Kansas; m in Kansas in 1870, Katherine Scouten (b March 6, 1848, Indiana; d April 4, 1915, Topeka, Kansas); d after 1915, most likely in Kern County, California. See next PA.3.2.7.7.

PA.3.2.7.2
OLIVER P. WILLETT
of Pennsylvania

Oliver P. Willett was born in 1834 in Pennsylvania.

He was a soldier in the Civil War. Lieutenant O. P. Willetts was recognized in a field report of Colonel Stephen H. Wattles, First Indian Home Guards, dated July 18, 1863, Cherokee Nation, which stated that, "*Of the latter who deserve honorable mentions are O. P. Willetts ...*" for his performance in the skirmish at Elk Creek (Part I, Volume 22, pages 455-456).

Captain O. P. Willets was killed December 18, 1863, during a skirmish near Shelton's Place, Barren Fork, in the Indian Territory. The December 18, 1863, report of Capt. Alexander C. Spillman, Third Indian Home Guards, Fort Gibson, Cherokee Nation, states that "*I regret that I must record the loss of Captain (O. P.) Willets, First Indian Regiment, who fell mortally wounded, while gallantly leading his men in the early part of the engagement*". The report was rendered to Col. William A. Phillips, Commanding First Brigade, Army of the Frontier (Part I, Volume 22, pages 781-782).

PA.3.2.7.3
HUMPHREY W. WILLETT and **SUSANNA E. SPARR**
of Lawrence, Douglas County, Kansas,
and Los Angeles, California

Humphrey W. (B.) Willett was born on August 29, 1835, in Fulton County, Pennsylvania. He was educated in the Fulton County schools, and after leaving school was engaged in teaching.

CIRCA 1910
HUMPHREY WILLETT

In 1856, Humphrey Willett removed to Kansas, arriving in Lawrence, Douglas County, Kansas, on May 23, 1856. Here he settled down and learned the carpenter's trade which he followed until 1861.

On October 7, 1861, he enlisted in the Eighth Kansas Regiment. *"They were finally consolidated into the Ninth Cavalry, and he was made Sergeant Major of Company A. On expiration of his enlistment, November, 1864, he returned to Lawrence"* (Andreas, page 1100).

He was a prominent Free State man, and took part in the Battles of Franklin, Fort Saunders, and Fort Titus.

In 1865, he took charge of the Lawrence House, and continued to operate it until 1867. He then returned to carpentry work until becoming postmaster in 1872.

Humphrey Willett married on May 28, 1866, Susanna ("Samantha") E. Sparr (b May 10, 1843, Ohio).

> *"H. W. Willett, Postmaster, and dealer in general merchandise, Media, was appointed Postmaster of Prairie City in 1872, and to his present post in 1879. The business was established in Prairie City in 1872, by H. W. Willett and Company, and moved to Media in 1879. He carries a stock of $3,500 to $4,000"* (Andreas, page 1100).

On May 23, 1883, Humphrey W. Willett (wife Susannah E.) of Kansas applied for and received a Civil War Military Pension, Certificate No. 862,056, for his service in Company A, 9th Kansas Cavalry ("Civil War Pension Applications").

At some point, they removed to California.

In 1910, Humphrey Willett and family were listed in the Los Angeles, Los Angeles County, California, census, as follows:

Willett	Humphrey W.	74	PA	
	Samantha E.	66	OH	wife

(*History of Kansas*, Douglas County, Andreas, page 1100; 1900, 1910 Los Angeles Township, Los Angeles County, California, census).

1. **Olive May WILLETT**:

PA.3.2.7.4

WILLIAM HENRY WILLETT and **MARY ELIZABETH ASKIN**
of Wells Township, Fulton County, and
Milford Township, Juniata County, Pennsylvania

William Henry ("Harry") Willett was born on February 4, 1841, in Wells Township, Fulton County, Pennsylvania. He attended the public schools in Wells Township, and in Rainesburg, Bedford County.

When the Civil War came, William Willett enlisted, on September 1, 1861, in Company F, Seventy-Seventh Pennsylvania Volunteers, and was mustered into service at Pittsburgh, Pennsylvania.

> "*He participated in the battles of Pittsburgh Landing, Stone River, Liberty Gap, Lookout Mountain, Nashville, and Resaca, and was with Sherman at the siege of Atlanta, where he received a wound in his right arm. He was in service three and a half years. He was a sergeant of his company and orderly sergeant, and was promoted to the rank of Second Lieutenant by Governor Curtin of Pennsylvania.*
>
> *He afterwards farmed in Fulton County until 1869, in Douglas County, Kansas, for eight years, then on the homestead until 1893, when he sold it and removed to Newton Hamilton. A year later he bought the Berdell Farm of 100 acres in Milford Township, where he has since resided.*
>
> *He is a Republican, and has been on the school board. He is a member of Wilson Post, Grand Army of the Republic, and of the Juniata Veteran Association*" (*Commemorative Biographical Encyclopedia of the Juniata Valley .... Pennsylvania*, pages 844-845).

William Willett married at Newton Hamilton, Pennsylvania, on December 21, 1865, Mary Elizabeth Askin (b 1841, Pennsylvania), the daughter of George and Matilda (Morrison) Askin. He was a member of the Methodist Episcopal church, a Sunday School teacher, and a steward.

In 1880, Harry W. Willett and family were listed in the Wells Township, Fulton County, Pennsylvania, census, page 3, dwelling 40-41, as follows:

Willett	Harry W.		35	PA
	Mary E.	wife	39	PA
	Ellwood V.	son	13	PA
	Maggie M.	daughter	12	PA
	Carrie F.	daughter	10	PA
	Laura C.	daughter	8	PA

On April 13, 1883, William H. Willett of Pennsylvania applied for and received a Civil War Military Pension, Certificate No. 374,155, for his service in Company F, 77th Pennsylvania Infantry ("Civil War Pension Applications").

William H. Willett died on October 29, 1928, in Valparaiso, Porter County, Indiana. His death certificate, signed (presumably) by his daughter, Miss Carrie Willett of 254 Hass Street, says his name was William "Harrison" Willett, the son of Allen Willett and Sarah Green.

(*The Willett Families*, 1985, pages 243-244; "Willett House" Quarterly, pages 243-244).

1. **Elwood V. WILLETT**: b 1867, Pennsylvania.

2. **Maggie M.** ("Myrtle") **WILLETT**: b 1868, Pennsylvania; a school teacher; m William McWhinney, of Boon Grove, Indiana.

3. **Carrie F. WILLETT**: b 1870, Pennsylvania.

4. **Laura C. WILLETT**: b 1872, Pennsylvania; m Foster Gallaher.

5. **Alda M. WILLETT**: b 1880.

PA.3.2.7.6
GEORGE A. WILLETT and MARY J. GROVE
of Peabody, Marion County, Kansas

George A. Willett was born on March 30, 1846, on the family farm in Fulton County, Pennsylvania.

George A. Willett married, most likely in Pennsylvania, in 1871 Mary J. Grove (b June 10, 1854, Pennsylvania; d March 26, 1938, buried Blackwell I.O.O.F. Cemetery, Blackwell, Kay County, Oklahoma).

They removed to Kansas after 1877.

In 1880, G. A. Willett and family were listed in the Palymra Township, Douglas County, Kansas census, as follows:

Willett	G. A.		34	PA
	M. J.	wife	26	PA
	Cora E.	daughter	7	PA
	William A.	son	5	PA
	Fannie	daughter	3	PA
Grail	B. F.	Si	19	PA

In 1900, George A. Willett and family were listed in the Peabody Township, Marion County, Kansas, census, at Walnut Street, as follows:

Willett	George A.	52	Mar 1847	PA
	Mary J.	46	Jun 1854	PA
	Lulu M.	19	Feb 1881	KS
	Claire G.	13	Jan 1887	KS
	Elizabeth	10	Aug 1890	KS
	Fay	8	Sep 1892	KS

In 1910, George Willett and family were listed in the Blackwell, Kay County, Oklahoma, census, as follows:

Willett	George	64	PA	head
	Mary	54	PA	wife
	Faye	17	KS	daughter
	Elizabeth	20	KS	daughter
	Clair	22	KS	son

George A. Willett died on January 21, 1914, and is buried in the Blackwell I.O.O.F. Cemetery, Kay County, Oklahoma, along with his wife.

(*The Willett Families*, 1985, page 244; Obituary, "Geo. A. Willett", 1914).

1. **Cora E. WILLETT**: b 1873, Pennsylvania; m H. P. Crego of Mangum, Greer County, Oklahoma.

2. **William A. WILLETT**: b 1875, Pennsylvania; of Topeka, Shawnee County, Kansas.

3. **Fannie WILLETT**: b 1877, Pennsylvania; married; of Elgin, Chautauqua County, Kansas.

4. **Lulu M. WILLETT**: b February, 1881, Kansas; m Albert Thompson; of Hutchinson, Reno County, Kansas.

5. **Charles** ("Claire") **WILLETT**: b January, 1887; of Oklahoma.

6. **Elizabeth WILLETT**: b August, 1890, Kansas; of Elgin, Chautauqua County, Kansas.

7. **Fay WILLETT**: b September, 1892, Kansas; of Blackwell, Kay County, Oklahoma.

PA.3.2.7.7
CAMBRIDGE W. WILLETT and KATHERINE SCOUTEN
of Shawnee County, Kansas

Cambridge W. (G.) Willett was born on May, 1848, in Pennsylvania.　He removed to Topeka, Shawnee County, Kansas.

Cambridge Willett married in Kansas in 1870, Katherine ("Kate") Scouten (b March 6, 1848, Terre Haute, Indiana; d April 4, 1915, Los Olivos, California, interred Topeka, Kansas).

In 1900, Cambridge G. Willett and family were listed in the Topeka, Shawnee County, Kansas, census, as residing at 521 Taylor Street, as follows:

Willett	Cambridge G.	52	May 1848	PA
	Kate E.	52	Mar 1848	IN
	Gertrude L.	24	May 1876	KS
	William B.	16	Mar 1884	KS

In 1910, they were residing with their son, William Willett, at Hurland, Kern County, California, as follows:

Willitt	Wm	26	KS	
	Constance	24	CA	wife
	Richard	NR	CA	son
	Cambridge	62	PA	father
	Kate	62	IN	mother

Cambridge Willett died after 1915.

1. **Gertrude L. WILLETT**: b May, 1876, Kansas.
2. **William B. WILLETT**: b March, 1884, Kansas; m abt 1904, Constance (b 1886, California). See next PA.3.2.7.7.2.

PA.3.2.7.7.2
WILLIAM B. WILLETT and CONSTANCE
of Hurland, Kern County, California

William B. Willett was born in March, 1884, Kansas.

William B. Willett married about 1904, Constance (b 1886, California).

In 1910, William <u>Willitt</u> and family were listed in the Hurland, Kern County, California, census, as follows:

Willitt	Wm	26	KS	
	Constance	24	CA	wife
	Richard	NR	CA	son
	Cambridge	62	PA	father
	Kate	62	IN	mother

1. **Richard WILLETT**: b before 1910, California.

PA.3.2.8
ELIZABETH WILLETT and **GREEN**
of Fulton County, Pennsylvania

Elizabeth ("Betsey", "Betty") Willett was born about 1818, Pennsylvania.

Miss Elizabeth Willett married about 1838, Green.

Her will is dated August 4, 1843, probated September 22, 1843. In it, she mentions daughter Sarah Jane Green, under 21. The will was witnessed by Samuel <u>Willet</u>, Jr., and William Alexander.

1. **Sarah Jane GREEN**: b 1840 in Pennsylvania. Listed in the 1850 Wells Township, Fulton County, Pennsylvania, census, in the household of her grandparents, Samuel Willett and Rachel.

PA.3.2.9
SAMUEL WILLETT
of Wells Township, Fulton County, Pennsylvania

Samuel Willett (II) was born in 1820 (1810), in Bedford County, Pennsylvania.

Samuel Willett married 1st about 1840, Elizabeth Lockard (b 1821 in Pennsylvania; d June 15, 1875, aged 54 years, 5 months, 25 days, buried Wells Valley E. U. B. Cemetery, Fulton County, Pennsylvania). They resided in Wells Valley, Fulton County, Pennsylvania.

On August 4, 1843, Samuel Willet, Jr., and William Alexander witnessed the will of his sister, Elizabeth Green, late of Wells Valley Township, Bedford County, Pennsylvania (*Bedford County Wills*, page 259).

In 1850, Samuel and Elizabeth, were listed in the Fulton County, Pennsylvania, census, page 94, dwelling 36-37, as follows:

Willet	Samuel	30	m	PA	farmer
	Elizabeth	27	f	PA	
	Hester A	4	f	PA	
	John W	1	m	PA	

In 1860, Samuel and Elizabeth, were listed in the Wells Township, Fulton County, Pennsylvania, census, No. 38, as follows:

Willet	Samuel	50	m	PA	farmer
	Elizabeth	38	f	PA	
	Hester A	14	f	PA	
	John W	12	m	PA	
	Samuel W	9	m	PA	
	Jacob A	6	m	PA	
	Alic J	3	f	PA	
Noggle	Elam I	18	m	PA	

Samuel Willett married 2d abt 1879, Maggie Edwards (b 1841, Pennsylvania).

Samuel Willett died in 1894.

(1870 Wells Township, Fulton County, Pennsylvania, census, page 7, dwelling 44-44, taken on June 8, 1870; 1880 Wells Township, Fulton County, Pennsylvania, census, page 6, dwelling 85-91).

1.   **Hester A. WILLETT**: b January 25, 1846, Pennsylvania; m Abel O. Griffith (b 1845; d 1921); d 1922. (1870 Fulton County census).

2.   **John W.** (R.) **WILLETT**: b July 24, 1848, Pennsylvania; farm laborer (1880); d 1904, California.   (1870 Fulton County, Pennsylvania, census; 1880 Fulton County, Pennsylvania, census; 1880 Downey Township, Los Angeles County, California, census, lists John R. Willett, born July, 1848, Pennsylvania, age 51, living alone).

3.   **Samuel W. WILLETT** (III): b April 3, 1851, Pennsylvania; d March 25, 1861, aged 9 years, 11 months, 21 days, buried E. U. B. Cemetery, Wells Valley, Fulton County.

4.   **Jacob A. WILLETT**: b June 11, 1854, Pennsylvania; changed his name (before 1870) to Albert John Willett; m 1st abt 1875, Theresa Rebecca Edwards (b 1856; d March 16, 1882); m 2d at Cromwell Township, Huntington County, Pennsylvania, on September 8, 1886, Mrs. Lydia Ann (nee Enyeart) Evans (b May 20, 1857; d November 30, 1940), widow of James Evans, and the daughter of Isaac and Margaret (Isenberg) Enyeart; d April 21, 1922.   See next PA.3.2.9.4.

5.   **Alice J. WILLETT**: b September 27, 1856, Pennsylvania; m Amon Edwards (b 1858; d 1942); d March 16, 1937. (1870, 1880 Fulton County census).

PA.3.2.9.4
JACOB A. WILLETT
of Fulton County, Pennsylvania

Jacob A. Willett was born on June 11, 1854, Pennsylvania. He changed his name (before 1870) to Albert John Willett.

Jacob Willett married 1st about 1875, Theresa ("Terrisse") Rebecca Edwards (b 1856, Pennsylvania; d March 16, 1882, aged 25 years, 11 months, 16 days, buried E. U. B. Cemetery, Wells Valley, Fulton County, Pennsylvania).

In 1880, <u>Albert J. Willett</u> and family were listed in the Wells Township, Fulton County, Pennsylvania, census, page 6, dwelling 84-90, as follows:

Willett	Albert J.		26	PA
	T. Rebecca	wife	23	PA
	Bruce W.	son	3	PA
	Viola Eliz	daughter	1	PA
Lockhard	Hannah	"A"	66	PA

Mrs. Terrisse Willett died on March 16, 1882, leaving Jacob Willett with 3 young children to raise.

Albert John Willett of Wells Valley, Fulton County, Pennsylvania, married 2d at Cromwell Township, Huntington County, Pennsylvania, on September 8, 1886, Mrs. Lydia Ann (Enyeart) Evans (b May 20, 1857, Pennsylvania; d November 30, 1940, Cambria County, Pennsylvania, buried Grandview Cemetery, Johnstown), the widow of James Evans (reported in the "Huntington Monitor," September 30, 1886), the daughter of Isaac and Margaret (Isenberg) Enyeart.

In 1900, A. J. Willett, resided in Cambria County, Pennsylvania (1900 Cambria County census).

A. J. Willett died on April 21, 1922.

(1900 Cambria County, Pennsylvania, census).

Children of Jacob A. Willett and his 1st wife, Theresa Rebecca Edwards:

1. **Bruce Watson WILLETT**: b October, 1876, Wells Tannery, Fulton County, Pennsylvania; m in Blair County, Pennsylvania, on August 21, 1902, Juniata Emma Powell (b circa 1880; d 1957), the daughter of William Powell; d 1934. See next <u>PA.3.2.9.4.1</u>.

2. **Viola May** ("Maggie) **WILLETT**: b October 26, 1879, Pennsylvania; m Herman B. Paul (b January 17, 1875; d November 28, 1946); d January 21, 1916. (1900 Cambria

County census).

3. Infant son **WILLETT**: b abt 1880, an infant death; buried E. U. B. Cemetery near mother, Terrisse R. Willett. Small stone inscribed, "Infant son of A. J. and T. R. Willett" (no dates).

4. **Bessie W. WILLETT**: b February 16, 1882; m Frederick Householder; d October 31, 1967.

Children of John Albert Willett and his 2d wife, Lydia Ann Enyeast:

5. **George Howard WILLETT**: b April 24, 1886, Pennsylvania; m April 27, 1910, Elizabeth Wilson (b October, 1881; d December 2, 1942); d August 12, 1953, Detroit, Wayne County, Michigan. (1900 Cambria County census). See next PA.3.2.9.4.5.

6. **Annie Zenobia WILLETT**: b September 22, 1890; m September 3, 1904, Mancill Leslie Smith; resided Elkton, Maryland; d June 19, 1980. (1900 Cambria County census).

7. **John Albert WILLETT**: b February 22, 1893; m Hazel Black. (1900 Cambria County census).

8. **Aline S. WILLETT**: b July, 1894, Pennsylvania. (1900 Cambria County census).

9. **David Enyeart WILLETT** ("Frank" in 1900 census): b March 17, 1897; resided Cocoa Beach, Florida; d June 14, 1978. (1900 Cambria County census).

10. **Ralph Rupert WILLETT**: b April 27, 1899, Johnstown, Cambria County, Pennsylvania; m 1st Marion E. Dixon (b August, 1902, Johnstown, Pennsylvania; d November 19, 1930, Windber, Pennsylvania, buried Grandview Cemetery, Johnstown), the daughter of Thomas and Ada (Foust) Dixon; m 2d Mary Frances Riddle (b November 16, 1900, Greensburg, Pennsylvania; d August 16, 1985, at home, Johnstown, Cambria County, Pennsylvania, buried Grandview Cemetery, Johnstown), the daughter of Emmett and Ellen (Taylor) Riddle; d October 9, 1962, at home, Johnstown, Cambria County, Pennsylvania, buried Grandview Cemetery, Johnstown. (1900 Cambria County census). No children.

11. **Margaret WILLETT**: m R. D. Fyock.

PA.3.2.9.4.1
BRUCE WATSON WILLETT and JUANITA EMMA POWELL
of Blair County, Pennsylvania

Bruce Watson Willett was born in October, 1876, at Wells Tannery, Fulton County, Pennsylvania.

In 1900, Bruce W. Willett resided a Main Street, Johnstown, Cambria County, Pennsylvania (1900 census).

Bruce W. Willett married at Altoona, in Blair County, Pennsylvania, on August 21, 1902, Juanita Emma Powell (b circa 1880; d 1957), the daughter of William Powell (*Marriage Application Records Hollidaysburg, Blair County, Pennsylvania*, Vol. 20, page 287).

They resided in Akron, Summit County, Ohio.

Bruce Willett died in 1934.

(1900 Johnstown, Cambria County, Pennsylvania, census; George E. Russell, *Powell Family of Allegheny County, Pennsylvania*, Catoctin Press, 1990, page 22).

1. **Robert Bruce WILLETT**: b February 22, 1907, Altoona, Blair County, Pennsylvania; m in 1930, Thelma Lambert (d 1978). See next PA.3.2.9.4.1.1.

2. **Ruth E. WILLETT**:

3. **Lois G. WILLETT**: m Trombley; resides (1993) Waterville, Maine.

PA.3.2.9.4.1.1
ROBERT BRUCE WILLETT and **THELMA LAMBERT**
of Summit County, Ohio

Robert Bruce Willett was born February 22, 1907, Altoona, Blair County, Pennsylvania.

Robert Bruce Willett married about 1930, Thelma Lambert (d 1978).

> *"Bob Willett obtained a degree in mechanical engineering from the University of Akron in 1928, and began his career with the Goodyear Tire and Rubber Company in 1925 as a member of the Co-op Squadron. His 43 year career included four years as personnel manager of the Goodyear Tire and Mechanical Goods Plant in Uitenhage, South Africa. He was production superintendent of Plastics and Metalcraft when he retired from Goodyear Aerospace in 1968. Following his retirement, Bob and Thelma traveled extensively, making a return visit to friends in South Africa, as well as camping throughout Mexico, Canada and the U.S., and rafting down the Colorado River through the Grand Canyon. Bob was also a master wood craftsman, and a musician who played several instruments by ear"* (Obituary, 1993, Robert B. Willett, Cuyahoga Falls, Ohio).

1. **Barbara WILLETT**: m Robert E. Jones; resides (1993) Parma, Ohio.

2. **Ruth WILLETT**: m Lawrence J. Anderson; resides (1993) Cuyahoga Falls, Summit County, Ohio.

PA.3.2.9.4.5
GEORGE HOWARD WILLETT and ELIZABETH WILSON
of Detroit, Wayne County, Michigan

George Howard Willett was born on April 24, 1886, Pennsylvania.

George H. Willett married on April 27, 1910, Elizabeth Wilson (b October, 1881; d December 2, 1942).

In 1912, George Howard Willett founded the Standard Fuel Engineering Company, of Detroit, Michigan.

George Howard Willett died on August 12, 1953.

1. **George Howard WILLETT** (II): b September 25, 1911; m April 21, 1934, Florence Harris Baker (b June 5, 1915). See next PA.3.2.9.4.5.1.

PA.3.2.9.4.5.1
GEORGE HOWARD WILLETT
and FLORENCE HARRIS BAKER
of Detroit, Wayne County, Michigan

George Howard Willett (II) was born on September 25, 1911, at Detroit, Wayne County, Michigan.

George H. Willett (II) married on April 21, 1934, Florence Harris Baker (b June 5, 1915).

George Willett was owner and president of Standard Fuel Engineering Company, Delray Investment Company, IPC Industries, and Zero Refractories.

He retired in 1971. He was a 32d degree Mason and member of the Detroit Commandry No. 1, The Old Guard, Moslem Shrine, Birmingham Lodge No. 44, F and AM, and Birmingham High Twelve Club.

George Howard Willett died in May, 1988, at Quail Ridge, Florida.

(REF: Obituary: 1988 George Howard Willett, Detroit, Michigan).

1. **Ann Harris WILLETT**: b April 8, 1938; m September 6, 1958, Harold A. Miller.

2. **George Howard WILLETT (III)**: b November 26, 1940; m June 29, 1963, Barbara Ann Morris (b May 7, 1940); resides at Grosse Point, Wayne County, Michigan (1981). See next PA.3.2.9.4.5.1.2.

3. **Gordon Henry WILLETT**: b April 17, 1946; m 1st July 2, 1969, Judith Lindell Ringiner; m 2d February 25, 1981, Ann Robinson (b August 3, 1945). See next PA.3.2.9.4.5.1.3.

PA.3.2.9.4.5.1.2
GEORGE HOWARD WILLETT and **BARBARA ANN MORRIS**
of Grosse Point, Wayne County, Michigan

George Howard Willett (III) was born on November 26, 1940.

George Howard Willett (III) married on June 29, 1963, Barbara Ann Morris (b May 7, 1940).

They reside at Grosse Point, Wayne County, Michigan (1981).

1. **Wendy Ann WILLETT**: b March 6, 1969.

PA.3.2.9.4.5.1.3
GORDON HENRY WILLETT
of Grosse Point, Wayne County, Michigan

Gordon Henry Willett was born on April 17, 1946.

Gordon Henry Willett married 1st July 2, 1969, Judith Lindell Ringiner.

Gordon H. Willett married 2d February 25, 1981, Ann Robinson (b August 3, 1945). They reside at Grosse Point, Wayne County, Michigan (1981).

1. **Michelle Leanna WILLETT**: b April 7, 1972.
2. **James Gordon WILLETT**: b August 2, 1979.

CHAPTER FOUR
BURGESS B. WILLETT AND SUSAN FORNWALT

INTRODUCTION

PA.0
HORATIO WILLETT
of Selins Grove, Northumberland County, Pennsylvania

Horatio Willett was born about 1786, in Montgomery County, Maryland.

In the 1790 Montgomery County, Maryland, census, page 87, he should be the male (age between 0-16) listed under his father, Ninian Willett.

In the 1800 Montgomery County, Maryland, census, Horatio Willett should be the male age 10-16, listed under his father, Ninian Willett.

Horatio Willett married, possibly in Pennsylvania, about 1806, Mrs. Mary Leckner, the widow of Frederick Leckner.

It is believed that about 1807, Horatio Willett settled in Selins Grove, Northumberland County, Pennsylvania, at the same time his brother, Dr. Robert White Willett settled there.

Horatio Willett's father, Ninian Willett, died intestate in Montgomery County, Maryland, on October 15, 1807, in possession of tracts "Sweepstakes", and "Jones Inheritance". His children, Catherine Jones, Sarah Leach, Polly Willett, sold their share of the estate to their brother, Burgess Willett (Book N, page 421, Land Office, Montgomery County, Maryland). Ninian Willett had left "Scotland" and the "Addition to Scotland", to his children who combined together (evidently including Horatio) on October 15, 1807, and sold the land to their brother Burgess Willett.

In August, 1808, John Grubb, plaintiff, summoned Horatio Willett, defendant, before the Northumberland County Court in Pennsylvania.

On December 9, 1809, Horatio Willetts (sic) and Mary, late widow and relict of Frederick Leckner of Tulpehown (sic) Township, Berks County, Pennsylvania, they of Township of Selinsgrove, Northumberland County, Pennsylvania, received of Jacob Leckner, executor of the estate of Frederick Leckner, 600 pounds of lawful money of the U.S. (Northumberland County, Pennsylvania, Deed Book "P", page 502).

Horatio Willett's mother, Mrs. Ann Willett, wrote her will on June 1, 1810, and left a silver watch to her son, Horatio Willett.

In 1810, "Rash" Willett and family were listed in the Selinsgrove, Northumberland County, census, page 312 (along with his brother Robert on the same page), as follows:

1 male	16-26	1784-1794	Horatio	age 24? b 1786?
1 female	16-26	1784-1794	Mrs. Leckner	
1 male	16-26	1784-1794		
1 female	0-10	1800-1810		
1 male	0-10	1800-1810	Burgess	age 0 b 1810

In August, 1811, Northumberland County Court, Jacob Hassinger, had a suit of "Capias" against Horatio Willett, defendant (Appearance Docket 139, page 161).

In November, 1811, in the Northumberland County Court, Jacob Hassinger, plaintiff, summoned Horatio Willett, defendant (Appearance Docket 79, page 198).

In August, 1812, in the Northumberland County Court, the Commonwealth declared that Horatio Willett, defendant, was insolvent (Appearance Docket 141, Northumberland County Court, page 24).

Horatio Willett's father's estate (Ninian Willett's) was not finally settled until August 10, 1817, when the executor, Burgess Willett, paid each heir $416.50. Horatio Willett was mentioned by name at this time.

In 1820, Horatio Willett may be one of the unnamed males, age 26-45, residing in the Robert Willett household in Selins Grove, Union County, Pennsylvania. Dr. Robert White Willett is presumed to be the brother of Horatio Willett.

The 1820 Selins Grove, Union County, Pennsylvania, census, lists the following information about Robert Willett, head of household:

1 male	45-up	bef. 1775	Robert	age 48 b 1772
1 female	26-45	1775-1794	Matilda	age 29 b 1791
1 male	26-45	1775-1794	Horatio?	age 34? b 1786?
1 male	26-45	1775-1794		
1 male	10-16	1804-1810	Fleming	age 13 b 1807
1 female	10-16	1804-1810	Ann	age 11 b 1809
1 female	0-10	1810-1820		
1 female	0-10	1810-1820	Harriet age 4 b 1816

NOTE: In attempting to reconstruct this family and prove its ancestry, the recollection of John C. Willett, "*said he remembers his grandfather (Horatio F. Willett) telling him that the Willett's originated from Northumberland County, and that they owned a big farm in that county*" (Transcribed tape taken on March, 1979, from Uncle Bill Willett to John

C. Willett)."

NOTE: In attempting to reconstruct this family and prove its ancestry, the recollection of Uncle William Horatio ("Bill") Willett may be important, "*Horatio Willette ... He was what they called a tanner. In other words, you bought the hide, cured them, tanned them and made leather that you used to repair harnesses, saddles, and made boots for your neighbors and all that kind of stuff. So that's what the original Horatio did.*

After the end of the Revolutionary War, he was supposed to have moved into Lancaster, Pennsylvania ...

They stayed until 1804, when they moved right below Cresson where the road turns left off 422 to go past Loretto to go to Carrolltown ...

They stayed there, I'm using they because they were a family shortly, they stayed there until 1840 or 1841 when they moved into the old stone house in Nolo (Indiana County, Pennsylvania). Now you remember us talking about the old stone house, John. It was an Inn before the Revolutionary War. They used to stop there (soldiers) a few days on their way to Pittsburgh to Philadelphia ..." (Transcribed tape taken on March, 1979, from Uncle Bill Willett to John C. Willett).

NOTE: The above family tradition seems to stray from the 1st Horatio Willett to his son, Burgess Willett, in the last paragraph cited.

Horatio Willett has not been "found" after 1817, when he is mentioned in the settlement of his father's estate.

1. **Burgess B. WILLETT**: b May 14, 1810. Speculated as the same as the Burgess B. Willett listed next as PA.4.

PA.4
BURGESS B. WILLETT and **SUSAN FORNWALT**
of Indiana County, Pennsylvania

Burgess B. Willett was born on May 14, 1810 (1808), in Pennsylvania. His birth year is 1810 according to the 1850 Blair County, Pennsylvania, census (i.e., he was age 40 in 1850) (and as stated from tombstone at Grandview Cemetery, Cambria County, Pennsylvania).

NOTE: The death certificate of his son, Horatio Willett, states, that Burgess Willett was born in Germany; the 1850 and 1860 Pennsylvania census records gives his place of birth as Pennsylvania, and this contemporary record of his place of birth is considered, by this researcher, to be the more accurate.

There is a Germany in Adams County, Pennsylvania, and in 1840 both Henry Willet and George Willet were heads of a household in Germany, which would have been a village or Township in Adams County.

In 1830, Germany (Township) in Adams County, Pennsylvania, both Jacob Willet and John Willet were heads of household.

In 1820, George, Henry, John, and the widow Rosannah Willet were heads of a household in Germany in Adams County.

In 1810, Rosannah Willet was the head of a household in Germany in Adams County.

On March 23, 1839, <u>B. Willett</u> owned lot No. 7, Claysburg, Greenfield Township, Huntington County, Pennsylvania (J. Simpson Africa, *History of Huntington and Blair Counties*, 1883, page 117). At that time, Claysburg was located in Huntington County. After 1846, Blair County would be created out of the western half of Huntington County, and the towns of Claysburg, and Hollidaysburg, would both fall in the newly formed Blair County.

> "*By mutual consent, the Partnership existing between Wolf and Willett has been dissolved. The business will be continued under Mr. Wolf*" ("Canal and Portage Register," dated September 9, 1840).

The "Canal and Portage Register" was published at Hollidaysburg, Huntington County, Pennsylvania, from 1836 to 1838.

The only known Mr. Wolf was a cabinet maker in Blair

County, Pennsylvania.

In 1841, B. B. Willett was a borough constable of Frankstown Village, Huntington (now Blair) County, Pennsylvania (J. Simpson Africa, *History of Huntington and Blair Counties*, 1883, page 106).

Later in the 1840s, Burgess Willett lived in Munster Township, Cambria County, Pennsylvania.

Mr. Burgess B. Willett married in Huntington County, Pennsylvania, on March 8, 1842, Miss Susan (Elizabeth) Fournwalt (b 1822; d February 19, 1870), all of Frankstown Township, Huntington County, Pennsylvania, by the Rev. J. P. Rockfeller ("Democratic Standard and Huntington County, Gazette," dated March 11, 1842; "Huntington Journal," dated March 16, 1842; and the "Hollidaysburg Register and Huntington County Inquirer" Newspaper, dated March 9, 1842. At that time, Hollidaysburg was in Huntington County).

In 1843, Burgess and Susan Willett were residents of Blair County, when their son George S. Willett was born.

> "*Dissolution of Partnership: By mutual consent, the partnership between M. Wolf and B. B. Willett has been dissolved. The business will be continued by M. Wolf*" ("Hollidaysburg Register and Huntington County Inquirer," dated January 8, 1845).

The "Hollidaysburg Register and Huntington County Inquirer" was published from 1842 to 1845. It was called the "Hollidaysburg and Blair County Inquirer" from 1846 to 1849. From 1849, it was called the "Hollidaysburg Register."

In the 1840s, Hollidaysburg fell in the original Huntington County; sometime about 1846 Blair County was created from the western part of Huntington County.

In 1846, Burgess Willett and family were residents of Cambria County, Pennsylvania, when their son Horatio F. Willett was born.

In 1850, Burgess Willett, laborer, and family were listed in the Blair County, Pennsylvania, census, page 60, dwelling 89-89, taken on August 16, 1850, as follows:

Burgess Willett	40	m	laborer
Susan Willett	28	f	
George S. Willett	7	m	
Oratio Willett	5	m	
Sarah L. Willett	3	f	
Matilda Willett	7/12	f	

In the 1850s, they lived in North Woodberry Township,

Blair County, Pennsylvania. In 1856, Burgess Willett was a resident of Taylor Township, Blair County, Pennsylvania.

After 1856, Burgess Willett removed to Indiana County, Pennsylvania. He had a general store in Nolo, Indiana County, Pennsylvania, and was employed extensively in the flour trade.

CIRCA 1868
SUSAN (FORNWALT) WILLETT
(Picture courtesy of Joan Grabenstein)

In 1860, B. B. Willett and family were listed in the Brush-valley P. O., Pine Township, Indiana County, Pennsylvania, census, No. 2342, as follows:

Willett	B. B.	52	PA	Store clerk
	Elisabeth	40	PA	

Horatio	10	PA
Elizabeth	7	PA
Emma J	5	PA
(male)	4	PA

In 1868, they removed to Ohio, settling near Jackson, Jackson County, Ohio, where he most likely engaged in the charcoal business along with his son, Horatio Fornwalt Willett.

Burgess Willett evidently moved back and forth across the state lines of Ohio and Pennsylvania as he followed in various business enterprises.

Burgess Willett died on February 19, 1870, and is buried in the Grandview Cemetery, Cambria County, Pennsylvania.

(REF: "Willett House" Quarterly, No. 4, 1987, pages 412-424).

1. **George S. WILLETT**: b January 2, 1843, Blair County, Pennsylvania; in 1860, he was enumerated with the Robert Crawford family; m 1866, Lunetta Hill (b March, 1850, Pennsylvania; d November 26, 1914, Thurston County, Washington, buried Mt. View Cemetery, Thurston County), the daughter of Samuel and Mary A. (Ferrier) Hill; removed to Ohio after the Civil War; returned to Pennsylvania; d July 3, 1922, Thurston County, Washington, buried Mt. View Cemetery, Thurston County. See next PA.4.1.

2. **Horatio** ("Oratio") **Fornwalt WILLETT**: b November 10, 1846 (1850), Munster, Cambria County, Pennsylvania; m at Nolo, Indiana County, Pennsylvania, on November 19, 1865, Emily Alice McKelvey (b March 17, 1848, Indiana County, Pennsylvania; d July 19, 1920, and buried on July 22, Cambria County, Pennsylvania), the daughter of Samuel A. McKelvy and Catherine Bennett; d September 1, 1927, Pennsylvania. See next PA.4.2.

3. **Sara Jane WILLETT**: b 1847, Pennsylvania.

4. **Matilda WILLETT**: b January, 1850, N. Woodberry Township, Blair County, Pennsylvania (age 7/12 months when the 1850 census was taken).

5. **Elizabeth WILLETT**: b 1853, Pennsylvania. (Possibly not a child of Burgess Willett).

6. **Emma Jane WILLETT**: b 1855, Pennsylvania. (Possibly not a child of Burgess Willett).

7. **Morris WILLETT**: b 1856, Pennsylvania. (Possibly not a child of Burgess Willett).

PA.4.1

GEORGE S. WILLETT and **LUNETTA HILL**
of Pine Township, Indiana County, Pennsylvania,
Ohio and Washington

George S. Willett was born on January 2, 1843, Blair County, Pennsylvania.

In 1860, he was a shoemaker's helper at Crawford's, Master Shoemaker, Indiana, Indiana County, Pennsylvania.

With the Civil War coming on, George S. Willett enlisted as a Private on September 19, 1861, in Company F, 55th Regiment Pennsylvania Volunteers. He had blue eyes, light complexion and stood 5 feet 9 inches. He served his tour of duty until he was mustered out on December 31, 1863, at Beauford, South Carolina. He immediately re-enlisted for 3 more years on January 1, 1864, at Beauford, South Carolina. At this time, he gave his home address as Chester County, Pennsylvania.

"On furlough since January 23, 1864, by reason of re-enlistment" according to the Company Muster Roll of Company F, 55th Regiment, Pennsylvania, Infantry.

In 1865, George S. Willett was mustered out with his company at the end of the war in Petersburg, Virginia.

In 1865, after the Civil War, he removed to Ohio, where he was a shoemaker.

George S. Willett married in 1866, Lunetta ("Sunella"; "Linetta") Hill (b March, 1850, Pennsylvania; d November 26, 1914, Thurston County, Washington, buried Mt. View Cemetery, Thurston County), the daughter of Samuel and Mary A. (Ferrier) Hill.

They returned to Pine Township, Indiana County, Pennsylvania, sometime after 1870.

In 1880, George Willett and family were listed in the Pine Street, Pine Township, Indiana County, Pennsylvania, census, as follows:

Willett	George	head	40	PA
	Lunetta	wife	30	PA
	S. B.	son	13	PA
	M. A.	daughter	9	PA
	E. E.	son	6	PA
	C. E.	daughter	5	PA

In 1900, they lived at 205 Irvin Hill, Curwensville, Clearfield County, Pennsylvania. He was an engineer.

George S. Willett died on July 3, 1922, age 79, at Thurston County, Washington, and is buried in the Mt. View Cemetery,

Thurston County, Washington.
(REF: "Willett House" Quarterly, No. 4, 1987, pages 452-453; 1900 205 Irvin Hill, Curvensville, Clearfield County, Pennsylvania, census).

1. **Burgess B. WILLETT**: b July, 1867, Curwensville, Clearfield County, Pennsylvania; m March 8, 1891, Sarah ("Sadie") Elma Doughman (b February, 1872, Pennsylvania), the daughter of Gideon P. and Eliz. E. (Walters) Doughman. See next PA.4.1.1.

2. **Maggie Alaska WILLETT**: b June 2, 1872, Curwensville, Clearfield County, Pennsylvania; m at Camden, New Jersey, on November 21, 1890, Lewis Paul Mullen (b April 15, 1871, Curwensville, Clearfield County, Pennsylvania; d October 31, 1944), the son of Hugh and Elizabeth C. (Ogden) Mullen; d November 18, 1957.

3. **E. C. WILLETT** (son): b 1874, Ohio (Pennsylvania, according to the 1880 census).

4. **Cora E. WILLETT**: b July, 1875, Ohio (Pennsylvania, according to the 1880 census); m 1898, Alcorn. (1900 Clearfield County census).

5. **Lewida WILLETT**: b March, 1880, Pennsylvania (1900 Clearfield County census).

6. **Josephine F. WILLETT**: b February, 1882, Pennsylvania (1900 Clearfield County census).

7. **Helena M. WILLETT**: b January, 1886, Pennsylvania (1900 Clearfield County census).

PA.4.1.1
BURGESS B. WILLETT and SARAH ELMA DOUGHMAN
of Clearfield County, Pennsylvania

Burgess B. Willett was born in July, 1867, in Ohio (Pennsylvania, according to the 1880 census). He was a laborer (1880).

Burgess Willett married on March 8, 1891, Sarah ("Sadie") Elma Doughman (b February, 1872, Pennsylvania), the daughter of Gideon P. and Eliz. E. (Walters) Doughman.

Burgess Willett was (1891) a stationary engineer.

In 1900, Burgess and family were residing at Penn Township, Clearfield County, Pennsylvania.

1. **Blaine G. WILLETT**: b June 19, 1891, Grampian, Clearfield County, Pennsylvania.

2. **George Vernon WILLETT**: b December 8, 1892, Grampian, Clearfield County, Pennsylvania.

3. **Dalphene** ("Daphne") **Elma WILLETT**: b June 8, 1895, Grampian, Clearfield County, Pennsylvania.

4. **Carroll WILLETT** (son): b September, 1898, Grampian, Clearfield County, Pennsylvania.

5. **Lyall WILLETT**: b 1901, Grampian, Clearfield County, Pennsylvania.

PA.4.2
HORATIO FORNWALT WILLETT
and **EMILY ALICE MCKELVEY**
of Pine Township, Indiana County, Pennsylvania

Horatio Fornwalt Willett was born on November 10, 1846, in Munster Township, Cambria County, Pennsylvania.

Horatio Willett, age 16, enlisted in the Union Army on April 15, 1862, for three years service, and assigned to the 6th Army Corps, 3rd Division, Company E, 67th Pennsylvania Infantry, Army of the Potomac. He had blue eyes, light hair, fair complexion, and stood 5'-4" tall. The regiment had a total 360 men at its maximum strength.

On April 3, 1862, the 67th Pennsylvania Volunteer Regiment was at Camac's Woods. It moved from Philadelphia by rail to Baltimore, and thence by water to Annapolis, Maryland, and at Camp Parole the 67th had guard duty.

Before Richmond under General George McClellan: On June 26, to July 1, 1862, the 67th Pennsylvania, was at the Seven Days Retreat, Richmond, Virginia. The 6th Corps was under Major General Franklin and suffered 245 killed, 1313 wounded, and 1179 missing.

On September 14, 1862, the 67th Pennsylvania, was at Turner's and Crampton's Gap, South Mount, Maryland, with the 6th Corps under Major General Franklin.

At Battle of Sharpsburg under General McClellan: On September 17, 1862, the 67th Pennsylvania, was at Antietam (Sharpsburg to the Confederate view), Maryland, with the 6th Corps under Major General Franklin.

At Battle of Fredericksburg under General Burnside: On December 13, 1862, the 67th Pennsylvania, was at Fredericksburg, Virginia, with the 6th Corps under Major General W. F. Smith.

In February, 1863, the 67th was moved to Harper's Ferry, and later was stationed at Berryville, Virginia, to patrol the lower Shenandoah Valley and its gaps.

At the Battle of Chancellorsville under General Hood: On May 1 to 4, 1863, the 67th Pennsylvania, was at Chancellorsville, Virginia, with the 6th Corps under Major General Sedgwick.

On June 13 to 15, 1863, the 67th Pennsylvania, was at Winchester, Virginia.

In June 15, 1863, the regiment was cut off from the main column by a large Confederate force, near Winchester, and was captured, with the exception of about 75 men. This was when the Confederates were moving north towards Harrisburg, Pennsylvania. The Confederates would stop short at Carlisle

Barracks, be recalled by General Lee, C.S.A., and the Battle of Gettysburg would be the result.

Horatio Willett was captured by the Confederates at Winchester, Virginia, and confined on June 24, 1863, in the Confederate Libby Prison, Richmond, and at Bell Island, Virginia. On July 19, 1863, after 4 weeks he was exchanged on parole at City Point, Virginia. He was reported at Camp Parole, Maryland, on July 25, 1863, and returned to his regiment four months later on October 5, 1863 (*War Department, Adjutant General's Office*, file dated March 2, 1883). Thus, he and his regiment missed participating in the Battle of Gettysburg on July 1, 2, and 3.

Private Horatio Willett was paroled and sent back to the Union Hospital to recuperate from his imprisonment.

On November 26 to 28, 1863, the 67th Pennsylvania, was at Mine Run, Virginia, with the 6th Corps.

In March, 1864, Private Horatio Willett was on leave, as were most of the 350 rank and file who had re-enlisted.

Horatio F. Willett, age 19, was officially mustered out on his 1st enlistment contract on April 1, 1864, at Brandy Station, Virginia. He immediately re-enlisted on April 2, 1864, as a "Vet Vol."

Under General Ulysses S. Grant: On May 5 to 7, 1864, the 67th Pennsylvania, was at Wilderness, Virginia, with the 6th Corps under Major General Sedwick.

On May 8 to 18, 1864, the 67th Pennsylvania, was at Spottsylvania, Virginia, with the 6th Corps under Major General Wright.

In June, the 67th was before Petersburg and served in the engagement at Reams' Station.

On August 15, 1864, the 67th Pennsylvania, was at Strasburg, Virginia, with the 6th Corps.

On August 21, 1864, the 67th Pennsylvania, was at Summit Point, Berryville, and Flowering Springs, Virginia, with the 6th Corps, 3rd Division.

On August 29, 1864, the 67th Pennsylvania, was at Smithfield, Virginia, with the 6th Corps, 3rd Division.

On October 29, 1864, the 67th Pennsylvania, was at Cedar Creek, Virginia, with the 6th Corps.

"On or about February 18, 1865, at Star Fort, Virginia, from over work and strain" Horatio was disabled and excused from manual labor by the Regimental Surgeon (*Declaration of Original Invalid Pension*, claim, dated March 17, 1881).

On April 2, 1865, the 67th Pennsylvania, was at the fall of Petersburg, Virginia, with the 6th Corps. The 67th participated in the forward movement which ended at Appomattox, after which it marched with the column sent to Danville,

Virginia, a precautionary measure which was ended by General Johnston's surrender upon April 26th.

Horatio Willett was promoted to Corporal on July 1, 1865, and discharged on July 14, 1865, at Halls Hill, Virginia.

By August 1, 1865, Horatio Willett was back home at Strongstown, Indiana County, Pennsylvania.

Horatio Willett married at Nolo, Indiana County, Pennsylvania, on November 19, 1865, Emily Alice McKelvey (b March 17, 1848, Indiana County, Pennsylvania; d July 19, 1920, Johnstown, and buried on July 22, in the Grandview Cemetery, Johnstown, Cambria County, Pennsylvania), the daughter of Samuel A. McKelvy and Catherine Bennett.

On November 21, 1865, they removed to Winchester, Jackson County, Ohio, and a little later to Keystone Furnace Post Office, Galia County, Ohio. In December, 1866, they were at Cadiz, Harrison County, Ohio, when their first child, Venora Alice Willett, was born. Horatio Willett was in the coal business, lumber, and a store merchant for over 25 years.

In December, 1870, they were residents of Winchester, Adams County, Ohio, when their son William Martin Willett, was born.

Harrison County, Ohio, is in the eastern central portion of the state and borders Pennsylvania. Both Jackson County and Adams County are in the southernmost portion of Ohio. Highland County adjoins Adams County to the north.

In 1875, Burgess Willett and family returned to Scottsdale, Westmoreland County, Pennsylvania.

He was active in the coal business in Fayette County, Pennsylvania. He then took up the coal and lumber trades in Clearfield County, Pennsylvania.

A recollection of Uncle Bill Willett to John C. Willett, March, 1979, probably relates to this time period. "*Granddad bought a shingle mill, that's to make the old clap board shingles and they traveled around various towns all over, especially Clearfield County and parts of Cambria County.*"

In 1878, they had moved back to Strongstown, Indiana County, Pennsylvania.

In 1880, H. F. Willett and family were listed in the Pine Street, Pine Township, Indiana County, Pennsylvania, census, as follows:

Willett	H. F.	head	33	PA
	Emily	wife	32	PA
	Venorah	daughter	13	PA
	H. E.	son	11	PA

Wm. M.	son	9	PA
C. C.	son	7	PA
Geo. R.	son	5	PA
Jas. H.	son	2	PA

On March 17, 1881, Horatio F. Willett filed for an "Invalid Pension" based on the deterioration of his health while imprisoned at Libby Prison in 1863. Evidently, this claim for a disability pension was accepted and at some point Certificate No. 946139 was issued.

In 1886, they had moved back to Curwensville, Clearfield County, Pennsylvania, where at some point he purchased 200 acres of coal lands.

In 1890, Horatio and family moved to Johnstown, Cambria County, and established a grocery store at 118 F Street, which he ran until his retirement in 1910.

In 1892, and 1894, Horatio Willett was queried by the United States Federal Government for more information on his claim to a disability pension, and again provided affidavits.

Horatio Willett was a member of the Grand Army of the Republic (G.A.R.) and has ribbons commemorating his attendance at the reunions they held on August 27, 1891, at Johnstown on September 17, 1895, at Indiana, Pennsylvania, on August 23, 1900, and at Indiana, on August 29, 1901.

In 1912, Mr. Willet sold his coal lands in Clearfield County consisting of 200 acres at $110.00 per acre.

NOTE: He was called "Rash", a diminutive of Horatio, possibly pronounced as "Ho Rashio" (according to his grandson, William Horatio Willett).

Horatio Willett died at his home at 137 M Street, Morrelville, on September 1, 1927, at age 80 years, 9 months, 22 days, at Johnstown, in Cambria County, Pennsylvania. Both he and his wife are buried at Grandview Cemetery, Johnstown, Pennsylvania.

(REF: "Willett House" Quarterly, No. 4, 1987, pages 453-455; September, 1927, Newspaper Obituary, Johnstown, Pennsylvania).

CIRCA 1895
HORATIO AND EMILY WILLETT FAMILY
(Picture courtesy of Nova Boyer)

Back porch of home on "M" Street, Morrellville, Johnstown,
Cambria County, Pennsylvania
From left to right - top to bottom

VENORA, EMILY (MOTHER), HORATIO (FATHER)
FRANK, WILLIAM, CHALMER
GEORGE, JAMES, OLIVER
VICTOR, EDWIN BURK

MRS. EMILY (MCKELVEY) WILLETT
CIRCA 1910

    1. **Venora** ("Venorah") **Alice WILLETT**: b December 25, 1866, Cadiz, Harrison County, Ohio; m John R. Wilkins (b February 4, 1857; d February 28, 1938) of Oakhurst; d in her sleep in Johnstown on January 12, 1918, buried Grandview Cemetery, Johnstown, Cambria County, Pennsylvania. See next PA.4.2.1.

2. **Franklin Emerson WILLETT**: b October 25, 1868, Ohio; unmarried; d April 10, 1948, age 79, Johnstown, Cambria County, Pennsylvania, buried Grandview Cemetery, Johnstown, Pennsylvania. See next PA.4.2.2.

3. **William Martin WILLETT**: b December 27, 1870, Winchester, Adams County, Ohio; m March 16, 1893, Anna ("Annie") Rodgers (b January 31, 1874, Johnstown, Cambria County, Pennsylvania; d May 16, 1948, Johnstown, Pennsylvania, buried Grandview Cemetery, Johnstown, Cambria County, Pennsylvania); d October 7, 1957, age 86, Johnstown, Cambria County, Pennsylvania. See next PA.4.2.3.

4. **Chalmer Cephas WILLETT**: b November 19, 1872, Keystone Furnace, Gallia County, Ohio; m in Morrellville (Johnstown) on December 27, 1894, Miss Edith Blanche Lucas (b December, 1876), the daughter of J. Emmet Lucas; d December 7, 1909, age 37, of Bright's Disease, Johnstown, Cambria County, Pennsylvania, buried Grandview Cemetery, Johnstown, Cambria County, Pennsylvania; no children. Mrs. Edith Blanche (Lucas) Willett married 2d in Pittsburgh on August 20, 1918, Wayne W. Wright of Chattanooga, Tennessee.

5. **George Raymond WILLETT**: b May 18, 1875, Keystone Furnace, Gallia County, Ohio; m in Dale Borough, Johnstown, Cambria County, Pennsylvania, in 1896, Carrie M. Smith (b October 10, 1879, Indiana County, Pennsylvania; d May 27, 1961, Johnstown, Cambria County, Pennsylvania, buried Grandview Cemetery, Johnstown, Pennsylvania), the daughter of Charles A. and Eliza Jane (Helman) Smith; d in an automobile accident on February 17, 1924, Pittsburgh, Pennsylvania, buried Grandview Cemetery, Johnstown, Pennsylvania. See next PA.4.2.5.

6. **James Buchanan WILLETT**: b July 28, 1878, Curwensville, Clearfield County, Pennsylvania; m in Cumberland, Maryland, on July 23, 1895, Emily Gertrude Wilson (b February 22, 1880, Indiana County, Pennsylvania; d November 7, 1948, Norristown, Montgomery County, Pennsylvania, buried in the Benshoff Hill Cemetery, Johnstown, Pennsylvania); d July 23, 1943, Johnstown, Cambria County, Pennsylvania, buried in the Benshoff Hill Cemetery, Johnstown, Pennsylvania. See next PA.4.2.6.

7. **Oliver Cromwell WILLETT**: b January 18, 1881, Johnstown, Cambria County, Pennsylvania; d April 4, 1915, near Armagh, Johnstown, Cambria County, Pennsylvania, in an automobile accident, buried, Grandview Cemetery, Johnstown, Cambria County, Pennsylvania.

8. **Edmund Burke** ("Burke") **WILLETT**: b November 14, 1883, Strongstown, Indiana County, Pennsylvania; m in

Johnstown on October 20, 1914, Mrs. Martha L. (Kase) Haas (b October 13, 1884, Elysburg, Pennsylvania; d April 7, 1954, Johnstown, buried Grandview Cemetery, Johnstown, Pennsylvania); d November 14, 1971, age 88, Shreveport, Louisiana, buried November 17, 1971, Grandview Cemetery, Johnstown, Cambria County, Pennsylvania. See next PA.4.2.8.

9. **Roscoe Samuel WILLETT**: b May 7, 1886; d May 7, 1886.

10. **Victor Jerald WILLETT**: b May 4, 1887, Clearfield County, Pennsylvania; m in Johnstown, Pennsylvania, on May 5, 1907, Olive Viola Zimmerman (b June 1, 1889, Ligonier, Westmoreland County, Pennsylvania; d September 4, 1987), the daughter of John H. Zimmermann and Emma M. Brant; d August 4, 1965, Johnstown, Cambria County, Pennsylvania, buried in the Grandview Cemetery, Johnstown, Cambria County, Pennsylvania. See next PA.4.2.10.

PA.4.2.1
VENORA ALICE WILLETT and **JOHN R. WILKINS**
of Indiana County, Pennsylvania

Venora ("Venorah") Alice Willett was born on December 25, 1866, at Cadiz, Harrison County, Ohio.

Miss Venora A. Willett married in 1892, John R. Wilkins (b February 4, 1857, Johnstown, Pennsylvania; d February 28, 1938, age 81 years, 24 days, buried Armagh Cemetery, Armagh, Pennsylvania) of Oakhurst.

Mrs. Venorah (Willett) Wilkins died in her sleep on January 12, 1918, age 52, and is buried Grandview Cemetery, Johnstown, Cambria County, Pennsylvania.

1. **Alice WILKINS**: b October 24, 1893, Pennsylvania; m A. H. Edberg.

2. **Horatio F. WILKINS**: b January 20, 1896, Butler County, Pennsylvania; m Grace Edna Tiffany; veteran of World War I; d July 4, 1952, Johnstown, Pennsylvania.

3. **Violet Venorah WILKINS**: b November 27, 1900, Pennsylvania; m Percy Everett Williams.

4. **Mary WILKINS**: b November 13, 1903, Johnstown, Pennsylvania; m 1st Joseph N. Winslow; m 2d Guy Brown; d March 31, 1989, Johnstown, buried Armagh Cemetery, Armagh, Pennsylvania.

5. **Jennings Bryan WILKINS**: b January 18, 1898, Connoquenessing, Pennsylvania; d June 14, 1984, Johnstown, Pennsylvania, buried Armagh Cemetery, Armagh, Pennsylvania.

PA.4.2.2
FRANKLIN EMERSON WILLETT
of Johnstown, Cambria County

Franklin Emerson Willett was born on October 25, 1868, in Ohio. He never married. He began work in the Johnstown Police Department in 1899.

Franklin Emerson Willett resided at 127 "M" Street, Johnstown, Pennsylvania (1927) and at 151 Garfield Street, Johnstown (1948) where he was living with his brother James B. Willett. He was active in the Fairfield Avenue Evangelical United Brethren (now part of the United Methodist Church) Church. He was Police Chief of Johnstown, Cambria County for many years. He retired from the Johnstown Police Department in 1948 after 50 years of service.

FRANKLIN EMERSON WILLETT
CIRCA 1940

Franklin Willett died on April 10, 1948, age 79, and is buried at the Grandview Cemetery, Johnstown, Cambria County, Pennsylvania.

PA.4.2.3
WILLIAM MARTIN WILLETT and ANNA RODGERS
of Pennsylvania

William Martin Willett was born on December 27, 1870, at Winchester, Adams County, Ohio.

William Martin Willett married March 16, 1893, Anna ("Annie") Rodgers (b January 31, 1874, Johnstown, Cambria County, Pennsylvania; d May 16, 1948, Johnstown, Cambria County, Pennsylvania, buried Grandview Cemetery, Johnstown, Cambria County, Pennsylvania), the daughter of Thomas and Anna (Hilliard) Rodgers.

1957, FIVE GENERATIONS
NOVA JANE (HEAD) BOYER - NEDA JOY (HEAD) RISCH
EMMA JANE (MISHLER, HEAD) GIVEN (HOLDING)
JUDITH ANN RISCH
WILLIAM MARTIN WILLETT
ETHEL ZOY (WILLETT) MISHLER (HOLDING)
CYNTHIA ANN BOYER
(Picture courtesy of Nova Boyer)

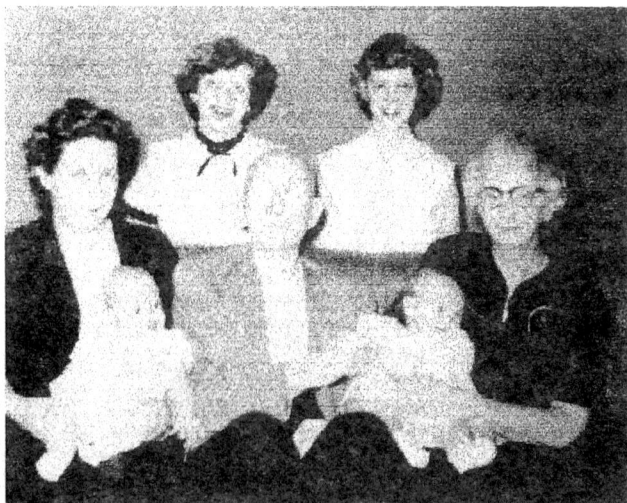

William Martin Willett died on October 7, 1957, age 86, at Johnstown, Cambria County, Pennsylvania, and is buried in the Grandview Cemetery, Johnstown, Cambria County, Pennsylvania.
("Willett House" Quarterly, No. 4, 1987, page 454).

1. **Ethel Zoy WILLETT**: b February 9, 1894, Johnstown, Cambria County, Pennsylvania; m at Johnstown, Cambria County, Pennsylvania, April 11, 1914, Harry Byron Mishler, Sr., (b April 17, 1894, North Ford [area], Somerset County, Pennsylvania; d September 25 [28], 1961, Foresthill, Placer County, California, buried Todd Valley Cemetery, Foresthill, Placer County, California), the son of Levi C. Mishler and Emma Jane Lohr; d December 23, 1986, Johnstown, Cambria County, Pennsylvania, buried Todd Valley Cemetery, Foresthill, Placer County, California. See next PA.4.2.3.1.

2. **Lillian Anne** ("Annie") **WILLETT**: b November 21, 1906, Johnstown, Cambria County, Pennsylvania; m Webster Bruce Rager (b July 19, 1900, Johnstown, Cambria County, Pennsylvania; d March 1, 1965, Johnstown, Cambria County, Pennsylvania, buried Benshoff Hill Cemetery, Johnstown), the son of E. Wallace Rager and Elsie May Noon; d July 5, 1978, Johnstown, Cambria County, Pennsylvania, buried Benshoff Hill Cemetery, Johnstown, Cambria County, Pennsylvania. See next PA.4.2.3.2.

3. **Horatio Franklin WILLETT**: b January 5, 1909, Johnstown, Cambria County, Pennsylvania; m in Johnstown, Cambria County, Pennsylvania, on August 28, 1930, Mary Ellen Gibson (b July 6, 1911, Johnstown, Cambria County, Pennsylvania; d 1993, Ohio), daughter of Harry and Mary Effie (Howard) Gibson; d abt 1983, Ohio. See next PA.4.2.3.3.

4. **William** ("Billy") **Sunday WILLETT**: b November 18, 1913, Johnstown, Cambria County, Pennsylvania; m at Johnstown, Cambria County, Pennsylvania, May 10, 1948, Mildred B. Sakal (b November 29, 1916; d February 28, 1993, age 76, Johnstown, Cambria County, buried Grandview Cemetery); d January 19, 1980, Johnstown, Cambria County, Pennsylvania, buried Grandview Cemetery, Johnstown, Cambria County, Pennsylvania. See next PA.4.2.3.4.

PA.4.2.3.1
ETHEL ZOY WILLETT and HARRY BYRON MISHLER

Ethel Zoy Willett was born February 9, 1894, Johnstown, Cambria County, Pennsylvania.

Miss Ethel Willett married in Johnstown, Cambria County, Pennsylvania, on April 11, 1914, Harry Byron Mishler, Sr. (b April 17, 1894, North Ford [area], Somerset County, Pennsylvania; d September 25 [or 28], 1961, Foresthill, Placer County, California, buried Todd Valley Cemetery, Foresthill, Placer County, California), the son of Levi C. Mishler and Emma Jane Lohr.

Mrs. Ethel Zoy (Willett) Mishler died December 23, 1986, Johnstown, Cambria County, Pennsylvania, and is buried in the Todd Valley Cemetery, Foresthill, Placer County, California.

1. **Emma Jane MISHLER:** April 29, 1915, Johnstown, Cambria County, Pennsylvania; m 1st at Cumberland, Allegany County, Maryland, February 2, 1935, Nathan Jehu Head (b December 29, 1914, Johnstown, Cambria County, Pennsylvania; d December 8, 1962, Johnstown, Cambria County, Pennsylvania), the son of Ralph and Anna M. (McGough) Head; m 2d at Cumberland, Allegany County, Maryland, on August 30, 1963, Robert Richard Given. See next PA.4.2.3.1.1.

2. **Dorothy Fern MISHLER:** b September 25, 1916, Johnstown, Cambria County, Pennsylvania; m at Cumberland, Allegany County, Maryland, on March 1, 1935, James Gradon Blanset; d August 8, 1986, at San Bernardino, San Bernardino County, California, buried Rose Hills, California. See next PA.4.2.3.1.2.

3. **Harry Byron MISHLER, Jr:** b April 7, 1918, Johnstown, Cambria County, Pennsylvania; m 1st at Johnstown, Cambria County, Pennsylvania, on January 28, 1938, Dorothy Lucille Govier; m 2d May 10, 1986, Betty (Walker) Replogle; d August 15, 1993, Johnstown, Pennsylvania. See next PA.4.2.3.1.3.

4. **William Ralph MISHLER:** b September 23, 1919, Johnstown, Cambria County, Pennsylvania; never married; d August 17, 1960, Sacramento, Sacramento County, California, buried Todd Valley Cemetery, Foresthill, Placer County, California.

5. **James Berwin MISHLER:** b January 22, 1921, Johnstown, Cambria County, Pennsylvania; m in Brooklyn, New York, on November 4, 1961, Gloria Ann Latting (b May 20, 1932, Queens, New York), the daughter of Walter and

Mary Agnes (Krumm) Latting. See next PA.4.2.3.1.5.

6. **Harold Paul MISHLER**: b August 22, 1922, Johnstown, Cambria County, Pennsylvania; m at Johnstown, Cambria County, Pennsylvania, on April 21, 1946, Annabel Johns (b September 20, 1924, Johnstown, Cambria County, Pennsylvania; d October 20, 1987, Erie, Erie County, Pennsylvania), the daughter of Clark B. and Leona (Wolford) Johns; d March 14, 1996, at Erie, Erie County, Pennsylvania. See next PA.4.2.3.1.6.

7. **Lillian Anna MISHLER**: b March 15, 1926, Johnstown, Cambria County, Pennsylvania; m at Johnstown, Cambria County, Pennsylvania, on January 14, 1949, Paul Gindleperger (b March 9, 1926, Johnstown, Cambria County, Pennsylvania), the son of Alvin S. and Violet (Melown) Gindlesperger; d on June 21, 1996. See next PA.4.2.3.1.7.

8. **Ruth Viola MISHLER**: b November 10, 1927, Johnstown, Cambria County, Pennsylvania; m at Winchester, Frederick County, Virginia, on September 5, 1947, Charles Parkinson, Jr. (b November 28, 1925, Johnstown, Cambria County, Pennsylvania), the son of Charles F. and Mary E. (Rowe) Parkinson, Sr. See next PA.4.2.3.1.8.

PA.4.2.3.1.1
EMMA JANE MISHLER
of Johnstown, Cambria County, Pennsylvania

Emma Jane Mishler was born April 29, 1915, Johnstown, Cambria County, Pennsylvania.

Miss Emma Jane Mishler married 1st at Cumberland, Allegany County, Maryland, on February 2, 1935, Nathan Jehu Head (b December 29, 1914, Johnstown, Cambria County, Pennsylvania; d December 8, 1962, Johnstown, Cambria County, Pennsylvania, and was buried in the Grandview Cemetery, Johnstown, Cambria County, Pennsylvania), the son of Ralph and Anna M. (McGough) Head.

Mrs. Emma J. (Mishler) Head married 2d at Cumberland, Allegany County, Maryland, on August 30, 1963, Robert Richard Given (b February 27, 1916).

1. **Nova Jane HEAD**: b January 7, 1936, Johnstown, Cambria County, Pennsylvania; m in Washington, D. C., on February 12, 1955, David George Boyer (b December 5, 1934, Johnstown, Cambria County, Pennsylvania), the son of Albert William and Lota Marie (Hostetler) Boyer. See next PA.4.2.3.1.1.1.

2. **Neda Joy HEAD**: b March 13, 1937, Johnstown,

Cambria County, Pennsylvania; m at North Fork (area),
Conemaugh Township, Somerset County, Pennsylvania, on
June 23, 1956, James Stanford Risch (b October 7, 1936,
Lewiston, Mifflin County, Pennsylvania) (now divorced), the
son of James Stanford and Cora (Meyers) Risch, Sr. See next
PA.4.2.3.1.1.2.

3. **Nanette Joan HEAD**: b January 13, 1940, Johnstown, Cambria County, Pennsylvania; m 1st at Winchester,
Frederick County, Virginia, on April 28, 1958, Charles Koontz
(b April 21, 1939, Jerome, Somerset County, Pennsylvania)
(divorced 1979), the son of Ralph and Etta (Oakman) Koontz;
m 2d in Las Vegas, Clark County, Nevada, on November 17,
1979, David Loren Reid (b March 21, 1940, Little Blue,
Jackson County, Missouri). See next PA.4.2.3.1.1.3.

4. **Norina Jen HEAD**: b August 18, 1946, Johnstown,
Cambria County, Pennsylvania; m 1st in Hagerstown,
Washington County, Maryland, on November 13, 1964,
Raymond Valosik (b June 20, 1944, Pittsburgh, Allegheny
County, Pennsylvania), the son of Joseph and Agnes
(McDowell) Valosik; m 2d in Gaithersburg, Montgomery
County, Maryland, on December 23, 1985, Paul Anghel. See
next PA.4.2.3.1.1.4.

PA.4.2.3.1.1.1
NOVA JANE HEAD and DAVID GEORGE BOYER
of Bowie, Prince Georges County, Maryland

Nova Jane Head was born January 7, 1936, Johnstown,
Cambria County, Pennsylvania.

Miss Nova Jane Head married in Washington, D. C., on
February 12, 1955, David George Boyer (b December 5, 1934,
Johnstown, Cambria County, Pennsylvania), the son of Albert
William and Lota Marie (Hostetler) Boyer.

1. **Cynthia Ann BOYER**: b November 20, 1956, Takoma
Park, Prince Georges County, Maryland; m in Bowie, Prince
George County, Maryland, on October 22, 1977, Jack Newport
Smith (b October 15, 1956, Washington, D. C.), the son of
Benjamin Bartlett and Doris Jean (Harris) Smith. See next
PA.4.2.3.1.1.1.1.

2. **Daniel Garland BOYER**: b February 18, 1959,
Cheverly, Prince Georges County, Maryland; m in Mitchellville,
Prince Georges County, Maryland, on September 21, 1985,
Loretta Jane Blue (b October 28, 1962, Washington, D. C.) the
daughter of Bobby Dean and Martha Lee (Ferrell) Blue. See
next PA.4.2.3.1.1.1.2.

PA.4.2.3.1.1.1.1
CYNTHIA ANN BOYER and JACK NEWPORT SMITH

Cynthia Ann Boyer was born on November 20, 1956, Takoma Park, Prince Georges County, Maryland.

Miss Cynthia Ann Boyer married in Bowie, Prince George County, Maryland, on October 22, 1977, Jack Newport Smith (b October 15, 1956, Washington, D. C.), the son of Benjamin Bartlett and Doris Jean (Harris) Smith.

    1. **Janice Norina SMITH**: b July 13, 1979, Washington, D. C.

    2. **Jason David SMITH**: b June 3, 1981, Cheverly, Prince Georges County, Maryland.

PA.4.2.3.1.1.1.2
DANIEL GARLAND BOYER and LORETTA JANE BLUE

Daniel Garland Boyer was born on February 18, 1959, Cheverly, Prince Georges County, Maryland.

Daniel Garland Boyer married in Mitchellville, Prince Georges County, Maryland, on September 21, 1985, Loretta Jane Blue (b October 28, 1962, Washington, D. C.) the daughter of Bobby Dean and Martha Lee (Ferrell) Blue.

    1. **Patrick Randall CARBERRY, Jr.** (stepson): b August 31, 1981, Cheverly, Prince Georges County, Maryland, the son of Patrick Randall Carberry and Loretta Jane Blue.

    2. **Kelly Nicole BOYER**: b June 13, 1987, Cheverly, Prince Georges County, Maryland.

    3. **Cara Danielle BOYER**: b August 28, 1988, Cheverly, Prince Georges County, Maryland.

PA.4.2.3.1.1.2
NEDA JOY HEAD and **JAMES STANFORD RISCH**
of Windber, Somerset County, Pennsylvania

Neda Joy Head was born on March 13, 1937, Johnstown, Cambria County, Pennsylvania.

Miss Neda Joy Head married at North Fork (area), Conemaugh Township, Somerset County, Pennsylvania, on June 23, 1956, James Stanford Risch (b October 7, 1936, Lewistown, Mifflin County, Pennsylvania) (now divorced), the son of James Stanford and Cora (Meyers) Risch, Sr.

1. **Judith Ann RISCH**: b February 5, 1957, Pittsburgh, Allegheny County, Pennsylvania; m in Greensburg, Westmoreland County, Pennsylvania, on September 11, 1982, Mark Christopher Donato (b November 22, 1957, Pittsburgh, Allegheny County, Pennsylvania), the son of Morgan Roy and Fyrn Jacquelyn (Hanford) Donato, Jr. See next PA.4.2.3.1.1.2.1.

2. **James Alan RISCH**: b May 6, 1958, Johnstown, Cambria County, Pennsylvania; m in Coatsville, Chester County, Pennsylvania, on July 18, 1987, Wendy Lynn McClure (b August 6, 1961, Coatsville, Chester County, Pennsylvania), the daughter of William Charles and Sandra Mae (Mendenhall) McClure, Jr. See next PA.4.2.3.1.1.2.2.

3. **Kerry Lauren RISCH**: b November 15, 1960, Washington, D.C.; m in Levittown, Bucks County, Pennsylvania, on June 1, 1985, Beth Ann Hower (b January 30, 1964, Easton, Northampton County, Pennsylvania), the daughter of James Thorton and Nancy Ann Louise (James) Hower, Sr. See next PA.4.2.3.1.1.2.3.

4. **Kelly Lee RISCH**: b February 13, 1962, Oil City, Venango County, Pennsylvania; m in Johnstown, Cambria County, Pennsylvania, on November 30, 1985, Dana Rachelle Hoffman (b December 28, 1965, Windber, Somerset County, Pennsylvania), the daughter of Gerald Clyde and Donna Raye (Dunmire) Hoffman. See next PA.4.2.3.1.1.2.4.

5. **Mark Stanford RISCH**: b December 2, 1964, Erie, Erie County, Pennsylvania; m in Johnstown, Cambria County, Pennsylvania, in November, 1987, Catalina Isip Sarmiento (b November 25, 1965, Santa Rita, Pampanga, Philippines), the daughter of Castor Salalila and Elena Santos (Isip) Sarmiento. See next PA.4.2.3.1.1.2.5.

6. **Chad J. RISCH**: b February 25, 1973, Somerset, Somerset County, Maryland.

PA.4.2.3.1.1.2.1
JUDITH ANN RISCH and MARK CHRISTOPHER DONATO
of Pittsburgh, Allegheny County, Pennsylvania

Judith Ann Risch was born on February 5, 1957, Pittsburgh, Allegheny County, Pennsylvania.

Miss Judith Ann Risch married in Greensburg, Westmoreland County, Pennsylvania, on September 11, 1982, Mark Christopher Donato (b November 22, 1957, Pittsburgh, Allegheny County, Pennsylvania), the son of Morgan Roy and Fyrn Jacquelyn (Hanford) Donato, Jr.

　　1. **Christopher Shane DONATO**: b February 19, 1986, Pittsburgh, Allegheny County, Pennsylvania.
　　2. **Lia Marie DONATO**: b May 18, 1989, Pittsburgh, Allegheny County, Pennsylvania.
　　3. **Michael Paul DONATO**: b March 31, 1996, Pittsburgh, Allegheny County, Pennsylvania.

PA.4.2.3.1.1.2.2
JAMES ALAN RISCH and WENDY LYNN MCCLURE
of Coatsville, Chester County, Pennsylvania

James Alan Risch was born on May 6, 1958, Johnstown, Cambria County, Pennsylvania.

James Alan Risch married in Coatsville, Chester County, Pennsylvania, on July 18, 1987, Wendy Lynn McClure (b August 6, 1961, Coatsville, Chester County, Pennsylvania), the daughter of William Charles and Sandra Mae (Mendenhall) McClure, Jr.

　　1. **Brianna Nicole RISCH**: b June 8, 1991, San Diego, San Diego County, California.
　　2. **Sean Michael RISCH**: b July 8, 1993, Huntsville, Madison County, Alabama.

PA.4.2.3.1.1.2.3
KERRY LAUREN RISCH and BETH ANN HOWER
of Virginia Beach, Virginia

Kerry Lauren Risch was born on November 15, 1960, Washington, D. C.

Kerry Lauren Risch married in Levittown, Bucks County, Pennsylvania, on June 1, 1985, Beth Ann Hower (b January 30, 1964, Easton, Northampton County, Pennsylvania), the daughter of James Thorton and Nancy Ann Louise (James) Hower, Sr.

    1. **Steven Thomas RISCH**: b September 30, 1985, Annapolis, Anne Arundel County, Maryland.
    2. **Ashley Marie RISCH**: b February 10, 1989, Annapolis, Anne Arundel County, Maryland.
    3. **Matthew James RISCH**: b February 11, 1994, Louisville, Jefferson County, Kentucky.

PA.4.2.3.1.1.2.4

KELLY LEE RISCH and **DANA RACHELLE HOFFMAN**

of Montgomery County, Maryland

Kelly Lee Risch was born on February 13, 1962, Oil City, Venango County, Pennsylvania.

Kelly Lee Risch married in Johnstown, Cambria County, Pennsylvania, on November 30, 1985, Dana Rachelle Hoffman (b December 28, 1965, Windber, Somerset County, Pennsylvania), the daughter of Gerald Clyde and Donna Raye (Dunmire) Hoffman.

    1. **Kayla Brittany RISCH**: b February 7, 1988, Silver Spring, Montgomery County, Maryland.
    2. **Jared Kelly RISCH**: b July 4, 1990, Silver Spring, Montgomery County, Maryland.
    3. **Zachary Todd RISCH**: b November 21, 1992, Silver Spring, Montgomery County, Maryland.

PA.4.2.3.1.1.2.5

MARK STANFORD RISCH and **CATALINA ISIP SARMIENTO**

of San Clemente, Orange County, California

Mark Stanford Risch was born on December 2, 1964, Erie, Erie County, Pennsylvania.

Mark S. Risch married in Johnstown, Cambria County, Pennsylvania, in November, 1987, Catalina Isip Sarmiento (b November 25, 1965, Santa Rita, Pampanga, Philippines), the daughter of Castor Salalila and Elena Santos (Isip) Sarmiento.

    1. **Justine Erica Sarmiento RISCH**: b July 20, 1988, San Diego, San Diego County, California.

PA.4.2.3.1.1.3
NANETTE JOAN HEAD
of Kent, King County, Washington

Nanette Joan Head was born on January 13, 1940, Johnstown, Cambria County, Pennsylvania.

Miss Nanette Joan Head married 1st at Winchester, Frederick County, Virginia, on April 28, 1958, Charles Koontz (b April 21, 1939, Jerome, Somerset County, Pennsylvania) (divorced 1979), the son of Ralph and Etta (Oakman) Koontz.

Mrs. Nanette Joan (Head) Koontz married 2d in Las Vegas, Clark County, Nevada, on November 17, 1979, David Loren Reid (b March 21, 1940, Little Blue, Jackson County, Missouri), the son of Cecil Harris and Helen Lucille (Ashcraft) Heath. David was adopted when he was 2 years old.

1. **Bret Lorin KOONTZ**: b February 19, 1960, Johnstown, Cambria County, Pennsylvania; m in Kirkland, King County, Washington, on December 31, 1988, Linda Kay West (b June 21, 1962, San Francisco, San Francisco County, California), the daughter of Lawrence J. and Kathyrn L. (Hooper) West. See next PA.4.2.3.1.1.3.1.

2. **Brian Lee KOONTZ**: b January 8, 1962, Johnstown, Cambria County, Pennsylvania; m in Windber, Somerset County, Pennsylvania, on May 20, 1989, Pamela Jean Noll (now divorced), the daughter of Wayne and Barbara Noll. See next PA.4.2.3.1.1.3.2.

3. **Lisa Renee KOONTZ**: b May 3, 1963, Johnstown, Cambria County, Pennsylvania; m 1st in Jerome, Somerset County, Pennsylvania, William Koss (b December 26, 19--), the son of Michael Drummond and Patricia Koss; m 2d in Lincoln, Lancaster County, Nebraska, on September 7, 1985, Lawrence Joseph Pospisil (b March 27, 1962, Lincoln, Lancaster County, Nebraska), the son of Leonard James and Dorothy Ann (Skoda) Pospisil. See next PA.4.2.3.1.1.3.3.

4. **Lara Rae KOONTZ**: b June 24, 1971, Johnstown, Cambria County, Pennsylvania; m in Las Vegas, Clark County, Nevada, on December 9, 1993, Todd Robert Lucas (b November 18, 1964, at Brewster, Okanogan County, Washington), the son of Robert W. and Anne (Miller) Lucas.

PA.4.2.3.1.1.3.1
BRET LORIN KOONTZ and LINDA KAY WEST
of Issaquah, King County, Washington

Bret Lorin Koontz was born on February 19, 1960, Johnstown, Cambria County, Pennsylvania.

Bret L. Koontz married in Kirkland, King County, Washington, on December 31, 1988, Linda Kay West (b June 21, 1962, San Francisco, San Francisco County, California), the daughter of Lawrence J. and Kathyrn L. (Hooper) West.

1. **Zena Quinelle KOONTZ**: b July 31, 1994, Issaquah, Kent County, Washington.

2. **Zachary Quinton KOONTZ**: b January 7, 1996, Issaquah, Kent County, Washington.

PA.4.2.3.1.1.3.2
BRIAN LEE KOONTZ and PAMELA JEAN NOLL
of Johnstown, Cambria County, Pennsylvania

Brian Lee Koontz was born on January 8, 1962, Johnstown, Cambria County, Pennsylvania;.

Brian Lee Koontz married in Windber, Somerset County, Pennsylvania, on May 20, 1989, Pamela Jean Noll (now divorced), the daughter of Wayne and Barbara Noll.

1. **Trevor Lee KOONTZ**: b January 12, 1990, Johnstown Cambria County, Pennsylvania.

2. **Devon Richard KOONTZ**: b May 17, 1993, Johnstown, Cambria County, Pennsylvania.

PA.4.2.3.1.1.3.3
LISA RENEE KOONTZ

Lisa Renee Koontz was born on May 3, 1963, Johnstown, Cambria County, Pennsylvania.

Miss Lisa Renee Koontz married 1st in Jerome, Somerset County, Pennsylvania, William Koss (b December 26, 19--), the son of Michael Drummond and Patricia Koss.

Mrs. Lisa Renee (Koontz) Koss married 2d in Lincoln, Lancaster County, Nebraska, on September 7, 1985, Lawrence Joseph Pospisil (b March 27, 1962, Lincoln, Lancaster County, Nebraska), the son of Leonard James and Dorothy Ann (Skoda) Pospisil.

1. **William Charles KOSS**: b August 4, 1980, Johnstown, Cambria County, Pennsylvania.

2. **Marissa Rachele POSPISIL**: b October 14, 1986, Lincoln, Lancaster County, Nebraska.

3. **MaLynda Rheanne POSPISIL**: b October 5, 1992, Lincoln, Lancaster County, Nebraska.

PA.4.2.3.1.1.4
NORINA JEN HEAD
of Gaithersburg, Montgomery County, Maryland

Norina Jen Head was born on August 18, 1946, Johnstown, Cambria County, Pennsylvania.

Miss Norina Jen Head married 1st in Hagerstown, Washington County, Maryland, on November 13, 1964, Raymond Valosik (b June 20, 1944, Pittsburgh, Allegheny County, Pennsylvania), the son of Joseph and Agnes (McDowell) Valosik. They divorced in 1980.

Mrs. Norina Jen (Head) Valosik married 2d in Gaithersburg, Montgomery County, Maryland, on December 23, 1985, Paul Anghel.

    1. **Lauren Rae VALOSIK**: b August 14, 1965, Munhall, Allegheny County, Pennsylvania; m 1st in Rockville, Montgomery County. Maryland, on June 26, 1987, Russell Todd Sisler (b November 26, 1963, New Mexico), the son of James and Mary Ellen (Smyth) Sisler. They divorced in 1989. Mrs. Lauren Rae (Valosik) Sisler married 2d at Rockville, Montgomery County, Maryland, on September 20, 1993, Richard Alan LaRiviere (b July 27, 1959, Bethesda, Montgomery County, Maryland), the son of Joseph and Elizabeth Lou (Shell) LaRiviere.

    1. **Maxwell Joseph LARIVIERE**: b December 22, 1993, Silver Spring, Montgomery County, Maryland.

PA.4.2.3.1.2
DOROTHY FERN MISHLER and **JAMES GRADON BLANSET**
of Johnstown, Cambria County, Pennsylvania

Dorothy Fern Mishler was born on September 25, 1916, Johnstown, Cambria County, Pennsylvania.

Miss Dorothy Fern Mishler married at Cumberland, Allegany County, Maryland, on March 1, 1935, James Gradon Blanset (b July 3, 1913, Johnstown, Cambria County, Pennsylvania), the son of Charles Isaac and Wilver (Pender) Blanset.

Mrs. Dorothy Fern (Mishler) Blanset died on August 8, 1986, at San Bernardino, San Bernardino County, California, and is buried at Rose Hills, California.

1. **Robert James BLANSET**: b September 21, 1935, Johnstown, Cambria County, Pennsylvania; m 1st at San Diego, San Diego County, Pennsylvania, on June 10, 1955, Raye Lee Heeb; m 2d at Incline Village, Washoe County, Nevada, on September 28, 1979, Irene Mae DuVall (b November 7, 1942, Brooklyn, New York; d August 5, 1995, Carthage, Jasper County, Missouri). See next PA.4.2.3.1.2..1.

2. **Walter Francis BLANSET**: b April 29, 1937, Johnstown, Cambria County, Pennsylvania; m at Carson City, Ormsby County, Nevada, on August 18, 1962, Barbara Wilcox. See next PA.4.2.3.1.2.2.

3. **William Sandfried BLANSET**: b March 30, 1938, Johnstown, Cambria County, Pennsylvania; m at San Fernando, Los Angeles County, California, on November 19, 1961, Mary Jo Shaffer. See next PA.4.2.3.1.2.3.

4. **Glenn Harry BLANSET**: b April 13, 1939, Johnstown, Cambria County, Pennsylvania; m at Sylmar, Los Angeles County, California, on May 28, 1966, Elizabeth Ruth Criglar. See next PA.4.2.3.1.2.4.

5. **Allan Harold BLANSET**: b November 25, 1944, Johnstown, Cambria County, Pennsylvania; m at Venice, Los Angeles County, California, on October 1, 1966, Eileen E. Sweezey. See next PA.4.2.3.1.2.1.

PA.4.2.3.1.2.1
ROBERT JAMES BLANSET
of Webb City, Jasper County, Missouri

Robert James Blanset was born on September 21, 1935, Johnstown, Cambria County, Pennsylvania.

Robert James Blanset married 1st at San Diego, San Diego County, California, on June 10, 1955, Raye Lee Heeb, the daughter of Glenn Heeb. They divorced in 1979.

Robert James Blanset married 2d at Incline Village, Washoe County, Nevada, on September 28, 1979, Irene Mae (Dominski) DuVall (b November 7, 1942, Brooklyn, New York), the daughter of Adam Chester and Rita (Byrnes) Dominski.

1. **Ronald L. BLANSET**: b January 7, 1956, San Diego, San Diego County, California; resides (1997) Hilo, Hawaii.

2. **Richard Lee BLANSET**: b March 28, 1957, San Diego, San Diego County, California; m February 14, 1980, Judith Garrett. See next PA.4.2.3.1.2.1.2.

3. **Roberta Jane BLANSET**: b April 14, 1958, San Diego, San Diego County, California; m Michael Fahey. See next PA.4.2.3.1.2.1.3.

4. **Rory Lane BLANSET**: b November 7, 1959, California; m at Covina, Los Angeles County, California, on March 6, 1982, Antonia (Nitsa) Kefalas; of (1997) Tampa, Hillsborough County, Florida.

5. **Robert Jay BLANSET**: b January 7, 1961, Covina, Los Angeles County, California; m at Covina, Los Angeles County, California, on June 7, 1980, Merrie McDavitt. See next PA.4.2.3.1.2.1.5.

PA.4.2.3.1.2.1.2
RICHARD LEE BLANSET and JUDITH GARRETT
of Joplin, Jasper County, Missouri

Richard Lee Blanset was born on March 28, 1957, San Diego, San Diego County, California

Richard Lee Blanset married on February 14, 1980, Judith Garrett.

1. **Jennifer BLANSET**: b May 25, 1983.

PA.4.2.3.1.2.1.3
ROBERTA JANE BLANSET and MICHAEL FAHEY
of Las Vegas, Clark County, Nevada

Roberta Jane Blanset was born on April 14, 1958, San Diego, San Diego County, California.

Roberta Jane Blanset married Michael Fahey.

1. **Sandra FAHEY** (twin):
2. **Jennifer FAHEY** (twin): died infant.
3. **Tiffany FAHEY**:

PA.4.2.3.1.2.1.5
ROBERT JAY BLANSET and MERRIE MCDAVITT
of Joplin, Jasper County, Missouri

Robert Jay Blanset was born on January 7, 1961, Covina, Los Angeles County, California.

Robert Jay Blanset married at Covina, Los Angeles County, California, on June 7, 1980, Merrie McDavitt.

1. **Jason BLANSET**:

PA.4.2.3.1.2.2
WALTER FRANCIS BLANSET and BARBARA WILCOX
of San Jose, Santa Clara County, California

Walter Francis Blanset was born on April 29, 1937, Johnstown, Cambria County, Pennsylvania.

Walter Francis Blanset married at Carson City, Ormsby County, Nevada, on August 18, 1962, Barbara Wilcox, the daughter of Wilbur and Annie Wilcox.

1. **Cynthia Lynn BLANSET**: b August 26, 1966, San Jose, Santa Clara County, California.
2. **Sandra Louise BLANSET**: b October 1, 1968, San Jose, Santa Clara County, California.

PA.4.2.3.1.2.3
WILLIAM SANDFRIED BLANSET and MARY JO SHAFFER
of Dickson, Dickson County, Tennessee

William Sandfried Blanset was born on March 30, 1938, Johnstown, Cambria County, Pennsylvania.

William Sandfried Blanset married at San Fernando, Los Angeles County, California, on November 19, 1961, Mary Jo Shaffer (b April 18, 1943, Lynnville, Jasper County, Iowa), the daughter of Clifford W. and Leona V. (Johnson) Shaffer.

1. **Jolene Michele BLANSET**: b October 12, 1966, San Fernando, Los Angeles County, California.
2. **Kelley Melissa BLANSET**: b October 29, 1969, Granada Hills, California; d October 29, 1969, and is buried in Glen Haven, San Fernando, Los Angeles County, California.

PA.4.2.3.1.2.4
GLENN HARRY BLANSET and **ELIZABETH RUTH CRIGLAR**
of Bishop, Inyo County, California

Glenn Harry Blanset was born on April 13, 1939, Johnstown, Cambria County, Pennsylvania.

Glenn Harry Blanset married at Sylmar, Los Angeles County, California, on May 28, 1966, Elizabeth Ruth Criglar (b September 21, 1943, Independence, Jackson County, Missouri), the daughter of Roy R. and Emma Ruth (Shrout) Criglar.

    1. **Todd William BLANSET**: b December 22, 1969, Panorama City, Los Angeles County, California.

    2. **Derk Glenn BLANSET**: b February 9, 1972, Panorama City, Los Angeles County, California.

PA.4.2.3.1.2.5
ALLAN HAROLD BLANSET and **EILEEN E. SWEEZEY**
of San Diego, San Diego County, California

Allan Harold Blanset was born on November 25, 1944, Johnstown, Cambria County, Pennsylvania.

Allan Harold Blanset married at Venice, Los Angeles County, California, on October 1, 1966, Eileen E. Sweezey (b July 16, 1947, Lincoln, Lancaster County, Nebraska), the daughter of Harvey F. Sweezey, Jr.

    1. **Anthony J. BLANSET**: b July 6, 1967, San Fernando, Los Angeles County, California.

    2. **Terrance R. BLANSET**: b March 27, 1969, San Fernando, Los Angeles County, California.

PA.4.2.3.1.3
HARRY BYRON MISHLER, JR.,
of Johnstown, Cambria County, Pennsylvania

Harry Byron Mishler, Jr., was born April 7, 1918, Johnstown, Cambria County, Pennsylvania.

Harry Byron Mishler, Jr., married 1st at Johnstown, Cambria County, Pennsylvania, on January 28, 1938, Dorothy Lucille Govier (b April 20, 1921, Johnstown, Cambria County, Pennsylvania; d November 20, 1982, Johnstown, Cambria County, Pennsylvania, buried at Grandview Cemetery, Johnstown, Cambria County, Pennsylvania), the daughter of Ralph and Mary (Hopkins) Govier.

Harry Byron Mishler, Jr., married 2d May 10, 1986, Betty (Walker) Replogle. He was a mail carrier for 32 years.

Harry B. Mishler, Jr., died August 15, 1993, Johnstown, Cambria County, Pennsylvania (cremated)

1. **Byron** ("Barry") **Lee MISHLER**: b June 12, 1939, Johnstown, Cambria County, Pennsylvania.   See next PA.4.2.3.1.3.1.
2. **Carol Ann MISHLER**: b September 20, 1943, Johnstown, Cambria County, Pennsylvania; m Heidenthal; resides (1993) Johnstown, Cambria County, Pennsylvania. See next PA.4.2.3.1.3.2.
3. **Debra Jane MISHLER**: b February 25, 1957, Johnstown, Cambria County, Pennsylvania; m Peter Karageanes. See next PA.4.2.3.1.3.3.

PA.4.2.3.1.3.1
BYRON LEE MISHLER

Byron ("Barry") Lee Mishler was born on June 12, 1939, Johnstown, Cambria County, Pennsylvania.

He resides (1993) in Maryland.

1. **Mark MISHLER**:
2. **Todd MISHLER**:

PA.4.2.3.1.3.2
CAROL ANN MISHLER and **HEIDENTHAL**

Carol Ann Mishler was born on September 20, 1943, Johnstown, Cambria County, Pennsylvania.

Miss Carol Ann Mishler married Heidenthal. They reside (1993) in Johnstown, Cambria County, Pennsylvania.

PA.4.2.3.1.3.3
DEBRA JANE MISHLER and **PETER KARAGEANES**

Debra Jane Mishler was born on February 25, 1957, Johnstown, Cambria County, Pennsylvania.

Miss Debra Jane Mishler married Peter Karageanes. They reside (1993) in Florida.

1. **Jennifer KARAGEANES**:
2. **Eric KARAGEANES**:

PA.4.2.3.1.5
JAMES BERWIN MISHLER and GLORIA ANN LATTING
of Davidsville, Somerset County, Pennsylvania

James Berwin Mishler was born on January 22, 1921, Johnstown, Cambria County, Pennsylvania.

James Berwin Mishler married in Brooklyn, New York, on November 4, 1961, Gloria Ann Latting (b May 20, 1932, Queens, New York), the daughter of Walter and Mary Agnes (Krumm) Latting.

1. **David James MISHLER**: b July 26, 1963, Auburn, Placer County, California.

2. **Barry Walter MISHLER**: b May 19, 1965, Roseville, Placer County, California.

PA.4.2.3.1.6
HAROLD PAUL MISHLER and ANNABEL JEAN JOHNS
of Erie County, Pennsylvania

Harold Paul Mishler was born on August 22, 1922, Johnstown, Cambria County, Pennsylvania. He graduated from Indiana University of Pennsylvania and the University of Kansas. He served in the U.S. Navy during World War II as a fighter pilot, attaining the rank of Lieutenant. He was awarded the World War II Victory Medal, American Theater Medal, Asiatic-Pacific Campaign Medal with three stars, Philippine Liberation Medal and the Air Medal with gold star.

Harold Paul Mishler married at Johnstown, Cambria County, Pennsylvania, on April 21, 1946, Annabel Jean Johns (b September 20, 1924, Johnstown, Cambria County, Pennsylvania; d October 20, 1987, Erie, Erie County, Pennsylvania), the daughter of Clark B. and Leona (Wolford) Johns.

He was employed by GTE as director of revenues and requirements.

Harold "Hud" Mishler died on March 14, 1996, at Erie, Erie County, Pennsylvania.

1. (Baby boy) **MISHLER**: b August 24, 1947, Johnstown, Cambria County, Pennsylvania; d August 24, 1947, Johnstown, Cambria County, Pennsylvania, buried Thompson Cemetery, Hillsdale, Indiana County, Pennsylvania.

2. **Clark Douglas MISHLER**: b January 4, 1951, Johnstown, Cambria County, Pennsylvania; m at Los Angeles, California, on December 10, 1980, Ilene Julie Kaufman (b September 21, 1957, Los Angeles, Los Angeles County,

California), the daughter of Arnold and Marilyn (Gordon) Kaufman. See next PA.4.2.3.1.6.2.

3. **Byron Kihm MISHLER**: b July 7, 1954, Corry, Erie County, Pennsylvania; m at Albion, Erie County, Pennsylvania, on November 17, 1970, Vicki Tortorelli. See next PA.4.2.3.1.6.3.

4. **Robert Paul MISHLER**: b April 21, 1960, Erie County, Pennsylvania.

PA.4.2.3.1.6.2
CLARK DOUGLAS MISHLER and ILENE JULIE KAUFMAN
of California

Clark Douglas Mishler was born on January 4, 1951, Johnstown, Cambria County, Pennsylvania.

Clark Douglas Mishler married at Los Angeles, Los Angeles County, California, on December 10, 1980, Ilene Julie Kaufman (b September 21, 1957, Los Angeles, Los Angeles County, California), the daughter of Arnold and Marilyn (Gordon) Kaufman.

1. **Matthew Erik MISHLER**: b July 9, 1981, Tarzana, California.

PA.4.2.3.1.6.3
BYRON KIHM MISHLER and VICKI TORTORELLI
of Erie County, Pennsylvania

Byron Kihm Mishler was born on July 7, 1954, Corry, Erie County, Pennsylvania.

Byron Kihm Mishler married at Albion, Erie County, Pennsylvania, on November 17, 1970, Vicki Tortorelli (b January 21, 1954, Albion, Erie County, Pennsylvania), the daughter of Victor and Virginia (Dysko) Tortorelli. They divorced in 1976.

1. **Jason Matthew MISHLER**: b May 19, 1971, Erie, Erie County, Pennsylvania.

PA.4.2.3.1.7

LILLIAN ANNA MISHLER and **PAUL GINDLESPERGER**

of Johnstown, Cambria County, Pennsylvania

Lillian Anna Mishler was born on March 15, 1926, Johnstown, Cambria County, Pennsylvania.

Miss Lillian Anna Mishler married at Johnstown, Cambria County, Pennsylvania, on January 14, 1949, Paul Gindlesperger (b March 9, 1926, Johnstown, Cambria County, Pennsylvania), the son of Alvin S. and Violet (Melown) Gindlesperger.

Mrs. Lillian (Mishler) Gindlesperger died on June 21, 1996, at Latrobe Hospital, Indiana County, Pennsylvania.

1. **Terry P. GINDLESPERGER**: b September 25, 1950, Johnstown, Cambria County, Pennsylvania; m at Johnstown, Cambria County, Pennsylvania, on June 24, 1972, Colleen D. Roberts (b August 5, 1952, Johnstown, Cambria County, Pennsylvania), the daughter of George F. and V. Faye (Cameron) Roberts, Jr. See next PA.4.2.3.1.7.1.

2. **Beverly D. GINDLESPERGER** (twin): b December 28, 1953, Johnstown, Cambria County, Pennsylvania; m at Johnstown, Cambria County, Pennsylvania, on August 12, 1972, Stanley C. Ziemba (b December 3, 1950, Johnstown, Cambria County, Pennsylvania), the son of Chester and Ruth (Miskowitz) Ziemba. See next PA.4.2.3.1.7.2.

3. **Kenneth R. GINDLESPERGER** (twin): b December 28, 1953, Johnstown, Cambria County, Pennsylvania; d December 29, 1953, at Johnstown, Cambria County, Pennsylvania.

4. **Judith A. GINDLESPERGER**: b September 4, 1959, Johnstown, Cambria County, Pennsylvania; m at Johnstown, Cambria County, Pennsylvania, on June 4, 1977, Nicky J. Cooper (b May 5, 1956, Johnstown, Cambria County, Pennsylvania), the son of Ray D. and Theresa (Duris) Cooper. See next PA.4.2.3.1.7.4.

PA.4.2.3.1.7.1

TERRY P. GINDLESPERGER and **COLLEEN D. ROBERTS**

of Johnstown, Cambria County, Pennsylvania

Terry P. Gindlesperger was born on September 25, 1950, Johnstown, Cambria County, Pennsylvania.

Terry P. Gindlesperger married at Johnstown, Cambria County, Pennsylvania, on June 24, 1972, Colleen D. Roberts (b August 5, 1952, Johnstown, Cambria County, Pennsylvania), the daughter of George F. and V. Faye (Cameron) Roberts,

Jr.

1. **Marcee Lynn GINDLESPERGER**: b January 31, 1980, Johnstown, Cambria County, Pennsylvania.
2. **Megan Faye GINDLESPERGER**: b October 15, 1982, Johnstown, Cambria County, Pennsylvania.

PA.4.2.3.1.7.2
BEVERLY D. GINDLESPERGER and **STANLEY C. ZIEMBA**
of Camp Hill, Cumberland County, Pennsylvania

Beverly D. Gindlesperger (twin) was born on December 28, 1953, Johnstown, Cambria County, Pennsylvania.

Miss Beverly D. Gindlesperger married at Johnstown, Cambria County, Pennsylvania, on August 12, 1972, Stanley C. Ziemba (b December 3, 1950, Johnstown, Cambria County, Pennsylvania), the son of Chester and Ruth (Miskowitz) Ziemba.

1. **Christopher Michael ZIEMBA**: b April 11, 1973, Pittsburgh, Allegheny County, Pennsylvania.
2. **Stephanie Lynn ZIEMBA**: b October 12, 1978, Harrisburg, Dauphin County, Pennsylvania.

PA.4.2.3.1.7.4
JUDITH A. GINDLESPERGER and **NICKY J. COOPER**
of Johnstown, Cambria County, Pennsylvania

Judith A. Gindlesperger was born on September 4, 1959, Johnstown, Cambria County, Pennsylvania.

Miss Judith A. Gindlesperger married at Johnstown, Cambria County, Pennsylvania, on June 4, 1977, Nicky J. Cooper (b May 5, 1956, Johnstown, Cambria County, Pennsylvania), the son of Ray D. and Theresa (Duris) Cooper.

1. **Nicole Marie COOPER**: b January 3, 1978, Johnstown, Cambria County, Pennsylvania.

PA.4.2.3.1.8
RUTH VIOLA MISHLER and CHARLES PARKINSON, JR.
of Johnstown, Cambria County, Pennsylvania

Ruth Viola Mishler was born on November 10, 1927, Johnstown, Cambria County, Pennsylvania.

Miss Ruth Viola Mishler married at Winchester, Frederick County, Virginia, on September 5, 1947, Charles Parkinson, Jr. (b November 28, 1925, Johnstown, Cambria County, Pennsylvania), the son of Charles F. and Mary E. (Rowe) Parkinson, Sr.

1. **Dawn Elaine PARKINSON**: b July 8, 1948, Johnstown, Cambria County, Pennsylvania; m Jack Parke.
2. **Kenneth Charles PARKINSON**: b March 4, 1950, Johnstown, Cambria County, Pennsylvania; single.
3. **Jeffrey Hal PARKINSON**: b August 16, 1952, Johnstown, Cambria County, Pennsylvania; m at Johnstown, Cambria County, Pennsylvania, on November 14, 1981, Michele Lovekin (b January 8, 1949, Johnstown, Cambria County, Pennsylvania), the daughter of Ira S. and Doris J. (Price) Lovekin. See next PA.4.2.3.1.8.3.
4. **Lorraine Joyce PARKINSON**: b July 21, 1957, Johnstown, Cambria County, Pennsylvania; m Robert Lewis Fisher.
5. **Brian Keith PARKINSON**: b August 17, 1959, Johnstown, Cambria County, Pennsylvania; m Melanie Dallope.

PA.4.2.3.1.8.3
JEFFREY HAL PARKINSON and MICHELE LOVEKIN

Jeffrey Hal Parkinson was born on August 16, 1952, Johnstown, Cambria County, Pennsylvania.

Jeffrey Hal Parkinson married at Johnstown, Cambria County, Pennsylvania, on November 14, 1981, Michele Lovekin (b January 8, 1949, Johnstown, Cambria County, Pennsylvania), the daughter of Ira S. and Doris J. (Price) Lovekin.

1. **Kevin S. PARKINSON**: b June 14, 1982, Hershey, Dauphin County, Pennsylvania.
2. **Christina A. PARKINSON**: b May 7, 1984, Lancaster, Lancaster County, Pennsylvania.

PA.4.2.3.2
LILLIAN ANNE WILLETT and WEBSTER BRUCE RAGER
of Johnstown, Cambria County, Pennsylvania

Lillian Anne ("Annie") Willett was born on November 21, 1906, Johnstown, Cambria County, Pennsylvania.

Miss Lillian Anne Willett married Webster Bruce Rager (b July 19, 1900, Johnstown, Cambria County, Pennsylvania; d March 1, 1965, Johnstown, Cambria County, Pennsylvania, buried Benshoff Hill Cemetery, Johnstown), the son of E. Wallace Rager and Elsie May Noon.

Mrs. Lillian Anne (Willett) Rager died on July 5, 1978, Johnstown, Cambria County, Pennsylvania, and is buried in the Benshoff Hill Cemetery, Johnstown, Cambria County, Pennsylvania.

1. **Gladys Jean RAGER**: m Frank Alter; d abt 1986.
2. **Robert Bruce RAGER**: m Stella.

PA.4.2.3.3
HORATIO FRANKLIN WILLETT and MARY ELLEN GIBSON
of Madison, Lake County, Ohio

Horatio Franklin Willett was born on January 5, 1909, at Johnstown, Cambria County, Pennsylvania.

Horatio F. Willett married at Johnstown, Cambria County, Pennsylvania, on August 28, 1930, Mary Ellen Gibson (b July 6, 1911, Johnstown, Cambria County, Pennsylvania; d 1993, Ohio), daughter of Harry and Mary Effie (Howard) Gibson.

Horatio F. Willett died about 1983 in Ohio.

1. **Arlen E. WILLETT**: b June 9, 1931, Johnstown, Cambria County, Pennsylvania; m Wanda M. Frye.
2. **David L. WILLETT**: b January 5, 1934, Johnstown, Cambria County, Pennsylvania; m Patricia Walsh.
3. **Raymond Vernon WILLETT**: b August 9, 1939, Johnstown, Pennsylvania; m Judith Lewis.
4. **Linda Mae WILLETT**: b May 1, 1942, Johnstown, Cambria County, Pennsylvania; m Devon West.
5. **Patricia Ann WILLETT**: b August 4, 1947, Johnstown, Cambria County, Pennsylvania.

PA.4.2.3.4
WILLIAM SUNDAY WILLETT and MILDRED B. SAKAL
of Johnstown, Cambria County, Pennsylvania

William ("Billy") Sunday Willett was born November 18, 1913, Johnstown, Cambria County, Pennsylvania. He was inducted December 18, 1942, and served as a Corporal during World War II.

William S. Willett married at Johnstown, Cambria County, Pennsylvania, on May 10, 1948, Mrs. Mildred B. (Lugar) Sakal (b November 29, 1916, Johnstown; d February 28, 1993, age 76, Johnstown, Cambria County, Pennsylvania, buried Grandview Cemetery), the daughter of Nicholas Lugar and Magdeline Sopric. Mildred Lugar had married 1st Louis Sakal.

William and Mildred resided Upper Yoder Township, Johnstown, Cambria County, Pennsylvania, where he worked for the "Tribune-Democrat" Newspaper from 1946 until his retirement in 1976. He was a past Vice President of the Johnstown Local 137, Typographical Union. They attended St. Clement's Catholic Church.

William S. Willett died January 19, 1980, age 66, Johnstown, Cambria County, Pennsylvania, and is buried in the Grandview Cemetery, Johnstown, Cambria County, Pennsylvania.

(REF: Obituary, Tribune-Democrat, 1980, "Former Printer Dies at 66!").

    1. **William Lee WILLETT**: b January 9, 1950; m Connie Speigel.

    2. **Diane M. SAKAL** (stepdaughter): b November 28, 1938.

    3. **Donald L. SAKAL** (stepson): b August 24, 1943; m April 23, --, Georgann Billetdeaux.

PA.4.2.5
GEORGE RAYMOND WILLETT and **CARRIE M. SMITH**
of Pittsburgh, Allegheny County, Pennsylvania

George Raymond Willett was born on May 18, 1875, at Keystone Furnace, Gallia County, Ohio.

George R. Willett married in Dale Borough, Johnstown, Cambria County, Pennsylvania, in 1896, Carrie M. Smith (b October 10, 1879, Indiana County, Pennsylvania; d May 27, 1961, Johnstown, Cambria County, Pennsylvania, buried Grandview Cemetery, Johnstown, Pennsylvania), the daughter of Charles A. and Eliza Jane (Helman) Smith.

He was employed by the Otis Elevator Company for 22 years in Pittsburgh, Allegheny County, Pennsylvania.

George R. Willett died in an automobile accident on February 17, 1924, in Pittsburgh, Pennsylvania, and was buried, on February 21, 1924, in Lot 372 of the Grandview Cemetery, Johnstown, Cambria County, Pennsylvania.

1. **Donald F. WILLETT**: b September 25, 1901, Pittsburgh, Pennsylvania; died of coronary occlusion on November 29, 1955, Johnstown, Cambria County, Pennsylvania, buried Grandview Cemetery, Johnstown, Cambria County, Pennsylvania.

2. **Claire Victor WILLETT**: b 1904, Pittsburgh, Pennsylvania; served as Second Lieutenant in World War II in the Army Air Corps; died September 11, 1943, age 39, from a fractured skull, in an airplane crash while test piloting at El Paso, Texas. His body was returned to Pennsylvania, and he was buried in the Grandview Cemetery, Johnstown, Cambria County, Pennsylvania.

PA.4.2.6
JAMES BUCHANAN WILLETT
and **EMILY GERTRUDE WILSON**
of Indiana County, Pennsylvania

James Buchanan Willett was born on July 28, 1878, at Curwensville, Clearfield County, Pennsylvania, according to his obituary. He came to Johnstown, Cambria County, with his parents in 1890.

1910
JAMES B. WILLETT CHILDREN
STANDING; VENORAH AND JOHN
SITTING: HARRY HOLDING BLANCHE
(Picture courtesy of Joan Grabenstein)

James Buchanan Willett married at Cumberland, Maryland, on July 23, 1895, Emily Gertrude Wilson (b February 22, 1880, Indiana County, Pennsylvania; d November 7, 1948, Norristown, Montgomery County, Pennsylvania, buried Benshoff Cemetery, Johnstown, Cambria County, Pennsylvania), the daughter of William and Jane (Sides) Wilson.

1916
JAMES B. WILLETT CHILDREN
STANDING: WILLIAM H., HARRY D.
COZETTA HOLDING ALVERTA,
AND VENORAH G.,
SITTING: JOHN C. AND CARRIE B.,
THE DOG IS "BOOTS"
(Picture courtesy of Joan Grabenstein)

Emma was 5'-3" and a large woman. She was a Sunday School teacher. Emily went to live with her son John in Essington, Tinicum Township, Pennsylvania, on July 18, 1948. She died of a heart attack while on a visit to Norristown.

James Willett resided in Morrelville and worked for the B. and O. Railroad for some time and then entered the employ of the Bethlehem Steel Company in Johnstown, Cambria County, Pennsylvania.

CIRCA 1940
JAMES B. WILLETT
(Picture courtesy of Joan Grabenstein)

James Buchanan Willett died of cancer a week after he retired from the steel plant, on July 23, 1943, age 63, at Johnstown, Cambria County, Pennsylvania, and is buried in the Benshoff Hill Cemetery, Johnstown, Cambria County, Pennsylvania.

(Obituary, James Buchanan Willett, July 23, 1943).

1.   **Cozetta** ("Coxetta", "Cozzetta") **Jane WILLETT**: b May 26, 1896, Johnstown, Cambria County, Pennsylvania; m January 12, 1918, Irvin Chester Ribblett (b September 14, 1895, Johnstown, Cambria County, Pennsylvania; d October 13, 1984, Milton, Wisconsin); d July 19, 1946, Johnstown, Cambria County, Pennsylvania, buried in the Benshoff Hill Cemetery, Johnstown, Cambria County, Pennsylvania.   See next PA.4.2.6.1.

2.   **Evelyn** ("Eveline") **WILLETT** (twin): b September 25, 1899; d August 18, 1900, buried Benshoff Cemetery, Johnstown, Cambria County, Pennsylvania.

3. **Emma Manilla WILLETT** (twin): b September 25, 1899; d August 18, 1900, buried Benshoff Cemetery, Johnstown, Cambria County, Pennsylvania.

4. **William Horatio WILLETT**: b October 14, 1901, Johnstown, Cambria County, Pennsylvania; m 1st Cora May Cassett (d 1936 of T. B., Johnstown, Cambria County, Pennsylvania, buried at Penn Run, Indiana County); m 2d abt 1937 Jessie Hahn; m 3d September 1, 1945, Helen Fox (b June 17, 1900, Pennsylvania; d August 30, 1979, Allentown, Pennsylvania), the daughter of James and Ellen (Mullen) Fox; d May 16, 1990, Allentown, Pennsylvania, age 89. See next PA.4.2.6.4.

5. **Venora** ("Venorah") **Gertrude WILLETT**: b April 3, 1906, Johnstown, Cambria County, Pennsylvania; m 1st in Johnstown, Pennsylvania, on June 9, 1925, Sanford Allen Mishler (b August 31, 1899, Johnstown, Cambria County, Pennsylvania; d May 13, 1980, California, buried Mt. View, California); divorced February 28, 1963; m 2d Kenneth C. Shaffer (d February 10, 1977, of heart attack); d April 12, 1993, Ebensburg, Pennsylvania, buried Benshoff Hill Cemetery, Johnstown. See next PA.4.2.6.5.

6. **Harry D.** ("Pete") **WILLETT**: b September 24, 1907, Johnstown, Cambria County, Pennsylvania; m in Johnstown, Cambria County, on May 16, 1927, Freida Arbutus Powell (b November 15, 1904, Somerset County, Pennsylvania; d July 14, 1992, Maryland); d of cancer of the liver on April 2, 1983, Canton, Stark County, Ohio, buried Sunset Hills Park, Canton, Ohio. See next PA.4.2.6.6.

7. **John Chalmer WILLETT**: b November 22, 1908, Johnstown, Cambria County, Pennsylvania; m in Johnstown, Cambria County, Pennsylvania, on November 18, 1936, Edna Grace Boring (b December 4, 1914, Johnstown, Cambria County, Pennsylvania; d June 24, 1994, age 79, at the Ingleside Care Center, Hockessin, Delaware, buried Glenwood Memorial Gardens, Broomall, Pennsylvania), the daughter of Claude D. Boring and Stella D. Ribblett; d October 6, 1995, Hockessin, Delaware. See next PA.4.2.6.7.

8. **Carrie Blanche WILLETT**: b November 7, 1910, Johnstown, Pennsylvania; joined the Marine Seabees during World War II; m 1st R. William Stufft (b October 11, 1911, Jenner Township, Johnstown, Pennsylvania; d July 22, 1980, Johnstown), the son of James B. and Edith (Risinger) Stufft; m 2d in Hagerstown, Washington County, Maryland, on March 30, 1947, Franklin Kaminsky (b April 9, 1921, South Fork, Cambria County, Pennsylvania), the son of Joseph and Sarah (Morgan) Kaminsky; she was a hairdresser. No children; d October 27, 1983, Long Beach, Los Angeles County, Califor-

nia, buried Forest Lawn Memorial Park, Cypress, California.

9. **Alverta June WILLETT**: b April 18, 1912 (or June 1, 1914); d April 18, 1916 (or April 20, 1916), buried Benshoff Cemetery, Johnstown, Cambria County, Pennsylvania.

10. **Charles Alexander WILLETT**: b February 23, 1917, Johnstown, Pennsylvania; m in Cumberland, Maryland, on September 5, 1936, Mildred Kinnery (d May, 1981, Pittsburgh, Pennsylvania); d November 12, 1942, in a motorcycle accident, in Baltimore, Maryland, buried Grandview Cemetery, Johnstown, Cambria County, Pennsylvania. See next PA.4.2.6.10.

PA.4.2.6.1
COZETTA JANE WILLETT and **IRVIN CHESTER RIBBLETT**
of Johnstown, Cambria County, Pennsylvania

Cozetta ("Cozzetta", Coxetta") Jane Willett was born on May 26, 1896, at Johnstown, Cambria County, Pennsylvania. Her name is spelled Cozzetta J. Willett in the family Bible and also spelled Coxetta in other records.

In 1903-1904, she attended the public school for one term.

On June 8, 1910, she sang and acted in the Carnegie Music Hall in the "Rose Maiden," Fortunia Fairy Queen. On June 8, 1911, she danced the Hungarian Dance No. 5, Brahms. She also played one of the Joyville Girls in "A Merry Company," by Collin Coe. William Willett, her brother, played a policeman/ On June 7, 1912, she played a solo "Nocturne" and brother William did a recitation of "Tweeny, Weeny Little Fellers." On December 23, 1913, she played the Goddess of Liberty and William played an aged man in "Trial by Jury, or Is Santa Claus a Fraud?"

Although not born blind, Cozetta gradually developed blindness by the age of 6. As soon as she was of school age, she was sent to the Blind Boarding School. She left school at age 19 and attended the Blind School in Pittsburgh, Pennsylvania.

Miss Cozetta Jane Willett married on January 12, 1918, Irvin Chester Ribblett (b September 14, 1895, Johnstown, Cambria County, Pennsylvania; d October 13, 1984, Milton, Wisconsin, buried Mauston Memorial Cemetery, Mauston, Juneau County, Wisconsin), the son of John Wesley Ribblett and Mary Ann Shirey. They resided (1943) Homer City.

During the depression, Cozetta (Willett) Ribblett received a $17.00 a month pension for the blind from the State of Pennsylvania which was paid out of the state Liquor Tax. Irvin Ribblett worked for Bethlehem Steel in Johnstown.

1927
VICTOR, IRVIN, HAROLD
CARL - IN HIGH CHAIR, EMILY JANE - STANDING
At Aunt Elsie's in Windber, Pennsylvania
(Picture courtesy of Pat Berzonsky)

Mrs. Cozetta (Willett) Ribblett died on July 19, 1946, at Johnstown, Pennsylvania, and is buried in the Benshoff Hill Cemetery, Johnstown, Cambria County.

"Grandfather was 60 when he left Pennsylvania and settled in Wisconsin. Pap was staying with his son, William ("Bill") Ribblett, moping around the house, and my aunt Betty said he needed a woman's touch. She sent his name into a Lonely Hearts Club. Before long, letters started to arrive from all over. He packed his bag and took off to Wisconsin where he married Maude Luke and stayed in Wisconsin. He loved it there. His daughter Shirley followed 26 years later" (Pat Berzonsky, November, 1994).

1. **Emily Jane RIBBLETT**: b December 9, 1918, Tanneryville (Johnstown), Cambria County, Pennsylvania; m 1st on August 7, 1935, George Dewey Wagner; m 2d at Elkins, West Virginia, on May 28, 1960, Edward Lee Ressler (b November 21, 1928, Cramer, Pennsylvania), the son of Lowry and Catherine (Wagner) Ressler; d January 27, 1996, Johnstown, Cambria County, Pennsylvania. See next PA.4.2.6.1.1.

1934
MRS. COZETTA JANE (WILLETT) RIBBLETT
Taken on the Saul Rue Place Farm,
Brush Valley, Pennsylvania
(Picture courtesy of Pat Berzonsky)

2. **Irvin James RIBBLETT**: b July 30, 1920, Tannery-ville, Johnstown, Cambria County, Pennsylvania; m 1st in Cumberland, Maryland, July 2, 1938, Louise Margaret Goaziou (b February 22, 1921, Barnesboro, Cambria County, Pennsylvania; d August 12, 1980, Johnstown, Pennsylvania, buried Benshoff Hill Cemetery, Johnstown, Cambria County, Pennsylvania), the daughter of Peter Goaziou and Ruth Green; m 2d in Bedford County, Pennsylvania, on August 16, 1981, Patricia Ann Jacoby (b November 6, 1943, Johnstown), the daughter of Samuel and Ethel (Berkbile) Jacoby. See next PA.4.2.6.1.2.

3. **Victor Gerald RIBBLETT**: b December 26, 1921, Johnstown, Cambria County, Pennsylvania; inducted in the US Army on June 8, 1942, took his basic training at Keesler Field, Mississippi, and served during World War II as a PFC in India; m in Columbus, Indiana, on August 7, 1944, Ruth Nadine Garland (b November 14, 1925, Vincennes, Indiana), the daughter of Charles and Mattie (Pittman) Garland; d March 14, 1994, Columbia, Indiana. See next PA.4.2.6.1.3.

4. **Harold Franklin RIBBLETT**: b April 9, 1924, Tan-neryville (Johnstown), Cambria County, Pennsylvania; World War II service; m in Huthwaite, England, on February 17,

1945, Enid Yvonne Allsop (b April 3, 1926, Huthwaite, England), the daughter of Jane Allsop; d July 3, 1992, Iselin, New Jersey. See next PA.4.2.6.1.4.

5. **Carl Eugene RIBBLETT**: b June 25, 1926, Tannery-ville (Johnstown), Cambria County, Pennsylvania; service during World War II at Ft. Riley, Kansas; m in Delton, Texas, on November 9, 1946, Betty Beasley (b April 13, 1930, Iowa; d April 21, 1995, Iselin, New Jersey), the daughter of Frank and Adeline (Storey) Beasley. See next PA.4.2.6.1.5.

6. **Ella Gertrude RIBBLETT**: b March 16, 1928, Johnstown, Cambria County, Pennsylvania; m 1st Leroy Lindsey; m 2d Melvin Burger (b May 20, 1924, Johnstown; d November 17, 1981, Galliee, buried Galliee cemetery, Galliee, Pennsylvania), the son of Calvin and Helen (Teeter) Berger. See next PA.4.2.6.1.6.

7. **William Allen RIBBLETT**: b May 9, 1930, Johnstown, Cambria County, Pennsylvania; m in Cambria County, Pennsylvania, on May 4, 1950, Betty Lou Teeter (b July 15, 1930, Johnstown), the daughter of Kenneth and Elsie (Rager) Teeter. See next PA.4.2.6.1.7.

8. **Ermald Blair RIBBLETT**: b August 4, 1933, Indiana, Indiana County, Pennsylvania; d August 7, 1933, Indiana, Indiana County, Pennsylvania, buried Benshoff Hill Cemetery, Johnstown, Cambria County, Pennsylvania.

9. **Shirley Norine** ("Narine") **RIBBLETT**: b January 8, 1934, Indiana County, Pennsylvania; m 1st February 9, 1951, Theodore ("Ted") Marlin Rose (b July 12, 1933, Johnstown, Pennsylvania; d June 26, 1981, Johnstown, Pennsylvania, buried Benshoff Hill Cemetery, Johnstown), the son of Theodore and Florence (Seeley) Rose; m 2d at Milton, Wisconsin, on October 16, 1976, Robert J. Pollock (b December 24, 1934, Mauston, Wisconsin), the son of Robert and Leila (Olson) Pollock. See next PA.4.2.6.1.9.

10. **Richard Quay RIBBLETT**: b June 20, 1935, Indiana, Indiana County, Pennsylvania; d at birth June 20, 1935, Indiana, Indiana County, Pennsylvania, buried Benshoff Hill Cemetery, Johnstown, Pennsylvania.

PA.4.2.6.1.1
EMILY JANE RIBBLETT
of Pennsylvania

Emily Jane Ribblett was born on December 9, 1918, Tanneryville (Johnstown), Cambria County, Pennsylvania.

Miss Emily Jane Ribblett married 1st on August 7, 1935, George Dewey Wagner.

Mrs. Emily Jane (Ribblett) Wagner married 2d at Elkins, West Virginia, on May 28, 1960, Edward Lee Ressler (b November 21, 1928, Cramer, Pennsylvania), the son of Lowery and Catherine Wagner Ressler. Edward retired from Bethlehem Steel; he loves to hunt and fish.

She was a master quilt maker. She was also interested in genealogy, stamp collecting, button and match book collecting, and post card collecting.

Mrs. Emily (Ribblett, Wagner) Ressler, age 77, died on January 27, 1996, in Johnstown, Cambria County, Pennsylvania and is buried in the Benshoff Hill Cemetery, Johnstown.

1. **Wilma Jean WAGNER:** b July 5, 1936, Indiana, Indiana County, Pennsylvania; m on August 10, 1953, Edward Stephen Chernay (b July 1, 1932, Johnstown), the son of John and Suzanna (Sojak) Chernay. See next <u>PA.4.2.6.1.1.1</u>.

PA.4.2.6.1.1.1
WILMA JEAN WAGNER and EDWARD STEPHEN CHERNAY

Wilma Jean Wagner was born on July 5, 1936, Indiana, Indiana County, Pennsylvania.

Miss Wilma Jean Wagner married on August 10, 1953, Edward Stephen Chernay (b July 1, 1932, Johnstown, Cambria County, Pennsylvania), the son of John and Suzanna (Sojak) Chernay.

1. **Gloria Jean CHERNAY:** b September 20, 1954, Johnstown, Cambria County, Pennsylvania; m in Johnstown, Cambria County, Pennsylvania, on July 22, 1974, John Gary Matolyak (b February 19, 1952, Johnstown), the son of John and Barbara (Babich) Matolyak. See next <u>PA.4.2.6.1.1.1.1</u>.

2. **Barbara Ann CHERNAY:** b September 20, 1956, Johnstown, Cambria County, Pennsylvania; m in Johnstown, Cambria County, on February 26, 1977, Edward Lewis Martinek (b December 10, 1956, Johnstown), the son of Andrew and Margaret (Lauchenbacker) Martinek. See next <u>PA.4.2.6.1.1.1.2</u>.

3. **Janet Lee CHERNAY:** b February 4, 1960, Johnstown, Cambria County, Pennsylvania; m December 29, 1984, Carl James Spishak (b August 16, 1955), the son of George and Mildred (Tarsovich) Spishak. See next PA.4.2.6.1.1.1.3.

4. **Edward Stephen CHERNAY, Jr:** b February 3, 1970, Johnstown, Pennsylvania; m in Savannah, Georgia, on November 24, 1992, Donna Christine Brownstein (b June 30, 1975, Savannah, Georgia), the daughter of Irving and Rosemary (More) Brownstein; Edward served in "Operation Desert Storm" during the Saudi-Iraqi War of 1991. He is serving in the US Coast Guard.

PA.4.2.6.1.1.1.1
GLORIA JEAN CHERNAY and JOHN GARY MATOLYAK

Gloria Jean Chernay was born on September 20, 1954, Johnstown, Cambria County, Pennsylvania.

Miss Gloria Jean Chernay married in Johnstown, Cambria County, Pennsylvania, on July 22, 1974, John Gary Matolyak (b February 19, 1952), the son of John and Barbara (Babich) Matolyak.

1. **Laura Lee MATOLYAK:** b January 6, 1975, Johnstown, Cambria County, Pennsylvania; m in Virginia Beach, Virginia, on July 11, 1993, Randall ("Randy") John Neatrour (b July 19, 1972), the son of John and Polly (Murton) Neatrour; remarried in Johnstown on November 18, 1995.

PA.4.2.6.1.1.1.2
BARBARA ANN CHERNAY and EDWARD LEWIS MARTINEK

Barbara Ann Chernay was born on September 20, 1956, Johnstown, Cambria County, Pennsylvania.

Miss Barbara Ann Chernay married in Johnstown, Cambria County, on February 26, 1977, Edward Lewis Martinek (b December 10, 1956, Johnstown), the son of Andrew and Margaret (Lauchenbacker) Martinek.

1. **Matthew Lewis MARTINEK**: b August 7, 1984, Johnstown, Cambria County, Pennsylvania.

PA.4.2.6.1.1.1.3
JANET LEE CHERNAY and CARL JAMES SPISHAK

Janet Lee Chernay was born on February 4, 1960, Johnstown, Cambria County, Pennsylvania.

Miss Janet Lee Chernay married on December 29, 1984, Carl James Spishak (b August 16, 1955), the son of George and Mildred (Tarsovich) Spishak.

1. **Ryan Keith SPISHAK**: b July 5, 1985, York, York County, Pennsylvania.
2. **Luke Evan SPISHAK**: b October 10, 1994, Johnstown, Cambria County, Pennsylvania.

PA.4.2.6.1.2
IRVIN JAMES RIBBLETT
of Johnstown, Cambria County, Pennsylvania

Irvin James Ribblett was born July 30, 1920, Tanneryville, Johnstown, Cambria County, Pennsylvania.

Irvin James Ribblett married 1st in Cumberland, Allegany County, Maryland, July 2, 1938, Louise Margaret Goaziou (b February 22, 1921, Barnesboro, Cambria County, Pennsylvania; d August 12, 1980, Johnstown, Cambria County, Pennsylvania), the daughter of Peter Goaziou and Ruth Green. She never wore make-up and had black curly hair. She was a den mother, and Irvin was a cub master. They did everything together.

WEDDING DAY JULY 2, 1938
MRS. RUTH GOAZIOU
LOUISE M. GOAZIOU - IRVIN JAMES RIBBLETT
(Picture courtesy of Pat Berzonsky)

He served during World War II as a Pvt. at Ft. McClellan, Alabama. He received a hardship discharge when his wife became sick; there were three children at home with one on the way.

Irvin worked for Bethlehem Steel. He quit the mines when he was badly burnt from the waist up in a coal mine fire. He bought a dump truck and hauled coal, ashes, wood, junk, for a while. His last place of employment was in the sanitation department with the City of Johnstown.

1980
IRVIN JAMES AND LOUISE RIBBLETT
(Picture courtesy of Pat Berzonsky)

Irvin James Ribblett married 2d in Bedford County, Pennsylvania, on August 16, 1981, Patricia Ann Jacoby (b November 6, 1943, Johnstown), the daughter of Samuel and Ethel (Berkbile) Jacoby.

NOVEMBER, 1986
IRVIN J. RIBBLETT AND MRS. PATRICIA (JACOBY) RIBBLETT
(Picture courtesy of Pat Berzonsky)

1. **Irvin James RIBBLETT**, Jr: b April 1, 1939, Barnes-boro, Cambria County, Pennsylvania; m July 10, 1961, Sarah Noreen Buchanan (divorced), the daughter of Price and Edna (Hershey) Buchanan; m 2d in Jerome, Pennsylvania, on May 5, 1996, Peggy Ann Buckingham (b December 19, 1944), the daughter of William A. and Dorothy E. Chaddock) Bucking-ham. See next PA.4.2.6.1.2.1.

2. **Patricia Louise RIBBLETT**: b June 27, 1941, Indiana, Indiana County, Pennsylvania; m 1st on January 26, 1961, Alan Wayne Dick (b October 22, 1941; d April 15, 1972, buried Forest Lawn Cemetery, Johnstown, Cambria County, Pennsylvania), the son of Harry and Margaret (Naugle) Dick; m 2d August 21, 1973 Ronald Joseph Berzonsky (b November 23, 1930, Bakerton, Pennsylvania), the son of Michael and Mary (Zavacky) Berzonsky. See next PA.4.2.6.1.2.2.

3. **John William RIBBLETT**: b December 19, 1943, Johnstown, Cambria County, Pennsylvania; m in Johnstown, Pennsylvania, on October 20, 1964, Roselyn Maloney (b July

5, 1944, Altoona, Pennsylvania), the daughter of Levi and Catherine (Hoover) Maloney. See next PA.4.2.6.1.2.3.

4. **Donald Francis RIBBLETT**: b November 10, 1944, Johnstown, Cambria County, Pennsylvania; m June 11, 1966, Elva Mae Stein (b May 21, 1946, Johnstown, Pennsylvania), the daughter of Walter and Elva (Wiedwald) Stein. See next PA.4.2.6.1.2.4.

5. **Elizabeth Ann RIBBLETT**: b May 4, 1946, Johnstown, Cambria County, Pennsylvania; m 1st William Youngblood; m 2d in Winchester, Virginia, on June 18, 1981, Raymond Leroy Smith (b October 23, 1940, Clearwater, Pinellas County, Florida) (divorced), the son of Roy and Lillian (Spivy) Smith. See next PA.4.2.6.1.2.5.

6. **Wanda Jean RIBBLETT**: b September 19, 1947, Johnstown, Cambria County, Pennsylvania; d November 1, 1947, buried Benshoff Hill Cemetery, Johnstown, Pennsylvania.

7. **Richard Earl RIBBLETT**: b May 13, 1949, Johnstown, Cambria County, Pennsylvania; unmarried (1993).

8. **Donna Jean RIBBLETT**: b May 3, 1952, Johnstown, Cambria County, Pennsylvania; m in Conemaugh, Pennsylvania, on June 21, 1975, David Molnar (b March 26, 1952, Johnstown, Cambria County, Pennsylvania), the son of Andrew and Annie (Slavich) Molnar. See next PA.4.2.6.1.2.8.

9. **Thomas Edward RIBBLETT**: b November 19, 1953, Johnstown, Cambria County, Pennsylvania; m in Cumberland, Maryland, on October 27, 1980, Kristine ("Kris") Minerva Doyle (b November 18, 1956, Johnstown, Cambria County, Pennsylvania), the daughter of Thomas and Dorothy (Blough) Doyle. See next PA.4.2.6.1.2.9.

10. **Pamela Ruth RIBBLETT**: b September 5, 1956, Johnstown, Cambria County, Pennsylvania; m in Johnstown, Pennsylvania, on September 14, 1975, Robert Wayne Miller (b July 1, 1954), the son of Yriah and Esther (Gensumer) Miller. She is in certified day care service. He is a Medic in the Navy. See next PA.4.2.6.1.2.10.

11. **Cheryl Lee RIBBLETT**: b March 8, 1959, Johnstown, Cambria County, Pennsylvania; m in Johnstown, Cambria County, Pennsylvania, on August 29, 1981, Edward Lee Conner (b August 30, 1958, Johnstown, Pennsylvania, the son of James and Lois (Price) Conner. She is a L.P.N. He is an automotive technician with a Ford dealer. See next PA.4.2.6.1.2.11.

PA.4.2.6.1.2.1
IRVIN JAMES RIBBLETT and SARAH NOREEN BUCHANAN

Irvin James Ribblett, Jr., was born on April 1, 1939, Barnesboro, Cambria County, Pennsylvania. Irvin J. Ribblett, Jr. married in Cumberland, Maryland, on July 10, 1961, Sarah Noreen Buchanan (b September 12, 1941, Johnstown, Cambria County, Pennsylvania) (divorced), the daughter of Price and Edna (Hershey) Buchanan. He is a steel worker.

Irvin J. Ribblett married 2d in Jerome, Pennsylvania, on May 5, 1996, Peggy Ann Buckingham (b December 19, 1944), the daughter of William A. and Dorothy E. Chaddock) Buckingham.

1. **James Irvin RIBBLETT**: b July 21, 1962, Johnstown, Cambria County, Pennsylvania.

2. **Karen Noreen RIBBLETT**: b October 6, 1964, Latrobe, Westmoreland County, Pennsylvania; m in Johnstown, Cambria County, Pennsylvania, on January 26, 1985, John Edward Remick (b September 22, 1955, Johnstown), the son of Edward and Mary Jane (Hale) Remick. See next PA.4.2.6.1.2.1.2.

3. **Susan Louise RIBBLETT**: b April 27, 1969, Johnstown, Cambria County, Pennsylvania; m in Johnstown, Pennsylvania, on January 20, 1996, Scott A. Constable (b August 30, 1965, Johnstown), the son of Alvin Blair Constable, Sr., and Genevieve Ruth Hutchinson. See next PA.4.2.6.1.2.1.3.

PA.4.2.6.1.2.1.2
KAREN NOREEN RIBBLETT and JOHN EDWARD REMICK

Karen Noreen Ribblett was born on October 6, 1964, Latrobe, Westmoreland County, Pennsylvania.

Miss Karen Noreen Ribblett married in Johnstown, Cambria County, Pennsylvania, on January 26, 1985, John Edward Remick (b September 22, 1955, Johnstown), the son of Edward and Mary Jane (Hale) Remick. She is a teacher at Johnstown, Vo-Tech. He is a draftsman.

    1. **Noreen Louise REMICK:** b August 22, 1987, Johnstown, Cambria County, Pennsylvania.

    2. **Jon James REMICK:** b July 11, 1990, Johnstown, Cambria County, Pennsylvania.

PA.4.2.6.1.2.1.3
SUSAN LOUISE RIBBLETT and SCOTT A. CONSTABLE

Susan Louise Ribblett was born on April 27, 1969, Johnstown, Cambria County, Pennsylvania.

Miss Susan Louise Ribblett was married in Johnstown, Pennsylvania, on January 20, 1996, Scott A. Constable (b August 30, 1965, Johnstown), the son of Alvin Blair Constable, Sr., and Genevieve Ruth Hutchinson.

    1. **Andrew Scott CONSTABLE:** b May, 1996, Johnstown, Pennsylvania.

PA.4.2.6.1.2.2
PATRICIA LOUISE RIBBLETT
of Johnstown, Cambria County, Pennsylvania

Patricia Louise Ribblett was born on June 27, 1941, Indiana, Indiana County, Pennsylvania.

1944
"PATTY" RIBBLETT
At Bob Hood's Farm, New Florence, Pennsylvania
(Picture courtesy of Pat Berzonsky)

Miss Patricia Louise Ribblett married 1st in Johnstown, Cambria County, Pennsylvania, on January 26, 1961, Alan Wayne Dick (b October 22, 1941, Cramer, Indiana County, Pennsylvania; d April 15, 1972, Johnstown, Cambria County, buried Forest Lawn Cemetery, Johnstown, Cambria County, Pennsylvania), the son of Harry and Margaret (Naugle) Dick.

Mrs. Patricia Louise (Ribblett) Dick married 2d in Winchester, Virginia, on August 21, 1973 Ronald Joseph Berzonsky (b November 23, 1930, Bakerton, Cambria County, Pennsylvania), the son of Michael and Mary (Zavacky) Berzonsky.

Children of Patricia Louise Ribblett and her 1st husband Alan Wayne Dick:

1. **Scott Alan DICK**: b July 24, 1961, Johnstown; d July 27, 1961, Johnstown, buried Forrest Lawn Cemetery, Johnstown, Cambria County, Pennsylvania.

2. **Shari Lynn DICK**: b November 3, 1962, Johnstown, Cambria County, Pennsylvania; m at the University Chapel, University of Pittsburgh, Johnstown Campus, Pennsylvania, on July 6, 1996, David Ross Bodin. Shari is a software engineer and David is in the US Navy. They reside (1997) at Crofton, Maryland.

3. **Jeffrey Alan DICK**: b September 21, 1967, Johnstown, Cambria County, Pennsylvania; m at Clark Air Force Base, Philippines, on November 8, 1988, Belinda Corpuz (b December 9, 1968, La Union, Philippines), the daughter of Natividad Torqueza and Angelino Corpuz. Jeffrey is an Assistant Manager of the Bon-Ton Department store. They reside (1997) at Oil City, Pennsylvania.

4. **Kerry Sue DICK**: b November 27, 1968, Johnstown, Cambria County, Pennsylvania; m at St. Nicholas Greek Orthodox Church, Pittsburgh, Pennsylvania, on September 3, 1994, Trifon George Dalson (b September 29, 1963, Pittsburgh, Pennsylvania), the son of George and Maria (Grecou) Dalson. She is a software engineer and Kerry is a computer programmer and paralegal. They reside (1997) at Columbia, Maryland.

5. **Jaime Alan DICK**: b July 19, 1971, Johnstown, Cambria County, Pennsylvania; graduate of Hagerstown Community College and Shippensburg University. Resides (1997) Crofton, Maryland.

Child of Patricia Louise Ribblett and her 2nd husband Ronald Joseph Berzonsky:

6. **Thomas Paul BERZONSKY**: b April 5, 1974, Johnstown, Cambria County, Pennsylvania; student at Indiana University of Pennsylvania.

PA.4.2.6.1.2.3
JOHN WILLIAM RIBBLETT and ROSELYN MALONEY

John William Ribblett was born on December 19, 1943, Johnstown, Cambria County, Pennsylvania.

John William Ribblett married in Johnstown, Cambria County, Pennsylvania, on October 20, 1964, Roselyn Maloney (b July 5, 1944, Altoona, Blair County, Pennsylvania), the daughter of Levi and Catherine (Hoover) Maloney.

1977
THE JOHN AND LYNN RIBBLETT FAMILY
STANDING BACK ROW - RAMI
CATHY, DAWN, LYNN AND JOHN
JOANN, BABY DENNIS, JOHN RUSSELL
(Picture courtesy of Pat Berzonsky)

1. **Rachelle Ann RIBBLETT** (adopted): b December 21, 1963, Altoona, Blair County, Pennsylvania; m at Lawrenceville, Georgia, on May 19, 1984, Michael Anthony Matuszak (b November 12, 1962), the son of Leon and Katherine Matuszak. See next PA.4.2.6.1.2.3.1.

2. **Catherine Louise RIBBLETT**: b February 18, 1966, Norfolk, Virginia; m 1st in Georgia, on July 19, 1984, Douglas Warren Bach (b June 12, 1963, St. Paul, Minnesota), the son of Warren D. and Marlene (Mann) Bach; m 2d in Atlanta, Fulton County, Georgia, on September 21, 1988, David Hagler

(b June 22, 1966, Selma, Alabama) (divorced), the son of Robert and Carolyn (Gurley) Hagler. See next PA.4.2.6.1.2.3.2.

3 **Dawn Marie RIBBLETT**: b December 13, 1967, Jacksonville, Florida; m in Lawrenceville, Georgia, on August 30, 198-, Michael A. Smith (b May 16, 1967, Atlanta, Georgia), the son of Kenneth and Diane (Peters) Hall Smith. See next PA.4.2.6.1.2.3.3.

4. **John Russell RIBBLETT**: b November 13, 1969, Japan; m in Snellville, Georgia, on October 21, 1995, Shannon Lee Vogel.

5. **Joanne Clare RIBBLETT**: b November 5, 1971, Japan; m September 5, 1989, Donald G. Hale (b September 18, 1971), the son of Donald and Cynthia Hale. See next PA.4.2.6.1.2.3.4.

6. **Dennis Irvin RIBBLETT**: b June 2, 1977, Florida.

PA.4.2.6.1.2.3.1
RACHELLE ANN RIBBLETT and
MICHAEL ANTHONY MATUSZAK

Rachelle Ann Ribblett (adopted) was born on December 21, 1963, Altoona, Blair County, Pennsylvania.

Miss Rachelle Ann Matuszak married on May 19, 1984, Michael Anthony Matuszak, the son of Leon and Katherine Matuszak.

1. **Michael Anthony MATUSZAK**: b December 14, 1985, Snellville, Georgia.

2. **Megan Catherine MATUSZAK**: b November 24, 1987, Snellville, Georgia.

3. **Mathew John MATUSZAK**: b April 9, 1990, Snellville, Georgia.

PA.4.2.6.1.2.3.2
CATHERINE LOUISE RIBBLETT

Catherine Louise Ribblett was born on February 18, 1966, Norfolk, Virginia.

Miss Catherine Louise Ribblett married 1st July 19, 1984, Douglas Warren Bach (b June 12, 1963, St. Paul, Minnesota), the son of Warren D. and Marlene (Mann) Bach.

Mrs. Catherine Louse (Ribblett) Bach married 2d in Atlanta, Fulton County, Georgia, on September 21, 1988, David Hagler (b June 22, 1966, Selma, Alabama), the son of Robert and Carolyn (Gurley) Hagler.

1. **Christopher Douglas BACH**: b May 23, 1985, Fort Benning, Georgia.
2. **Caitlyn Louise HAGLER**: b January 18, 1990, Snellville, Georgia.
3. **David Allen HAGLER**: b January 4, 1994, Georgia.

PA.4.2.6.1.2.3.3
DAWN MARIE RIBBLETT and MICAHEL A. SMITH

Dawn Marie Ribblett was born on December 13, 1967, Jacksonville, Florida.

Miss Dawn Marie Ribblett married in Lawrenceville, Georgia, on August 30, 198-, Michael A. Smith (b May 16, 1967, Atlanta, Georgia), the son of Kenneth and Diane (Peters) Hall Smith.

1. **Michael C. SMITH**: b February 15, 1989, Snellville, Georgia.
2. **Charles Justin SMITH**: b May 7, 1990, Snellville, Georgia.
3. **Kristine Nicole SMITH**: b January 7, 1992, Snellville, Georgia.

PA.4.2.6.1.2.3.4
JOANNE CLARE RIBBLETT and DONALD G. HALE

Joanne Clare Ribblett was born on November 5, 1971, Japan.

Miss Joanne Clare Ribblett married on September 5, 1989, Donald G. Hale (b September 18, 1971), the son of Donald and Cynthia Hale.

1. **Mandie Lyn HALE**: b April 2, 1990, Snellville, Georgia.

PA.4.2.6.1.2.4
DONALD FRANCIS RIBBLETT and **ELVA MAE STEIN**

Donald Francis Ribblett was born on November 10, 1944, Johnstown, Cambria County, Pennsylvania.

Donald Francis Ribblett married in Johnstown, Cambria County, Pennsylvania, on June 11, 1966, Elva Mae Stein (b May 21, 1946, Johnstown, Cambria County, Pennsylvania), the daughter of Walter and Elva (Wiedwald) Stein. He is an U.P.S. supervisor.

1. **Brian David RIBBLETT**: b April 22, 1967, Annapolis, Maryland; received a B. S. from Maryland State University; paralegal; m in Millersville, Maryland, on August 10, 1996, Susanna Rose Galu.

2. **Brenda Jean RIBBLETT**: b March 22, 1969, Shevely, Maryland; attending college; m in Millersville, Maryland, on October 7, 1995, Matthew Manogian.

3. **Sandra Louise RIBBLETT**: b January 20, 1973, Shevely, Maryland; employed by NASA; attended college; m at Millersville, Maryland, on October 7, 1995, Jamie A. Nimmo.

4. **Kevin Francis RIBBLETT**: b July 20, 1977, Annapolis, Maryland; student.

PA.4.2.6.1.2.5
ELIZABETH ANN RIBBLETT
of Oak Harbor, Washington

Elizabeth Ann Ribblett was born on May 4, 1946, Johnstown, Cambria County, Pennsylvania.

Miss Elizabeth Ann Ribblett was married 1st William Youngblood.

Mrs. Elizabeth Ann (Ribblett) Youngblood married 2d in Winchester, Virginia, on June 18, 1981, Raymond Leroy Smith (b October 23, 1940, Clearwater, Pinellas County, Florida) (divorced), the son of Roy and Lillian (Spivy) Smith.

1. **Amy Marie YOUNGBLOOD**: b October 13, 1967, Oak Harbor, Washington; m on December 9, 1987, Robin Tandy (b March 21, 1962, Redmond, Oregon), the son of Edwin and Donna (Zedwick) Tandy.

2. **Beth Ann YOUNGBLOOD**: b October 9, 1969, Oak Harbor, Washington; m at Fort Lewis, Washington, on April 30, 1994, Reginald Dale (b December 27, 1971, DeKalb), the son of Charles E. and Ilet (Little) Dale. See next PA.4.2.6.1.2.5.2.

PA.4.2.6.1.2.5.2
BETH ANN YOUNGBLOOD and REGINALD DALE

Beth Ann Youngblood was born on October 9, 1969, Oak Harbor, Washington.

Miss Beth Ann Youngblood married at Fort Lewis, Washington, on April 30, 1994, Reginald Dale (b December 27, 1971, DeKalb), the son of Charles E. and Ilet (Little) Dale. They reside (1997) at Fort Lee, Virginia.

1. **Marice E. JONES**: b January 29, 1988, Johnstown, Cambria County, Pennsylvania.
2. **Marie E. JONES**: b October 30, 1990, Johnstown, Cambria County, Pennsylvania.
3. **Devon Marquis DALE**: b February 12, 1996, Fort Lewis, Washington.

PA.4.2.6.1.2.8
DONNA JEAN RIBBLETT and DAVID MOLNAR
of Johnstown, Cambria County, Pennsylvania

Donna Jean Ribblett was born on May 3, 1952, Johnstown, Cambria County, Pennsylvania.

Miss Donna Jean Ribblett married in Conemaugh, Cambria County, Pennsylvania, on June 21, 1975, David Molnar (b March 26, 1952, Johnstown, Cambria County, Pennsylvania), the son of Andrew and Annie (Slavich) Molnar. He is a supervisor for M. Glosser and Sons, Inc., Windber, Pennsylvania.

1. **Peter Andrew MOLNAR**: b October 3, 1976, Johnstown, Cambria County, Pennsylvania.
2. **Nicole Louise MOLNAR**: b October 1, 1979, Johnstown, Cambria County, Pennsylvania.

PA.4.2.6.1.2.9
THOMAS EDWARD RIBBLETT
and KRISTINE MINERVA DOYLE
of Johnstown, Cambria County, Pennsylvania

Thomas Edward Ribblett was born on November 19, 1953, Johnstown, Cambria County, Pennsylvania.

Thomas Edward Ribblett married in Cumberland County, Maryland, on October 27, 1980, Kristine ("Kris") Minerva Doyle (b November 18, 1956, Johnstown, Cambria County, Pennsylvania), the daughter of Thomas and Dorothy (Blough) Doyle. He is a salesman for an Electric Company and is an electrician. Kris is an aide in the Johnstown School District.

1. **Chastity Ann RIBBLETT** (adopted): b September 13, 1979, Johnstown, Cambria County, Pennsylvania.
2. **Chad Thomas RIBBLETT**: b March 19, 1983, Johnstown, Cambria County, Pennsylvania.

PA.4.2.6.1.2.10
PAMELA RUTH RIBBLETT and ROBERT WAYNE MILLER

Pamela Ruth Ribblett was born on September 5, 1956, Johnstown, Cambria County, Pennsylvania.

Miss Pamela Ruth Ribblett married in Johnstown, Pennsylvania, on September 14, 1975, Robert Wayne Miller (b July 1, 1954), the son of Uriah and Esther (Gensumer) Miller. She is in certified day care service. He is a Medic in the Navy.

1. **Robert Jason MILLER**: b June 15, 1977, Gambrills, Anne Arundel County, Maryland.

PA.4.2.6.1.2.11
CHERYL LEE RIBBLETT and EDWARD LEE CONNER

Cheryl Lee Ribblett was born on March 8, 1959, Johnstown, Cambria County, Pennsylvania.

Miss Cheryl Lee Ribblett married in Johnstown, Cambria County, Pennsylvania, on August 29, 1981, Edward Lee Conner (b August 30, 1958, Johnstown), the son of James and Lois (Price) Conner. She is a L.P.N. He is an automotive technician with a Ford dealer.

1. **Jessica Elaine CONNER**: b May 16, 1984, Columbia, Maryland.
2. **Michelle Ann CONNER**: b June 27, 1987, Columbia, Maryland.

PA.4.2.6.1.3
VICTOR GERALD RIBBLETT and **RUTH NADINE GARLAND**
of Columbus, Indiana

Victor Gerald Ribblett was born on December 26, 1921, Tanneryville (Johnstown), Cambria County, Pennsylvania. He was inducted in the US Army on June 8, 1942, took his basic training at Keesler Field, Mississippi, and served during World War II as a PFC in India.

Victor Gerald Ribblett married in Columbus, Bartholomew County, Indiana, on August 7, 1944, Ruth Nadine Garland (b November 14, 1925, Vincennes, Indiana), the daughter of Charles and Mattie (Pittman) Garland.

Victor Gerald Ribblett died on March 14, 1994, at Columbus, Indiana, and is buried in Columbus.

1. **Denise Lynn RIBBLETT**: b December 11, 1957, Columbus, Indiana; m in Columbus, Indiana, on June 10, 1976, Gary Lynn Gill (b April 30, 1957), the son of Gary and Wanda (Duncan) Gill. See next PA.4.2.6.1.3.1.

2. **Donna Jean RIBBLETT**: b February 24, 1960, Columbus, Indiana; m 1st 1977, Rodger Rumbley (b December 12, 1961) (divorced), the son of Merle and Marjie Rumbley; m 2d in Tennessee on May 30, 1981, Marvin R. Harris (b December 12, 1961), the son of Delbert and Julia (Bowman) Harris. See next PA.4.2.6.1.3.2.

PA.4.2.6.1.3.1
DENISE LYNN RIBBLETT and **GARY LYNN GILL**

Denise Lynn Ribblett was born on December 11, 1957, Columbus, Indiana.

Miss Denise Lynn Ribblett married in Columbus, Indiana, on June 10, 1976, Gary Lynn Gill (b April 30, 1957), the son of Gary and Wanda (Duncan) Gill.

1. **Benjamin Arthur GILL**: b February 10, 1980, Columbus, Indiana.

2. **Nichole Joann GILL**: b February 12, 1982, Columbus, Indiana.

PA.4.2.6.1.3.2
DONNA JEAN RIBBLETT

Donna Jean Ribblett was born on February 24, 1960, Columbus, Indiana.

Miss Donna Jean Ribblett married 1st 1977, Rodger Rumbley (b December 12, 1961) (divorced), the son of Merle and Marjie Rumbley.

Mrs. Donna Jean (Ribblett) Rumbley married 2d in Tennessee on May 30, 1981, Marvin R. Harris (b December 12, 1961), the son of Delbert and Julia (Bowman) Harris.

1. **Matthew Dean RUMBLEY**: b September 7, 1977, Indiana.
2. **Kristin Ann MCELRAVY**: b December 13, 1988, Silver Springs, Maryland.
3. **Aaron Mike MCELRAVY**: b April 2, 1993, Prince Frederick, Maryland.

PA.4.2.6.1.4
HAROLD FRANKLIN RIBBLETT and ENID YVONNE ALLSOP

Harold Franklin Ribblett was born on April 9, 1924, Tanneryville (Johnstown), Cambria County, Pennsylvania.

He had service during World War II. Harold F. Ribblett enlisted April 30, 1943, at New Cumberland, Pennsylvania, and was posted to England prior to "D" Day. He jumped onto Omaha Beach at the Normandy invasion with the 101st Airborne Division, later in the 82nd Airborne Division at Bastogne, Belgium, serving in the European Theater of Operations until June 21, 1945. He had a further 2 months in British Guyana, leaving service as a PFC at Greensboro, North Carolina, on November 24, 1945.

Harold Franklin Ribblett married in Huthwaite, England on February 17, 1945, Enid Yvonne Allsop (b April 3, 1926, Huthwaite, England; d April 21, 1995, Iselin, New Jersey, and is buried in the Rosedale Cemetery, Linden, New Jersey), the daughter of Jane Allsop.

He was active in the Veterans of Foreign Wars (VFW) serving as a Chaplain and in the Color Guard.

Harold F. Ribblett died on July 3, 1992, at Iselin, New Jersey and is buried in the Rosedale Cemetery, Linden, New Jersey.

1. **Harold Glen RIBBLETT**: b November 19, 1947, Rahway, New Jersey.

PA.4.2.6.1.5
CARL EUGENE RIBBLETT and **BETTY BEASLEY**
of Johnstown, Cambria County, Pennsylvania

Carl Eugene Ribblett was born on June 25, 1926, Johnstown, Cambria County, Pennsylvania. He had service during World War II at Ft. Riley, Kansas.

1938
CARL EUGENE RIBBLETT
(Picture courtesy of Pat Berzonsky)

Carl Eugene Ribblett married in Delton, Texas, on November 9, 1946, Betty Beasley (b April 13, 1930, Iowa), the daughter of Frank and Adeline (Storey) Beasley. They reside in Long Beach, California. He is a foreman for McDonald Douglas Aircraft.

1. **Daniel Eugene RIBBLETT**: b February 5, 1949, Iowa, Pennsylvania; m in Torrance, California, on March 30, 1971, Diane Cattani (b March 30, 1953), the daughter of Elmo and Gloria (Freed) Cattani. See next PA.4.2.6.1.5.1.

2. **Deborah Jean RIBBLETT**: b January 15, 1952, Johnstown, Pennsylvania; d October 22, 1990, California.

3. **Diane Lynn RIBBLETT**: b February 25, 1954, Johnstown, Pennsylvania; m in Las Vegas, Nevada, on December 2, 1972, Michael Keith Egbert (b November 24, 1951, Salt Lake City, Utah), the son of Keith and Afton Mae (Houter) Egbert. See next PA.4.2.6.1.5.3.

4. **Karen Sue RIBBLETT**: b August 5, 1955, Tucson, Arizona; m 1st on January 12, 1974, Ronald E. Tune (b June 25, 1953), the son of John and Dorothy (Long) Tune; m 2d on October 18, 1980, Ralph Van Der Mulen (b January 4, 1951), the son of Dictus and Tina (Spellman) Van Der Mulen. See next PA.4.2.6.1.5.4.

5. **Gary Lee RIBBLETT**: b February 26, 1957, Tucson, Arizona, m at the Chapel of the Bells, Las Vegas, Nevada, on March 5, 1983, Jani Michelle McInerney (b January 3, 1966), the daughter of John and Bonnie (Charley) McInereny.

PA.4.2..6.1.5.1

DANIEL EUGENE RIBBLETT and **DIANE CATTANI**

Daniel Eugene Ribblett was born on February 5, 1949, Iowa.

Daniel Eugene Ribblett married in Torrance, California, on March 30, 1971, Diane Cattani (b March 30, 1953), the daughter of Elmo and Gloria (Freed) Cattani.

1. **Jaime Lee RIBBLETT**: b April 9, 1982, Whittier, Los Angeles County, California.

PA.4.2.6.1.5.3
DIANE LYNN RIBBLETT and MICHAEL KEITH EGBERT

Diane Lynn Ribblett was born on February 25, 1954, Johnstown, Pennsylvania.

Diane Lynn Ribblett married in Las Vegas, Nevada, on December 2, 1972, Michael Keith Egbert (b November 24, 1951, Salt Lake City, Utah), the son of Keith and Afton Mae (Houter) Egbert.

1. **Michael Keith EGBERT**: b October 29, 1972, Lakewood, Orange County, California.

2. **Joshua Eugene EGBERT**: b November 21, 1980, Fontana, California.

PA.4.2.6.1.5.4
KAREN SUE RIBBLETT

Karen Sue Ribblett was born on August 5, 1955, Tucson, Arizona.

Miss Karen Sue Ribblett married 1st on January 12, 1974, Ronald E. Tune (b June 25, 1953), the son of John and Dorothy (Long) Tune.

Mrs. Karen Sue (Ribblett) Tune married 2d on October 18, 1980, Ralph Van Der Mulen (b January 4, 1951), the son of Dictus and Tina (Spellman) Van Der Mulen.

1. **Stephen E. TUNE (VAN DER MULEN)** (stepson): b March 25, 1973. Adopted by his stepfather. Wife: Stephine Needham, the daughter of Richard and Cindy (Algire) Needham.

1. **Steven Andrew TUNE (VAN DER MULEN)**: b November 26, 1990, California.

PA.4.2.6.1.6
ELLA GERTRUDE RIBBLETT

Ella Gertrude Ribblett was born on March 16, 1928, Johnstown, Cambria County, Pennsylvania.

Miss Ella Gertrude Ribblett married 1st Leroy Lindsey.

Mrs. Ella G. (Ribblett) Lindsey married 2d Melvin Burger (b May 20, 1924, Cambria County, Pennsylvania; d November 12, 1981, Galillee, buried Galliee cemetery, Galliee, Pennsylvania), the son of Calvin and Helen (Teeter) Berger.

1. **Adrian Wayne RIBBLETT**: b March 6, 1943, Indiana County, Pennsylvania; m 1st Delores E. Heilman (b January 11, 1944), the daughter of Edward and Vivian (Galbraith) Heilman; m 2d Pat. See next PA.4.2.6.1.6.1.
2. **Margie Elaine LINDSEY**: b August 10, 1944.
3. **Judy Ann LINDSEY**: b June 2, 1946.
4. **Edward Eugene LINDSEY**: b September 17, 1947.
5. **Shirley E. LINDSEY**: b June 10, 1948, Johnstown, Cambria County, Pennsylvania; m June 10, 1967, Fred Lee Dick, Jr., the son of William and Sarah (Wiley) Dick. See next PA.4.2.6.1.6.5.
6. **Melvin James LINDSEY**: b June 28, 1950; m in Pine Mill, Pennsylvania, on October 19, 1971, Connie Marie Young (b April 19, 1951), the daughter of Jessie and Grace (Eldred) Young. See next PA.4.2.6.1.6.6.

PA.4.2.6.1.6.1
ADRIAN WAYNE RIBBLETT

Adrian Wayne Ribblett was born on March 6, 1943, Indiana County, Pennsylvania.

Adrian Wayne Ribblett married 1st Delores E. Heilman (b January 11, 1944), the daughter of Edward and Vivian (Galbraith) Heilman.

Adrian Wayne Ribblett married 2d Pat.

1. **Edward Allen RIBBLETT**: b February 16, 1962; m July 10, 1982, Dawn S. Sheard (b February 23, 1962), the daughter of Alfreda and Leanna (Diehl) Sheard. See next PA.4.2.6.1.6.1.1
2. **Cordell Tyrone RIBBLETT**: b April 28, 1963, Randolph, New York; m October 17, 1982, Colleen L. Doak (b October 6, 1963), the daughter of William and Joan (Francher) Doak. See next PA.4.2.6.1.6.1.2.
3. **Adrienne Lynn RIBBLETT**: b March 18, 1964; m at

Randolff, New York, on November 5, 1983, James Robert Lynn (b June 7, 1963), the son of Robert E. and Eleanor (Curthoys) Lynn. See next PA.4.2.6.1.6.1.3.

4. **Erick Wayne RIBBLETT**: b July 4, 1967.
5. **Charlyn Kay RIBBLETT**: b January 13, 1973.

PA.4.2.6.1.6.1.1
EDWARD ALLEN RIBBLETT and DAWN S. SHEARD

Edward Allen Ribblett was born on February 16, 1962.

Edward Allen Ribblett married on July 10, 1982, Dawn S. Sheard (b February 23, 1962), the daughter of Alfreda and Leanna (Diehl) Sheard.

1. **Stephen Michael RIBBLETT**: b December 21, 1985.
2. **April Lee RIBBLETT**: b April 8, 1988.

PA.4.2.6.1.6.1.2
CORDELL TYRONE RIBBLETT and COLLEEN L. DOAK

Cordell Tyrone Ribblett was born on April 28, 1963, Randoplh, New York.

Cordell Tyrone Ribblett married on October 17, 1982, Colleen L. Doak (b October 6, 1963), the daughter of William and Joan (Francher) Doak.

1. **Joshua Paul RIBBLETT**: b February 27, 1982.
2. **Jessica Lynn RIBBLETT**: b April 14, 1983.

PA.4.2.6.1.6.1.3
ADRIENNE LYNN RIBBLETT and JAMES ROBERT LYNN

Adrienne Lynn Ribblett was born on March 18, 1964.

Miss Adrienne Lynn Ribblett married at Randolff, New York, on November 5, 1983, James Robert Lynn (b June 7, 1963), the son of Robert E. and Eleanor (Curthoys) Lynn.

1. **Craig Robert LYNN**: b March 24, 1984.

PA.4.2.6.1.6.5
SHIRLEY E. LINDSEY and FRED LEE DICK

Shirley E. Lindsey was born on June 10, 1948, Johnstown, Cambria County, Pennsylvania.

Miss Shirley E. Lindsey married in Blairsville, Pennsylvania, on June 10, 1967, Fred Lee Dick, Jr. (b November 7, 1946), the son of William and Sarah (Wiley) Dick.

1. **Fred Lee DICK, Jr**: b December 13, 1967.

2. **Alesha Ann DICK**: b August 21, 1979.

PA.4.2.6.1.6.6
MELVIN JAMES LINDSEY and CONNIE MARIE YOUNG

Melvin James Lindsey was born June 28, 1950.

Melvin James Lindsey married in Pine Mill, Pennsylvania, on October 19, 1971, Connie Marie Young (b April 19, 1951), the daughter of Jessie and Grace (Eldred) Young.

1. **Andrew Austin LINDSEY**: b May 1, 1975.

PA.4.2.6.1.7
WILLIAM ALLEN RIBBLETT and BETTY LOU TEETER

William Allen Ribblett was born on May 9, 1930, Johnstown, Cambria County, Pennsylvania.

William Allen Ribblett married in Cambria County, Pennsylvania, on May 4, 1950, Betty Lou Teeter (b July 15, 1930, Johnstown), the daughter of Kenneth and Elsie (Rager) Teeter.

1. **Elsie Marie RIBBLETT** (adopted): b August 23, 1949, Cambria County, Pennsylvania; m June 27, 1970, Donald Wickett, Sr. (August 22, 1949), the son of Carl and Alice (Frey) Wickett.   Resides (1994) Holland, New York.   See next PA.4.2.6.1.7.1.

2. **Patricia Jane RIBBLETT**: b February 8, 1951, Cambria County, Pennsylvania; m July 13, 1971, Terry Lee Green (b July 27, 1951), the son of Neil and Ella (Tinue) Green. See next PA.4.2.6.1.7.2.

3. **William Allen RIBBLETT, Jr**: b August 6, 1953, Johnstown, Cambria County, Pennsylvania; m 1st in Springville, New York, on September 25, 1971, Denise Louise Lochte (b April 17, 1951, New York), the daughter of Howard Lochte; m 2d November 20, 1975, Kim Louise ByRoods (b April 12, 1956), the daughter of Harold and Donna ByRoods. See next PA.4.2.6.1.7.3.

4. **Albert Roy RIBBLETT**: b April 16, 1956; m Sheryl Lynn Mitchell (b November 27, 1959), the daughter of Edward and Lillian Mitchell. See next PA.4.2.6.1.7.4.

5. **Leonard Lee RIBBLETT**: b June 21, 1967.

PA.4.2.6.1.7.1
ELSIE MARIE RIBBLETT

Elsie Marie Ribblett (adopted) was born on August 23, 1949, Cambria County, Pennsylvania.

Miss Elsie Marie Ribblett married on June 27, 1970, Donald Wickett, Sr. (August 22, 1949), the son of Carl and Alice (Frey) Wickett. Resides (1994) Holland, New York.

1. **Donald Lee WICKETT, Jr**: b September 27, 1973, New York.

PA4.2.6.1.7.2
PATRICIA JANE RIBBLETT and TERRY LEE GREEN

Patricia Jane Ribblett was born on February 8, 1951, Cambria County, Pennsylvania.

Miss Patricia Jane Ribblett married on July 13, 1971, Terry Lee Green (b July 27, 1951), the son of Neil and Ella (Tinue) Green.

1. **Terry Lee GREEN, Jr**: b December 13, 1971.
2. **Lori Kay GREEN**: b September 5, 1973.
3. **Todd Allen GREEN**: b June 30, 1980.

PA.4.2.6.1.7.3
WILLIAM ALLEN RIBBLETT

William Allen Ribblett, Jr., was born on August 6, 1953, Johnstown, Cambria County, Pennsylvania.

William Allen Ribblett, Jr., married 1st in Springville, New York, on September 25, 1971, Denise Louise Lochte (b April 17, 1951, New York), the daughter of Howard Lochte.

William Allen Ribblett married 2d November 20, 1975, Kim Louise Byroads (b April 12, 1956), the daughter of Harold and Donna Byroads.

1. **Jodi Ann RIBBLETT**: b June 19, 197-
2. **William Allen RIBBLETT**, III: b May 31, 1973.
3. **Jennifer Ann RIBBLETT**: b January 9, 1978.
4. **Jason Allen RIBBLETT**: b March 2, 1981.

PA.4.2.6.1.7.4
ALBERT ROY RIBBLETT and SHERYL LYNN MITCHELL

Albert Roy Ribblett was born on April 16, 1956.

Albert Roy Ribblett married Sheryl Lynn Mitchell (b November 27, 1959), the daughter of Edward and Lillian Mitchell.

1. **Andrew James RIBBLETT**: b December 8, 1981.
2. **Mathew James RIBBLETT**: b June 6, 198-.

PA.4.2.6.1.9
SHIRLEY NORINE RIBBLETT

Shirley Norine ("Noreen") Ribblett was born on January 8, 1934, Indiana County, Pennsylvania.

Miss Shirley Norine Ribblett married 1st February 9, 1951, Theodore ("Ted") Marlin Rose (b July 12, 1933, Johnstown, Pennsylvania; d June 26, 1981, Johnstown, Pennsylvania, buried Benshoff Hill Cemetery, Johnstown), the son of Theodore and Florence (Seeley) Rose.

Mrs. Shirley (Ribblett) Rose married 2d in Milton, Wisconsin, on October 16, 1976, Robert J. Pollock (b December 24, 1934, Mauston, Wisconsin), the son of Robert and Leila (Olson) Pollock.

1. **Theodore Marlin ROSE, Jr**: b October 3, 1953; m 1st on July 22, 1972, Donna Lee Gerez (b March 6, 1954); m 2d at Jonesville, Wisconsin, on July 20, 1985, Mary Ruth Weissinger (b March 17, 1963), the daughter of Hubert J. and Ellen (Hill) Weissinger.

    1. **Belinda Ann ROSE**: b April 17, 1973.
    2. **Amanda Jo ROSE**: b January 28, 1987.

2. **Barry Lee ROSE**: b November 8, 1956, California; m on December 17, 1977, Christol Pollock (b July 3, 1959), the daughter of Ira and Patricia (Wahankee) Pollock; reside Wisconsin.

    1. **Jamie Lynn ROSE**: b September 13, 1978.
    2. **Lisa Marie ROSE**: b November 15, 1979.

3. **Lorrie Norine ROSE**: b September 30, 1960, Mauston, Wisconsin; d November 11, 1973, in Mauston, Wisconsin, when hit by automobile while riding her bike; buried Mauston Cemetery, Mauston, Wisconsin.

4. **Regina Louann ROSE**: b December 21, 1969, Wisconsin; m in Edgerton, Wisconsin, on September 26, 1992, Jamie Scott Kruger, the son of Gary Kruger; reside Wisconsin.

PA.4.2.6.4
WILLIAM HORATIO WILLETT
of Cambria County, Pennsylvania

William Horatio Willett was born on October 14, 1901, in Johnstown, Cambria County, Pennsylvania.

In 1921, he graduated from Western Pennsylvania School for the Blind.

1921
WILLIAM HORATIO WILLETT
(Picture courtesy of Joan Grabenstein)

William Willett married 1st Cora May Cassett (d 1936, Johnstown, Pennsylvania, of T. B., buried Penn Run, Indiana County, Pennsylvania), the daughter of William and Emma (Hagens) Cassett.

William Willett married 2d about 1937 Jessie Hahn.

William Horatio Willett married 3d at St. Patrick's Catholic Church, on September 1, 1945, Helen Fox (b June 17, 1900, Pennsylvania; d August 30, 1979, Allentown, Pennsylvania), the daughter of James and Ellen (Mullen) Fox.

He retired from the Cambria County Branch Association for the Blind where he taught Braille and piano.

William Willett died on May 16, 1990, Allentown, Pennsylvania, at the age 89.

1. **James William WILLETT**: b March 4, 1930, Johnstown, Pennsylvania; m Twilla.

2. **Robert Merl** ("Tony") **WILLETT**: b April 12, 1931, Johns-town, Pennsylvania; m Lea Jean Teeter (b Johnstown, Pennsylvania, on September 18, 1937), the daughter of Kenneth M. and Elsie Alvera (Rager) Teeter; reside Collins, Erie County, New York. See next PA.4.2.6.4.2.

3. **Leo Earl WILLETT**: b February 3, 1935, Johnstown, Pennsylvania.

PA.4.2.6.4.2

ROBERT MERL WILLETT and **LEA JEAN TEETER**
of New York

Robert Merl ("Tony") Willett was born on April 12, 1931, at Johnstown, Cambria County, Pennsylvania.

Robert M. Willett married Lea Jean Teeter (b Johnstown, Pennsylvania, on September 18, 1937), the daughter of Kenneth M. and Elsie Alvera (Rager) Teeter.

They reside at Collins, Erie County, New York.

1. **Robert Lee WILLETT**: b February 6, 1957, North Collins, Erie County, New York; m Cyndie Mary Ackles (b October 8, 1959), the daughter of Paul and Barbara (Borden) Ackles. See next PA.4.2.6.4.2.1.

2. **John Erick WILLETT**: b April 3, 1962, New York; m Debra V. Intrabartols (b December 25, 1953). See next PA.4.2.6.4.2.2.

3. **Paul Andrew WILLETT**: b April 26, 1967, New York.

4. **Scott Patrick WILLETT**: b May 9, 1971, New York.

5. **Daniel Thomas WILLETT**: b August 6, 1980, New York.

PA.4.2.6.44.2.1
ROBERT LEE WILLETT and CYNDIE MARY ACKLES

Robert Lee Willett was born on February 6, 1957, North Collins, Erie County, New York.

Robert Lee Willett married Cyndie Mary Ackles (b October 8, 1959), the daughter of Paul and Barbara (Borden) Ackles.

1. **Branden WILLETT**: b October 1, 1980, New York.

PA.4.2.6.4.2.2
JOHN ERICK WILLETT and DEBRA V. INTRABARTOLS

John Erick Willett was born on April 3, 1962, New York

John Erick Willett married Debra V. Intrabartols (b December 25, 1953).

1. **Renee Dawn WILLETT**: b May 28, 1991, New York.

PA.4.2.6.5
VENORAH GERTRUDE WILLETT
Johnstown, Cambria County, Pennsylvania

Venorah Gertrude Willett was born on April 3, 1906, at Johnstown, Cambria County, Pennsylvania.

Miss Venorah G. Willett married 1st at Johnstown, Cambria County, Pennsylvania, June 9, 1925, Sanford Allen Mishler (b August 31, 1899, Johnstown, Cambria County, Pennsylvania; d May 13, 1980, Barstow, California, buried Mt. View, California), the son of Allen Mishler and Mary Miller. They were divorced February 28, 1963, at Johnstown, Cambria County.

Mrs. Venorah (Willett) Mishler married 2d Kenneth C. Shaffer (d February 10, 1977 [or August 25], of heart attack).

Mrs. Venorah G. (Willett, Mishler) Shaffer died April 12, 1993, at Laurel Crest, Ebensburg, Pennsylvania, and is buried in the Benshoff Hill Cemetery, Johnstown, Cambria County, Pennsylvania.

1. **Franklin Emerson MISHLER, Sr**: b September 18, 1925, Johnstown, Cambria County, Pennsylvania; served in World War II receiving the Purple Heart; m Aleene Blough (b May 30, 1928), the daughter of Sylvester and Ida Rebecca (Shaffer) Blough; resided Somerville, New Jersey; d February 26, 1984, Somerville, New Jersey, buried Lake Nelson Memorial Park, New Jersey. See next PA.4.2.6.5.1.

2. **Sanford** ("Mike") **A. MISHLER**: b November 24, 1926, Johnstown, Cambria County, Pennsylvania; resided Russell Avenue, Johnstown, Pennsylvania; m Evelyn J. Houraluck; member of Somerset American Legion; d May 31, 1991, Johnstown, Pennsylvania, buried Forest Lawn Cemetery, Johnstown, Cambria County, Pennsylvania. See next PA.4.2.6.5.2.

3. **Harry Arnold** ("Pete") **MISHLER**: b September 28, 1930, Johnstown, Cambria County, Pennsylvania; served in the Army during World War II; m Joan Chapin, the daughter of George Chapin; killed in a plane crash on October 26, 1968, Phillipsburg, Pennsylvania, buried Elan Memorial Park, Bloomsburg, Pennsylvania. See next PA.4.2.6.5.3.

4. **Mary Gertrude** ("Tillie") **MISHLER**: m 1st Chad Filmore; resided Gardena, California; m 2d Pearce; d October 26, 1968. See next PA.4.2.6.5.4.

PA.4.2.6.5.1
FRANKLIN EMERSON MISHLER and ALEENE BLOUGH
of Somerville, New Jersey

Franklin Emerson Mishler was born on September 18, 1925, Johnstown, Cambria County, Pennsylvania. He served in World War II receiving the Purple Heart.

Franklin Emerson Mishler married Aleene Blough (b May, 1928), the daughter of Sylvester and Ida Rebecca (Shaffer) Blough. They resided at Somerville, New Jersey.

Franklin Emerson Mishler died on February 26, 1984, New Jersey, and is buried in the Lake Nelson Memorial Park, New Jersey.

1. **Raymond Leslie MISHLER**: b June 17, 1947, Johnstown, Cambria County, Pennsylvania; m 1st at Somerville, New Jersey, on March 25, 1967, Lillian Young (b March 18, 1949), the daughter of Francis and Mary Anna (Tilletsk) Young; m 2d on June 19, 1985, Mary Lou MacIntosh. See next PA.4.2.6.5.1.1.

2. **Franklin Emerson MISHLER**: b March 27, 1949, Johnstown; unmarried.

3. **Tami Alene MISHLER**: b October 31, 1961, Somerville, New Jersey; m at Somerville, New Jersey, on February 26, 1983, Thomas M. Nemeth (b August 7, 1962, Brooklyn, New York), the son of Raymond J. and Ernestine (Gannone) Nemeth.

    1. **Lorien M. NEMETH**: b February 10, 1988, Somerville, New Jersey.

    2. **Megan E. NEMETH**: b March 2, 1989, Somerville, New Jersey.

    3. **Michael D. NEMETH**: b April 11, 1992, Somerville, New Jersey.

PA.4.2.6.5.1.1
RAYMOND LESLIE MISHLER and LILLIAN YOUNG

Raymond Leslie Mishler was born on June 17, 1947, Johnstown, Cambria County, Pennsylvania.

Raymond Leslie Mishler married 1st at Somerville, New Jersey, on March 25, 1967, Lillian Young (b March 18, 1949), the daughter of Francis and Mary Anna (Tilletsk) Young.

Raymond Leslie Mishler married 2d on June 19, 1985, Mary Lou MacIntosh.

1. **Penny Lee MISHLER**: b March 27, 1968, Perth Amboy, New Jersey; m at Hazlet, New Jersey, on June 8, 1985, Richard Slutter; m 2d on July 31, 1992, William Biggins. See next PA.4.2.6.5.1.1.1.

2. **Sherry Ann MISHLER**: b March 27, 1968, Perth Amboy, New Jersey; m at Chester, Pennsylvania, on February 2, 1991, Terry Sellers.

PA.4.2.6.5.1.1.1
PENNY LEE MISHLER of New Jersey

Penny Lee Mishler was born on March 27, 1968, Perth Amboy, New Jersey.

Miss Penny Lee Mishler married at Hazlet, New Jersey, on June 8, 1985, Richard Slutter.

Mrs. Penny Lee (Mishler) Slutter married 2d on July 31, 1992, William Biggins.

1. **Adam J. SLUTTER**: b February 11, 1985, Hazlet, New Jersey.

2. **Crystal A. SLUTTER**: b February 15, 1986, Hazlet, New Jersey.

PA.4.2.6.5.2
SANFORD A. MISHLER and EVELYN J. HOURALUCK
of Cambria County, Pennsylvania

Sanford ("Mike") A. Mishler was born on November 24, 1926, Johnstown, Pennsylvania. He resided at Russell Avenue, Johnstown, Pennsylvania.

Sanford Mishler married Evelyn J. Houraluck. He was a member of Somerset American Legion. He was employed for 38 years with the US Steel Corporation.

Sanford A. Mishler died on May 31, 1991, Johnstown, Pennsylvania, and is buried in the Forest Lawn Cemetery, Johnstown, Cambria County, Pennsylvania.

1. **Keith MISHLER**: m Theresa Forosisky.

   1. **Michael MISHLER**:
   2. **Nathan MISHLER**:
   3. **Samuel MISHLER**:
   4. **David MISHLER**:

PA.4.2.6.5.3
HARRY ARNOLD MISHLER and JOAN CHAPIN

Harry Arnold ("Pete") Mishler was born on September 28, 1930, Johnstown, Cambria County, Pennsylvania. He served in the Army during World War II.

Harry Arnold Mishler married Joan Chapin, the daughter of George Chapin.

Harold Mishler was killed in a plane crash on October 25, 1968, Phillipsburg, Pennsylvania, and is buried Elan Memorial Park, Bloomsburg, Pennsylvania.

1. **Scott MISHLER**:
2. **Brian MISHLER**:

PA.4.2.6.5.4
MARY GERTRUDE MISHLER

Miss Mary Gertrude ("Tillie") Mishler married 1st Chad Filmore. They resided at Gardena, California.

Mrs. Mary G. (Mishler) Filmore married 2d Pearce.

Mrs. Mary G. (Mishler, Filmore) Pearce died on October 26, 1968.

1. **Patricia FILLMORE**:
2. **William P. FILLMORE**:
3. **Chad FILLMORE**:

PA.4.2.6.6
HARRY D. WILLETT and FREIDA ARBUTUS POWELL
of Canton, Ohio

Harry D. ("Pete") Willett was born on September 24, 1907, Johnstown, Cambria County, Pennsylvania.

Harry D. Willett married in Johnstown, Cambria County, Pennsylvania, on May 16, 1927, Freida Arbutus Powell (b November 15, 1904, Somerset County, Pennsylvania; d July 14, 1992, Maryland, of heart failure), the daughter of Sylvester and Quinnie (Rodgers) Powell.

They moved to Ohio in 1942. He is a World War II veteran.

Harry D. ("Pete") Willett was employed by the Tournoux-McDowell Plymouth Agency. He attended the Methodist Church.

HARRY D. WILLETT AND FREIDA ARBUTUS POWELL
(Picture courtesy of Joan Grabenstein)

Harry Willett died of cancer of the liver on April 2, 1983, at Canton, Stark County, Ohio, and is buried in the Sunset Hills Burial Park, Canton, Ohio. At the time of his death, Harry Willett had 11 grandchildren, and 11 great-grandchildren.

1. **Gussie Cozetta WILLETT**: b February 3, 1928, Shade Township, Somerset County, Pennsylvania; m in Stark County, Ohio, on July 19, 1946, John Underwood; resides Phoenix, Arizona.

2. **Flora Nell** ("Pat") **WILLETT**: b June 24, 1930, Johnstown, Cambria County, Pennsylvania; m 1st Richard E. Oldfield (b December 15, 1928), the son of Richard E. Oldfield; m 2d Nelson John Hainsey (b May 5, 1932), the son of Nelson J. Hainsey. See next PA.4.2.6.6.3.

3. **Wilma Jane WILLETT**: b December 19, 1932, Johnstown, Pennsylvania; m 1st in Sebring, Ohio, on April 9, 1949, William Vernon Kennedy (b October 29, 1927, Alliance, Monroe County, Ohio), the son of William V. Kennedy; m 2d in Las Vegas, Nevada, on August 22, 1970, Richard Lee Bates (b June 18, 1942, Centerville, Iowa). See next PA.4.2.6.6.3.

4. **Roger Delroy WILLETT**: b November 26, 1935, Johnstown, Cambria County, Pennsylvania; reside Williamsport, Maryland; m at Canton, Stark County, Ohio, on September 11, 1954, Donna Jean Gilbert (b March 20, 1937, Louisville, Ohio. See next PA.4.2.6.6.4.

PA.4.2.6.6.3
FLORA NELL WILLETT

Flora Nell ("Pat") Willett was born on June 24, 1930, Johnstown, Cambria County, Pennsylvania.

Miss Flora Nell Willett married 1st Richard E. Oldfield (b December 15, 1928), the son of Richard E. Oldfield.

Mrs. Flora Nell (Willett) Oldfield married 2d Nelson John Hainsey (b May 5, 1932), the son of Nelson J. Hainsey; resides Sacramento, California.

1. **Christopher J. OLDFIELD**: b September 18, 1949; d June 11, 1967.

2. **Christine J. OLDFIELD**: b February 5, 1942; m Gary D. Owen.

3. **Richard E. OLDFIELD**: b July 2, 1954; d June 11, 1967.

4. **Nelson John HAINSEY**, III: b September 4, 1959.

PA.4.2.6.6.3
WILMA JANE WILLETT

Wilma Jane Willett was born on December 19, 1932, Johnstown, Pennsylvania.

Miss Wilma Jane Willett married 1st in Sebring, Ohio, on April 9, 1949, William Vernon Kennedy (b October 29, 1927, Alliance, Monroe County, Ohio), the son of William V. Kennedy.

Mrs. Wilma (Willett) Kennedy married 2d in Las Vegas, Nevada, on August 22, 1970, Richard Lee Bates (b June 18, 1942, Centerville, Iowa). She resides in Alibia, Iowa.

1. **Patrick John KENNEDY**: b February 14, 1950, Ohio; m Maloni Lai Ganoi.
2. **Janie Helen KENNEDY**: b July 27, 1951, California; m Horace Y. Downing.
3. **Vernon Dale KENNEDY**: b December 22, 1954, California; m Debra Turry.
4. **Brenda Mae KENNEDY**: b August 24, 1961, California.
5. **Ricky Lee BATES**: b February 28, 1971, California.

PA.4.2.6.6.4
ROGER DELROY WILLETT and DONNA JEAN GILBERT
of Ohio and Maryland

Roger Delroy Willett was born on November 26, 1935, Johnstown, Cambria County, Pennsylvania.

Roger D. Willett married at Canton, Stark County, Ohio, on September 11, 1954, Donna Jean Gilbert (b March 20, 1937, Louisville, Ohio).

They reside in Williamsport, Maryland.

1. **Timothy James WILLETT**: b April 23, 1956, Fort Worth, Texas; m at Alliance, Monroe County, Ohio, on October 4, 1976, Essiree Elane Kindler. See next PA.4.2.6.6.4.1.
2. **Vicky Lynn WILLETT**: b January 19, 1958, Canton, Stark County, Ohio; m at Canton, Ohio, on March 25, 1976, Ronald Gary Sheckel (b May 6, 1958, Alliance, Monroe County, Ohio. See next PA.4.2.6.6.4.2.
3. **Erick John WILLETT**: b January 8, 1965, Canton, Stark County, Ohio.

PA.4.2.6.6.4.1

TIMOTHY JAMES WILLETT and ESSIREE ELANE KINDLER

Timothy James Willett was born on April 23, 1956, Fort Worth, Texas.

Timothy James Willett married at Alliance, Monroe County, Ohio, on October 4, 1976, Essiree Elane Kindler.

1. **Joshua Jacob WILLETT**: b 1975.
2. **Angela Marie WILLETT**: b April 11, 1980, Ohio.

PA.4.2.6.6.4.2

VICKY LYNN WILLETT and RONALD GARY SHECKEL

Vicky Lynn Willett was born on January 19, 1958, Canton, Stark County, Ohio.

Vicky Lynn Willett was married at Canton, Ohio, on March 25, 1976, Ronald Gary Sheckel (b May 6, 1958, Alliance, Monroe County, Ohio.

1. **Nicholas Jonathan SHECKEL**: b November 4, 1976.
2. **Erik Ryan SHECKEL**: b September 12, 1979.

PA.4.2.6.7
JOHN CHALMER WILLETT and EDNA GRACE BORING
of Johnstown, Pennsylvania

John Chalmer Willett was born on November 22, 1908, Johnstown, Cambria County, Pennsylvania, the son of James B. and Emily G. (Wilson) Willett. In 1928, he graduated from Johnstown High School. In 1933, he received a Bachelor of Science degree in Education from Temple University, Philadelphia, Pennsylvania.

1928 JOHNSTOWN HIGH SCHOOL
JOHN CHALMER WILLETT
(Picture courtesy of Joan Grabenstein)

John C. Willett married in Johnstown, on November 18, 1936, Edna Grace Boring (b December 4, 1914, Johnstown, Cambria County, Pennsylvania; d June 24, 1994, age 79, at the Ingleside Care Center, Hockessin, Delaware, buried Glenwood Memorial Gardens, Broomall, Pennsylvania), the daughter of Claude D. and Stella D. (Ribblett) Boring. Edna suffered from neurofibromatosis, and all her male children inherited it.

John Willett suffered from the eye disease, Retinities Pigmentosa, which causes blindness, and is incurable. He went blind in 1936. This is an affliction which all the children of James Buchanan and Emma (Wilson) Willett share.

1952: JOHN CHALMER WILLETT CHILDREN
GEORGE C., JOHN C., CARL E., CHARLES W., and JOAN E.
(Picture courtesy of Joan Grabenstein)

"From Classic to Corn"

Lovers of music will be amply rewarded by a visit to the new Oak Room of the Fort Stanwix Hotel.

Seated inconspicuously in a corner of the room is John Willett, local blind pianist, who plays the most exciting piano you can possibly imagine.

Barrelhouse, boogie-woogie, blues, classics, or corn - whatever your mood this deft-touch artist can satisfy. If you feel like singing such stuff as "Sweet Adeline," you'll get that too.

Talented 34 year old John Willett has been playing piano since he was eight. His first lessons were at the Pittsburgh Blind School, where he spent four years on technical work and finger exercises. Since then, it's been a matter of constant practice and picking up tunes by ear.

There were a couple of years of study at Temple University, too, where the young musician struggled with advanced harmony and even managed to pass a course in sight reading, thanks to his knowledge of Braille ..." (1942

Newspaper article).

They moved to Essington in 1944 where he worked as a piano tuner for the Lester Piano Company, Lester, Pennsylvania, from which he retired in 1961. Mr. Willett owned and operated Willett's Professional Piano Tuning, Chester, Pennsylvania, for several years before working for the Wilmington Piano Company, Wilmington, Delaware for 12 years. In 1988, after working for 8 years, he retired from the Lanning Piano Company.

John Chalmer Willett died on October 6, 1995, age 86, at Hockessin, Delaware, and is buried in the Glenwood Memorial Gardens (Cemetery), Broomall, Pennsylvania.

(REF: "Willett House" Quarterly, No. 4, 1987, page 457-458).

1970
JOHN C. AND EDNA G. WILLETT
(Picture courtesy of Joan Grabenstein)

1. **George Chalmer WILLETT**: b September 9, 1937, Johnstown, Cambria County, Pennsylvania; m June 18, 1960, Mary Theresa Panaro (b June 16, 1942), the daughter of Daniel James and Ann May (Johnson) Panaro; resides (1994) Newark, New Jersey. See next PA.4.2.6.7.1.

2. **Joan Edna WILLETT**: b May 7, 1940, Johnstown, Cambria County, Pennsylvania; m in Lester, Pennsylvania, on

November 28, 1959, Robert Carl Grabenstein (b February 14, 1936, Philadelphia, Pennsylvania). See next PA.4.2.6.7.2.

3. **John** ("Jack") **Claude WILLETT**: b May 23, 1942, Johnstown, Cambria County, Pennsylvania; m 1st 1965, Carol B. Marchiani (divorced 1969, New Orleans); m 2d in New Orleans, Louisiana, on August 21, 1970, Delores Roche (divorced March 3, 1987, Wisconsin); m 3d in Burlington, Wisconsin, on November 27, 1991, Barbara Reynolds (b April 24, 1962), the daughter of Charles Kalscheur and Clara Belle (Farrell) Reynolds. See next PA.4.2.6.7.3.

4. **Carl Edward WILLETT**: b May 15, 1945, Philadelphia, Pennsylvania; m in Elkton, Maryland, on November 18, 1977, Barbara Ann Riddle (b October 24, 1953, Ashe County, North Carolina); resides (1995) Delaware City, Delaware. See next PA.4.2.6.7.4.

5. **Charles** ("Chuck") **William WILLETT**: b November 22, 1947, Philadelphia, Pennsylvania; raised in Essington, Pennsylvania; unmarried; removed to Delaware in the 1960s; resided (1994) Hockessin, Delaware; d February 22, 1995, of heart failure, Hockessin, Delaware, buried Glenwood Memorial Gardens, Brommall, Pennsylvania (Obituary, 1995, "Charles W. Willett").

PA.4.2.6.7.1
GEORGE CHALMER WILLETT and **MARY TERESA PANARO**
of Wilmington, Delaware

George Chalmer Willett was born on September 9, 1937, at Johnstown, Cambria County, Pennsylvania.

George Chalmer Willett married in Wilmington, Delaware, on June 18, 1960, Mary Theresa Panaro (b June 16, 1942, Wilmington, Delaware), the daughter of Daniel James and Ann May (Johnson) Panaro. They reside (1994) in Newark, Delaware.

1. **Jennifer WILLETT**: b April 14, 1962, Wilmington, Delaware; m 1st in California on August 22, 1981, Frank D. Lewis (divorced 1983); m 2d Mark Smith; m 3d at Elkton, Maryland, on September 27, 1986, Edward Wesley (divorced 1988). See next PA.4.2.6.7.1.1.

2. **Monica WILLETT**: b July 3, 1964, Wilmington, Delaware; m December 17, 1983, William Wallace Wipf (divorced 1984). See next PA.4.2.6.7.1.2.

3. **Cynthia WILLETT**: b July 2, 1965, Wilmington, Delaware; m at Elkton, Maryland, on October 6, 1990, Patrick Bredbenner, Jr. (divorced 1991).

4. **Jason Eric WILLETT**: b July 24, 1966, Wilmington, Delaware; m at Sierra Madre, California, on March 4, 1989, Lisa Marie Switzer (divorced).

5. **George Chalmer WILLETT** (II): b June 24, 1969, Wilmington, Delaware; m Jennifer Reynolds. See next PA.4.2.6.7.1.5.

PA.4.2.6.7.1.1
JENNIFER WILLETT

Jennifer Willett was born on April 14, 1962, Wilmington, Delaware.

Miss Jennifer Willett married 1st in California on August 22, 1981, Frank D. Lewis (divorced 1983), the son of Frank L. and Shirley Lewis.

Mrs. Jennifer (Willett) Lewis married 2d Mark Smith.

Mrs. Jennifer (Willett, Lewis) Smith married 3d at Elkton, Maryland, on September 27, 1986, Edward Wesley (divorced 1988).

1. **Jessica N. LEWIS**: b January 21, 1981, California.
2. **Bret SMITH**: b September 27, 1985, Tucson, Arizona.

PA.4.2.6.7.1.2
MONICA WILLETT and WILLIAM WALLACE WIPF

Monica Willett was born on July 3, 1964, Wilmington, Delaware.

Mrs. Monica Willett married in Wilmington, Delaware, on December 17, 1983, William Wallace Wipf (divorced 1984), the son of John and Emma Wipf.

1. **William Charles WIPF**: b March 26, 1982.
2. **Daniele N. WIPF**: b February 22. 1984, Wilmington, Delaware.

PA.4.2.6.7.1.5
GEORGE CHALMER WILLETT and JENNIFER REYNOLDS

George Chalmer Willett (II) was born on June 24, 1969, Wilmington, Delaware.

George Chalmer Willett married Jennifer Reynolds.

1. **Jessica Alyse WILLETT**: b November, 1993.

PA.4.2.6.7.2

JOAN EDNA WILLETT and **ROBERT CARL GRABENSTEIN**

of Wilmington, Delaware

Joan Edna ("Mamie") Willett was born on May 7, 1940, Johnstown, Cambria County, Pennsylvania. She attended Essington Public Grade School and Ridley Park High School, Ridley Park, Pennsylvania.

It should not be forgotten, that Joan E. Willett of the 8th grade Essington School, was crowned as May Queen of Essington.

JOAN E. WILLETT AND GEORGE C. WILLETT, 1942
(Picture courtesy of Joan Grabenstein)

Miss Joan Edna Willett married in Lester, Pennsylvania, on November 28, 1959, Robert Carl Grabenstein (b February

14, 1936, Philadelphia, Pennsylvania), the son of Franz Carl Grabenstein and Marie Wallen.

They resided in Essington, Pennsylvania, until 1966, and then in Chester, Pennsylvania. In 1968, they removed to Delaware.

Bob Grabenstein works for Boeing Helicopter Company, Ridley Township, Delaware County, Pennsylvania.

They attend the Roman Catholic Church.

JOAN AND BOB GRABENSTEIN
MAY, 1987
(Picture courtesy of Joan Grabenstein)

1. **Dawn Marie GRABENSTEIN**: b March 13, 1962, Ridley Park, Delaware County, Pennsylvania; m at Christ Our King, Roman Catholic Church, Wilmington, Delaware, on September 30, 1989, Michael John Hamill (b August 31, 1956, Wilmington, Delaware); reside Newark, Delaware, the son of Joseph and Shirley L. (Smith) Hamill. Both are Collection Specialist for P. N. C. Bank, Wilmington, Delaware.

2. **Joan Ann GRABENSTEIN**: b March 28, 1963, Ridley Park, Delaware County, Pennsylvania; 1980 joined the Navy; m in Key West, Florida, on September 19, 1985, Danny Hugh Jones (b July 28, 1961, Sylacauga, Alabama). See next PA.4.2.6.7.2.1.

3. **Shirl Lynn GRABENSTEIN**: b January 21, 1965,

Ridley Park, Delaware County, Pennsylvania; m at Immaculate Heart of Mary Catholic Church, Wilmington, Delaware, on September 10, 1994, Michael John Sotak (b June 21, 1963, Greensburg, Westmoreland County, Pennsylvania), the son of Ralph and Catharine (Stenson) Sotak of Greensburg, Pennsylvania. Michael is an Aeronautical Engineer at Atlantic Aviation. He attended Greensburg Catholic High School and Embry Riddle Aeronautical University, Daytona Beach, Florida. Shirl Lynn is an Interior Designer, self employed.

4. **Robert Carl GRABENSTEIN** (Jr.): b May 8, 1967, Upland, Pennsylvania; d infant May 8, 1967, buried Holy Cross Cemetery, Yeador, Pennsylvania.

PA.4.2.6.7.2.1
JOAN ANN GRABENSTEIN and DANNY HUGH JONES

Joan Ann Grabenstein was born on March 28, 1963, at Ridley Park, Pennsylvania. In 1980, she joined the Navy while still in high school under the delayed-entrance program. She entered into Naval active duty nine months after graduation.

Joan Ann Grabenstein married in Key West, Florida, on September 19, 1985, Danny Hugh Jones (b July 28, 1961, Sylacauga, Alabama), the son of Hugh and Gloria (Gaither) Jones. They divorced on October 20, 1992, Charleston, South Carolina.

Joan left the Navy on November 30, 1993, after 12 years of service. She is now (1997) employed by Lockeed-Martin in New Jersey, and resides in Burlington, New Jersey.

1. **Daniel Braxton JONES**: b March 18, 1986, Key West, Florida.

2. **Lindsay Renee JONES**: b January 4, 1990, Charleston, South Carolina.

FOUR GENERATIONS OF THE WILLETT FAMILY, 1986
JOHN C. WILLETT AND WIFE EDNA
JOAN WILLETT GRABENSTEIN, JOAN GRABENSTEIN JONES
DANIEL BRAXTON JONES
(Picture courtesy of Joan Grabenstein)

PA.4.2.6.7.3
JOHN CLAUDE WILLETT
of Burlington, Racine County, Wisconsin

John ("Jack") Claude Willett was born on May 23, 1942, at Johnstown, Cambria County, Pennsylvania.

Jack Willett married 1st in 1965, to Carol B. Marchiani (divorced 1969, New Orleans).

Jack Willett married 2d in New Orleans, Louisiana, on August 21, 1970, Delores Roche (divorced March 3, 1987, Wisconsin).

Jack Willett married 3d in Burlington, Racine County, Wisconsin, on November 27, 1991, Barbara Reynolds (b April 24, 1962), the daughter of Charles Kalscheur and Clara Belle (Farrell) Reynolds. They reside (1994) in Burlington, Wisconsin.

Children of John Claude and his 1st wife, Carol B. Marchiani:

1. **John Claude WILLETT** (III): b December 2, 1965, Wilmington, Delaware.

2. **Ann Marie WILLETT**: b August 15, 1966, Wilmington, Delaware.

Child of John Claude and his 3rd wife, Barbara Reynolds:

3. **Edna Jean WILLETT**: b March 30, 1992, Wisconsin.

PA.4.2.6.7.4
CARL EDWARD WILLETT and BARBARA ANN RIDDLE

Carl Edward Willett was born on May 15, 1945, at Philadelphia, Pennsylvania.

Carl Willett married in Elkton, Maryland, on November 18, 1977, Barbara Ann Riddle (b October 24, 1953, Ashe County, North Carolina), the daughter of Edison Ford and Catherine (Davis) Riddle. They reside (1995) in Delaware City, Delaware. He works for Sun Oil County, Marcus, Pennsylvania.

    1. **Sandy Lynn LAMBERT WILLETT** (adopted stepdaughter): b November 29, 1971, Wilmington, Delaware; m William Francis McDowell.

    2. **Lisa Ann LAMBERT WILLETT** (adopted stepdaughter): b May 22, 1973, Wilmington, Delaware; m on January 24, 1990, Harry Anderson (b June 29, 1969, Delaware); reside (1994) Smyrna, Delaware. PA.4.2.6.7.4.2.

    3. **Carl Edward WILLETT** (Jr.): b May 26, 1978, Wilmington, Delaware.

PA.4.2.6.7.4.2
LISA ANN LAMBERT WILLETT and HARRY ANDERSON

Lisa Ann LAMBERT WILLETT (stepdaughter, adopted) was born on May 22, 1973, Wilmington, Delaware.

Miss Lisa Ann Lambert Willett married on January 24, 1990, Harry Anderson (b June 29, 1969, Delaware), the son of Frederick and Nacy (Stapleton) Anderson. They reside (1994) Smyrna, Delaware.

    1. **John Fred ANDERSON**: b November 8, 1989, Stanton, Delaware.

PA.4.2.6.10
CHARLES ALEXANDER WILLETT and MILDRED KINNERY
of Baltimore, Maryland

Charles Alexander Willett was born on February 23, 1917, Johnstown, Cambria County, Pennsylvania.

In 1934, he graduated from Johnstown High School.

Charles A. Willett married in Cumberland, Maryland, on September 5, 1936, Mildred Kinnery (d May, 1981, Pittsburgh, Pennsylvania).

During the war, Charles Willett worked for the Glenn Martin Bomber Factory, in Baltimore, Maryland. He was accidentally killed in an motorcycle accident in Baltimore on November 12, 1942, at age 25, and is buried in the Grandview Cemetery, Johnstown, Cambria County, Pennsylvania.

CIRCA 1940
CHARLES ALEXANDER AND MILDRED (KINNERY) WILLETT
(Picture courtesy of Joan Grabenstein)

(Obituary, "Charles Willett, Son of West End Couple, is Killed" "The Johnstown Tribune," dated November 14, 1942).

1. **Erick Thomas WILLETT**: b July 21, 1937, Pennsylvania.
2. **Charles Alexander WILLETT** (Jr.): b October 17, 1938, Pennsylvania.
3. **Kenneth WILLETT**: b May 22, 1940, Pennsylvania.

CIRCA 1944
CHARLES ALEXANDER WILLETT CHILDREN
THOMAS, ALEXANDER, AND KENNETH
(Picture courtesy of Joan Grabenstein)

PA.4.2.8
EDMUND BURKE WILLETT and **MARTHA L. KASE HAAS**
of Pennsylvania and Louisiana

Edmund Burke ("Bert") Willett was born on November 14, 1883, in Strongstown, Indiana County, Pennsylvania.

Edmund Burke Willett married in Johnstown, Cambria County, on October 20, 1914, Mrs. Martha L. (Kase) Haas (b October 13, 1884, Elysburg, Pennsylvania; d April 7, 1954, age 69, Johnstown, and is buried in the Grandview Cemetery, Johnstown, Pennsylvania), the daughter of Simon P. and Martha Kase.

Edmund Willett was a contractor. They resided at 137 "M" Street, Johnstown, Pennsylvania (1927).

In 1956, they removed to Shreveport, Louisiana. He was a plasterer and contractor.

Edmund Willett died on November 14, 1971, at Shreveport, Louisiana, and is buried November 17, 1971, in the Grandview Cemetery, Johnstown, Cambria County, Pennsylvania.

1. **Franklin Emerson WILLETT**: b February 10, 1917, Johnstown, Cambria County, Pennsylvania; m October 31, 1945, Vivian Jacqutia Rogers (b May 17, 1923, Vivian, Louisiana), the daughter of Edward and Hattie (Burton) Rogers; d November 3, 1975, Shreveport, Louisiana, buried Forest Park Cemetery, Louisiana. See next PA.4.2.8.1.

2. **Chalmer WILLETT**: died as an infant May 21, 1915, at 151 Garfield Street, Johnstown, Cambria County, Pennsylvania, buried Grandview Cemetery, Johnstown. Death due to Septehaemia.

PA.4.2.8.1
FRANKLIN EMERSON WILLETT
and **VIVIAN JACQUTIA ROGERS**
of Shreveport, Louisiana

Franklin Emerson Willett was born on February 10, 1917, at Johnstown, Cambria County, Pennsylvania.

He worked for the Bethlehem Steel Corporation prior to military service with the Army Corps, Armored Field Artillery.

Franklin Emerson Willett married on October 31, 1945, Vivian Jacqutia Rogers (b May 17, 1923, Vivian, Louisiana), the daughter of Edward and Hattie (Burton) Rogers.

CIRCA 1942
FRANKLIN E. WILLETT
(Picture courtesy of Joan Grabenstein)

He was the sheriff of Shreveport, Louisiana, and resided Shreveport.

Franklin E. Willett died on November 3, 1975, in Shreveport, Louisiana, and is buried in the Forest Park Cemetery, Louisiana.

    1. **Sandra Kay WILLETT**: b August 4, 1946, Shreveport, Louisiana; m 1st Hawkins; m 2d Carl B. Arnold.   See PA.4.2.8.1.1.

    2. **Edmond Franklin WILLETT**: b June 6, 1949, Shreveport, Louisiana; m Carol Giddengs. See PA.4.2.8.1.2.

    3. **Susanne WILLETT**: b October 14, 1952, Shreveport, Louisiana.

PA.4.2.8.1.1
SANDRA KAY WILLETT

Sandra Kay Willett was born on August 4, 1946, Shreveport, Louisiana.

Miss Sandra Kay Willett married 1st Hawkins.

Mrs. Sandra Kay (Willett) Hawkins married 2d Carl B. Arnold.

    1. **Trey Willett HAWKINS**:

    2. **Parker Christian HAWKINS**:

    3. **Jennifer Susanne HAWKINS**:

PA.4.2.8.1.2
EDMOND FRANKLIN WILLETT and CAROL GIDDENGS

Edmond Franklin Willett was born on June 6, 1949, Shreveport, Louisiana.

Edmond Franklin Willett married Carol Giddengs.

    1. **Michael Brent WILLETT**:

PA.4.2.10
VICTOR JERALD WILLETT and OLIVE VIOLA ZIMMERMAN
of Cambria County, Pennsylvania

Victor Jerald ("Jugo") Willett was born on May 4, 1887, in Clearfield County, Pennsylvania.

Victor J. Willett married in Johnstown, Pennsylvania, on May 5, 1907, Olive Viola Zimmerman (b June 1, 1889, Ligonier, Westmoreland County, Pennsylvania; d September 9, 1987, age 98, Johnstown, Cambria County, Pennsylvania, buried Grandview Cemetery, Johnstown, Cambria County, Pennsylvania), the daughter of John H. Zimmermann and Emma M. Brant.

They resided at 113 Spring Street, Johnstown (1927). He retired as a plasterer and contractor.

Victor Jerald Willett died on August 4, 1965, age 78, at Johnstown, Cambria County, Pennsylvania, and is buried in the Grandview Cemetery, Johnstown, Cambria County, Pennsylvania.

1. **Willa Mildred WILLETT**: b September 23, 1908, Pennsylvania; m May 28, 1936, John W. Fitzpatrick (b September 24, 1904, Johnstown, Cambria County, Pennsylvania; d June 3, 1978, Johnstown); resided at 373 McKee Avenue, Johnstown, Pennsylvania (1965). See next PA.4.2.10.1.

2. **Emily Louise WILLETT**: b November 21, 1920, Johnstown, Pennsylvania; m April 14, 1946, John Cole Hoover (b April 30, 1918, Johnstown, Pennsylvania; d June 6, 1987, Laurel Crest Manor, Ebensburg, Pennsylvania), the son of Clarence W. and Ophelia G. (Cole) Hoover; resided at 115 Spring Street, Johnstown, Cambria County (1965); d August 10, 1979, Johnstown, buried Grandview Cemetery, Johnstown, Cambria County, Pennsylvania. See next PA.4.2.10.2.

PA.4.2.10.1
WILLA MILDRED WILLETT and JOHN W. FITZPATRICK

Willa Mildred Willett was born on September 23, 1908, Pennsylvania.

Miss Willa Mildred Willett married on May 28, 1936, John W. Fitzpatrick (b September 24, 1904, Johnstown, Cambria County, Pennsylvania; d June 3, 1978, Johnstown). They resided at 373 McKee Avenue, Johnstown, Pennsylvania (1965).

1. **John Walter FITZPATRICK**: b December 18, 1939, Pennsylvania; d December 23, 1939, buried Grandview Cemetery, Johnstown, Cambria County, Pennsylvania.

2. **Walter John FITZPATRICK**: b May 16, 1942, Pennsylvania; m Nancy A. Sperber (b June 1, 1945, Pittsburgh, Pennsylvania), the daughter of Howard F. and Sarah Eliz (Kramer) Sperber; resides (1994) Butler County, Pennsylvania. See next PA.4.2.10.1.2.

PA.4.2.10.1.2
WALTER JOHN FITZPATRICK and NANCY A. SPERBER
of Butler County, Pennsylvania

Walter John Fitzpatrick was born on May 16, 1942, Pennsylvania.

Walter John Fitzpatrick married Nancy A. Sperber (b June 1, 1945, Pittsburgh, Pennsylvania), the daughter of Howard F. and Sarah Eliz (Kramer) Sperber.

They reside (1994) in Butler County, Pennsylvania where he is a professor at Butler County Community College.

1. **Shannon Ann FITZPATRICK**: b February 25, 1977, Pittsburgh, Pennsylvania.

2. **Justin Quinn FITZPATRICK**: b April 2, 1979, Pittsburgh, Pennsylvania.

PA.4.2.10.2
EMILY LOUISE WILLETT and JOHN COLE HOOVER

Emily Louise Willett was born on November 21, 1920, Johnstown, Pennsylvania.

Miss Emily Louise Willett married on April 14, 1946, John Cole Hoover (b April 30, 1918, Johnstown, Pennsylvania; d June 6, 1987, Laurel Crest Manor, Ebensburg, Pennsylvania), the son of Clarence W. and Ophelia G. (Cole) Hoover.

They resided at 115 Spring Street, Johnstown, Cambria County (1965).

Mrs. Emily (Willett) Hoover died on August 10, 1979, at Johnstown, and is buried in the Grandview Cemetery, Johnstown, Cambria County, Pennsylvania.

1. **Nancy Louise HOOVER**: b July 8, 1949, Johnstown, Cambria County, Pennsylvania.

2. **Donald John HOOVER**: b January 4, 1952, Johnstown, Cambria County, Pennsylvania; m 1st Debra Lynn Salem; m 2d Diane Rella Gray.

1. **Abigail Dianne HOOVER**: b July 18, 1991, Johnstown, Cambria County, Pennsylvania.

CHAPTER FIVE
WILLIAM WILLETT (1775-1856)

PA.5
WILLIAM WILLETT and **ORSILLA THOMPSON**
of Allegheny County, Pennsylvania

William Willett was born in 1775 in Maryland (born Maryland according to the 1850 census).

In 1804, William Willett purchased land in Allegheny County, Pennsylvania, and settled there for the rest of his life. This is the first mention of William Willett in Pennsylvania.

William Willett married about 1804 Orsilla Thompson (b 1786, Pennsylvania; d August 3, 1866. Allegheny County, Pennsylvania), the daughter of William Thompson, pioneer of Allegheny County, Pennsylvania.

In 1810, William Willet and family are listed in the St. Clair, Allegheny County, Pennsylvania, census, page 161, as follows:

3-0-2-1-0 0-0-1-0-0

1 male	26-45	1765-1784	*William*	*age 35*	*b 1775*
1 female	16-26	1784-1794	*Orsilla*	*age 24*	*b 1786*
1 male	16-26	1784-1794			
1 male	16-26	1784-1794			
1 male	0-10	1800-1810	*John*	*age 7?*	*b 1803?*
1 male	0-10	1800-1810	*William*	*age 5?*	*b 1805?*
1 male	0-10	1800-1810	*Samuel*	*age 2?*	*b 1808?*

In 1820, William Willet and family are listed in the St. Clair, Allegheny County, Pennsylvania, census, page 120, as follows:

1 male	45-up	bef.-1775	*William*	*age 44**	*b 1776**
1 female	26-45	1775-1794	*Orsilla*	*age 34*	*b 1786*
1 male	10-16	1804-1810	*John*	*age 17?*	*b 1803?*
1 male	10-16	1804-1810	*William*	*age 15?*	*b 1805?*
1 male	10-16	1804-1810	*Samuel*	*age 12?*	*b 1808?*
1 female	0-10	1810-1820	*Sarah*	*age 5*	*b 1815*
1 male	0-10	1810-1820	*Hezekiah*	*age 4*	*b 1816*
1 female	0-10	1810-1820	*Elizabeth*	*age 1*	*b 1819*

In 1830, William Willett and family are listed in the Mifflin Township, Allegheny County, Pennsylvania, census, page 247, as follows:

1 male	50-60	1770-1780	*William*	*age 54 b 1776*
1 female	30-40	1790-1800	*Orsilla*	*age 44* b 1786**
1 male	20-30	1800-1810	*William*	*age 25? b 1805?*
1 male	20-30	1800-1810	*Samuel*	*age 22? b 1808?*
1 female	15-20	1810-1815	*Sarah*	*age 15 b 1815*
1 male	15-20	1810-1820	*Hezekiah*	*age 14 b 1816*
1 female	10-15	1815-1820	*Elizabeth*	*age 11 b 1819*
1 female	5-10	1820-1825	*Emeline*	*age 6 b 1824*
1 male	0-5	1825-1853	*Uriah*	*age 3 b 1827*
1 female	0-5	1825-1830		

In 1840, William Willett and family are listed in the Mifflin Township, Allegheny County, Pennsylvania, census, page 145, as follows:

1 male	60-70	1770-1780	*William*	*age 64 b 1776*
1 female	50-60	1780-1790	*Orsilla*	*age 54 b 1786*
1 female	15-20	1820-1825	*Elizabeth*	*age 21* b 1819**
1 female	15-20	1820-1825	*Emeline*	*age 16 b 1824*
1 male	10-15	1825-1830	*Uriah*	*age 13 b 1827*

In 1850, William Willett and family are listed in the Baldwin Township, Allegheny County, Pennsylvania, census, dwelling 145-145, page 135, as follows:

Willett	William	74	m	MD farmer $3,500
	Ursula	64	f	PA
	Emeline	25	f	PA
	Urriah	23	m	PA

Also in 1850, his son, Hezekiah and family were listed beside him, as follows:

Willett	Hezekiah	35	m	PA farmer
	Elizabeth	35	f	PA
	Martha Jane	13	f	PA
	Isabella	5	f	PA
	William	1	m	PA

William Willett died on July 25, 1856 at Baldwin, Allegheny County, Pennsylvania.

William Willett, Sr., will directed that the coal on his estate be sold to the highest bidder and that a portion of the proceeds go to his wife, Orsilla, and daughter, Emeline. The remainder of the money was to be divided amongst his grandchildren, who are not named in the will. At his death, William Willett had thirty grandchildren and one of his daughters was pregnant; the estate was therefore divided thirty-one ways. One grandson, James, was a son of John Willett and had predeceased his grandfather.

1. **John WILLETT**: b 1803, Mifflin, Allegheny County, Pennsylvania; m abt 1832 Eliza A. (b 1808; d November 27, 1879, Pittsburgh, Allegheny County, Pennsylvania); d May 8, 1839, Beaver County, Pennsylvania. See next PA.5.1.

2. **William WILLETT** (II): b abt 1805? Mifflin Township, Allegheny County, Pennsylvania; m in Pennsylvania on December 4, 1833, Jane McGibbeny; died before 1856 (predeceased his father), Lewis County, Missouri. See next PA.5.2.

3. **Samuel WILLETT**: b December (20), 1808, St. Clair, Allegheny County, Pennsylvania; m at Sangamon County, Illinois, on January 14, 1834 Mariah Cummins (b August 1, 1815, Dayton, Ohio; d March 6, 1902 , buried in the Hebron Cemetery, Morgan County, Illinois); d January 5, 1892, Morgan County, Illinois, buried in the Hebron Cemetery, Morgan County, Illinois. See next PA.5.3.

4. **Sarah WILLETT**: b 1815, St. Clair Township, Allegheny County, Pennsylvania; m December 5, 1833, Alfred Sheich; d May 2, 1891, Knoxville (now part of Pittsburgh), Pennsylvania. See next PA.5.4.

5. **Hezekiah WILLETT**: b 1816, Allegheny County, Pennsylvania; m abt 1835 Elizabeth Stewart (b 1815, St. Clair Township, Allegheny County, Pennsylvania); resided Allegheny County, Pennsylvania; d in Americus, Grand Forks County, North Dakota. See next PA.5.5.

6. **Elizabeth Jane WILLETT**: b 1819, St. Clair Township, Allegheny County, Pennsylvania; m abt 1845 Joel Sickman; resided in Allegheny County, Pennsylvania.

7. **Emeline** (Emaline) **WILLETT**: b 1824, St. Clair Township, Allegheny County, Pennsylvania; still unmarried when her mother died in 1866. Possibly the Emeline Willett who married in Allegheny County, Pennsylvania, on February 11, 1869, as his 2d wife the Hon. Matthew P. McClanahan (b January 2, 1806, Sewickley, Westmoreland County, Pennsylvania; d June 3, 1881); d after 1882.

8. **Uriah WILLETT**: b 1827, St. Clair, Township, Allegheny County, Pennsylvania; m abt 1851 Elizabeth Craft (b 1828, Pennsylvania; d February 8, 1923, Pittsburgh, Allegheny County, Pennsylvania); d February 4, 1874, Pittsburgh, Allegheny County, Pennsylvania. See next PA.5.8.

PA.5.1
JOHN WILLET and ELIZA A.
of Fallston, Beaver County, Pennsylvania

John Willet was born in 1803 at Mifflin, Allegheny County, Pennsylvania.

John Willett married about 1832 Eliza A. (b 1808; d November 27, 1879, Pittsburgh, Allegheny County, Pennsylvania).

Beaver County, Pennsylvania, Tax Lists show John Willett residing in Fallston from 1836 to 1838.

John Willet died on May 8, 1839, of lockjaw ("Beaver Argus" Newspaper, Beaver County, Pennsylvania, May 8, 1839) (Beaver County Register Docket I, page 21, "Estate Record"; Beaver County Orphan's Court, Volume 3, page 121, 1841; Beaver County, Estate Notice, Charles Lukens, Admr., May 15, 1839, February 3, 1841).

In 1840, E. A. Willet, female head of household, age 30-40, and family, were enumerated in New Brighton Bor., Beaver County, Pennsylvania, page 2, as follows:

1 female	30-40	1800-1810 *E. A.*	*age 38?b 1802?*
1 female	15-20	1820-1825	*age 16?b 1824?*
1 female	5-10	1830-1835 *Maria Ann*	*age 10 b 1830*
1 male	0-5	1835-1840 *(James)*	*age 4? b 1836?*
1 female	0-5	1835-1840 *Emma*	*age 2 b 1838*

After John Willett died (1839), Mrs. E. A. Willett, went to Pittsburgh, Pennsylvania with their two daughters and married a man by the name of Haggerty and had more children.

In 1856, Mrs. Elizabeth Haggerty (mother of James Willett who had predeceased his grandfather, William) received her deceased child's portion of the estate.

1. **Maria Ann WILLETT**: b 1830, Pennsylvania; m before 1851, Charlton; d July 19, 1904, Pittsburgh, Allegheny County, Pennsylvania. See next PA.5.1.1.

2. **James WILLETT**: b 1836, Pennsylvania; d 1840. James Willett, son of John Willett, had predeceased his grandfather (i.e., died before 1856).

3. **Emma WILLETT**: b 1838, Pennsylvania; m before 1864, Hodgson. See next PA.3.1.3.

PA.5.1.1
MARIA ANN WILLETT and MR. CHARLTON
of Allegheny County, Pennsylvania

Maria Ann Willett was born in 1830, Pennsylvania.
Miss Maria Ann Willett married before 1851, Mr. Charlton.
Mrs. Maria Ann (Willett) Charlton died on July 19, 1904, Pittsburgh, Allegheny County, Pennsylvania.

1. **William CHARLTON**: b 1851, Pittsburgh.
2. **Charles CHARLTON**: b 1855, Pittsburgh.

PA.5.1.3
EMMA WILLETT and MR. HODGSON

Emma Willett was born in 1838, Pennsylvania.
Miss Emma Willett married before 1864, Mr. Hodgson.

1. **Ian HODGSON**: b abt 1864.

PA.5.2
WILLIAM WILLETT and JANE MCGIBBNEY
of Allegheny County, Pennsylvania

William Willett was born about 1805? Pennsylvania.
William Willett married in Pennsylvania on December 4, 1833 Jane McGibbeny.
In 1840, William Willett and family are listed in the Mifflin Township, Allegheny County, Pennsylvania, census, page 145, as follows:

1 male	20-30	1810-1820	*William*	*age 25? b 1805?*
1 female	20-30	1810-1820	*Jane*	
1 female	15-20	1815-1820		
1 female	5-10	1830-1835	*Kesiah*	*age 5* *b 1835*
1 female	0-5	1835-1840	*Mary O.*	*age 3* *b 1837*
1 male	0-5	1835-1840	*William A*	*age 1* *b 1839*

From 1843 to 1848, William Willett, Jr., and family owned land in Washington County, Pennsylvania.
William Willett and family have not been found in the 1850 census.
William Willett, Jr., predeceased his father, William Willett, Sr. (i.e., he died before 1856) in Lewis County, Missouri.

1   **Kesiah WILLETT**: b 1835, Pennsylvania; in (1856) Missouri with the James Bell family.

2   **Mary O. WILLETT**: b 1837, Pennsylvania; in (1856) Missouri with the James Bell family.

3.   **William A. WILLETT**: b 1839, Pennsylvania; in (1856) Illinois.

4.   **Emaline WILLETT**: b abt 1841, Pennsylvania; in (1856) Illinois.

5.   **George Oliver WILLETT**: b 1846, Pennsylvania; in (1856) Missouri with the James Bell family; George O. Willett married in Lewis County, Missouri, on March 10, 1875, Elizabeth ("Lizzie") D. Woods (b 1853, Kentucky), the daughter of William Woods. See next PA.5.2.5.

6.   **Frances Jane WILLETT**: b abt 1847, Pennsylvania; in (1856) Missouri with the James Bell family.

PA.5.2.5
GEORGE OLIVER WILLETT and ELIZABETH D. WOODS
of Clark County, Missouri

George Oliver Willett was born in 1846, Pennsylvania.

In (1856) Missouri with the James Bell family.

George O. Willett married in Lewis County, Missouri, on March 10, 1875, Elizabeth ("Lizzie") D. Woods (b 1853, Kentucky), the daughter of William Woods.

In 1880, George Willett and family were enumerated in the William Woods household in Clay Township, Clark County, Missouri, census, as follows:

Willett	George	head	34	PA
	Elizabeth	daughter	27	KY
	Cecil	grandson	2	MO

1.   **Cecil WILLETT**: b 1878, Missouri.

PA.5.3
SAMUEL WILLETT and MARIAH CUMMINS
of Sangamon County, Illinois

Samuel Willett was born in 1808, St. Clair, Allegheny County, Pennsylvania.

Samuel Willett married in Sangamon County, Illinois, on January 14, 1834, Mariah Cummins (b August 1, 1815, Dayton, Ohio; d March 2, 1902, buried in the Hebron Cemetery, Morgan County, Illinois) (Sangamon County Marriage Record, #026507).

In 1850, Samuel <u>Willet</u> and family are listed in the Morgan County, Illinois, census, as follows:

Willet	Samuel	head	43	PA	farmer
	Maria	wife	35	OH	
	Henry	son	8	IL	
	Zach	son	1	IL	

In 1870, Samuel Willett and family are listed in the Latesville Precinct, Morgan County, Illinois, census, page 684, dwelling 944-94, as follows:

Willet	Samuel	head	64	PA	farmer, $10,000
	Maria	wife	53	OH	
	Taylor	son	21	IL	
	Mary	d-i-l	20	IL	
	Margaret	gdau	1	IL	
Owens	Eliza	ad dau	11	IL	

In 1880, Samuel <u>Willett</u> and family are listed in the Town 16, Morgan County, Illinois, census, as follows:

Willett	Samuel	head	72	m	PA
	Mariah	wife	64	f	OH
	Taylor	son	31	m	IL
	Mary	d-i-l	30	m	IL
	Margaret	gdau	11	f	IL
	William	gson	9	m	IL
	Anna	gdau	7	f	IL
	John	gson	3	m	IL
	Lily	gdau	1	f	IL
Owens	Eliza	ad. dau	20	f	IN

Samuel Willett died on January 5, 1892, and is buried in the Hebron Cemetery, Morgan County, Illinois.

1. **Henry Clay WILLETT**: b 1842, Morgan County, Illinois; enlisted on September 7, 1861, in Company I, 14th Illinois Infantry; d January 25 (31), 1865, age 22 years, 11 months, as a soldier in the Civil War and is buried in the Hebron Cemetery, Morgan County, Illinois. See next PA 5.3.1.

2. **Zachary** (Uriah) **Taylor WILLETT**: b April 25, 1849, Morgan County, Illinois; m abt 1867, Mary E. Ratliff (b February 4, 1850, Illinois; d July 8, 1909); d January 31, 1911, buried Yatesville Cemetery, Morgan County, Illinois. See next PA.5.3.2.

A. **Eliza OWENS (WILLETT)** (adopted); b 1860, Indiana.

PA.5.3.1
HENRY CLAY WILLETT
of Illinois

Henry Clay Willett was born in 1842, Morgan County, Illinois.

Henry Clay Willett married about 1861 (wife's name unknown).

Henry Clay Willett enlisted on September 7, 1861, in Company I, 14th Illinois Infantry.

Henry Clay Willett died on January 25 (31), 1865, age 22 years, 11 months, as a soldier in the Civil War and is buried in the Hebron Cemetery, Morgan County, Illinois. Hebron Cemetery is 6 miles northeast of Jacksonville, Illinois.

1. **Samuel WILLETT**: b 1863; d May 26, 1885; age 22 years, 4 months, 3 days, and is buried in the Hebron Cemetery, Morgan County, Illinois.

PA.5.3.2
ZACHARY TAYLOR WILLETT and MARY E. RATLIFF
of Morgan County and Cass County, Illinois

Zachary (Uriah) Taylor Willett was born on April 25, 1849, Morgan County, Illinois.

Zachary Taylor Willett married about 1867, Mary E. Ratliff (b February 4, 1850, Illinois; d July 8, 1909).

In 1870, Taylor Willett and family are listed in the household of his parents in the Latesville Precinct, Morgan County, Illinois, census, page 684, dwelling 944-94, as follows:

Willet   Samuel   head   64 PA farmer, $10,000

	Maria	wife	53	OH	
	Taylor	**son**	**21**	**IL**	
	Mary	**d-i-l**		**20**	**IL**
	Margaret	**gdau**	**1**	**IL**	
Owens	Eliza	ad dau	11	IL	

In 1880, Taylor <u>Willett</u> and family are listed in the household of his father, Samuel Willett, in the Town 16, Morgan County, Illinois, census, as follows:

Willett	Samuel	head	72	m	PA
	Mariah	wife	64	f	OH
	Taylor	**son**	**31**	**m**	**IL**
	Mary	**d-i-l**	**30**	**m**	**IL**
	Margaret	**gdau**	**11**	**f**	**IL**
	William	**gson**	**9**	**m**	**IL**
	Anna	**gdau**	**7**	**f**	**IL**
	John	**gson**	**3**	**m**	**IL**
	Lily	**gdau**	**1**	**f**	**IL**
Owens	Eliza	ad. dau	20	f	IN

Zachary Taylor Willett died on January 31, 1911, and is buried in the Yatesville Cemetery, Morgan County, Illinois. Also buried in the same graveyard are two children: Jenie Willett and Georgie Willett, both noted as children of Taylor and Mary Willett. None of the family remember these children, and presumably they are infant deaths.

1. **Margaret WILLETT**: b 1869, Illinois.
2. **William WILLETT**: b 1871, Illinois.
3. **Anna Elizabeth WILLETT**: b September 25, 1872, Yatesville, Morgan County, Illinois; m on January 16, 1895, William Elmer Ratliff (b November 14, 1872; d April 30, 1938, buried in the Yatesville Cemetery, Morgan County, Illinois); d January 5, 1957, buried in the Yatesville Cemetery, Morgan County, Illinois. See next <u>PA.5.3.2.3</u>.
4. **John WILLETT**: b 1877, Illinois.
5. **Lillian ("Lily") WILLETT**: b 1879, Illinois; m Albert Doyle (b July 28, 1877; d January 12, 1971).
6. **Nellie WILLETT**: b October 10, 1882, Prentice, Morgan County, Illinois; m Arthur Hiles. See next <u>PA.5.3.2.6</u>.
7. **Lou Pearl WILLETT**: b May 28, 1883 (Illinois); m on November 18, 1903, Walter Long (b October 24, 1880; d November 2, 1953); d September 5, 1915. See Next <u>PA.5.3.2.7</u>.
8. **Beulah WILLETT**:

PA.5.3.2.3
ANNA ELIZABETH WILLETT and WILLIAM ELMER RATLIFF
Morgan County, Illinois

Anna Elizabeth Willett was born on September 25, 1872, Yatesville, Morgan County, Illinois.

Miss Anna Elizabeth Willett married on January 16, 1895, William Elmer Ratliff (b November 14, 1872; d April 30, 1938, buried in the Yatesville Cemetery, Morgan County, Illinois).

He was a farmer.

Mrs. Anna Elizabeth (Willett) Ratliff died on January 5, 1957, buried in the Yatesville Cemetery, Morgan County, Illinois.

1. **Gladys C. RATLIFF**: b December 7, 1898, Illinois; d April 12, 1899, buried in the Yatesville Cemetery, Morgan County, Illinois.

2. **Ellen Elizabeth RATLIFF**: b March 27, 1900, Illinois; m on January 7, 1919, Jess McNeely (b November 22, 1898; d November 13, 1981); d December 30, 1989, buried in Jacksonville, Morgan County, Illinois. See next PA.5.3.2.3.2.

3. **Walter E. RATLIFF**: b March 7, 1903, Illinois; d September 18, 1909, buried in the Yatesville Cemetery, Morgan County, Illinois.

4. **Frank Harold RATLIFF**: b January 26, 1906, Virginia, Cass County, Illinois; m September 30, 1933, Ersle Briney (b January 7, 1911, Schuyler County, Illinois; d January 27, 1989); d at Beardstown, Illinois, on August 28, 1988. See next PA.5.3.2.3.4.

5. **Hazel M. RATLIFF**: b August 16, 1908, Illinois; d March 9, 1909, buried in the Yatesville Cemetery, Morgan County, Illinois.

PA.5.3.2.3.2
ELLEN ELIZABETH RATLIFF and JESS MCNEELY

Ellen Elizabeth Ratliff was born on March 27, 1900, Illinois.

Miss Ellen Elizabeth Ratliff married on January 7, 1919, Jess McNeely (b November 22, 1898; d November 13, 1981).

Mrs. Ellen Elizabeth (Ratliff) McNeely died on December 30, 1989, and is buried in Jacksonville, Morgan County, Illinois.

1. **Margaret Elizabeth MCNEELY**: b October 3, 1924, Jacksonville, Illinois; m on May 6, 1944, Rainer Broekel (b March 24, 1923, Dresden, Germany).

The photographs were taken on their wedding day.
ANNA ELIZABETH WILLETT   WILLIAM ELMER RATLIFF

(Pictures courtesy of Krista Holst)

WILLIAM AND ANNA RATLIFF
HAROLD AND ELLEN

PA.5.3.2.3.4
FRANK HAROLD RATLIFF and ERSLE BRINEY
of Ashland, Cass County, Illinois

Frank Harold Ratliff was born on January 26, 1906, Virginia, Cass County, Illinois.

Frank Harold Ratliff married on September 30, 1933, Ersle Briney (b January 7, 1911, Schuyler County, Illinois; d January 27, 1989, buried in the Yatesville Cemetery, Morgan County, Illinois). Ersle graduated from Beardstown High School in 1929.

Frank Harold Ratliff died on August 28, 1988, and is buried in the Yatesville Cemetery, Morgan County, Illinois.

1. **Betty JoAnn RATLIFF**: b July 30, 1936, Beardstown, Cass County, Illinois; m at Beardstown, Cass County, Illinois, on April 17, 1954, Howard Laverne Senters. See next PA.5.3.2.3.4.1.

2. **Barbara Jean RATLIFF**: b November 16, 1937, Beardstown, Cass County, Illinois; m in Corinth, Mississippi, on June 18, 1955, Cosby Earl Willis (b May 25, 1937; d September 10, 1997, Decatur, Illinois, and is buried in Pleasant Plains, Illinois). See next PA.5.3.2.3.4.2.

3. **James William RATLIFF**: b April 15, 1939, Beardstown, Cass County, Illinois; m at Ashland, Illinois, on November 25, 1967, Shirley Prather McCaw; d January 16, 1997. No children.

4. **Darrell Eugene RATLIFF**: b October 15, 1944, Beardstown, Cass County, Illinois; m in Ashland, Illinois, on December 5, 1961, Virginia Alan (b April 9, 1947; d April 17, 1997). See next PA.5.3.2.3.4.4.

PA.5.3.2.3.4.1
BETTY JOANN RATLIFF and HOWARD LAVERNE SENTERS
of Bourbon, Missouri

Betty JoAnn Ratliff was born on July 30, 1936, Beardstown, Cass County, Illinois.

Miss Betty JoAnn Ratliff married at Beardstown, Cass County, Illinois, on April 17, 1954, Howard Laverne Senters. See next PA.5.3.2.3.4.1.

1. **Dale Alan SENTERS**: b November 23, 1954, Springfield, Sangamon County, Illinois.

2. **Robi Lari SENTERS**: b April 8, 1956, Springfield, Sangamon County, Illinois.

3. **Joni Jean SENTERS**: b February 17, 1958, Springfield, Sangamon County, Illinois.

4. **Jeffrey Lynn SENTERS**: b March 20, 1960, Springfield, Sangamon County, Illinois.

5. **Brian Keith SENTERS**: b February 23, 1960, Springfield, Sangamon County, Illinois.

6. **Bradley Ray SENTERS**: b August 3, 1963, Springfield, Sangamon County, Illinois.

PA.5.3.2.3.4.2
BARBARA JEAN RATLIFF and COSBY EARL WILLIS
Pleasant Plains, Illinois

Barbara Jean Ratliff was born on November 16, 1937, Beardstown, Cass County, Illinois.

Miss Barbara Jean Ratliff married in Corinth, Mississippi, on June 18, 1955, Cosby Earl Willis (b May 25, 1937, Christine, Kentucky; d September 10, 1997, Decatur, Illinois, and is buried in Pleasant Plains, Illinois), the son of Henry Fayette Willis and Angie Lettie Farris.

1. **Terri Dean WILLIS**: b August 17, 1956, Springfield, Sangamon County, Illinois; d August 20, 1957, buried Pleasant Plains, Illinois..

2. **Kim Earleen WILLIS**: b June 14, 1958, Springfield, Sangamon County, Illinois; m at Houston, Texas, on August 6, 1988, Gary Linn Yokie (b January 7, 1956) . See next PA.5.3.2.3.4.2.2.

3. **Kara Lynne WILLIS**: b July 31, 1961, Springfield, Sangamon County, Illinois; m at Pleasant Plains, Illinois, on June 19, 1982, Robert Stephen Kummerow (b September 4, 1960), the son of Wilbur Kummerow and Margaret Hayes. See next PA.5.3.2.3.4.2.3.

4. **Krista Lea WILLIS**: b May 17, 1963, Peoria, Peoria County, Illinois; m at Pleasant Plains, Illinois, on May 28, 1988, Timothy Charles Holst (b September 21, 1963, Waukegan, Illinois), the son of James Wesley Holst and Marion Caroline Scholler. See next PA.5.3.2.3.4.2.4.

PA.5.3.2.3.4.2.2
KIM EARLEEN WILLIS and GARY LINN YOKIE
of Houston, Texas

Kim Earleen Willis was born on June 14, 1958, at Springfield, Sangamon County, Illinois.

Miss Kim Earleen Willis married at Houston, Texas, on August 6, 1988, Gary Linn Yokie (b January 7, 1956).

1. **William Michael YOKIE** (adopted): b August 30, 1990, Houston, Texas.

PA.5.3.2.3.4.2.3
KARA LYNNE WILLIS and ROBERT STEPHEN KUMMEROW
of Elmhurst, Illinois

Kara Lynne Willis was born on July 31, 1961, at Springfield, Sangamon County, Illinois.

Miss Kara Lynne Willis married at Pleasant Plains, Illinois, on June 19, 1982, Robert Stephen Kummerow (b September 4, 1960), the son of Wilbur Kummerow and Margaret Hayes.

1. **Kayla Jean KUMMEROW**: b February 3, 1991, Elmhurst, Du Page County, Illinois.

PA.5.3.2.3.4.2.4
KRISTA LEA WILLIS and TIMOTHY CHARLES HOLST
of Grayslake, Illinois

Krista Lea Willis was born on May 17, 1963, at Peoria, Peoria County, Illinois.

Miss Krista Lea Willis married at Pleasant Plains, Illinois, on May 28, 1988, Timothy Charles Holst (b September 21, 1963, Waukegan, Illinois), the son of James Wesley Holst and Marion Caroline Scholler.

1. **Codi Caroline HOLST**: b March 6, 1991, Racine, Wisconsin.

PA.5.3.2.3.4.4
DARRELL EUGENE RATLIFF and VIRGINIA ALAN
Irving, Texas

Darrell Eugene Ratliff was born on October 15, 1944.

Darrell Eugene Ratliff married in Ashland, Illinois, on December 5, 1961, Virginia Alan (b April 9, 1947; d April 17, 1997).

1. **Darrell Eugene RATLIFF**, Jr: b October 17, 1966, Peoria, Peoria County, Illinois.
2. **Anthony Joseph RATLIFF**: b February 7, 1969, Peoria, Peoria County, Illinois.
3. **Angela Lynne RATLIFF**: b December 15, 1969, Peoria, Peoria County, Illinois.
4. **Paula Dianne RATLIFF**: b August 2, 1971, Peoria, Peoria County, Illinois.

PA.5.3.2.6
NELLIE WILLETT and ARTHUR HILES

Nellie Willett was born on October 10, 1882, in Prentice, Morgan County, Illinois.

Miss Nellie Willett married Arthur Hiles.

1. **Leo HILES**: b March 8, 1902; d March 26, 1956.

PA.5.3.2.7
LOU PEARL WILLETT and WALTER LONG

Lou Pearl Willett was born on May 28, 1883.

Miss Lou Pearl Willett married on November 18, 1903, Walter Long (b October 24, 1880; d November 2, 1953).

Mrs. Lou Pearl (Willett) Long died on September 5, 1915.

1. **Helen Louise LONG**: b October 29, 1904.
2 **Walter Myron LONG**: b February 16, 1906; d March 28, 1954.
3. **Raymond Eugene LONG**: b August 31, 1908.
4. **William Gerald LONG** (twin): b May 3, 1915.
5. **James Harold LONG** (twin): b May 3, 1915.

PA.5.4
SARAH WILLETT and ALFRED SCHEICK
of Allegheny County, Pennsylvania

Sarah Willett was born in 1815, St. Clair Township, Allegheny County, Pennsylvania.

Miss Sarah Willett married on December 5, 1833, Alfred Sheick.

Mrs. Sarah (Willett) Scheick died on May 2, 1891, Knoxville (now part of Pittsburgh), Pennsylvania.

1. **William SCHEICK**: b 1835; m Martha Linhart (b 1842).
2. **Caroline SCHEICK**:
3. **Sarah Ann SHEICK**:
4. **Uriah SCHEICK**: b 1843.
5. **Orsilla SCHEICK**: b 1850; d 1893.
6. **Jacob SCHEICK**: b 1855; m Ellen Olenhausen (b 1851); d 1924.

PA.5.5
HEZEKIAH WILLETT and ELIZABETH STEWART
of Allegheny County, Pennsylvania

Hezekiah Willett was born in 1816, in Mifflin Township, Allegheny County, Pennsylvania.

Hezekiah Willett married about 1835 Elizabeth Stewart (b 1815, St. Clair Township, Allegheny County, Pennsylvania), the daughter of John Stewart and Sarah who were Irish immigrants.

In 1840, Hezekiah Willett and family are listed in the Mifflin Township, Allegheny County, Pennsylvania, census, page 145, as follows:

1 male	20-30	1810-1820	*Hezekiah*	*age 24*	*b 1816*
1 female	20-30	1810-1820	*Elizabeth*	*age 25*	*b 1815*
1 male	20-30	1810-1820			
1 female	0-5	1835-1840	*Martha J*	*age 4*	*b 1836*
1 male	0-5	1835-1840			

In 1850, Hezekiah Willett and family are listed in the Baldwin Township, Allegheny County, Pennsylvania, census, page 135, as follows:

Willett	Hezekiah	35	m	PA	farmer
	Elizabeth	35	f	PA	
	Martha Jane	13	f	PA	
	Isabella	5	f	PA	
	William	1	m	PA	

His father, William Willett, and family were listed next.

In 1860, Hezekiah Willett and family are listed in the Library P.O., Baldwin Township, Allegheny County, Pennsylvania, census, dwelling 428, as follows:

Willett	Hezekiah	49	m	PA	farmer
	Eliz.	41	f	PA	
	Isabella	16	f	PA	
	William	11	m	PA	
	Urzella F	8	-	PA	
	Bateman K	4	-	PA	
	Garner	1	-	PA	

His brother, Uriah and family were listed beside him (dwelling 429), as follows:

Willett	Uriah	33	m	PA	farmer

Eliz.	28	f	PA
Wm J	8	m	PA
Robt W	6	m	PA
Oliver	4	m	PA
Walter F	1/12	m	PA

In 1870, Hezekiah Willett and family are listed in the Little Beaver Township, Lawrence County, Pennsylvania, census (taken July 11, 1870), as follows:

Willett	Hezekiah	60	m	PA	farmer
	Elizabeth	60	f	PA	wife
	William	21	m	PA	son
	Frances	18	f	PA	daughter
	Eshmore	14	m	PA	son
	Verner	10	m	PA	son
McGibbney,	Anne	14	f	PA	g.dau
	George	10	m	PA	g.son
	Margaret	6	f	PA	d.dau

At some point, before 1880 but mostly likely late in 1879 or early in 1880, Hezekiah Willett, his family, and at least two adult families of children, went out to the Dakota Territory.

In 1880, Hezekiah Willett and family are listed in the Americus, Grand Forks County, Dakota Territory, census, dwelling 90-94, as follows:

Willett	Hezekiah	67	m	PA	farmer
	Elizabeth	67	f	PA	wife
	Vernon	20	m	PA	son
McGibbney,	Margaret	18	f	PA	granddaughter

On January 28, 1881, Hezekial Willett received a certificate for land from the U. S. Government at Grand Forks County, North Dakota, at NE 1/4, Sec. 23, Town 149, Range 50 (Book D, page 81).

William Willett died in Americus, Grand Forks County, North Dakota.

(Ohliger file; 1920 Grand Forks County, North Dakota, census).

1. **Martha Jane WILLETT**: b July 1, 1836, Mifflin Township, Allegheny County, Pennsylvania; m 1st George W. Gibbney (d abt 1863); m 2d abt 1864 Thomas W. Martin (widowed); m 3d September 10, 1876, Matthew MacDonald; d at Pittsburgh, Pennsylvania, on November 30, 1912, buried West Liberty Cemetery. See next PA.5.5.1.

2. **Isabella WILLETT**: b 1844, Baldwin Township, Allegheny County, Pennsylvania.

3. **William WILLETT**: b 1849, Baldwin Township, Allegheny County, Pennsylvania; m 1st (wife's name unknown); m 2d 1880 Mary Elizabeth (b 1850, Pennsylvania; d 1926, Beaver County, Pennsylvania); d 1929, Beaver County, Pennsylvania. See next PA.5.5.3.

4. **Orzilla Frances WILLETT**: b 1852, Allegheny County, Pennsylvania; m abt 1875 Louis Schnick (b 1843, New York). (1880 Americus, Grand Forks County, Dakota Territory, census, dwelling 94-98). See next PA.5.5.4.

5. **Edward Ethmore Hannah Stewart WILLETT**: b August, 1856 (1860), Allegheny County, Pennsylvania; m in Minnesota in 1882 Martha N. Euphemy Dunlap (June 20, 1866, Centre County, Pennsylvania; d March 7, 1947, Milwaukee, Wisconsin) the daughter of George W. Dunlap and Francis Louisa Gordon; d before 1947. See next PA.5.5.5.

6. **Vernon** ("Garner", "Varner") **WILLETT**: b 1859, Allegheny County, Pennsylvania. Varner was the surname of a prominent family in Baldwin. One Varner was a Justice of the Peace and witnessed one of William Willett's deed transfers. See next PA.5.5.1.

PA.5.5.1
MARTHA JANE WILLETT
of Pittsburgh, Pennsylvania.

Martha Jane Willett was born on July 1, 1836, Mifflin Township, Allegheny County, Pennsylvania.

Miss Martha Jane Willett married 1st George W. McGibbney (d abt 1863).

Mrs. Martha Jane (Willett) McGibbney married 2d abt 1864 Thomas W. Martin (widowed).

In 1870, M. J. McGibbney and family are listed in the Washington Boro, Allegheny County, Pennsylvania, census (taken June 21, 1870), as follows:

McGibony	M. J.	34	f	PA	mother
	A. E.	14	f	PA	daughter
	Samuel	13	m	PA	son
	George	10	m	PA	son
	M. A.	7	f	PA	daughter
	Thomas	3	m	PA	son
Martin	Thomas	12	m	PA	boarder
Biven	Wm.	16	m	PA	boarder

Just three weeks earlier Anne, George, and Margaret McGibbney were recorded with their grandfather (Hezekiah Willett) in Lawrence County, Pennsylvania.

Mrs. Martha Jane (Willett, McGibbney) Martin married 3d September 10, 1876, Matthew MacDonald.

Mrs. Martha Jane (Willett, McGibbney) Martin died at Pittsburgh, Allegheny County, Pennsylvania, on November 30, 1912, and is buried West in the West Liberty Cemetery.

Children of Martha Jane Willett and her 1st husband, George McGibbney:

1. **Ann Eliza MCGIBBNEY**: b 1855, Baldwin, Allegheny County, Pennsylvania; m William John Shawhan (d 1909).

2. Samuel MCGIBBNEY: b abt 1857, Baldwin, Allegheny County, Pennsylvania; m in Pittsburgh, Allegheny County, Pennsylvania, on July 29, 1880, Elisabetha Luffy.

3. **George W. MCGIBBNEY**: b February 25, 1860, Baldwin, Allegheny County, Pennsylvania.

4. **Margaret Jane MCGIBBNEY**: b 1862, Baldwin, Allegheny County, Pennsylvania. In 1880, enumerated with her grandparents, in Grand Forks County, Dakota Territory.

Children of Martha Jane Willett and her 2nd husband, Thomas W. Martin:

5. **Thomas MARTIN**: b November 2, 1865, Allegheny County, Pennsylvania; m at Pittsburgh, Allegheny County, Pennsylvania, on July 14, 1887, Elizabeth Katherine Neumeyer (b September 13, 1867, Lower St. Clair, Allegheny County, Pennsylvania; d October 9, 1952, Pittsburgh, Allegheny County, Pennsylvania); d October 23, 1906, New Castle, Lawrence County, Pennsylvania, buried South Side Cemetery, Pittsburgh, Pennsylvania. See next <u>PA.5.5.1.5</u>.

6. **William MARTIN**: 1872, Mount Washington, Allegheny County, Pennsylvania; m Ida C. Gettler; d after 1952.

PA.5.5.1.5
THOMAS MARTIN and **ELIZABETH KATHERINE NEUMEYER**
of Pittsburgh, Allegheny County, Pennsylvania

Thomas Martin was born on November 2, 1865, Allegheny County, Pennsylvania.

Thomas Martin married at Pittsburgh, Allegheny County, Pennsylvania, on July 14, 1887, Elizabeth Katherine Neumeyer (b September 13, 1867, Lower St. Clair, Allegheny County, Pennsylvania; d October 9, 1952, Pittsburgh, Allegheny County, Pennsylvania).

Thomas Martin died on October 23, 1906, at New Castle, Pennsylvania, and is buried in the South Side Cemetery, Pittsburgh, Allegheny County, Pennsylvania.

1. **Verner MARTIN:**
2. **Viola May MARTIN:** b July 21, 1890, Pittsburgh, Allegheny County, Pennsylvania; m at Pittsburgh, Allegheny County, Pennsylvania, on July 14, 1910, George B. Wessa; d March 15, 1960, Fort Lauderdale, Florida, buried Allegheny County, Pennsylvania, Memorial Park. No children.
3. **Ellsworth Thomas MARTIN:** b January 21, 1894, Pittsburgh, Allegheny County, Pennsylvania; d April 23, 1956, Pittsburgh, Pennsylvania, buried McCandless, Allegheny County, Pennsylvania, Memorial Park.
4. **Lillian Belle MARTIN:** b November 27, 1896, Pittsburgh, Allegheny County, Pennsylvania; m at Wellsburg, West Virginia, on July 6, 1920, Herbert Henry Ohliger; d September 14, 1984, Mt. Lebanon, Pennsylvania, buried Allegheny County, Pennsylvania, Memorial Park. See next PA.5.5.1.5.4.
5. **Mary Elizabeth MARTIN** (twin): b March 23, 1900, Pittsburgh, Allegheny County, Pennsylvania; m at Pittsburgh, Pennsylvania, on April 21, 1921, Edward Richard Diegelman; d December 21, 1991, Fort Lauderdale, Florida.
6. **ReuEmah Jane MARTIN** (twin): b March 23, 1900, Pittsburgh, Allegheny County, Pennsylvania; m at Pittsburgh, Pennsylvania, on July 20, 1921, Henry P. Ludwig; d May 19, 1987, Fort Lauderdale, Florida.

PA.5.5.1.5.4
LILLIAN BELLE MARTIN
and HERBERT HENRY OHLIGER
of Allegheny County, Pennsylvania

Lillian Belle Martin was born on November 27, 1896, Pittsburgh, Allegheny County, Pennsylvania.

Miss Lillian Belle Martin married at Wellsburg, West Virginia, on July 6, 1920, Herbert Henry Ohliger; d September 14, 1984, Mt. Lebanon, Pennsylvania, buried Allegheny County, Pennsylvania, Memorial Park.

1. **Herbert Henry OHLIGER**, Jr: b April 23, 1923, Pittsburgh, Allegheny County, Pennsylvania; m at Pittsburgh on February 15, 1958, Mary Margaret Mehaffey; d May 18, 1990, Mt. Lebanon, Allegheny County, Pennsylvania. See next PA.5.5.1.5.4.

PA.5.5.1.5.4
HERBERT HENRY OHILGER
and MARY MARGARET MEHAFFEY
of Allegheny County, Pennsylvania

Herbert Henry Ohliger, Jr., was born on April 23, 1923, Pittsburgh, Allegheny County, Pennsylvania.

Herbert Henry Ohliger married at Pittsburgh on February 15, 1958, Mary Margaret Mehaffey.

Herbert Ohliger died on May 18, 1990, Mt. Lebanon, Allegheny County, Pennsylvania.

1. **Herbert Henry OHLIGER** (III): b on January 25, 1960, Pittsburgh, Allegheny County, Pennsylvania; m in Scott Township, Allegheny County, Pennsylvania, on August 3, 1996, Danielle Lynette Barnett.

2. **David Alan OHLIGER**: b September 6, 1967, Mt. Lebanon, Allegheny County, Pennsylvania; m in Finleyville, Washington County, Pennsylvania on August 5, 1995, Amy Lynn Steedle (b January 30, 1970, Miami, Dade County, Florida), the daughter of James William Steedle and Mary Rita Forsythe.

1. Karl Herbert Peter **OHLIGER**: b May 30, 1997.

PA.5.5.3
WILLIAM WILLETT
of Americus, Grand Forks County, Dakota Territory
and Beaver County, Pennsylvania

William Willett was born in 1849, in Baldwin Township, Allegheny County, Pennsylvania.

William Willett married 1st (wife's name unknown).

William Willett married 2d 1880 Mary Elizabeth (b 1850, Pennsylvania; d 1926, buried in the Reformed Presbyterian Church Cemetery, Beaver County, Pennsylvania).

William Willett and family went out to the Dakota Territory and stayed a while.

In 1880, William Willett and family are listed at Americus Township, Grand Forks County, in the Dakota Territory, dwelling 94-98, as follows:

Willett	William	head	30	PA
	Mary Elizabeth,	wife	30	PA
	Lillie Olive	daughter	5	PA
	Harry Angus	son	9/12	Dakota

At some point, they left the Dakota Territory and returned to Pennsylvania where they settled in Beaver County.

William Willett died in 1929 and he was buried in the Reformed Presbyterian Church Cemetery, Beaver County, Pennsylvania.

Child of William Willett and his 1st wife:

1. **Lillie Olive WILLETT**: b 1875, Pennsylvania.

Stepchild of William Willett and his 2d wife, Mary Elizabeth:

2. **Harry ANGUS WILLETT** (stepson): b September 14, 1879, Dakota; d December 22, 1929, buried in the Reformed Presbyterian Church Cemetery, Beaver County, Pennsylvania.

Child of William Willett and his 2d wife, Mary Elizabeth:

3. **Clarence David WILLETT**; b 1883; d 1920, buried in the Reformed Presbyterian Church Cemetery, Beaver County, Pennsylvania.

PA.5.5.4

ORZILLA FRANCES WILLETT and **LOUIS SCHNICK**

Beaver County, Pennsylvania, and
of Americus, Grand Forks County, Dakota Territory

Orzilla Frances Willett was born in 1852, in Allegheny County, Pennsylvania.

Miss Orzilla F. Willett married about 1875 Louis Schnick (b 1843, New York).

In 1880, Louis Schnick and family are listed in the Americus, Grand Forks County, Dakota Territory, census, dwelling 94-98, as follows:

Schnick	Louis	head	37	NY Bavaria, Bav.
	Orizilla F.	wife	27	PA PA PA
	Elizabeth B., daughter		3	PA NY PA
	Willett L.	son	1	PA NY PA

1. **Elizabeth B. SCHNICK**: b 1877, Pennsylvania,
2. **Willett L. SCHNICK**: b 1879, Pennsylvania.

PA.5.5.5

EDWARD ETHMORE HANNAH STEWART WILLETT
and **MARTHA N. E. DUNLAP**

of Appleton, Outagamie County, Wisconsin

Edward Ethmore (Etmore) Hannah Stewart Willett was born in August, 1856 (1860), Allegheny County, Pennsylvania.

In 1870, <u>Esthmore</u> Willett, age 14, born Pennsylvania, is listed in his father's, Hezekiah Willett, age 60, household in the Little Beaver Township, Lawrence County, Pennsylvania, census (taken July 11, 1870).

About 1879 or 1880, Hezekiah Willett and two of his sons and their families removed to North Dakota. It must be around this time that Edward Ethmore Willett removed to Minnesota.

Edward Ethmore H. S. Willett married in Minnesota in 1882 Martha N. Euphemy Dunlap (b June 20, 1866, Centre County, Pennsylvania; d March 7, 1947, Milwaukee, Wisconsin) the daughter of George W. Dunlap and Francis Louisa Gordon.

By 1885, they were in Waterville, Le Seur County, Minnesota, through the 1920s. By the turn of the century they took up residence in Hill City, Aitkin County, Minnesota, remaining there until the Rabey Rail Line closed sometime before 1935. Then they removed to Appleton, Outagamie

County, Wisconsin.

Edward Willett was a railroad worker on the Rabey Rail Line.

Edward Ethmore Willett died before 1947 (exact date and place unknown; he may be buried in Hill City, Aitkin County, Minnesota).

("Martha N. Euphemy Dunlap", 8 pages, typescript, no date).

1. **Howard H. WILLETT**: b August, 1884, Minnesota; unmarried; d October 24, 1904, Brainerd, Crow County, Minnesota - died as a young man of a gun shot wound.

2. **Walter WILLETT**: b November 15, 1885, Waterville, Le Seur County, Minnesota; m abt 1905 Sena Marie Klippenes (b August 7, 1889, Minneapolis, Minnesota; d December 10, 1979, Crosby, Minnesota), the daughter of Charles Klippenes and Josephine; d January 30, 1959, Brainerd, Crow County, Minnesota. See next PA.5.5.5.2.

3. **Raymond Guy WILLETT**: b January, 1888, Waterville, Le Seur County, Minnesota; m abt 1911 Minnie Rauch (b January 8, 1893, Little Falls, Minnesota; d January 17, 1987, age 94, at the Virginia Medical Center, Minnesota, buried Maple Hill Cemetery, Hibbing, Saint Louis County, Minnesota), the daughter of Anne Hartun; d October 27, 1940, at Kinmount, Minnesota. See next PA.5.5.5.3.

4. **Roy Lee WILLETT**: b April 1, 1889, Minnesota; m abt 1910 Ethel Maude Johnson (b December 17, 1890; d October 28, 1980); d March 8, 1944, Minnesota. See next PA.5.5.5.4.

5. **Verner WILLETT**: b September, 1885, Minnesota.

6. **Blanche Belle WILLETT**: b July 23, 1897, Hill City, Aitkin County, Minnesota; m in Hill City, Aitkin County, Minnesota, on October 23, 1916, Clarence William Wilkinson; d November 4, 1977, Brainerd, Crow County, Minnesota. See next PA.5.5.5.6.

7. **Joseph WILLETT**: b 1897, Minnesota; unmarried; disappeared.

8. **Peasley WILLETT**: b December, 1899, Minnesota; died as an infant.

9. **Ruth WILLETT**: b 1902, Minnesota.

10. **Lillian WILLETT**: b 1910, Minnesota; m Clarence Kurtz; resided once in Milwaukee, Minnesota; d abt 1985. No children.

PA.5.5.5.2
WALTER WILLETT and SENA MARIE KLIPPENES
of Brainerd, Crow County, Minnesota

Walter Willett was born on November 15, 1885, Waterville, Le Seur County, Minnesota.

Walter Willett married about 1905 Sena Marie Klippenes (b August 7, 1889, Minneapolis, Minnesota; d December 10, 1979, Crosby, Minnesota), the daughter of Charles Klippenes and Josephine.

Walter Willett died on January 30, 1959, Brainerd, Crow County, Minnesota.

("Martha N. Euphemy Dunlap", 8 pages, typescript, no date).

1. **Walter Edward WILLETT**: b July 29, 1909, Minnesota; m in Brainerd, Crow County, Minnesota, on February 16, 1948, Jeanette Mary Radtke (b June 22, 1921, Sanborn, Minnesota); d May 20, 1968, St. Paul, Minnesota. See next PA.5.5.5.2.1.

2. **Margaret WILLETT**: b May 18, 1914, Minnesota; m Thomas Mulholland (b 1900, Nokay Lake, Minnesota; d 1976, Crosby, Minnesota); d May 2, 1944. No children.

3. **Lloyd E. WILLETT**: b December 14, 1917, Minnesota; m Louise Goble; d July 23, 1966, Duluth, Saint Louis County, Minnesota. No children.

4. **Ronald WILLETT**: b 1920, Minnesota; m Mary; d 1991, St. Paul, Minnesota. No children.

5. **Deloris Eleanor WILLETT**: b April 5, 1928, St. Paul, Minnesota; m on June 28, 1947, Loren Louis Radtke (b June 10, 1926, Riverton, Minnesota); d December 19, 1988, Hoyt Lakes, Minnesota.

6. **Laurence Eugene WILLETT**: b March 12, 1924, St. Paul, Minnesota; m in Brainerd, Minnesota, on August 28, 1950, Janine Jacquiline Morison; d July 25, 1986, Brainerd, Minnesota. See next PA.5.5.5.2.6.

PA.5.5.5.2.1
WALTER EDWARD WILLETT
and JEANETTE MARY RADTKE
of Brainerd, Crow County, Minnesota

Walter Edward Willett was born on July 29, 1909, Minnesota.

Walter Edward Willett married in Brainerd, Crow County, Minnesota, on February 16, 1948, Jeanette Mary Radtke (b June 22, 1921, Sanborn, Minnesota).

Walter Edward Willett died on May 20, 1968, St. Paul, Minnesota.

("Martha N. Euphemy Dunlap", 8 pages, typescript, no date).

1. **James Allen WILLETT**: b April 30, 1948, Brainerd, Crow County, Minnesota; m 1st May 10, 1968, Karen Tacheny (divorced February, 1975); m 2d April 30, 1975, Lynn J. Darson (b May 13, 1949). See next PA.5.5.5.2.1.1.

2. **Kathleen Rene WILLETT**: b September 8, 1952, Brainerd, Crow County, Minnesota; m on April 20, 1977, George Arthur Franis (b November 30, 1947, St. Paul, Minnesota). See next PA.5.5.5.2.2.1.2.

3. **Debbie Jean WILLETT**: b January 12, 1961, St. Paul, Minnesota; m at Forest Lake, Minnesota, on September 25, 1982, Richard John Lindorifer (b May 1, 1958, St. Paul, Minnesota).

PA.5.5.5.2.1.1
JAMES ALLEN WILLETT
of St. Paul, Minnesota

James Allen Willett was born on April 30, 1948, Brainerd, Crow County, Minnesota.

James Allen Willett married 1st May 10, 1968, Karen Tacheny (divorced February, 1975).

James Allen Willett married 2d April 30, 1975, Lynn J. Darson (b May 13, 1949).

("Martha N. Euphemy Dunlap", 8 pages, typescript, no date).

1. **Jeffrey D. WILLETT**: b September 24, 1967, St. Paul, Minnesota.

2. **Lisa Jeanette WILLETT**: b January 4, 1968, St. Paul, Minnesota.

    1. **Courtney Jean WILLETT**: b April 22, 1989, Chisago, Minnesota.

3. **Jamie E. WILLETT**: b December 21, 1969, St. Paul, Minnesota.

4. **Joseph E. WILLETT**: b March 10, 1971, St. Paul, Minnesota.

5. **Jeremy E. WILLETT**: b July 26, 1975, St. Paul, Minnesota.

6. **Lori D. WILLETT**: b March 29, 1976, St. Paul, Minnesota.

PA.5.5.5.2.2.1.2
KATHLEEN RENE WILLETT and GEORGE ARTHUR FRANIS
of St. Paul, Minnesota

Kathleen Rene Willett was born on September 8, 1952, Brainerd, Crow County, Minnesota.

Kathleen Rene Willett married on April 20, 1977, George Arthur Franis (b November 30, 1947, St. Paul, Minnesota).

1. **Lanette Theresa FRANIS**: b June 24, 1974, St. Paul, Minnesota.

2. **Rene Kathleen FRANIS**: b April 18, 1978, St. Paul, Minnesota.

PA.5.5.5.2.6
LAURENCE EUGENE WILLETT
and JANINE JACQUILINE MORISON
of Brainerd, Crow County, Minnesota

Laurence Eugene Willett was born on March 12, 1924, St. Paul, Minnesota.

Laurence Eugene Willett married in Brainerd, Minnesota, on August 28, 1950, Janine Jacquiline Morison; d July 25, 1986, Brainerd, Minnesota.

("Martha N. Euphemy Dunlap", 8 pages, typescript, no date).

    1. **Russell LeRoy WILLETT**: b July 19, 1951, Brainerd, Crow County, Minnesota.

    2. **Bruce Eugene WILLETT**: b August 4, 1952, Brainerd, Crow County, Minnesota; m in Aurora, Minnesota, on February 10, 1979, Kayla Renee Wilcox (b August 19, 1960, Virginia, Minnesota). See next PA.5.5.5.2.6.2.

    3. **Mark Lyle WILLETT**: b January 5, 1956, Brainerd, Crow County, Minnesota; m July 31, 1976, Barbara Lucille Bogart (b December 12, 1957, Virginia, Minnesota).

        1. **Mark Eric WILLETT**: b July 1, 1977, Duluth, Saint Louis County, Minnesota.

        2. **Mindy Lynn WILLETT**: b December 1, 1978, Aurora, Minnesota.

PA.5.5.5.2.6.2
BRUCE EUGENE WILLETT and KAYLA RENE WILCOX
of Virginia, Minnesota

Bruce Eugene Willett was born on August 4, 1952, Brainerd, Crow County, Minnesota.

Bruce Eugene Willett married in Aurora, Minnesota, on February 10, 1979, Kayla Renee Wilcox (b August 19, 1960, Virginia, Minnesota).

    1. **John Laurance WILLETT**: b April 18, 1980, Virginia, Minnesota.

    2. **Michael Gene WILLETT**: b November 6, 1981, Virginia, Minnesota.

PA.5.5.5.3
RAYMOND GUY WILLETT and MINNIE RAUCH

Raymond Guy Willett was born in January, 1888, Waterville, Le Seur County, Minnesota.

Raymond Guy Willett married about 1911 Minnie Rauch (b January 8, 1893, Little Falls, Minnesota; d January 17, 1987, age 94, at the Virginia Medical Center, Minnesota, buried Maple Hill Cemetery, Hibbing, Saint Louis County, Minnesota), the daughter of Mr. Rauch and Anne Hartun.

In 1925 or 1926, they resided at Kelly Lake, Saint Louis County, Minnesota. While they were visiting Minnie's parents in St. Paul, their house burned down and they lost everything. They had a small guest house which they lived in for a while, but because of the tragedies associated with Kelly Lake, in 1927 "Bill" quit his 21 year job as a brakeman and moved to Ray, Minnesota.

They resided variously at Hill City, St. Paul, Brainerd, Ray, Kinmount, and the Kabetogama Lake area, Minnesota. He was a brakeman for the Great Northern Railroad Company and moved around quite a bit as the railroad sent him to work at various locations.

Raymond Guy Willett died on October 27, 1940, age 53, of a heart attack, at Kinmount, Minnesota, and is buried in the Maple Hill Cemetery, Hibbing, Saint Louis County, Minnesota.

("Martha N. Euphemy Dunlap", 8 pages, typescript, no date).

1. **Raymond J. WILLETT**: b 1913, St. Paul, Minnesota; d July, 1925, Kelly Lake, Saint Louis County, Minnesota. He drowned and was buried in a family plot at Maple Hill Cemetery, Hibbing, Saint Louis County, Minnesota.

2. **John WILLETT**: b January 9, 1915, Hill City, Aitkin County, Minnesota; m Vivian; d October, 1978, at St. Marys Hospital, Duluth, Saint Louis County, Minnesota, buried at Oneath Cemetery, Duluth, Saint Louis County, Minnesota. See next PA.5.5.5.3.2.

3. **Lillian M. WILLETT**: b December 14, 1917, St. Paul, Minnesota; m at International Falls, Koochiching County, Minnesota, on September 10, 1938, William Tuohinen; resides (1997) Orr, Minnesota. No children.

4. **Lucille WILLETT**: b October 26, 1919, St. Paul, Minnesota; m 1st Emil Roethler; m 2d Edgar Molmon; d January 2, 1985, at St. Marys Hospital, Duluth, Saint Louis County, Minnesota, and is buried in the Maple Hill Cemetery, Hibbing, Saint Louis County, Minnesota. See next PA.5.5.5.3.4.

5. **Betty WILLETT**: b February 24, 1924, Stuntz Township, St. Louis, Missouri; m Eugene Filori. See next PA.5.5.5.3.5.

6. **Marcella WILLETT**: b September 19, 1923; m Lawrence Vidor; d December 26, 1991, at St. Marys Hospital, Duluth, Saint Louis County, Minnesota, and is buried in the Maple Hill Cemetery, Hibbing, Saint Louis County, Minnesota. No children.

7. **Royden Joseph WILLETT**: b October 1, 1925, Kelly Lake, Saint Louis County, Minnesota; m 1st in International Falls, Minnesota, to _____ (divorced); m 2d Eileen; d January 16, 1988, Duluth, Saint Louis County, Minnesota, of a heart attack and is buried at the Oneota Cemetery, Duluth, Saint Louis County, Minnesota. See next PA.5.5.5.3.7.

8. **Eileen WILLETT**: b July 26, 1927, Kelly Lake, Saint Louis County, Minnesota; m Edward Benoit; reside (1996) Duluth, Saint Louis County, Minnesota.

9. **Delores Mary WILLETT**: b January 12, 1929, International Falls, Minnesota; m 1952 Joseph S. Kosluchar (divorced 1965); resides Angora (1996), Saint Louis County, Minnesota.

10. **Kenneth WILLETT**: b August 15, 1932, International Falls, Minnesota; m Darlene; resides (1996) Hibbing, Saint Louis County, Minnesota.

11. **Flora Mae WILLETT**: b May 11, 1936, Ray, Minnesota; m Stanley Martinson (d February 2, 1977, Cook, Saint Louis County, Minnesota); resided (1996) Angora, Saint Louis County, Minnesota; d March 5, 1997, Angora, St. Louis County, Minnesota, and is buried at the Sand Lake Chapel Cemetery, Britt, Minnesota.

12. **Lucille WILLETT**: d 1985, Duluth, Saint Louis County, Minnesota.

PA.5.5.5.3.2
JOHN WILLETT and VIVIAN

John Willett was born on January 9, 1915, Hill City, Aitkin County, Minnesota.

John Willett married Vivian.

John Willett died on October, 1978, at St. Marys Hospital, Duluth, Saint Louis County, Minnesota, and is buried at Oneath Cemetery, Duluth, Saint Louis County, Minnesota.

1. **John WILLETT**, Jr: d abt 1979? in Superior, Wisconsin

PA.5.5.5.3.4
LUCILLE WILLETT
of Saint Louis County, Minnesota

Lucille Willett was born on October 26, 1919, St. Paul, Minnesota.

Miss Lucille Willett married 1st Emil Roethler.

Mrs. Lucille (Willett) Roethler married 2d Edgar Mohlmon.

Mrs. Lucille (Willett, Roethler) Mohlmon died on January 2, 1985, at St. Marys Hospital, Duluth, Saint Louis County, Minnesota, and is buried in the Maple Hill Cemetery, Hibbing, Saint Louis County, Minnesota.

    1. **Emil ROETHLER**, Jr: m Debbie; resided (1996) New Holstein, Wisconsin.

    2. **Duane ROETHLER**: d March, 1997.

    3. **Lloyd MOHLMON**: m Renee.

PA.5.5.5.3.5
BETTY WILLETT and EUGENE FILORI
of Startup, Washington

Betty Willett was born on February 24, 1924., in Stuntz Township, St. Louis County, Minnesota.

Miss Betty Willett married at Hibbing, Minnesota, to Eugene Filori (d August 3, 1984).

Mrs. Betty (Willett) Flori died on November 8, 1996, of a heart attack, and is buried in the Marysville Cemetery, Snohomish County, Washington.

    1. **Darlene Marie FILORI**: b June 10, 1946, Oakland, California; m in Snohomish County, Washington, on June 2, 1967, John T. Falls (b November 9, 1944, Spokane, Washington); resides (1997) Marysville, Washington.

    2. **Marilyn FILORI**:

    3. **John FILORI**:

    4. **Robert FILORI**:

PA.5.5.5.3.7
ROYDEN JOSEPH WILLETT and EILEEN
of Saint Louis County, Minnesota

Royden Joseph Willett was born on October 1, 1925, at Kelly Lake, Saint Louis County, Minnesota. Royden J. Willett married 1 st _____ (divorced).

Royden Joseph Willett married 2d Eileen.

Royden Joseph Willett died on January 16, 1988, Duluth, Saint Louis County, Minnesota, of a heart attack and is buried at the Oneota Cemetery, Duluth, Saint Louis County, Minnesota.

1. **Royden Joseph WILLETT**, Jr: resides in Minneapolis, Minnesota.
2. **Joseph Michael WILLETT**:

PA.5.5.5.4
ROY LEE WILLETT and **ETHEL MAUDE JOHNSON**
of Minnesota

Roy Lee Willett was born on April 1, 1889, Minnesota.

Roy Lee Willett married about 1910 Ethel Maude Johnson (b December 17, 1890; d October 28, 1980).

Roy Lee Willett died on March 8, 1944, Minnesota.

("Martha N. Euphemy Dunlap", 8 pages, typescript, no date).

1. **Lila Leona WILLETT**: b December 30, 1912, Minnesota; m Charles Newville; d before 1982.
2. **Geraldine Mardell WILLETT**: b September 20, 1914, Minnesota; m Edward T. Klarkowski; d before 1992.
3. **Lorraine Eleanore WILLETT**: b December 2, 1916, Minnesota; m on December 2, 1960, Ambrose J. Drobinski. No children.
4. **Myron WILLETT**: b December 18, 1918; d December 31, 1918.
5. **Melvin LeRoy WILLETT**: b September 17, 1920, Minnesota; m Elfrida Delores Belisle; d April 8, 1977, St. Paul, Minnesota. See next PA.5.5.5.4.5.
6. **Richard Warren WILLETT**: b June 4, 1929; m Jeanne. See next PA.5.5.5.4.6.
7. **Glenn Ethmore Stuart WILLETT**: b November 29, 1938; m Sally; d abt 1989, Texas. See next PA.5.5.5.4.7.

PA.5.5.5.4.5.
MELVIN LEROY WILLETT and **ELFRIDA DELORES BELISLE**
of St. Paul, Minnesota

Melvin LeRoy Willett was born on September 17, 1920, Minnesota.
Melvin LeRoy Willett married Elfrida Delores Belisle.
Melvin LeRoy Willett died on April 8, 1977, St. Paul, Minnesota.

1. **Roy Lee WILLETT**: b June 23, 1947, St. Paul, Minnesota; m in Hawaii, on June 16, 1969, Julie Ann McNulty (b August 1, 1948, Winona, Minnesota). See next PA.5.5.5.4.5.1.

2. **Michael Melvin WILLETT**: b January 17, 1949, St. Paul, Minnesota; m in North St. Paul, Minnesota, on April 30, 1971, Jeanette Stroeing (b January 6, 1950). See next PA.5.5.5.4.5.2.

3. **Roxanne WILLETT**: b January 12, 1953, St. Paul, Minnesota; m in North St. Paul, Minnesota, on March 10, 1973, Steven Melvin Eisenschenk (b August 9, 1953, Minnesota).

4. **Renee WILLETT**: b August 11, 1958, St. Paul, Minnesota; m in St. Paul, Minnesota, on July 2, 1983, Thomas Otto Vujovich (b March 4, 1957).

5. **Marla WILLETT**: b January 2, 1959, St. Paul, Minnesota; m in Brainerd, Crow County, Minnesota, on September 10, 1983, Bret Gary Cummings (b May 23, 1958).

6. **Maureen WILLETT**: b August 2, 1961, St. Paul, Minnesota; m in Brainerd, Crow County, Minnesota, on September 10, 1983, Curtis James Pickars (b August 30, 1958, Brainerd, Minnesota).

7. **Paula WILLETT**: b July 23, 1963, St. Paul, Minnesota; m in Lake Tahoe, California (or Nevada), on January 27, 1990, Robert Charles Johnson (b December 2, 1958, St. Paul, Minnesota).

PA.5.5.5.4.5.1
ROY LEE WILLETT and JULIE ANN MCNULTY
of St. Paul, Minnesota

Roy Lee Willett was born on June 23, 1947, St. Paul, Minnesota.

Roy Lee Willett married in Hawaii, on June 16, 1969, Julie Ann McNulty (b August 1, 1948, Winona, Minnesota).

1. **Jennifer Lynn WILLETT**: b May 9, 1972, St. Paul, Minnesota.

2. **Trisha Lee WILLETT**: b June 6, 1975, St. Paul, Minnesota.

3. **Kristine Ann WILLETT**: b December 5, 1981, St. Paul, Minnesota.

PA.5.5.5.4.5.2
MICHAEL MELVIN WILLETT and JEANETTE STROEING
of St. Paul, Minnesota

Michael Melvin Willett was born on January 17, 1949, St. Paul, Minnesota.

Michael Melvin Willett married in North St. Paul, Minnesota, on April 30, 1971, Jeanette Stroeing (b January 6, 1950).

1. **Eric Michael WILLETT**: b May 28, 1975, St. Paul, Minnesota.

PA.5.5.5.4.6
RICHARD WARREN WILLETT and JEANNE

Richard Warren Willett was born on June 4, 1929.
Richard Warren Willett married Jeanne.

    1. **Richard Warren WILLETT**, Jr: b August 29, 1952; d October 26, 1976.
    2. **Daniel WILLETT**:
    3. **David WILLETT**:
    4. **Diane WILLETT**:

PA.5.5.5.4.7
GLENN ETHMORE STUART WILLETT and SALLY

Glenn Ethmore Stuart Willett was born on November 29, 1938.
Glenn Ethmore Stuart Willett married Sally.
Glenn E. S. Willett died about 1989, Texas.

    1. **Pamela WILLETT:**

PA.5.5.5.6
BLANCHE BELLE WILLETT
and CLARENCE WILLIAM WILKINSON

Blanche Belle Willett was born on July 23, 1897, Hill City, Aitkin County, Minnesota.

Miss Blanche Belle Willett married in Hill City, Aitkin County, Minnesota, on October 23, 1916, Clarence William Wilkinson.

Mrs. Blanche Belle (Willett) Wilkinson died on November 4, 1977, Brainerd, Crow County, Minnesota.

1. **Doris WILKINSON**: b 1917; m Defazio; d February 10, 1962.

    1. Kathy Defazio.

2. **Eileen WILKINSON**: b July 8, 1919, Duluth, Saint Louis County, Minnesota; m Dalton D. Bradfield (d December, 1995); resides (1996) Niles, Michigan 49120.

    1. Craig Douglas **BRADFIELD**:
    2. Gary Alan **BRADFIELD**:
    3. Janis **BRADFIELD**:

3. **Geraldine WILKINSON**: b 1925; m Blakeney; resides (1996) Sequim, Washington.

    1. Diane **BLAKENEY**:
    2. Claudia **BLAKENEY**:
    3. Michael **BLAKENEY**:
    4. Brian **BLAKENEY**:

4. **Judith WILKINSON**: b 1942.

    1. Lisa **WEYGANT**: b February, 1962.
    2. Christopher **WEYGANT**: b January, 1963.
    3. Peter **WEYGANT**: b December, 1963.
    4. William **WEYGANT** (twin):
    5. Jonathon **WEYGANT** (twin)

PA.5.8
URIAH WILLETT and ELIZABETH CRAFT
of Allegheny County, Pennsylvania

Uriah Willett was born in 1827, St. Clair Township, Allegheny County, Pennsylvania.

Uriah Willett married about 1851 Elizabeth Craft (b 1828, Pennsylvania; d February 8, 1923, Pittsburgh, Allegheny County, Pennsylvania).

In 1860, Uriah Willett and family are listed in the Library P. O., Baldwin Township, Allegheny County, Pennsylvania, census, dwelling 429, as follows:

Willett	Uriah	33	m	PA	farmer
	Eliz	28	f	PA	
	Wm J	8	m	PA	
	Robt W	6	m	PA	
	Oliver	4	m	PA	
	Walter F	1/12	m	PA	

His brother, Hezekiah Willett and family were listed beside him in the 1860 census.

In 1870, Uriah Willett and family are listed in the Birmingham, Allegheny County, Pennsylvania, census, page 386, dwelling 86-106, as follows:

Willett	Uriah	44	m	PA	nut maker
	Elizabeth	42	f	PA	house keeper
	Wm J	18	m	PA	at home
	Wilbert W.	15	m	PA	at home
	Oliver	14	m	PA	at home
	Miller F	9	m	PA	at home
	Mary A.	7	f	PA	at home

Uriah Willett died on February 4, 1874, at Pittsburgh, Allegheny County, Pennsylvania. He committed suicide by hanging.

1. **William John WILLETT**: b 1852, Baldwin, Allegheny County, Pennsylvania; d February 1, 1872, Pittsburgh, Allegheny County, Pennsylvania.

2. **Wilbert Uriah WILLETT**: b June 15, 1853, Baldwin, Allegheny County, Pennsylvania; m before 1875, Fannie A. (b March, 1853, Pennsylvania). See next PA.5.8.2.

3. **Oliver James WILLETT**: b 1856, Baldwin, Allegheny County, Pennsylvania; m in Pittsburgh on November 29, 1877 to Jennie Getting (b 1859, Pennsylvania); d November 13,

1899, Pittsburgh. (1880 1415 Bingham, Pittsburgh, Allegheny County, Pennsylvania, census).

    1. **Mary WILLETT**: b 1878, Pennsylvania.

    4. **Miller Franklin WILLETT**: b 1860, Baldwin, Allegheny County, Pennsylvania; m in Pittsburgh, on April 15, 1885, Tillie Lenore Crothers; d June 21, 1896, Pittsburgh.
    5. **Mary Ann WILLETT**: b 1863, Baldwin, Allegheny County; d December 2, 1878, Pittsburgh, Allegheny County, Pennsylvania.

PA.5.8.2
WILBERT URIAH WILLETT and FANNIE A,
of Allegheny County, Pennsylvania

    Wilbert Uriah Willett was born on June 15, 1853, Baldwin, Allegheny County, Pennsylvania.
    Wilbert Uriah Willett married before 1875, Fannie A. (b March, 1853, Pennsylvania).

    1. **Hamilton Uriah WILLETT**: b January, 1876, Pittsburgh, Allegheny County, Pennsylvania; in Allegheny County, Pennsylvania, in 1900, Stella Aikman (d before 1953).
    2. **Harriett H. WILLETT**: b July, 1879, Pittsburgh, Allegheny County, Pennsylvania; m in Allegheny County, Pennsylvania, James McKibben.
    3. **Wilbert W. WILLETT**: b March, 1880; m in Allegheny County, Pennsylvania, in 1900, Grace Black.
    4. **Alicia A. WILLETT**: b August, 1882, Pittsburgh, Allegheny County, Pennsylvania; in   Allegheny County in 1909, Edward J. Kaufmann.
    5. **Frank M. WILLETT**: b July, 1885, Pittsburgh, Allegheny County, Pennsylvania; m in Pittsburgh, Allegheny County, Pennsylvania, in 1903, Margaret Speicher; d March 5, 1953, Pennsylvania.

    1. **Wilbert Uriah WILLETT**: b December 23, 1904, Pittsburgh, Allegheny County, Pennsylvania; d April, 1966, Fort Lauderdale, Florida.
    2. **James N. WILLETT**: b abt 1910, Allegheny County, Pennsylvania

CHAPTER SIX
WILLIAM WILLETT (C1768-C1845)

PA.6
WILLIAM WILLETT
of Rush Township, Northumberland County, Pennsylvania

William Willet was born about 1768?

William Willet married about 1790? (wife's name un-known).

William <u>Willet</u>, taylor, and family are listed in the 1820 Rush Township, Northumberland County, Pennsylvania, census, page 49, as follows:

0-2-0-0-1 0-2-0-1

male	45-up	bef.-1775	*William*	*52?*	*b 1768?*
Female	26-45	1775-1794		*43?*	*b 1777?*
male	10-16	1804-1810		*15?*	*b 1805?*
male	10-16	1804-1810	*Thomas*	*13*	*b 1807*
female	10-16	1804-1810		*12?*	*b 1808?*
female	10-16	1804-1810		*10?*	*b 1810?*

In 1830, William <u>Willett</u> and family are listed in the Rush Township, Northumberland County, Pennsylvania, census, page 247, as follows:

0-0-0-0-2-0-0-0-1 0-1-1-1-0-0-0-1

male	60-70	1760-1770	*William*	*62?*	*b 1768?*
Female	50-60	1770-1780		*53?*	*b 1777?*
male	20-30	1800-1810		*25?*	*b 1805?*
male	20-30	1800-1810	*Thomas*	*23*	*b 1807*
female	15-20	1810-1815		*20?*	*b 1810?*
female	10-15	1815-1820	*Sarah?*	*13?*	*b 1817?*
female	5-10	1820-1825		*9?*	*b 1821?*

In 1840, William <u>Willett</u> and family are listed in the Rush Township, Northumberland County, Pennsylvania, census, page 207, as follows:

male	60-70	1760-1770	*William*	*72?b 1768?*
female	50-60	1780-1790		*63?b 1777?*
female	15-20	1820-1825		

William Willett died about 1845. At least, neither he nor a female who could have been his wife are listed in the 1850 Pennsylvania census.

1. (son) **WILLETT**: b abt 1805? (between 1800-1810).
2. **Thomas WILLETT**: b 1807; died Thomas Willit, the son of William Willett, about age 27, on June 26, 1834, Rush Township, Northumberland County, Pennsylvania ("Danville Intelligencer" present day Montour County).
3. (daughter) **WILLETT**: b abt 1810? (between 1810-1815).
4. **Sarah WILLETT**: b abt 1817; m Miss Sarah Willet of Derry Township on January 7, 1834, to William Berry ("Danville Intelligencer" present day Montour County).

CHAPTER SEVEN
THOMAS WILLETT (1767-1828)

PA.7
THOMAS WILLET
of Northumberland County, Pennsylvania

Thomas Willet was born on January 25, 1767 (Willett-Truex Family Bible record; Thura Truax Hires Manuscripts). It is thought that Thomas Willett may have come from New Jersey, but not necessarily have been born there.

Thomas Willett may have married 1st (speculation) about 1793 Anna (b November 4, 1775).

In 1810, Thomas Willits, carp(enter), and family were listed in the Shamokin Township, Northumberland County, Pennsylvania, census, page 272. From the following reconstructed census, it is almost certain that this is the family of our Thomas Willet:

```
2-1-0-0-1 3-0-0-1-0
```

1 male	45-up	bef.-1765	*Thomas*	*age 43 b 1767**	
1 female	26-45	1775-1794	*Anna*		
1 male	10-16	1794-1800	*Henry*	*age 15*	*b 1795*
1 female	0-10	1800-1810	*Anne*	*age 11*	*b 1799*
1 male	0-10	1800-1810	*David*	*age 9*	*b 1801*
1 female	0-10	1800-1810	*Martha*	*age 7*	*b 1803*
1 female	0-10	1800-1810	*Catherine*	*age 4*	*b 1806*
1 male	0-10	1800-1810	*Nicholas*	*age 2*	*b 1808*

Thomas Willet, age 48, married 2d on December 7, 1815, Mary Slaugh(t), age 37, (b December 3, 1778; d January, 1860) (Clara Ivey Truex questionnaire). This 2nd marriage is speculated from a reading of the census records; there is also the possibility that this recorded marriage could be Thomas Willett's third marriage.

It appears (as speculation) that most the of Thomas Willett's children by his first wife were left in Northumberland County, Pennsylvania, most likely with their maternal relatives when Thomas Willett decided to immigrate westward to Franklin County, Indiana. The only male child to move westward about the same time was Henry C. Willett and family who removed to Butler County, Ohio.

In 1820, Thomas Willitt, and family were listed in the Bath Township, Franklin County, Indiana, census, page 196. From the following reconstructed census, it is almost certain that this is the family of our Thomas Willet:

```
1-0-0-0-0-1 0-0-0-1-0 0-0-0-1
1 male      45-up   bef.-1775   Thomas    age 53  b 1767
1 female    26-45   1775-1794   Mary      age 42  b 1778
1 male       0-10   1810-1820   Isaac     age 3   b 1817
```

Thomas Willet died in October, 1828 (Willett-Truex Family Bible record).

It is presumed that with the death of her husband in 1828, Mrs. Mary Willett, widow, left the unsettled-untamed frontier of Indiana, and returned to Ohio, to be near her son Isaac Willett.

In 1830, Mary Willets, and family were listed in the Congress, Richland County, Ohio, census, page 76. From the follow-ing reconstructed census, it is almost certain that this is the family of the widow, Mary Willet:

```
0-0-1-0-0-0 0-0-1-0-0-0-0-1
1 female    50-60   1770-1780   Mary       age 52  b 1778
1 male      10-15   1815-1820   Isaac      age 13  b 1817
1 male      10-15   1815-1820   Mary Ann   age 11  b 1819
```

In 1840, Mary Willet and family were listed in the Congress, Richland County, Ohio, census, page 215, as follows:

```
0-0-0-0-0-0-0 0-0-0-0-1-0-0-1-0
1 female    50-60   1790-1800   Mary       age 62* b 1778*
1 female    20-30   1810-1820   Mary Ann   age 21  b 1819
```

This might be the mother, Mary Willett, widow, and possibly her daughter, Mary Ann Willett. Her son, Isaac Willett and family are listed on the same page.

(Thura Truax Hires Manuscripts, Volume 1, edited by Everett and Sandra Truax, Hamilton, Ontario, Canada, 1983).

Children of Thomas Willet and his 1st wife, Anna:

1. **Samuel WILLET**: b January 23, 1794 (Willett-Truex Family Bible record) (Pennsylvania); m abt 1818 (wife's name unknown); remained in Northumberland County, Pennsylvania until at least 1840. See next PA.7.1.

2. **Henry C. WILLET**: b October 6, 1795 (Willett-Truex Family Bible record), New Jersey (born New Jersey from 1850

and 1860 Butler County, Ohio, census records); m 1st March 25, 1819, Hannah Robertson (Family Bible record); m 2d Butler County, Ohio, on October 2, 1845, Jane O'Hara; d after 1860 most likely in Butler County, Ohio. See next PA.7.2.

3. **Eliza WILLET**: b September 4, 1798 (Willett-Truex Family Bible record) (Pennsylvania).

4. **Ann WILLET**: b July 1, 1799 (Willett-Truex Family Bible record), Pennsylvania.

5. **David WILLET**: b September 19, 1801 (Willett-Truex Family Bible record) (Pennsylvania).

6. **Martha WILLET**: b September 7, 1803 (Willett-Truex Family Bible record) (Pennsylvania); m in Franklin County, Indiana, on August 31, 1823, Moses Thirston (Thurston) (Family Bible record; IGI).

7. **Catharine WILLET**: b January 30, 1806 (Willett-Truex Family Bible record), Pennsylvania.

8. **Nicholas WILLET**: b December 24, 1808 (Willett-Truex Family Bible record), Pennsylvania (born Pennsylvania according to 1850 and 1860 Northumberland County, Pennsylvania, censuses); m in Northumberland County, Pennsylvania, on October 29, 1829, Rachel Arter (b July 13, 1799, Pennsylvania; d July 2, 1866, buried Shamokin Valley Baptist Church Cemetery, Northumberland County) of Shamokin Township. See next PA.7.8.

Children of Thomas Willet and his 2d wife Mary Slaught:

9. **Isaac WILLET**: b May 10, 1817 (Willett-Truex Family Bible record), (a native of or born Ohio); m in Knox County, Ohio, November 26, 1839, Susannah Pershing (Persing) (b February 10, 1813), the daughter of John Pershing and Ann Larkins. See next PA.7.9.

10. **Mary Ann WILLET**: b August 30, 1819 (Willett-Truex Family Bible record), Hamilton County, Indiana (Hires Manuscript) or Cincinnati, Hamilton County, Ohio (Orilla Truex Wisler questionnaire); married in Richland County, Ohio, on October 29, 1842, Benjamin Truex, son of William Truex (Richland County, Ohio, record). See next PA.7.10.

11. **Jonathan WILLET**: b December 8, 1821 (Willett-Truex Family Bible record), (Indiana).

PA.7.1
SAMUEL WILLETT
of Rush Township, Northumberland County, Pennsylvania

Samuel Willet was born January 23, 1794 (place unknown, but possibly New Jersey or Pennsylvania).

Samuel Willet married about 1818 (wife's name unknown, but possibly Mary, born 1786).

In 1830, Samuel Willet and family are listed in the Rush Township, Northumberland County, Pennsylvania, census, page 165. If he is the same Samuel Willet (b in 1794) then the following is possible:

male	40-50	1780-1790	*Samuel*	*age 34*	*b 1784*
female	20-30	1800-1810			
male	5-10	1820-1825	*(John)*	*age 8*	*b 1822*
female	0-5	1825-1830	*(Ann)*	*age 4*	*b 1826*
female	0-5	1825-1830			

In 1840, Samuel Willet and family are listed in the Rush Township, Northumberland County, Pennsylvania, census, page 199, as follows:

male	40-50	1790-1800	*Samuel*	*age 44*	*b 1794*
female	30-40	1800-1810			
male	15-20	1820-1825	*(John)*	*age 18*	*b 1822*
female	10-15	1825-1830	*(Ann)*	*age 14*	*b 1826*
female	5-10	1830-1835			
female	0-5	1835-1840			

1. **(John WILLETT)**: The following is very speculative, based solely on the fact that both families are associated with Rush Township. Possibly the John Willett listed next who was born February 13, 1822, Pennsylvania; m abt 1846 Mary E. Dimmick (b June 6, 1826, Pennsylvania; d April 8, 1896, in Gearhart Township, Northumberland County, Pennsylvania, buried St. Luke's Plum Creek, Rockafellar Township, Northumberland County, Pennsylvania). See next PA.7.1.1.

2. **(Ann WILLETT)**: b 1826, Pennsylvania.

PA.7.1.1
JOHN WILLETT and **MARY E. DIMMICK**
of Rush Township, Northumberland County, Pennsylvania

John Willett was born on February 13, 1822, in Pennsylvania.

John Willett married about 1846 Mary E. Dimmick (b June 6, 1826, Pennsylvania; d April 8, 1896, in Gearhart Township, Northumberland County, Pennsylvania, and is buried at St. Luke's Plum Creek, Rockafellar Township, Northumberland County, Pennsylvania).

In 1850, John <u>Willet</u> and family are listed in the Rush Township, Northumberland County, Pennsylvania, census, page 151, dwelling 31-31, as follows:

Willet	John	29	m	PA	laborer, $150
	Mary	24	f	PA	
	Helen?	1	f	PA	
Johnston, Samuel		27	m	PA	laborer
	Ann	24	f	PA	
	Elizabeth?	1	f		
Willet	Washington	2	m		

In 1860, John Willett, and family are listed in the Rush Township, Northumberland County, Pennsylvania, census, No. 42, as follows:

Willett	John	38	m	PA	laborer
	Mary E	35	f	PA	
	female	11	f	PA	
	David	9	m	PA	
	Christian	6	m	PA	
	Adam N	4	m	PA	
	Sarah C	1	f	PA	

In 1860, living nearby is, Mary Willet, age 74, born New Jersey, in the same Rush Township [M653, R1149, page 509, dwelling no. 92], as follows:

Willet	Mary	74	f	NJ
Robbins	Mary	78	f	NJ
McCloughan, Rebecca		45	f	PA

In 1870, John Willett, and family are listed in the Rush Township, Northumberland County, Pennsylvania, census, page 8, dwelling 57-57, as follows:

Willett	John	48	m	PA	laborer
	Mary E	44	f	PA	
	David T.	19	m	PA	
	Sarah C.	12	f	PA	
	Margaret J.	5	f	PA	

John Willett died on December 19, 1891, and is buried at St. Luke's, Plum Creek, Rockefellar Township, Northumberland County, with his wife. Also buried there is an Anna Willett (b February 29, 1784; d May 12, 1849) who may be his mother.

(*The Willett Families*, page 246).

1. **Washington WILLETT**: b 1848, Pennsylvania.
2. **Helen M. WILLETT**: b 1849 in Pennsylvania.
3. **David T. WILLETT**: b 1851 in Pennsylvania.
4. **Christian WILLETT** (female): b 1854 in Pennsylvania.
5. **Adam N. WILLETT**: b 1856 in Pennsylvania; m abt 1878 Laura (b 1859, Pennsylvania). In 1870, Adam Willett, age 15, was a farm laborer. See next PA.7.1.1.5.
6. **Sarah Catherine** ("Kate") **WILLETT**: b June 22, 1858, Pennsylvania; m George Young Weimar.

    1. **Elijah G. R. WEIMAR**.

7. **Margaret Jane WILLETT**: b 1865, Pennsylvania.

PA.7.1.1.5
ADAM N. WILLETT and **LAURA**
of Danville, Montour County, Pennsylvania

Adam N. Willett was born in 1856 in Pennsylvania.

Adam Willett married about 1878 Laura (b 1859, Pennsylvania). In 1870, Adam Willett, age 15, was a farm laborer (1870 Northumberland County census, page 382).

In 1880, Adam Willett and family are listed in the Danville City, Montour County, Pennsylvania, census, as follows:

Willet	Adam	head	24	PA
	Laura	wife	21	PA
	Margaret	daughter	1	PA

1. **Margaret WILLETT**: b 1879, Pennsylvania.

PA.7.2
HENRY C. WILLET
of Oxford Township, Butler County, Ohio

Henry C. Willet was born on October 6, 1795 (Willett-Truex Family Bible record) (New Jersey).

Henry C. Willet married 1st on March 25, 1819, Hannah Robertson (Family Bible record).

In 1830, Henry C. Willet and family were listed in the Oxford Township, Butler County, Ohio, census, page 113. From the following reconstructed census, it is almost certain that this is the family of this Henry C. Willet:

1-0-0-0-0-1 1-1-0-0-0-1-0

1 male	30-40	1790-1800	*Henry C*	*age 35 b 1795*
1 female	30-40	1790-1800	*Hannah*	*age 35?b 1795?*
1 female	5-10	1820-1825		
1 female	0-5	1825-1830		
1 male	0-5	1825-1830		

In 1840, Henry C. Willet and family were listed in the Madison Township (Mad River), Clark County, Ohio, census, as follows:

1 male	40-50	1790-1800	*Henry C*	*age 45 b 1795*
1 male	20-30	1810-1820		
1 female	15-20	1820-1825		
1 female	10-15	1825-1830		

Henry C. Willet married 2nd in Butler County, Ohio, on October 2, 1845, Jane O'Harra (IGI).

In 1850, Henry C. Willet and family are listed in the Oxford Township, Butler County, Ohio, census, page 412, dwelling 499-521, as follows:

Willet	Henry C.	56 m	NJ	toll gateman
	Jane	40 f	NJ	
	Eliza Jane	1 f	OH	
Harrow	Mary E	14 f	NJ	
	John	6 m	NJ	

In 1860, H. C. Willet and family are listed in the Oxford Township, Butler County, Ohio, census, No. 360, as follows:

Willet	H. C.	65 m	NJ	toll Gate Keeper
	Jane	50 f	NJ	
	Eliza	12 f	OH	

Rebecca	9 f	OH
Harriette	8 f	OH

1. **Eliza Jane WILLETT**: b 1849, Ohio.
2. **Rebecca WILLETT**: b 1851, Ohio.
3. **Harriette WILLETT**: b 1852, Ohio.

PA.7.8
NICHOLAS WILLET and RACHEL ARTER
Shamokin Township, Northumberland County, Pennsylvania

Nicholas Willet was born on December 24, 1808, in Pennsylvania (born Pennsylvania according to 1850 and 1860 censuses) (Willett-Truex Family Bible record).

Nicholas Willets married in Northumberland County, Pennsylvania, on October 29, 1829, Rachel Arter (b July 13, 1799, Pennsylvania; d July 2, 1866, buried Shamokin Valley Baptist Church Cemetery, Northumberland County) of Shamokin Township ("Danville Intelligencer" present day Montour County).

In 1840, Nicholas Willett and family were listed in the Augusta Township, Northumberland County, Pennsylvania, census, page 197, as follows:

1 male	30-40	1800-1810 *Nicholas*	*age 32 b 1808*
1 female	30-40	1800-1810 *Rachel*	*age 41* b 1799**
1 male	5-10	1830-1835 *Joshua*	*age 6 b 1834*
1 male	0-5	1835-1840 *David J*	*age 4 b 1836*
1 female	0-5	1835-1840 *Catherine*	*age 1 b 1839*
1 male	0-5	1835-1840	

In 1850, Nicholas Willet and family are listed in the Shamokin Township, Northumberland County, Pennsylvania, census, page 277, dwelling 270-270, as follows:

Willet	Nicholas	40	m	PA
	Rachel	39	f	PA
	Joshua	15	m	PA
	Daniel?	13	m	PA
	Cathrine	11	f	PA
	Amanda	9	f	PA

He was a farmer (1860).

In 1860, Nicholas Willett and family are listed in the Shamokin Township, Northumberland County, Pennsylvania, census, dwelling 1149, as follows:

Willett	Nicholas	51	m	PA	farmer
	Rachael	50	f	PA	
	David J.	25	m	PA	
	Lucinda	18	f	PA	
	William	6	m	PA	

Nicholas Willet died on January 11, 1866 (tombstone), age 57 years, and 17 days, and is buried in the Shamokin Valley Baptist Church Cemetery, Northumberland County ("The Sunbury Gazette," January 20, 1866).

Will of Nicholas Willet,
1st, Joshua Willet, executor ...
2d, Rachel Willet, beloved wife, all my ...
Son, David J. Willet the sum of one hundred dollars ...
Daughter, Cather L., now married to Simon C. Rem, $100.00
...
Daughter, Lucinda now married to Edward C. Logan, $100.00 ...
Balance: to son Joshua Willet.
Wife Rachel to reside with son Joshua.

Dated December 13, 1865.

On January 22, 1866, Joshua Willet qualified as the executor of the estate of Nicholas Willet, deceased (Northumberland County, Pennsylvania, *Index to Registers ....* *Prior to 1930, Northumberland County,* File No. 308).
On July 9, 1866, Joshua Willet qualified as the Administrator of the estate of Rachel Willet, deceased (Northumberland County, Pennsylvania, *Index to Registers .... Prior to 1930, Northumberland County,* File No. 313).

1. **Joshua WILLET**: b 1834, Pennsylvania; m abt 1855 Rebecca P. (b 1836, Pennsylvania); will dated October 1, 1884. See next PA.7.8.1.
2. **David J. WILLET**: b 1836, Pennsylvania. Possibly the "Mr. David Willet" was married "on Thursday, Dec. 3d, at the Baptist parsonage, near Reeds station, by the Rev. J. R. Shanafelt, Mr. David Willet, to Miss Matilda Price, both of Shamokin Township". David Willett's tombstone only has the initials "G.A.R." (Grand Army of the Republic), buried Shamokin Valley Baptist Church Cemetery, Northumberland. See next PA.7.8.2.
3. **Cathrine WILLET**: b 1839, Pennsylvania; m (before 1865) Simon C. Rem.

4. **Lucinda** (Amanda in 1850 census) **WILLET**: b 1841, Pennsylvania; called "Lucinda" in 1860 Northumberland County census and in father's will of 1865; m (before 1865) Edward C. Logan.

5. **William WILLET**: b 1854, Pennsylvania. Possibly a grandchild as his surname was unreadable on the microfilm, and he is not mentioned in Nicholas Willet's will of 1865.

PA.7.8.1
JOSHUA WILLET
Shamokin Township, Northumberland County, Pennsylvania

Joshua Willet was born in 1834, Pennsylvania.

Joshua Willet married about 1855 Rebecca P. (b 1836, Pennsylvania). He was a blacksmith (1860).

In 1860, Joshua Willet and family were listed in the Upper Augusta Township, Northumberland County, Pennsylvania, census, dwelling 656, as follows:

Willet	Joshua	30	m	PA	blacksmith
	Rebecca	28	f	PA	
	John A	2	m	PA	
	Rachael	10/12	f	PA	

In 1870, Joshua Willet and family were listed in the Shamokin Township, Northumberland County, Pennsylvania, census, page 415, dwelling 278-297, as follows:

Willet	Joshua	36	m	PA	blacksmith
	Rebecca	35	f	PA	
	John	12	m	PA	
	Rachel J.	10	f	PA	
	Sarah	8	f	PA	
	Emma E.	6	f	PA	
	Eleanor	4	f	PA	

In 1880, Joshua Willett and family were listed as residing at Elysberry, Shamokin Township, Northumberland County, Penn-sylvania, census 59-62-7-42, as follows:

Willet	Joshua	46	PA	
	Rebecca P	44	PA	wife
	Rachel J	20	PA	daughter
	Sarah D	18	PA	daughter
	Ellen E	14	PA	daughter
	Calvin A	2	PA	son

Joshua Willett married 2d about 1882? Sarah A.

Will No. 24, I Joshua Willet of Bloomsburg, Columbia County, Penna. Make this my last Will ...

First: To my wife Sarah A. I bequeath my personal and real estate to be held by her as long as she shall remain my widow. The foregoing provisions to be in lieu of her right of dower in my real and personal estate during her widowhood.

Second: I give and devise all the real and personal Estate of which I shall die Seized of to my children, to be equally divided between them to be held by them and their heirs, to their use and behoof forever ...

Third: wife executrix.
Witnesses: K. Appleman
Chas. R. Housel
Dated October 1, 1884, Bloomsburg

First Account: March 17, 1887
Final Account: May 9, 1887

1. **John A. WILLET**: b 1858, Pennsylvania. The following record has been assigned based solely on similarity of name and approximate age. See next PA.7.8.1.1.
2. **Rachel J. WILLET**: b late 1859 or early 1860, Pennsylvania.
3. **Sarah D. WILLET**: b 1862, Pennsylvania.
4. **Ellen Emma WILLET**: b 1864, Pennsylvania.
5. **Eleanor WILLETT**: b 1866, Pennsylvania.
6. **Calvin A. WILLET**: b 1878, Pennsylvania.

PA.7.8.1.1
A. JOHN WILLETT and ANNIE
of Northumberland County, Pennsylvania

A. John Willett was born in 1855 in Pennsylvania.

A. John Willett married about 1875 Annie (b 1856, Pennsylvania).

In 1880, A. J. Willett and family were listed in the Rush Township, Northumberland County, Pennsylvania, census, as follows:

Willett	A. J.	25	1855	PA	
	Annie	24	1856	PA	wife
	Lizzie R.	4	1876	PA	daughter
	Ida M.	2	1878	PA	daughter

In 1900, <u>John H.</u> Willett and family were listed in the Gearhart Township, Northumberland County, Pennsylvania, census, as follows:

Willett	John H.	42	Aug 1857	PA	
	Anna	45	May 1855	PA	wife
	Ida M.	20	Aug 1879	PA	daughter
	John	17	Aug 1882	PA	son
	Samuel	14	Oct 1885	PA	son
	Franklin	12	Feb 1888	PA	son
	Mary	10	Nov 1890	PA	daughter
	Clara	7	May 1893	PA	daughter

1. **Lizzie R. WILLETT**: b 1876, Pennsylvania.
2. **Ida M. WILLETT**: b August, 1879, Pennsylvania.
3. **John WILLETT**: b August, 1882, Pennsylvania.
4. **Samuel WILLETT**: b October, 1885, Pennsylvania.
5. **Franklin WILLETT**: b February, 1888, Pennsylvania.
6. **Mary WILLETT**: b November, 1890, Pennsylvania.
7. **Clara WILLETT**: b May, 1893, Pennsylvania.

PA.7.8.2
DAVID J. WILLET
of Northumberland County, Pennsylvania

David J. Willet was born in 1836, in Pennsylvania.

He is mentioned in the household of his parents in the 1850 and 1860 Northumberland County, Pennsylvania, census.

Possibly the "Mr. David Willet" was married "on Thursday, Dec. 3d, at the Baptist parsonage, near Reeds station, by the Rev. J. R. Shanafelt, Mr. David Willet, to Miss Matilda Price, both of Shamokin Township" ("The Sunbury Gazette," December 12, 1863).

David J. Willet most likely enlisted in the Union Army and served a one to three year tour of duty. This Civil War duty can be inferred from the fact that his gravestone has the initials "G.A.R." carved on them (Grand Army of the Republic).

David J. Willet of Snydertownborough, Northumberland County, Pennsylvania, laborer, will is dated December 7, 1881, and was recorded on January 7, 1882. There is no mention of wife or children. Everything is left to Harriet E. Alexander "who is now keeping house for me ..."

On January 7, 1882, J. M. Wolverton qualified as the executor of the estate of David J. Willett, deceased (Northumberland County, Pennsylvania, *Index to Registers .... Prior to 1930, Northumberland County*, File No. 435).

David J. Willet's tombstone only has the initials "G.A.R." (Grand Army of the Republic), buried Shamokin Valley Baptist Church Cemetery, Northumberland.

PA.7.9
ISAAC WILLETT and SUSAN PERSHING
of Ohio and Henry County, Illinois

Isaac Willett was born May 10, 1817 (Willett-Truex Family Bible record), (born Ohio) (*Memoirs of Lenawee County, Michigan,* 1909, page 832).

Isaac Willett married in Knox County, Ohio, on November 26, 1839, Susannah Pershing (Persing) (b February 10, 1813), the daughter of John Pershing and Ann Larkins (IGI record). Actually the record says Susan Persing married <u>Mr. Willitt</u>. There is no date associated with this Northumberland County, Pennsylvania, newspaper (undated, paper not noted) entry and it was an newspaper article recording the marriage of a former resident.

In 1840, there is an Isaac <u>Willet</u> and family listed in the Washington, Erie County, Pennsylvania, census, page 34 (not copied). This census may belong to a different Isaac Willet and family.

In 1840, there is an Isaac <u>Willet</u> and family residing in Congress, Richland County, Ohio, page 215, as follows:

1 male	20-30	1810-1820	*Isaac*	*age 23 b 1817*
1 female	20-30	1810-1820	*Susannah*	
1 male	0-5	1835-1840		

On the same page is listed Mary Willet who most likely is his sister, Mary Willett. The census listing for Mary Willett in Congress, Richland County, Ohio, page 215, is as follows:

1 female	40-50	1810-1820	*Mary*	*age 62* b 1778**
1 female	20-30	1810-1820	*Mary*	*age 21 b 1819*

FOR THE RECORD: In 1850, there is an Isaac <u>Willet</u> and family residing at Washington Township, Erie County, Pennsylvania, page 324, dwelling 115-116, as follows:

Willet	Isaac	44	NY	farmer
	Relief	33	NY	
	Eveline	5	PA	
	Vincent	8	PA	

The census record of the Isaac Willet family above belongs to a different branch of the Willet family (see *The Willett Families,* page 230).

Isaac and Susannah Willett (reputedly) lived in Ohio, and in 1851 located in Henry County, Illinois.

FOR THE RECORD: In 1860, there is an Isaac <u>Willett</u> and family residing at Washington Township, Erie County, Pennsylvania, dwelling 894, as follows:

Willet	Isaac	46	NY	farmer
	female	40	NY	(might be Relief)
	male	19	PA	(this is Vincent)
	female	16	PA	

FOR THE RECORD: In 1870, there is an Isaac <u>Willett</u> and family residing at Washington Township, Erie County, Pennsylvania, dwelling 894, as follows:

Willet	Isaac	59	NY	farmer
	Relief	53	NY	(might be Relief)
	Vincent	29	PA	

It is unlikely that the above census records belong to Isaac Willett and Susan Pershing.

FOR THE RECORD: In 1880, there is an Isaac <u>Willett</u> and family residing at Washington Township, Erie County, Pennsylvania, dwelling 34-175, as follows:

Willet	Isaac	70	NY	
	Relief	60	NY	wife
	Vincent	9	PA	son
	Deelt?	31	PA	daughter-in-law
	Claude	3	PA	grandson

It is unlikely that the census record above belongs to Isaac Willett and Susan Pershing.

Both Isaac and Susan Willet had died by 1909 (*Memoirs of Lenawee County, Michigan,* 1909, page 832).

(*The Willett Families,* 1985, page 930).

1. **John L. WILLETT**: b February 12, 1844, in Ohio; m in Fulton County, Ohio, on January 12, 1871, Jennie S. Reynolds (b March 25, 1842, in Ohio). See next <u>PA.7.9.1</u>.

PA.7.9.1
JOHN L. WILLETT and JENNIE S. REYNOLDS
of Dover Township, Lenawee County, Michigan

John L. Willett was born on February 12, 1844, in Ohio.

John L. Willett married in Fulton County, Ohio, on January 12, 1871, Jennie S. Reynolds (b March 25, 1842, in Ohio).

They resided in Illinois until 1873, when they returned to Ohio for a year, and then moved to Dover Township, Lenawee County, Michigan, where they purchased 80 acres in Section 35.

In 1880, John L. Willet and family were enumerated in the Dover Township, Lenawee County, Michigan, census, as follows:

Willett	John L.	35	OH
	Jennie	36	OH
	Frank	8	IL
	Wendel	2	MI

(*Memoirs of Lenawee County, Michigan*, 1909, page 832; *The Willett Families*, 1985, page 931; 1900, 1910 Dover Township, Lenawee County, Michigan, census).

1. **Frank J. WILLETT**: b November 30, 1871, in Henry County, Illinois; m February 2, 1899, Florence Parker, the daughter of Julia A. Parker (b 1853, Michigan) of Madison Township, Lenawee County, Michigan. (1900 Madison Township, Lenawee County, Michigan, census; 1910 Lenawee County, Michigan, census). See next PA.7.9.1.1.

2. **Wendell D. WILLETT**: b October 22, 1877; resided in Adrian.

3. **Lloyd** ("Londe") **W. WILLETT**: b June 13, 1880; resided with his parents in Lenawee County, Michigan in 1909; m Marel (b 1885, Michigan). (1900 Madison Township, Lenawee County, Michigan, census; 1910 Lenawee County, Michigan, census).

PA.7.9.1.1
FRANK J. WILLETT and FLORENCE PARKER
of Adrian, Lenawee County, Michigan

Frank J. Willett was born on November 30, 1871, in Henry County, Illinois.

Frank J. Willett married on February 2, 1899, Florence Parker, the daughter of James and Julia (Carpenter) Parker. (*The Willett Families*, 1985, page 931).

> "*Frank J. Willett received his earliest education in the district schools of Dover township, later attended the normal department of Adrian College, in which school he graduated with the class of 1891. He then taught school for 2 years. Not finding the work of teaching congenial, he returned home and worked with his father for 6 or 7 years, in fact remained at home until the time of his marriage*" (*Memoirs of Lenawee County, Michigan*, 1909, pages 832-833).

The Willetts are members of the Baptist Church and also members of the local Grange.

(1900 Madison Township, Lenawee County, Michigan, census; 1910 Lenawee County, Michigan, census).

PA.7.10
MARY ANN WILLET and BENJAMIN TRUEX
of Morrow County, Ohio, and Labette County, Kansas

Mary Ann Willet was born August 30, 1819 (Willett-Truex Family Bible record), Hamilton County, Indiana (Hires manuscript), or near Cincinnati, Hamilton County, Ohio (Orilla Truex Wisler questionnaire). Born Indiana agrees with the 1850 Lincoln Township, Morrow County, Indiana, census; born Ohio also agrees with the 1860 and 1870 Lock Township, Elkhart County, Indiana, census records. In 1820, most of central Indiana was divided between the "unorganized" counties of Wabash and Delaware, it is unlikely that Mary Ann Willett could have been born in that portion of the state in 1819. Hamilton County, Indiana, was not in existence in 1820, was largely unpopulated and still primarily Indian lands, therefore, it is more likely that Mary Ann Willett was born in Hamilton County, Ohio.

Miss Mary Ann Willet registered to marry in Richland County, Ohio, on October 15, 1842, and did married on November 29, 1842, Benjamin Truex (d October 27, 1882, Emporia, Lyon County, Kansas) (Lyon County, Kansas, record; Richland County, Ohio, record), son of William Truex. Marriage date is from a Justice of the Peace record, and the marriage is also recorded in Morrow County, Ohio.

In 1850, Benjamin Truex and family were listed in the Lincoln Township, Morrow County, Ohio, census, (between pages 24 and 25), dwelling 333-336, as follows:

Truex	Benjamin	30	PA
	Mary (Ann Willet)	30	IA

(In 1850, "IA" is the abbreviation for Indiana)

Judson	7	OH
Amanda	5	OH
Thomas	2 1/2	OH

In 1860, Benjamin Truex and Mary (Willett) were listed in the Goshen Post Office, Lock Township, Elkhart County, Indiana, census.

In 1870, Benjamin Truex and Mary (Willett) appear in the Wakarusa Post Office, Lock Township, Elkhart County, Indiana, census.

Sometime after 1870, Mrs. Mary Ann (Willet) and her husband separated.

In 1882, Benjamin Truex died intestate. Probate records

name his wife, Sarah J., and six children: Judson L. Truax, Thomas L. Truax, William W. Truax, Louisa J. McCoy, Orilla C. Truax, and Amanda D. Truax, as heirs. His place of burial is not known.

Mrs. Mary Ann (Willet) Truex died on May 4, 1888, at Parsons, Labette County, Kansas, and is buried in Block 39, Lot 9, of the Oakwood Cemetery, Parsons, Labette County, Kansas (tombstone record).

(Thura Truax Hines Manuscripts, Volume I, Pennsylvania to Ohio, Truax/Truex genealogy).

1. **Judson Adoniram TRUEX**: b November 6, 1843, Mt. Gilead, Morrow County, Ohio; m at Carmel, Charlotte, Eaton County, Michigan, on November 6, 1876, Mary Adelaide Merriam (b July 5, 1846/1847, LaGrange, Lorain County, Ohio; d July 31, 1906, West Plains, Howell County, Missouri), the daughter of Marshall S. Merriam and Rebecah H. Goss; d April 25, 1912, Kansas City, Wyandotte County, Kansas. See next PA.7.10.1.1.

2. **Amanda Dunreath TRUEX**: b 1845, Ohio; m Nathan Williams.

3. **Thomas L. TRUEX**: b 1850, Ohio; unmarried.

4. **Louisa Jane TRUEX**: m Eldridge McCoy.

5. **William Willard TRUEX**: m Clara Melissa Ivey.

6. **James B. TRUEX**: died in infancy.

7. **Orilla C. TRUEX**: m John W. Wisler.

8. **Mary Ada TRUEX**: died in infancy.

PA.7.10.1.1
JUDSON ADONIRAM TRUEX
and MARY ADELAIDE MERRIAM

Judson Adoniram Truex was born on November 6, 1843, Mt. Gilead, Morrow County, Ohio.

Judson A. Truex married at Carmel, Charlotte, Eaton County, Michigan, on November 6, 1876, Mary Adelaide Merriam (b July 5, 1846/1847, LaGrange, Lorain County, Ohio; d July 31, 1906, West Plains, Howell County, Missouri), the daughter of Marshall S. Merriam and Rebecah H. Goss.

Judson A. Truex died on April 25, 1912, Kansas City, Wyandotte County, Kansas.

1. **Howard Eugene TRUEX**: b November 16, 1877,, Junction City, Geary County, Kansas; m in Chicago, Cook County, Illinois, on July 27, 1909, Frances ("Helene") Casey (b February 5, 1888, Illinois; d February 19, 1942, Wichita Falls, Wichita County, Texas), the daughter of John Casey and Anna Dobbie; d November 26, 1943, San Antonio, Bexar County, Texas.

    1. **Howard Francis LEBARON**: b August 19, 1912, Kansas City, Jackson County, Missouri; m in San Antonio, Bexar County, Texas, on May 10, 1937, Dorothy Louise Huggins (b November 5, 1915, Yoakum, Lavaca County, Texas).

        1. **Juliette Anne LEBARON**: b December 2, 1939, Forth Worth, Tarrant County, Texas; m in Houston, Harris County, Texas, on June 29, 1963, Anthony Frank Garito.

CHAPTER EIGHT
LEWIS F. WILLET (1809-1865)

PA.8

LEWIS F. WILLET and **MARGARET LONGSHORE**
of Newcumberland, Cumberland County, Pennsylvania

Lewis F. Willet was born on December 28, 1809 (1811) in Pennsylvania (birth date take from tombstone).

Lewis F. Willet married in 1833 Margaret Longshore (b January 9, 1816, Pennsylvania; d May 29, 1895, age 79 years, 6 months, 11 days, buried Mt. Olivet Cemetery, New Cumberland, Cumberland County).

On February 18, 1848, George Crist and wife Ann of New Cumberland sold to Lewis Willet of New Cumberland, purchase land (evidently the house and lot on Bridge Street near corner with Second Street) (Deed Abstract).

In 1850, Lewis Willet and family are listed in the Newcumberland Township, Cumberland County, Pennsylvania, census, page 383 dwelling 13-15, as follows:

Willet	Lewis	39	m	PA	cooper, $700
	Margaret	36	f	PA	wife
	Theodore	16	m	PA	storekeeper
	Martha	11	f	PA	daughter
	Catharine	8	f	PA	daughter
	Mary	6	f	PA	daughter
Willet	John Arthur	8/12	m	PA	son

Lewis Willett was a cooper (1850, spring of 1857).

Lewis Willett was an inmate at the Harrisbury Lunatic Asylum from November 14, 1857, until May 27, 1862. On November 14, 1857, it was recorded at the asylum, "*Lewis Willet, 45, married, born and resides in Cumberland County, has been a cooper until this spring when he moved on a town stand and exchanged a life of activity for one of inaction. Had been in good health and had no relations troubled with mental disorder, is naturally quiet. This attack came on some five months ago; his neglect of business, inaction, and ...*"

In 1860, (Mrs.) M.(argaret) Willet and family are listed in the Borough of New Cumberland, Cumberland County, Pennsylvania, census, page 112 dwelling 1313-1327, as follows:

Willet	M. (Margaret)	45	m	PA	1,000/3,00
	K. (Katherine)	18	f	PA	teacher
	M. (Mary)	15	f	PA	
	A. (Arthur)	11	m	PA	
	H. (Harriet)	8	f	PA	

Lewis F. Willet died on January 11, 1865, age 55 years, 15 days. He is buried in the Mt. Olivet Cemetery, New Cumberland, Cumberland County, Pennsylvania (death date take from tombstone).

In 1870, Margaret Willett and family are listed in the Borough of New Cumberland, Cumberland County, Pennsylvania, census, as follows:

Willett	Margaret	f	55	keeping house
	Halley	f	17	at home

In 1880, Margaret Willet and family are listed in the Borough of New Cumberland, Cumberland County, Pennsylvania, census, as follows:

Willett	Margaret	f	64	keeping house
Balsley	Halley	f	28	daughter
	Russell	m	4	grandson

1. **Theodore WILLET**: b 1834, Pennsylvania; storekeeper (1850); m abt 1856 Sarah E. (b 1838; d October 14, 1865, age 28 years, 9 months, 4 days, buried Mt. Olivet Cemetery, New Cumberland, Cumberland County). See next PA.8.1.

2. **Mary E. WILLET**: b 1838; d June 16, 1842, age 5 years, 3 months, 15 days, buried Mt. Olivet, New Cumberland, Cumberland County Cemetery, with her parents and siblings (tombstone).

3. **Martha WILLET**: b 1839, Pennsylvania.

4. **Catherine WILLET**: b 1842, Pennsylvania; teacher (1860).

5. **Mary WILLET**: b 1844, Pennsylvania.

6. **Elizabeth WILLET**: b 1847, Pennsylvania; d July 27, 1849, age 2 years, 4 months, 26 days, buried Mt. Olivet Cemetery, New Cumberland, Cumberland County (tombstone).

7. **John Arthur WILLET**: b October 14, 1849 (Cumberland County), Pennsylvania; m abt 1872 Elsetta Kohler (b February 17, 1854, Lancaster County, Pennsylvania; d January 24, 1933, Oak Hill Cemetery, Lawrence, Douglas County, Kansas); in 1879 removed to Lawrence, Kansas; d October 14, 1914, Oak Hill Cemetery, Lawrence, Douglas County, Kansas. See next PA.8.7.

8. **Harriet** ("Halley") **WILLET**: b 1852 (Cumberland County), Pennsylvania; m Balsley.

    1. **Russell BALSLEY**: b 1876.

PA.8.1
THEODORE WILLET and SARAH E.
of Cumberland County, Pennsylvania

Theodore Willet was born in 1834, Pennsylvania.
He was a storekeeper (1850).
Theodore Willet married about 1856 Sarah E. (b 1838; d October 14, 1865, age 28 years, 9 months, 4 days, buried Mt. Olivet Cemetery, New Cumberland, Cumberland County, Pennsylvan-ia). Mrs. Sarah E. Willett died in a train accident in Lancaster County, Pennsylvania (New Cumberland Histori-cal Society, Newspaper notice).
In 1860, T. Willet and family are listed in the Borough of New Cumberland, Cumberland County, Pennsylvania, census, page 262 dwelling 1285-1298, as follows:

Willet	T.	24	m	PA	merchant
	S.	21	f	PA	
	T. H.	3	m	PA	
	E.	3/12	m	PA	
Roth	D.	21	f	PA	servant
Barshaw	M.	33	m	GER	Segar Maker
Hess	J.	19	m	PA	clerk

    1. **T. H. WILLET** (male): b 1857, Pennsylvania.
    2. **Elmer S. WILLET**: b 1859, Pennsylvania; d May 8, 1859, age 1 month, buried Mount Olivet Cemetery, Fairview Township, New Cumberland, Cumberland County, Pennsylva-nia.
    3. **E. WILLET** (male): b (April), 1860, Pennsylvania.
    4. **Frank H. WILLET**: b 1862; d December 4, 1862, age 5 years, 3 months, 27 days, buried Mt. Olivet Cemetery, New Cumberland, Cumberland County, Pennsylvania.

PA.8.7

JOHN ARTHUR WILLETT and **ELSETTA KOEHLER**

of Lawrence, Douglas County, Kansas

John Arthur Willett was born on October 14, 1849, (Cumberland County) Pennsylvania, the son of Lewis Willett and Margaret Longshore.

John Arthur Willett married about 1872 Elsetta Kohler (b February 17, 1854, Lancaster County, Pennsylvania; d January 24, 1933, Fishing River, Clay County, Missouri, buried in the Oak Hill Cemetery, in Lawrence, Douglas County, Kansas [1933 Death Certificate, Elsetta Willett]), the daughter of William Koehler and Leah Hoffman.

Family tradition states that either he or his brother Theodore worked in or owned a quarry near Harrisburg, Pennylvania (i.e., Dauphin, Cumberland or York county).

In 1879, John Arthur Willett and family removed to Lawrence, Douglas County, Kansas, where he was employed as a dry goods salesman. He was associated with the Innes Store as the manager of the Silk Department for many years until failing health compelled him to relinquish active business.

In 1880, John A. Willett and family are listed at Massachusetts Street, Lawrence, Douglas County, Kansas, census, as follows:

Willett	John A.	head	29	PA
	Electra (sic)	wife	25	PA
	Carroll	son	7	PA

In 1900, John A. Willett and family are enumerated at 905 Ohio Street, Lawrence, Douglas County, Kansas, census, as follows:

Willett	John A.	head	Sep 1848	51	PA
	Elsetta	wife	Feb 1854	46	PA
	Carlton L.	son	May 1874	26	PA
	William A.	son	Apr 1892	8	KS

John Arthur Willett died at home at 905 Ohio Street, Lawrence, on October 14, 1914, age 60, and is buried in the Oak Hill Cemetery, Lawrence, Douglas County, Kansas.

(1914 Death Certificate, John A. Willett, Douglas County, Kansas; 1914 Obituary, J. A. Willet [Douglas County, Kansas]).

1. **Carlton** ("Carroll") **Alonzo WILLETT**: b May, 1874, Pennsylvania.

2. **William Arthur WILLETT**: b April 20, 1892, Law-rence, Douglas County, Kansas; m on April 21, 1917, Florence Amelia Baehler (b June 30, 1896; d November 13, 1979); resided (1933) Fort Wayne, Indiana; d October 21, 1970, Riverside, California, cremated and interred at Evergreen Cemetery (1970 Death Certificate, William Arthur Willett). See next PA.8.7.2.

PA.8.7.2
WILLIAM ARTHUR WILLETT
and **FLORENCE AMELIA BAEHLER**
of Illinois, Wisconsin and California

William Arthur Willett was born on April 20, 1892, Lawrence, Douglas County, Kansas. He went to High School in 1907-1909. He quit before graduating because of the death of his father and went to work selling the Saturday Evening Post. He attended a business college in Lawrence, Kansas, from 1911 to 1912. He worked for General Cigar Company from 1915 to 1945.

William Arthur Willett married at his bride's home in Kansas City, Missouri, on April 21, 1917, Florence Amelia Baehler (b June 30, 1896, Jefferson City, Missouri; d November 13, 1979, at the age of 85), the daughter of August Eugene Baehler of St. Louis and Augusta Caroline Weber of Fairbury, Illinois. They resided in Oklahoma City, Chicago, Fort Wayne, Indiana (1933) and from 1935-1945 in Milwaukee, Wisconsin.

In 1945, they removed to Santa Barbara, California, where he was employed as a wholesale tobacco dealer until he retired. In 1953, they moved to Sacramento, California, then to Riverside, California, in 1960 until his death.

William Arthur Willett died on October 21, 1970, at Riverside, California; he was cremated and interred at Evergreen Cemetery, Riverside, California (1970 Death Certificate, Riverside, California, William Arthur Willett).

1. **Florence Marie WILLETT**: b May 2, 1930, Chicago, Cook, County, Illinois; m in Sacramento, California, on November 12, 1955, US Air Force Major William Daniel Hempy (b January 3, 1931; d June 27, 1992) (divorced 1980); resides (1996) Riverside, California. See next PA.8.7.2.1.

PA.8.7.2.1
FLORENCE MARIE WILLETT and **WILLIAM DANIEL HEMPY**
of Riverside, California

Florence Marie Willett was born on May 2, 1930, Chicago, Cook, County, Illinois. Florence graduated from Santa Barbara High School. She graduated cum laude from University of California, at Santa Barbara, with a M. A. in Speech, and from U.C.L.A with a M. A. in Theater Arts.

Miss Florence Marie Willett married in Sacramento, California, on November 12, 1955, US Air Force Major William Daniel Hempy (b January 3, 1931; d June 27, 1992) (divorced 1979).

Mrs. Florence Marie (Willett) Hempy resides (1996) at Riverside, California. She has been a California Real Estate broker for over 20 years. Her interests include photography, travel and gardening. Marie is a talented lady with membership in Mensa, Riverside Community Players, Riverside Art Alliance, Riverside Folk Song Society, Why Nots, Actor's Company (*Who's Who in California*, 19th edition).

1. **Daniel Willett HEMPY**: b October 8, 1956, Sacramento, California; graduated (1979) from Pomona College with a B. A., and from (1980) San Diego State with a M. S. in Geology; m 1st in Riverside, California, on September, 1980, Natalie Herring (divorced January, 1991); m 2d in Pacific Palisades, California, on April 20, 1996, Lisa Jane Morrisson (b on November 15, 1958, in Cleveland, Ohio).

2. **David William HEMPY**: b June 25, 1958, Sacramento, California; graduated from Cal Poly, Pomona, with a B. S. in Mechanical Engineering; m in Yorba Linda, California, on January 12, 1984, Cynthia Helen Tahse (b August 5, 1960). See next PA.8.7.2.1.2.

3. **Robert Michael HEMPY**: b January 13, 1961, Riverside, California; m on September 1, 1984, Linda Staroba (divorced 1987). See next PA.8.7.2.1.3.

PA.8.7.2.1.2
DAVID WILLIAM HEMPY and CYTHNIA TAHSE
of Riverside, California

David William Hempy was born on June 25, 1958, Sacramento, California. He graduated from Cal Poly, Pomona, with a B. S. in Mechanical Engineering.

David William Hempy married in Yorba Linda, California, on January 12, 1984, Cynthia Helen Tahse (b August 5, 1960).

1. **Alexander James HEMPY**: b April 1, 1986, Riverside, California.

2. **Taylor HEMPY**: b November 24, 1988, Riverside, California.

PA.8.7.2.1.3
ROBERT MICHAEL HEMPY and LINDA STAROBA

Robert Michael Hempy was born on January 13, 1961, Riverside, California.

Robert Michael Hempy married on September 1, 1984, Linda Staroba (divorced 1987).

Linda married 2d Don Kalinsky of Dallas, Texas.

1. **Elizabeth Katherine Carol HEMPY**: b December 18, 1986, Redlands, California. Since remarriage of her mother, Elizabeth has been adopted by her stepfather, Don Kalinsky.

ABOUT THE INDEX

This is not an every name index. The only names indexed are those that are listed in **Bold** and are also "Capitalized" in the **"Title Line"** of each heading and those names in the **"List of Children"**. This indexing preference was chosen so that an individual will be led only to those persons who are directly related to the Willett family. By using this convention to index names, a researcher can expect that everyone listed in the Index is related by either marriage, adoption, or blood to one of the Willett families of Pennsylvania.

If a name is listed twice on a page, there will be only one index page number reference to that name. When names have a Jr., Sr., I, or II, added to their name, only the Christian and Surname is indexed.

When searching for an individual either a Willett or related to the Willett family, that individual will be listed no more than twice in the index - once as a child of a parent, and potentially once under a separate heading.

One shortcoming of this indexing method is that when a person has more than one spouse, the spouse will not be listed in the index. However, any children of that spouse will be listed alleviating the absence of some surnames of spouses.

The index lists all alternative Willett surnames under the spelling **Willet/t** thus enabling someone to find a person who may have used **Willit**, **Willette**, etc., under one index heading. This choice to index all alternative Willett surnames has been made since the record of a particular spelling of a name may not have been consistent neither in the distant past are even the usage in the more recent past.

The index lists all alternative spellings of the Willetts surname as **Willet/t/s** thus the spelling of **Willets**, **Willits**, and **Willitts** are also found under the index heading Willet/t/s.

Just because a person is not found in the index on first looking for him, does not mean he is not there. When looking for a particular individual consider all alternative spellings and ways of listing a persons name. Spellings of a name are as found or reported. Thus, **Philip** is normally spelled with one "l" but **Phillip** Willett (page 55) is spelled with two "ll"s.

Sometimes a person has an initial as part of his name, thus **Wheeler** Willett (page 52) is listed in the index under **B. Wheeler** Willett. Some names can commonly have letters substituted for each other, thus if a person is not found in the index under **Cathy** then check for the spelling of **Kathy**. Other names can be shorten; thus if a person is not found under the listing **Abraham**, check under **Abram**, and vice versa. Also consider "nicknames" deriving from a given name; thus if **James** is not found check under **Jim**; if **Polly** is not found, check under **Mary**.

THE INDEX

Heritage Books by Albert James Willett, Jr.:

Abraham Willett (c1735–c1805) of Onondaga County, New York

The Martin Family of the Poquoson District, York County, Virginia
Albert James Willett, Jr. and Dr. Fred William Martin, Ph.D.

*Poquoson Families, Volume I: The Forrest Family
of the Poquoson District, York County, Virginia*

*Poquoson Families, Volume II: The Holloway, Messick, and Linton Families
of the Poquoson District, York County, Virginia*

*Poquoson Families, Volume III: The Topping, Rollins, and Carmines Families
of Poquoson District, York County, Virginia*

*Poquoson Families, Volume IV: The Amory, Insley, Firman, and Firth Families
of the Poquoson District, York County, Virginia*

*Poquoson Families, Volume V: The Gilbert and Hopkins Families
of the Poquoson District, York County, Virginia*

*Poquoson Families, Volume VI: The Patrick, Evans and Lawson Families
of the Poquoson District, York County, Virginia*

CD: Willett Family of Pennsylvania

Willett House Collection [Willett Family of Pennsylvania]

www.ingramcontent.com/pod-product-compliance
Lightning Source LLC
Chambersburg PA
CBHW071826270326
41929CB00013B/1906